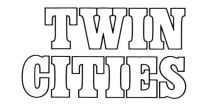

TWIN CITIES

A Pictorial History
of Saint Paul
and Minneapolis

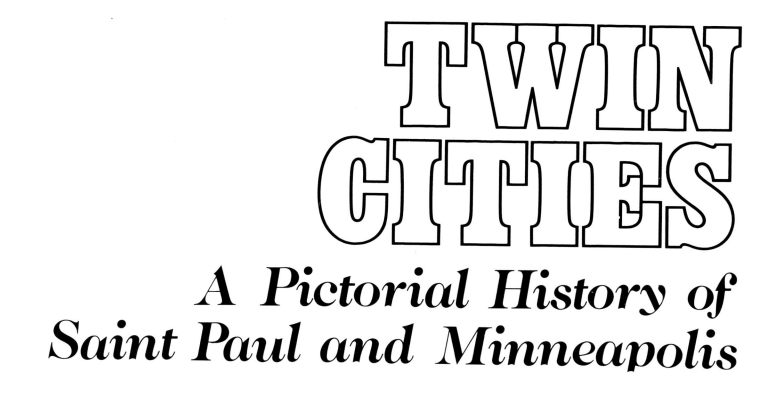

TWIN CITIES

A Pictorial History of Saint Paul and Minneapolis

Lucile M. Kane and Alan Ominsky

MINNESOTA
HISTORICAL
SOCIETY
PRESS
ST. PAUL
1983

Copyright © 1983 by the MINNESOTA HISTORICAL SOCIETY

Library of Congress Cataloging in Publication Data

Kane, Lucile M.
  Twin Cities.

  Bibliography: p.
  Includes index.
   1. Saint Paul (Minn.)—History—Pictorial works.
2. Minneapolis (Minn.)—History—Pictorial works.
3. Saint Paul (Minn.)—Description—Views. 4. Minneapolis (Minn.)—Description—Views. I. Ominsky,
Alan. II. Title.
F614.M6K36   1983   977.6'579   83-21929

International Standard Book Number 0-87351-165-4

Table of Contents

Acknowledgments   vii

Introduction   1

1838-65

River Cities   4

1920-29

The Jazz Age   154

1865-80

The Railroad Age   44

1929-45

Depression and War   189

1880-95

The Golden Age   79

1945-83

Metropolis   230

Epilogue

The Cities
Remember   270

1895-1920

Passage to the
Twentieth Century   116

Reference Notes   279

Picture Credits   289

Index   295

Acknowledgments

The authors gratefully acknowledge the contributions of many people to the preparation and production of *Twin Cities: A Pictorial History of Saint Paul and Minneapolis.* Bonnie G. Wilson and her staff in the Minnesota Historical Society's Special Libraries Department were unfailing in their efforts to help the authors tap the rich resources on the Twin Cities in the picture collection and explore the data on the photographs and photographers available in the department's files. Jon L. Walstrom, the department's map librarian, guided the authors along the intricate pathways of geographic research. Elizabeth Hall Wehrwein, chief photographer, and her assistant Shirley Lofgren produced most of the prints used in the book.

Several members of the society's Publications and Research Division staff were also deeply involved. Kenneth A. Carley did extensive research on photographs and shared with the authors his knowledge of sports and the arts. Bruce M. White, a former staff member, researched pictures, assisted in the selection of photographs, and provided guidance to sources on popular culture. Jean A. Brookins, assistant director for publications and research, advised the authors during various stages of book preparation, a counseling role played by the late June Drenning Holmquist in the project's initial phase. Ann Regan was the editor in charge of the book. Anne R. Kaplan worked with her, as did Sarah P. Rubinstein, who with Helen T. Katz prepared the index. June Sonju typed the final draft of the manuscript.

Other MHS staff members who gave generous assistance, often beyond the call of duty, were Patricia C. Harpole, Alissa L. Wiener, Wiley R. Pope, Faustino J. Avaloz, Alice M. Grygo, and Louis M. deGryse (former staff member) of the Reference Library; Ruth E. Bauer, Ruby J. Shields, and Bonnie Palmquist of the Division of Archives and Manuscripts; Thomas O'Sullivan and Albert E. Galbraith, Jr., of the Field Services, Historic Sites, and Archaeology Division; and John A. Dougherty of the newspaper microfilming project. Also helpful were the staffs of other institutions providing pictures used in the book, particularly the Hennepin County Historical Society, the Minneapolis Public Library and Information Center, the National Archives, and the Library of Congress.

The authors called upon family and friends as volunteers in the cause. Leona Kane Eder typed drafts of the manuscript and photocopied a mountain of research notes; Sister Alora Kane helped in research; Elizabeth A. Knight assisted in producing contemporary photographs of the cities. Television station KSTP also joined the ranks of volunteers when its helicopter and pilot carried photographer Alan Ominsky aloft.

Last, but far from least, the authors salute the four critics who read the manuscript, shared their extensive knowledge of the Twin Cities, and saved them from many a slip: Virginia Brainard Kunz, executive director of the Ramsey County Historical Society; Dorothy M. Burke, head of the Minneapolis History Collection of the Minneapolis Public Library and Information Center; Russell W. Fridley, director of the Minnesota Historical Society; and Robert Hoag, formerly on the staff of the St. Paul Public Library and now a volunteer in the society's Special Libraries Department.

Introduction

THIS BOOK IS A HISTORY in pictures and words of St. Paul, St. Anthony, and Minneapolis—triplet towns that developed from clusters of frontier cabins into a cosmopolitan urban center in the Upper Midwest. St. Paul, founded at the head of practical navigation on the Mississippi River, drew its initial strength from commerce, while St. Anthony and Minneapolis, established upriver at the Falls of St. Anthony, exploited the cataract's water power to become manufacturing towns. When Minneapolis and St. Anthony merged in 1872, the triplets became twins, both of which developed into commercial-manufacturing centers. In a race that has been called "one of the more enduring standoffs in American municipal history," the cities forged bonds that gave them a common identity but retained individual characteristics that marked them as distinct. Today they are nonidentical twins, they are an urban center, and they are the core cities of a metropolitan area embracing ten counties with a population of over two million people.[1]

Much of the cities' history throughout a century and a half has been captured in images — paintings, drawings, maps, photographs, advertisements, and broadsides. Those chosen for this book range from panoramas to streetscapes to candid shots of the cities' people. Others document more unusual events: the aftermath of the Washburn A mill's explosion in Minneapolis; J. Edgar Hoover returning Alvin "Creepy" Karpis, "Public Enemy Number 1," to St. Paul for trial; the celebration of V-J Day; presidential visits, antiwar demonstrations, construction and demolition of major city buildings. The pictures offer readers an opportunity to wander back in time — to catch vivid glimpses of the 1950s rock 'n' roll era, of two World Wars and the Great Depression, of the Gay '90s, and of the three towns' early years. The artist and the photographer recorded many facets of urban life: clothing styles, recreation spots, amusements, sports, workplaces, and homes; business and industrial districts, residential neighborhoods, and cityscapes; steamboats, railroads, horsecars, streetcars, balloons, automobiles, buses, trucks, and airplanes.

Artists and map makers provided images of St. Paul and St. Anthony in their years of birth and earliest development. Although photographers William H. Jarvis and Joel E. Whitney moved to St. Paul in 1850, no surviving photographs of the towns are known to have been made before 1851. The work of early cameramen contrasts with the sketches by artists of the period: the 1851 photo of St. Paul's Baptist Hill has a rude frontier look compared to Jean Baptiste Wengler's picturesque sketch of the town in the same year (page 14). Although early artists conveyed some information about the landscape, even such a careful draftsman as Seth Eastman, a trained military artist and commandant at Fort Snelling in the 1840s, failed to depict the raw, unpainted look of the town — including the mud.[2]

Early photographers, too, were limited in their capabilities to capture what they saw. The painstaking process of taking and developing pictures — which required that subjects sit or stand still for twenty seconds to several minutes of exposure — made photographers very selective in choosing images to record. In addition, social and artistic considerations influenced their choice of subject matter. In order to attract the buying public, photographers found "suitable subjects" in people, buildings, and views that customers found pleasing. In judging the quality of photographic composition, photographers continued to draw upon the aesthetics of the artist.[3]

By the 1860s two significant developments had taken place in American photography. Technical advancement came with the maturation of the wet-plate process which, unlike the making of a daguerreotype, yielded a negative that could produce many prints of the same image. Armed with this equipment, American photographers became journalists on the battlefields of the Civil War, taking pictures of events, not simply of people or things. The images, speedily made into engravings and published in the popular press, projected great immediacy. Local examples of this new kind of picture taking are found in the photo-documents made of the recurring collapse of the riverbed at the Falls of St. Anthony in the 1860s and of St. Paul's retail districts in the early 1870s (pages 66, 67).

In about 1880 prepared dry plates of glass, which did not require immediate processing after exposure as did wet plates, became available. Freed from the burden of carrying a darkroom tent, photographers began to take more photos and to pursue more diverse subjects. In the Twin Cities, several photographers of this period shot numerous storefronts with the proud owners and their employees standing on porches or sidewalks, providing the fine sequence of images on pages 100 and 101.

The growing popularity of photography caught the attention of the Minnesota Historical Society, and the institution's interest in documentation through photographs dates from the 1870s. "Photography is one of the most valuable aids in preserving history which we have," J. Fletcher Williams, the society's secretary, commented in 1875. He appealed for donations to the small collection, citing the need to record the "ever changing and rapidly growing towns and cities" of the state. Among the donors who responded to Williams' frequent appeals was St. Paulite Charles A. Zimmerman, who contributed pictures from his "justly famous gallery" and who was designated the society's official photographer in 1875.[4]

Other photographers donated the pictures they collected as well as those they took. Much of the early photographers' work now in the collections of both the Minnesota Historical Society and the Minneapolis Public Library exists because of the efforts of Edward A. Bromley, a Twin Cities newspaperman and pioneer photojournalist. In 1878 Bromley purchased negatives of Benjamin F. Upton's photographs, and subsequently he acquired work by Joel E. Whitney, William H. Illingworth, and others important in documenting the Twin Cities in the nineteenth century.[5]

Although photography had become simpler, most who practiced the art were professionals or dedicated amateurs. But that began to change in 1888, when George Eastman introduced snapshot roll-film cameras. For $25 anyone could buy a camera containing enough film for a hundred exposures; for another $10 the photographer could have the pictures processed and receive a reloaded camera. Unhampered by social conventions or artistic fashion, the new photographers casually snapped pictures of family, friends, places, and things they wanted to remember. Photography — now in the hands of people like the high-school graduate adjusting his camera on page 147 — headed into a new era.[6]

Just as the snapshot camera was introduced, printers developed the halftone process, by which photographs could be reproduced directly in published materials. The *Minneapolis Journal* may have been the first newspaper in the country to print halftone cuts regularly, beginning in July, 1896. Over the next generation, newspapers and magazines slowly began to realize the potential of the innovative process in illustrating news reports. By the 1920s, the timely newsphoto began to emerge as a way of documenting local, national, and world events.[7]

Throughout the twentieth century, the technology of photography underwent steady development. As films became more sensitive to light, lenses faster, and cameras easier for both amateurs and professionals to use, pictures could be taken under previously impossible conditions. In 1931 a news photographer took one such photograph — using only existing indoor light — of Governor Floyd B. Olson addressing the legislature (page 190).

The Minnesota Historical Society kept pace with the expanding field of photography and continued its efforts to acquire the work of other Twin Cities photographers and collectors. The institution now holds the work of Charles Norton and Clifford Peel, who began their partnership as commercial photographers in 1925 and accumulated a voluminous store of photographs during their forty years in business together. Included in the Norton and Peel Collection of 75,000 photographs and negatives were those of Charles J. Hibbard, for whom the partners worked before 1925, and those Hibbard had collected. Other important preservationists and photographers were Kenneth M. Wright, who in 1930 acquired the work of Charles P. Gibson, and Louis D. Sweet, who preserved negatives of William H. Jacoby, some of which traveled to the society via Bromley.[8]

During the 1940s and 1950s picture magazines such as *Life* and *Look* combined the informal spontaneity of the snapshot with the stylistic techniques of news photography to achieve what historian Nathan Lyons has called "an unprecedented mirroring of things in our culture." Many staff photographers of Twin Cities newspapers were undoubtedly influenced by the picture magazines. Their photographs and negatives, transferred to the society by the newspapers, are, like the Norton and Peel Collection, an impressive cultural resource.[9]

Following World War II, Americans began to use finely engineered hand cameras, developed first in Europe and later in Japan. Newspaper photographers slowly moved from sheet-film press cameras to twin-lens reflex cameras and finally, as it was perfected, to the thirty-five millimeter single-lens reflex camera. The latter allowed professional as well as amateur photographers unprecedented freedom to photograph images of almost anything on which a camera could be focused. A variety of lenses, from wide-angle to telephoto, permitted an interesting variation on artistic license: photographers could stretch or compress space, asking people to see and believe in something not visible to the eye alone. Examples of this exaggerated perspective are shown in several pictures in Chapters 7 and 8, including the photograph on page 255 of freeways near downtown St. Paul.

SELECTING PHOTOGRAPHS for this book from the abundance of Twin Cities images accessible to the authors was both frustrating and rewarding. The society's holdings of about 250,000 photographs — many of them of the Twin Cities and their residents — provided a fine core collection. The Hennepin County Historical Society and the Minneapolis Public Library provided other photos. A few more came from the Library of Congress, the National Archives, and other institutions, as well as from businesses and individuals.

In preparing a pictorial history, the arrangement of the illustrations is as important an editorial consideration as their selection. In this book each chapter presents an era; images are arranged topically, enabling the reader to explore various subjects in more depth than a strict chronology would allow. The authors have combined images with one another and with informative captions in ways that will expand on the information conveyed by individual images alone. For instance, the 1857 panoramas of St. Anthony and St. Paul have each been reproduced in part many times and as a whole occasionally. The two have never before, however, been presented with other supporting images and text (pages 17-35).

By showing two or more views of the same subject taken from different vantage points or eras, the authors hope to make these places more accessible to the reader. Such a synthesis occurs on page 41, where a photo of the wooden, two-story Spooner Building appears next to reproductions of advertisements for goods and services that people purchased at the location. The ads project the bustle of business and amusements, and the photo shows the space and scale in which it took place. The image of St. Paul's Jackson Street Methodist Church in mid-twentieth-century surroundings (page 21) makes the 1857 picture of the same building less remote and implies a century of people coming and going.

Readers should keep in mind that the scope of history presented in these pictures is limited to existing images and to the number feasible for inclusion in a moderate-sized volume. On those pages presenting the cities' early days, for example, there are few pictures showing action, people at work or play, or close-up images of everyday items. In later chapters covering more recent years, the crush of people, commerce, and institutions offers greater pictorial diversity but requires more arbitrary standards of selection. Throughout, the authors have aimed for as broad a representation as possible, allowing the supporting text to "frame" the images with information from city documents, histories of different aspects of city life, and accounts from newspapers and letters.

The picture captions are not annotated, but the information on which they are based is in the Twin Cities Pictorial History files at the Minnesota Historical Society's Division of Archives and Manuscripts. Research on the photographs took the authors to contemporary newspaper accounts, plat and insurance maps, other photographs, business records, ephemeral publications, and manuscript collections. City directories provided information for most of the photographs, including addresses contemporary with the images.

This book can be read, or looked at, on many levels. Many of the photographs are beautiful as well as interesting; some are simply humorous. Readers will find a special challenge: those who study the images will see much more than is at first apparent. Their reward will be a more comprehensive and more visceral understanding of how St. Paul and Minneapolis have grown, changed, and prospered.

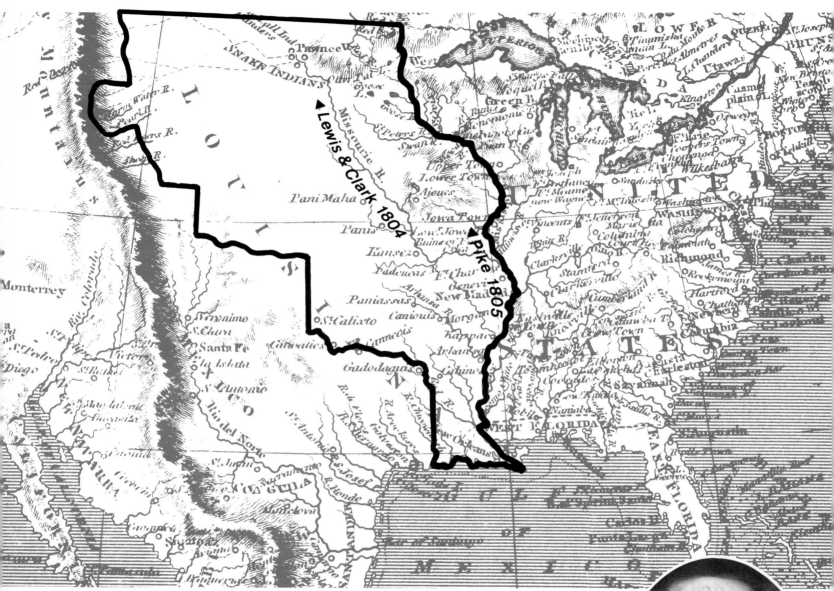

In 1803, through the Louisiana Purchase, the United States bought almost 900,000 square miles of new land from France. A few of those square miles, lying west of the Mississippi River near its confluence with the "St. Peters" (later Minnesota) River, would become part of the Twin Cities. The cities' development depended on the exploitation of resources in the northern reaches of the purchase, extension of railroads into the area, and access to navigation on the Mississippi.

President Thomas Jefferson, who acquired the vast domain for the United States, was keenly interested in learning more about it. He speculated that when the land east of the Mississippi was filled up, "we may lay off a range of States on the western bank from the head to the mouth, and so, range after range, advancing compactly as we multiply."

F OR THE tiny communities of St. Paul and St. Anthony, huddled in 1849 on the bank of the frozen Mississippi River, spring seemed a long time in coming. Their residents eagerly awaited important news from Washington, D.C., and "Expectation was on the tip toe" when early April thaws opened the way for the steamboats that would bring the long-delayed mails. Late in the day on April 9, during a violent thunderstorm, St. Paulites heard the shrill whistle of a steamboat, and a lightning flash illuminated the "Dr. Franklin No. 2," heading for the levee. People ran through the raging storm to the landing and boarded the boat before it was tied fast to the moorings. A cheer echoed from the "beetling bluffs and rolling hills" when they learned that on March 3 the bill creating Minnesota Territory had become law, and St. Paul was named capital of the commonwealth.[1]

The news spread from St. Paul to Fort Snelling and Mendota, six miles upriver, and then nine miles farther to St. Anthony. Fort Snelling, the great stone bastion that had risen in the early 1820s on the heights overlooking the junction of the Mississippi and Minnesota rivers, was the center from which the other settlements had sprung. The post's broad military reservation, purchased by Lieutenant Zebulon M. Pike from the Dakota Indians in 1805, had boundaries that were ill-defined for many years. The fur-trading hamlet of Mendota, which by 1849 wore "something of an ancient aspect," had grown up on the reservation close to the fort in the 1820s. In the succeeding three decades the federal government's management of the reservation helped scatter the seeds of settlement from the fort and Mendota to the sites of the future cities of St. Paul, St. Anthony, and Minneapolis.[2]

Major Joseph Plympton set the process in motion when he arrived to take command of Fort Snelling in 1837. Disturbed by the presence of settlers on the reservation, he had the area mapped and in 1838 warned the squatters that they were intruders on the military reserve. Some of the settlers, heeding his words, moved across the Mississippi to a point three miles below the fort near Fountain Cave, where the whisky seller Pierre Parrant had a hovel. The whisky business continued to thrive at the site, and the outraged commandant, faced with "beastly scenes of in-toxication" among the soldiers, drew a new map that brought the Fountain Cave settlement within the reservation's limits. In 1840, at Plympton's orders, Fort Snelling soldiers destroyed the harried squatters' cabins. Again on the move, the settlers planted themselves downriver at the present location of downtown St. Paul. The settlement originally borrowed Parrant's nickname of "Pig's Eye," but it acquired a more dignified designation when the Chapel of St. Paul was built in 1841.[3]

Less confusion but more excitement attended the birth of St. Anthony. The 1837 boundary line excluded from the reservation the east bank of the Mississippi at the Falls of St. Anthony. Plympton's motive in juggling the line quickly became clear. The land abutting the falls carried with it the right to develop water power. This critical piece of real estate, no longer part of the reservation, reverted to Indian ownership, and upon ratification of treaties negotiated in 1837 with the Dakota and Ojibway it was opened to pre-emption claims. When news of ratification arrived on July 15, 1838, Captain Martin Scott led a detachment from the fort to stake a claim for Plympton. Already in residence on this early morning, however, was Franklin Steele, the post sutler, who had stolen a march on competitors by making a night trip to the falls. Outmaneuvered but game, Scott, Plympton, and others staked claims nearby.[4]

Voyageurs, traders, scouts, soldiers, merchants, whisky sellers, farmers, and others drifted into the settlements. Since these people had claimed the land before the federal government offered it for sale, they often had trouble holding it against intruders. Steele, for example, had to buy off a claim jumper who moved into his cabin while the man he had hired to occupy it was gone. A dispute between Pierre Parrant and Michel Le Claire over the boundaries of their claims in St. Paul was settled in a more novel way—an eight-mile foot race. Although Parrant's "avarice nerved up his strength," the younger Le Claire outdistanced him. Arriving at the finish line "sick, mad and furious," Parrant found that the winner had already driven the stakes securing the claim.[5]

Claim holders also feared that speculators might try to outbid them when the lands were formally sold in 1848 at St. Croix Falls, Wisconsin. During the sale Henry H. Sibley, the tall, commanding squire of Mendota who represented the claimants to the St. Paul townsite and others, was "invariably surrounded by a number of men with huge bludgeons." As the crier announced the land parcels up for sale, however, the property, including the townsites of St. Paul and St. Anthony, passed to the claimants without bloodshed. In the following year, more than a decade after the first claim stakes were driven, St. Paul was incorporated as a town. Although St. Anthony was not formally incorporated, its plat was registered and it took on characteristics of a frontier village.[6]

Meanwhile across the river from St. Anthony wily strategists laid the foundations for a settlement that would be called Minneapolis. Their objective was to get control of land on the military reservation, particularly the area abutting the falls that shared with Steele's property the rights to the water power. From 1836 several bold men, including Sibley, tried in vain to acquire the saw and grist mills that soldiers had built by the falls in the early 1820s. Success came in 1849 to Robert Smith, an Illinois congressman who deviously claimed that he planned to make Minnesota his new home (which he did not do) and thus obtained a lease on the mills. In the same year John H. Stevens, Steele's bookkeeper, offered to operate a free ferry at the falls for the troops in exchange for land near the mills. Other settlers later joined him on the west bank, and the drums began to beat for reduction of the 34,000-acre reservation.[7]

THE NEWS carried by the "Dr. Franklin No. 2" introduced a period of tremendous growth. From 1849 until a severe panic struck in 1857, the year before the territory became a state, Minnesota's population mushroomed from 4,131 to 150,037; the growth rate then slowed, and the state had about 264,600 residents by 1865. The same years witnessed the rise and fall of St. Anthony. From a village of 248 people concentrated at the falls in the summer of 1849, the town spread out onto the beautiful prairie. Incorporated as a city in 1855, it had a population of 4,689 two years later. Then its population, hard hit by the panic and other economic problems, dwindled to 3,499 by 1865.[8]

While St. Anthony became so lethargic that it was called a "city of the unburied dead," the infant community born on the military reservation across the river climbed from its cradle. Campaigns for reduction of the reservation succeeded in 1852, and soon settlers were able to buy the prized real estate. Unlike St. Anthony, named for the falls, and St. Paul, named for the chapel after a brief dalliance with "Pig's Eye," the community debated about what to call itself. After

considering such names as West St. Anthony, All Saints, Albion, Winona, and Lowell, it settled the matter by combining "Minnehaha," the Dakota word for "laughing waters," with "polis," the Greek word for "city," to make Minneapolis. Although Minneapolis was so dilatory about municipal organization that it was not incorporated as a city until 1867, its population grew from an estimated 300 in 1854 to 3,391 by 1857 and to 4,607 by 1865.[9]

Minneapolis was in the ascendancy at the falls by 1865, but it was no match for its neighbor downriver. Incorporated as a city in 1854, St. Paul skyrocketed in population from 910 in the summer of 1849 to 9,973 by 1857, then climbed to 12,976 by 1865. Minnesota's dominant city, infected by the buoyant optimism of the West, sprawled upward from the lowlands on the Mississippi onto the amphitheater of hills overlooking the river.[10]

The nature of the river was a vital element in the development of the three communities. The chief resource of St. Anthony and Minneapolis was the falls, with a power potential great enough, it was claimed in euphoric days, "to turn all the spindles and water wheels of New England." Nicollet and Hennepin islands divided the river at the falls, and in 1847 and 1848 Steele took the lead in creating power by damming the eastern channel. The water power was used for fledgling industries that would reign supreme at the falls for many years: Steele and his partners built sawmills and a grist and flour mill, other investors constructed a flour mill on Hennepin Island, and the west-side owners remodeled the government mills twice in the early 1850s.[11]

The pace of development quickened after Smith and his partners incorporated the Minneapolis Mill Company and the Steele group organized the St. Anthony Falls Water Power Company in 1856. From 1856 to 1858 the firms together constructed a dam that channeled the water into their millponds. The Minneapolis firm's powerful stockholders, including Dorilus Morrison and brothers William D. and Cadwallader C. Washburn, made it more successful than the trouble-ridden St. Anthony company. While the city of St. Anthony suffered from its company's chaotic fortunes, the well-managed business across the river laid a solid base for industrial expansion in Minneapolis.[12]

As firms producing sashes, doors, blinds, paper, ironware, and other products joined flour and lumber mills at the falls, the promising industrial communities coveted the commercial advantages that easy access to Mississippi River navigation would give them. But the shallow, swift water below the cataract, running over rocks left as the falls receded through the centuries from the vicinity of Fort Snelling, denied the residents this access. When most steamboat captains refused to make the difficult trip, the struggle for river improvements that would bring regular navigation to the falls became a civic obsession.[13]

What the river denied Minneapolis and St. Anthony it gave to St. Paul. Although the absence of water power slowed the growth of manufacturing, the city's position at the head of practical navigation made it an important commercial center. A growing number of steamboats moored at the Lower Levee, at the foot of Jackson Street, and the Upper Levee, at the foot of Chestnut. The steamboat traffic, increasing overland transportation, and the vast western country opening to settlement lent eloquence to the pens of prophets. As early as 1849, for example, a local booster predicted that St. Paul "must necessarily supply the trade of all the vast regions north of it to the rich plains of the Selkirk Settlement [on the Red River], and west to the Rocky Mountains, and east to the basin of the great lakes." Even before railroads replaced stages, wagons, and other limited forms of overland transportation, St. Paul's northwestern trade flourished, with caravans of oxcarts arriving annually from the Red River. The carts carried furs and other cargo to St. Paul for transshipment downriver, while on the return trip they hauled a wide variety of general merchandise.[14]

The busy Lower Levee, where a "brazier filled with blazing pine knots . . . lighted the black stevedores as they bore the cargo aboard on their calloused shoulders," was also a major gateway for immigrants to Minnesota. A great wave of settlers moved to the newly opened lands, especially after 1851, when the Dakota Indians signed treaties ceding millions of acres. Although many migrants traveled overland in wagons laden with their worldly goods, thousands debarked from steamboats at St. Paul.[15]

The *Minnesota Weekly Times* on May 9, 1857, described a morning scene at the Lower Levee after some 3,000 people had arrived within four days. "Here, upon the left, is an emigrant family very quietly eating breakfast in the open air. A table has been disentangled from the heaps of furniture and set on its legs; edibles, none the better for age, have been dragged from the musty depths of mysterious-looking boxes, and distributed along the board; the children, a score or so, are mustered around the unsavory breakfast, and they partake of it under the shadow of the bluff, with the awakening clang and bustle on every side, and nothing but the blue sky to bless them with its benediction. Further along is a woman holding a coffee-mill in her lap, and grinding some 'pure Java' for breakfast. They slept here last night . . . gathered in clusters under this grateful canvas stretched across the barrels, or huddling in that empty nook that has escaped the crowding merchandise of yesterday."

SWIFT GROWTH taxed the young communities' capacities for providing necessities of urban life like streets, public buildings, bridges, crime control, fire protection, sanitation, street lighting, and schools. Minneapolis, with its delayed municipal organization, was somewhat negligent, but the citizens of St. Anthony and St. Paul made vigorous efforts to meet urban needs through a combination of public funding, private capital, and volunteer participation.

Among the needs none was more pressing than opening streets. St. Paul had the most severe problem: it was platted "with the same lawlessness the bird exemplifies in its path through the fenceless air" over a rugged terrain that was, to say the least, well watered. The tasks of blasting, grading, and draining begun by the municipal government in the 1850s made the city look like the "vicinity of Etna after an eruption — big ditches, ponderous piles, fearful precipices, yawning chasms and mountains of volcanic rock making it the very picture of desolation and ruin." On the more hospitable prairie at the falls, the city of St. Anthony pushed improvements so aggressively that at one point taxpayers cried for a respite. Minneapolis town, despite its lagging civic organization and resistance to taxation for public improvements, joined the others in surveying and grading streets.[16]

St. Paul, seat of Ramsey County and center for the commonwealth's government, was soon ornamented with public buildings — a territorial capitol, county courthouse, city hall, and jails. Although Minneapolis as seat of Hennepin County acquired a combined courthouse and jail, and St. Anthony built a jail, neither had a municipal hall. The prominence of jails indicated the difficulty of preserving the peace. Law enforcement officials struggled to control common offenses like violence, drunkenness, prostitution, and disorderly conduct. "Gamblers, con-men, thieves, and bad women thronged the hotels and streets," a chronicler of St. Paul crime wrote of the 1850s. "St. Paul had grown to be the 'fastest' town on the river." In an outburst of moral indignation, the *Minnesota Republican* called on St. Anthony citizens to strike at the roots of crime by tearing down the "rummeries and harlot-hells." Reflecting the same concern for disorder in Minneapolis, the newspaper lamented the fate of young men who were "silly dupes of the liquor-seller and of 'the strange woman.'"[17]

While citizens contributed somewhat to law enforcement as vigilantes and as home guards during the Civil War, their role was vital in fire fighting. The cities purchased equipment, but the force was composed of volunteers organized into companies. For battling the frequent fires with engines, hook and ladder trucks, hoses, buckets, and axes, the volunteers were rewarded only with exemptions from road work, jury duty, and some kinds of military service. But the men took great pride in their accomplishments. When the towns' bells rang out the alarms, the companies usually worked together with good spirit, combining their forces to fight major fires. They also held balls, paraded in their brightly colored uniforms, and competed with one another in water-throwing contests.[18]

Private capitalists joined volunteers in helping form the urban landscapes of the three towns. Bridge-building companies during the 1850s spanned the Mississippi at the falls with a "spider-like creation" suspended from cables, put up two additional bridges above and below the cataract, and built still another at Wabasha Street in St. Paul with assistance from the municipal government. The St. Paul Gas Light Company contracted with the city in 1857 to furnish the municipality with street lighting. Although lamp-lighters became a familiar sight in St. Paul, the communities at the falls had no street lights for at least another thirteen years.[19]

In several other respects the communities remained in darkness. For example, little effective attention was given to the quality of the water supply drawn from the river, springs, and wells or to waste disposal and drainage. Officials, aware of the link between sanitation and health, urged remedial action to prevent epidemics, established quarantines, and fitted up pest houses during times of contagion. A historian of public health in Minnesota points out that as late as 1872, the communities' residents "depended upon a sturdy constitution to breathe successfully the pestilential air from reeking yards, alleys, and privy vaults, to drink water polluted by sewage carelessly and promiscuously dumped, and to leap over filthy mudholes in poorly drained streets."[20]

Other social needs were little better met. For want of a better solution, persons in St. Paul judged insane were lodged for a time in jail; orphans, paupers, and the "indigent sick," caught in an ambiguous legal situation, received limited support from municipal governments of St. Paul and St. Anthony. In the 1850s the St. Paul Common Council tried to cut off the "diseased and destitute" at the levee by making steamboat captains and others who brought them to the city choose between returning the dependents to the place from which they came or caring for them.[21]

Although the local governments were slow in responding to the residents' health needs, private enterprise filled some of the gaps. The ailing could seek care at St. Joseph's and St. Luke's hospitals, founded by religious denominations in St. Paul, or from private physicians, who had grown numerous enough in the 1850s to warrant organization of medical societies. They could also resort to a variety of panaceas advertised in their newspapers, including Dr. McLane's Liver Pills, the Perry Davis Vegetable Pain Killer, Cephalic Pills, Celebrated Female Pills, Dr. Weaver's Canker and Salt Rheum Syrup, Bryan's Pulmonic Wafers, and Pesiguagomik, a preparation made from Minnesota plants and recommended for cholera morbus, dysentery, and diarrhea.[22]

Private enterprise also joined public efforts for education, producing a mosaic of public, parochial, and "select" schools in the communities. The establishment in 1851 of the University of Minnesota was a significant achievement in laying the foundations for public education. The university, it was predicted seven years later, would become "a central sun of science and a temple of light radiating the whole Northwest." Catholics built parochial schools in both St. Paul and St. Anthony, while the "select" institutions prided themselves on offering "all the accomplishments taught in the best Eastern schools." Their curricula included subjects like French, Latin, Greek, "epistolary correspondence," "Belles Lettres," drawing, painting, and music.[23]

The interest Minnesota's early white citizens showed in education exemplified their vigor in transplanting the society they had known in their old homes to a new setting. No part of the culture was of greater concern than religion. "You will need to be doubly watchful in those ends of the Earth lest you let down your standard. *Take heed*," a Michigan friend wrote to Sibley in 1835 soon after the latter's arrival in Mendota. The "full blaze of the Gospel" that Sibley's friend hoped would soon light the "dark corners of the Earth" on the frontier was kindled in the 1830s and early 1840s at Fort Snelling and Mendota, in the Dakota Indian villages at Lake Calhoun, Lake Harriet, and Kaposia, and at St. Paul's mission chapel. Keeping pace with community growth, religious denominations — including Catholic, Presbyterian, Episcopal, Congregational, Methodist, Lutheran, and Baptist — by 1860 had built thirty-five churches in St. Paul, St. Anthony, and Minneapolis.[24]

The influence of religion in the communities was pervasive. Clergymen like Edward D. Neill, who was also an educator and historian, helped foster cultural life. Many citizens concerned with morality lobbied for territorial legislation promoting temperance and the serenity of the Lord's day. The founders of the Protestant Orphan Asylum presaged the strong role religion would play in social welfare. Activities like church festivals and donation parties enlivened social life, while immigrant churches offering services in the languages of their foreign-born worshipers eased transition to a new society.[25]

MIGRANTS from the eastern United States were especially quick to establish other cultural traditions in their new homes. They sought reading materials from bookstores that operated rental libraries, subscribed to newspapers from their old homes as well as those published locally, bought such magazines as the *Scientific American, Godey's Lady's Book,* and *Harpers Monthly,* and passed around a new book like *David Copperfield* until it was "worn to rags." They also founded private library groups, among them the Minneapolis Athenaeum and the St. Paul Library Association, that were forerunners of the cities' public libraries.[26]

Music lovers orchestrated the beginnings of the fine arts in the communities. Vocal and instrumental music groups proliferated: brass bands, cotillion bands, a quintet club, a philharmonic society, choral societies, and glee clubs. The performances did not always win critical acclaim, as in the instance of the German band that in 1852 "bored the ears of St. Paul for three hours, with a most villainous compound of offensive noises." The object of the serenade, a new bride, made her critical comment by throwing hot water out the window on the unlucky players.[27]

Residents' thirst for entertainment was as strong as their yen for the homegrown arts. Crowding into halls and other places of amusement, they applauded traveling troupes of performers. "St. Paul was never so blessed (cursed?) with amusement and 'places of entertainment' as just at present," the *Minnesota Republican* reported on July 30, 1857. "Theatres, elephants, 'monsters', equestrians, concerts, clowns and claquers, bears, beauties, bands, ballads and banjosies *[sic]* lurk on every corner and under every tented canvass to entrap the unwary and take their dimes." Seekers of unusual sights viewed not only the trivial curiosity of a seven-legged calf but such major events as a balloon ascension, which they greeted with "deafening cheers" as the "grand bubble" floated aloft.[28]

Other activities strengthened the bonds of community life. The residents formed groups of Odd Fellows, Masons, and temperance crusaders, shot off cannons and paraded on the Fourth of July, skimmed over the snow during the long winters to the merry jingle of sleigh bells, danced at grand balls, and entertained visitors in their homes. On festive occasions they often celebrated in hotels and public halls, consuming formidable feasts served with a wide assortment of wines.[29]

The interests common to migrants from a particular place inspired new associations among thousands of people who had come from many parts of the nation and Europe. For example, New Englanders, who with other newcomers from the eastern states were influential community members, formed a society. German Turners paraded in their white uniforms, and Irishmen with shamrocks on their hats and green scarves over their shoulders marched in celebration of St. Patrick's Day. Ethnic loyalties, however, sometimes created friction: a street fight broke out in 1858 when

Minneapolis pranksters hung an effigy of St. Patrick with a string of potatoes around its neck. A local newspaper commented that the conflict began "with a trick perpetrated by some sportive boys from a love of mischief, which unlettered superstition, and blind veneration for a patron saint easily tortured into malice."[30]

THE CIVIL WAR generally contributed to the sense of community, although there were some conflicts between "patriotic" citizens and "traitorous" talkers. Crowds turned out to bid the soldiers the first of many farewells at the departure on June 22, 1861, of the First Minnesota Volunteer Regiment, which included companies from the three communities. Families and friends from many parts of the state gathered at Fort Snelling to see the soldiers board the "War Eagle" and the "Northern Belle." The regiment, led by Colonel Willis A. Gorman, debarked at St. Paul and marched through the streets before proceeding farther downriver. At Gorman's side was Chaplain Edward D. Neill, "who with his determined countenance and simple costume . . . looked as if he had been resurrected from one of Cromwell's regiments."[31]

Rallying on the home front, the St. Anthony and St. Paul city councils voted funds to support soldiers' families and to pay enlistment bounties. Volunteers assembled bedding and clothing that would protect the troops from the hot southern sun; they prepared food like jellies, preserved tomatoes, and pickles; and they gave fund-raising entertainments. At a more somber meeting held in St. Anthony in 1861, city leaders considered ways to recover the bodies of those from the city who had fallen "in the late desperate conflict near Manassas." Local residents also rallied to provide assistance to refugees from the Dakota War, waged in 1862 when the Indians, outraged by their treatment at the hands of the whites, attacked settlements in southern Minnesota.[32]

IN SOME RESPECTS the communities were ambivalent about the kind of society they were shaping on the new urban frontier. While local newspapers often boasted of the raw energy of the West, they also remarked on the towns' progress toward the "customs and observances of the *beau monde* of fashionable life." Dancers no longer stamped their feet to the beat of the music at balls, they noted, nor would society accept a gentleman professing "refined manners" if he appeared in "slouchy, uncouth garments, hanging about his person like a sheet on a fence post." Another plane of the prism reflected their mixed feelings about the East. Smarting under Easterners' condescension, for example, newspaper editors contrasted the Westerners' friendliness, frankness, and sincerity with the formal, affected, and deceitful manners of Easterners — but at the same time the editors relished western imitations of the older culture.[33]

The communities' attitudes toward one another were perhaps more complex than their self-images. They had shared the same experiences as they grew from rude settlements to small cities with great expectations. As the largest urban center in the Northwest, they also shared ambitions for the conquest of a hinterland that stretched to the Pacific Coast; they hoped to exclude their rival Chicago, whose influence was creeping westward over rails pointed toward Minnesota and the land beyond. As a St. Paul newspaper put it in 1853, the "sister cities" in coming years would be "viewed as the upper and lower towns of the same great metropolis, which will be to the Northwest what New Orleans is to the South, and St. Louis to the centre — a railroad and commercial terminus, a grand centre of trade, and . . . the manufactory and workshop of the West."[34]

And yet for all the ties that bound them, the cities were rivals, polarized into dual centers as the falls communities united to confront St. Paul in a battle for supremacy. While each center initially based its claim to superiority on the advantages bestowed by the Mississippi River, both also tried, with some success, to become combined commercial-manufacturing cities. The rivalry was bitter and pervasive, and local newspapers piled fuel onto the blaze as they espoused the causes of their cities.[35]

The cargo of the steamboat "Alhambra," arriving in St. Paul on September 9, 1861, set off changes that would both sharpen the cities' rivalry and strengthen their common bonds. On board and on barges, the boat carried railroad cars, track iron, and the locomotive "William Crooks." The track was laid between St. Paul and St. Anthony, and on June 28, 1862, St. Paul Mayor John S. Prince, the city's aldermen, and a gala crowd of about a hundred boarded the cars for the falls. "Let it be recorded for the benefit of the future historian of the vast Northwest," the *St. Paul Daily Press* pontificated, "that . . . [on this day] the first link in the great chain of railroads which will . . . spread all over this State from the valley of the Mississippi to the Red River of the North, and from Lake Superior to the Iowa boundary line, was completed, and a passenger train started from St. Paul in the direction of Puget Sound!"[36]

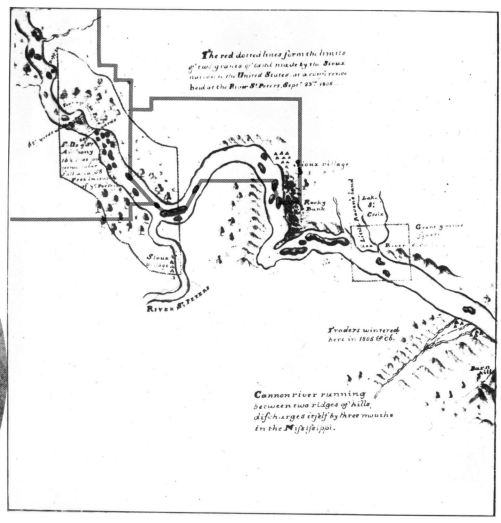

The red dotted lines form the limits of two grants of land made by the Sioux nation to the United States, at a conference held at the River St. Peters, Sept' 23'' 1805.

Cannon river running between two ridges of hills, discharges itself by three mouths in the Mississippi.

In 1805-06 Lieutenant Zebulon M. Pike led an expedition to explore the Upper Mississippi region, part of it in the Louisiana Purchase. Like the Lewis and Clark expedition, which took place in the same years, Pike's journey was intended to satisfy Jefferson's and the nation's curiosity about the new western domain. At the future site of the Twin Cities metropolitan area, the explorer diligently noted the characteristics of the river, the dimensions of the Falls of St. Anthony, fur traders' establishments, Dakota Indian villages, and sites for establishing forts.

A map drawn by a government cartographer from Pike's notes shows the sites for military posts that the explorer acquired from the Dakota. Pike negotiated the treaty for the cession on an island later named for him at the junction of the Mississippi and Minnesota rivers. Fort Snelling was built on these lands, as were parts of the Twin Cities. Gray lines show the approximate boundaries of the present Twin Cities.

Kaposia, the village of a succession of Dakota chiefs named Little Crow, was located on the Mississippi near present-day South St. Paul. The Little Crow of the early 1800s, Che-tan-wakan-mani, was one of the signers of the treaty Pike negotiated.

Fort Snelling, first called Fort St. Anthony and shown here about 1850, was named for Colonel Josiah Snelling, the energetic commandant under whose direction it was built. Snelling wrote in 1824 that the post "commands the channels of both rivers and the adjacent country within point blank distance; its peculiar form was chosen to adapt to the shape of the ground on which it stands; on the north side the hill is a perpendicular bluff, on the south the ascent is steep and a road has been cut by which stores, wood etc. are conveyed from the landing to the garrison."

Franklin Steele, observed a contemporary soon after this sketch was made in 1856, had not been such a well-dressed man when he staked the first claim at the Falls of St. Anthony in 1838. His costume at that time included "a pair of pantaloons in a state of disorganization, a coat somewhat the worse for wear, over the reddest of the red, red shirts of that red-shirted age."

When this portrait was made in 1849, Henry H. Sibley, Steele's brother-in-law, was playing important roles in purchasing the St. Paul townsite from the government and in persuading Congress to reduce the size of the Fort Snelling military reservation. From Mendota, where he lived from 1834 until moving to St. Paul in 1862, the urbane fur trader and frontiersman wielded great influence in Minnesota's affairs.

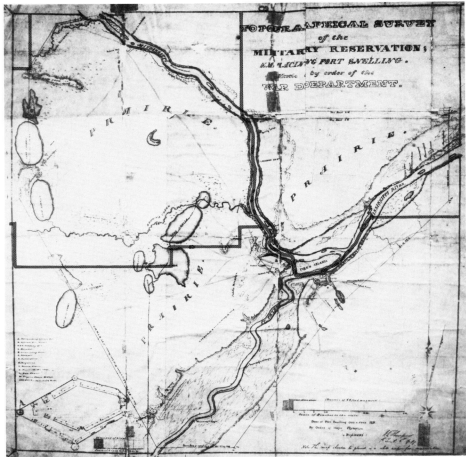

This map of the Fort Snelling military reservation, made by Lieutenant James L. Thompson in 1839 on the order of Major Joseph Plympton, shows the extension of the reservation boundary on the east side of the river to the whisky-sellers' settlement at Fountain Cave. Plympton transmitted the map to the War Department with the comment that if the reservation boundaries could be extended farther on the east side, "it would no doubt add to the quiet of this command." Approximate present-day city boundaries are superimposed in gray.

This ferry, crossing between Fort Snelling and the road to St. Paul in about 1867, was the only means of traversing the Mississippi River at this point until a bridge was completed in 1880.

The "Virginia" inaugurated steamboat service on the Upper Mississippi River in May, 1823. Passing the site of the future city of St. Paul, the 118-foot stern-wheeler carried its freight and passengers to Fort Snelling. The craft, here depicted by a latter-day artist, made one more trip to the post before it sank in September, 1823. After the "Virginia" had "cut its way . . . against the current of the great river," other boats came whenever there was cargo for them. When regular service was established in 1847, the growing business center of St. Paul, rather than Fort Snelling, became the port.

The Chapel of St. Paul was built in 1841 between present-day Cedar and Minnesota streets. Father Lucien Galtier, who located the chapel near a good spot for a steamboat landing, gave the settlement its name. "St. Paul, applied to a town or city, seemed appropriate," he wrote. "The monosyllable is short, sounds well, and is understood by all denominations of Christians." A marker on Kellogg Boulevard at the foot of Minnesota Street now commemorates the chapel.

"My! how this town is growing," commented a St. Paulite who saw smoke rising from eighteen chimneys one winter's morning in 1848. That same year Seth Eastman, commandant of Fort Snelling, made this sketch of the settlement.

Cloudman's Dakota village at Lake Calhoun — now within the Minneapolis city limits — was called "Eatonville" by Major Lawrence Taliaferro, the local Indian agent who in the 1820s persuaded the band to found an agricultural colony there. Gideon and Samuel Pond established a Protestant mission at the lake in 1834, hoping to further encourage the Dakota to adopt "civilized life."

The frame sawmill and stone grist mill built on the west bank of St. Anthony Falls were the first to use the cataract's power. Snelling claimed in 1824 that "the flour manufactured last year was equal to any in the world" and that 3,500 board feet of pine plank were sawed in one twenty-four-hour period. The mills remained in use after Robert Smith acquired the property, but they were deteriorating by the time this photograph was taken in 1857.

In 1849-50 John H. Stevens built his house (visible in the background of this daguerreotype made in about 1854) near the Falls of St. Anthony on the future site of Minneapolis. There, he later recalled, Dakota, Ojibway, or Winnebago Indians often moved in during the night and erected their tepees while the Stevens family slept.

St. Paul was booming in 1851, enjoying the effects of the creation of Minnesota Territory. "Every day makes it clearer, that St. Paul is destined to more importance as a city than the most sanguine have dared to anticipate," the *Minnesota Pioneer* commented in a typical burst of optimism. The First Presbyterian Church looms over the town in a sketch by an artist who was facing east; the First Baptist Church stands out in a photograph looking south.

When this daguerreotype was made in about 1855, the cataract flowed freely, not yet harnessed by the dam that would be built across the river. The logs that marred the scene of primitive beauty probably had escaped from the booms that stored them for the nearby sawmills. This industrial development would bring great danger to the fragile limestone sheath holding the falls in place.

St. Anthony in 1851 was entering its brief period of prosperity. Four sawmills on the dam Steele had built across the eastern channel were daily producing thousands of board feet of lumber, and a grist and flour mill on the shore beside the row of sawmills began operating. The newly founded *St. Anthony Express* voiced the community's ambitions to overcome the "strenuous rivalry" of the dominant town of St. Paul. Hennepin Island is in the left foreground.

The "Milwaukee" was among the many steamboats that tied up at St. Paul during the 1850s. Known as "one of the crack boats of the Minnesota Packet Company," it offered its passengers the comfort of a luxurious cabin.

The "Ben Campbell," an elegant steamboat with fifty large staterooms, began navigating the Upper Mississippi in 1852; there were 171 steamboat arrivals that year at St. Paul. In 1856, about the year this photograph was taken at the Upper Levee, the number had grown to 857.

In the 1850s and early 1860s other flour mills joined the "government mill" and the mill Steele and his partners had built at the falls. The structures included the Island or Minnesota mill, built on Hennepin Island in 1854. In a daguerreotype taken inside the mill about 1858 are Francis and I. P. Hill. One of them is recutting ("dressing") grooves in a millstone while leaning on a cushion called a "bist."

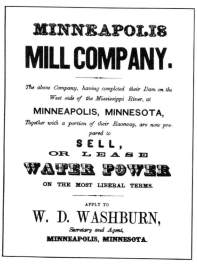

The Minneapolis Mill Company issued this advertisement in 1859-60, when it had dug a 215-foot raceway or canal along the west bank to make water power accessible. The canal, later extended, was the key to an efficient water-distribution system that made Minneapolis the pre-eminent industrial city at the falls. Flour mills were concentrated at the canal; most of the sawmills, however, were built in a row on the dam.

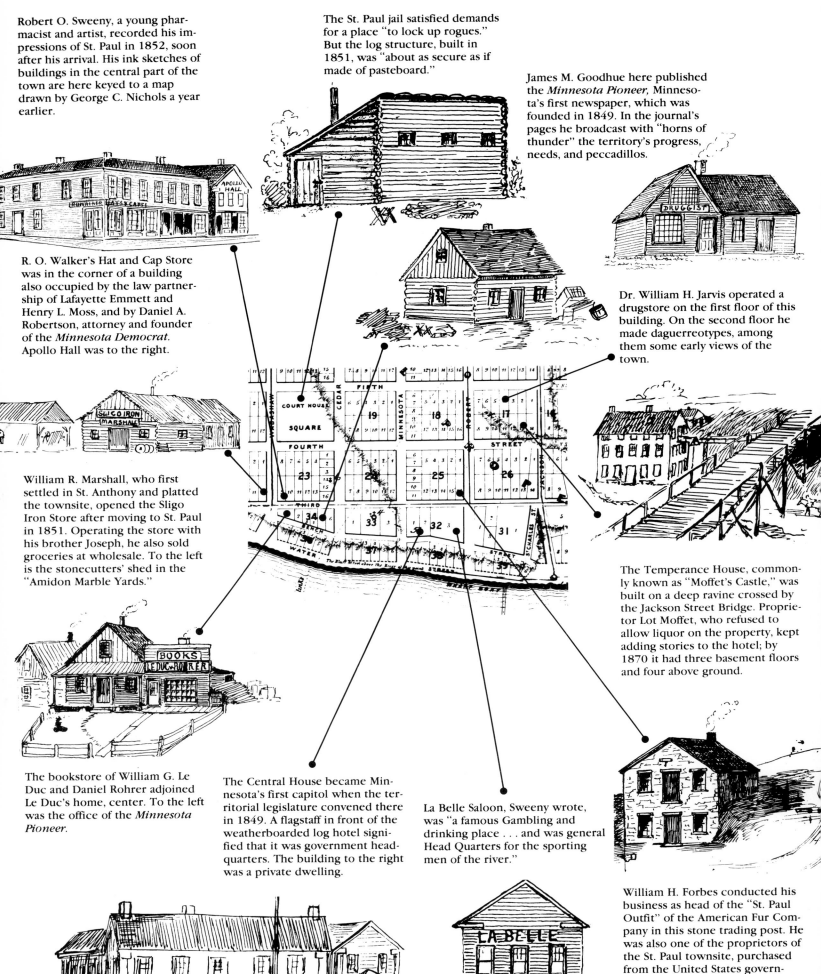

Robert O. Sweeny, a young pharmacist and artist, recorded his impressions of St. Paul in 1852, soon after his arrival. His ink sketches of buildings in the central part of the town are here keyed to a map drawn by George C. Nichols a year earlier.

The St. Paul jail satisfied demands for a place "to lock up rogues." But the log structure, built in 1851, was "about as secure as if made of pasteboard."

James M. Goodhue here published the *Minnesota Pioneer,* Minnesota's first newspaper, which was founded in 1849. In the journal's pages he broadcast with "horns of thunder" the territory's progress, needs, and peccadillos.

R. O. Walker's Hat and Cap Store was in the corner of a building also occupied by the law partnership of Lafayette Emmett and Henry L. Moss, and by Daniel A. Robertson, attorney and founder of the *Minnesota Democrat.* Apollo Hall was to the right.

Dr. William H. Jarvis operated a drugstore on the first floor of this building. On the second floor he made daguerreotypes, among them some early views of the town.

William R. Marshall, who first settled in St. Anthony and platted the townsite, opened the Sligo Iron Store after moving to St. Paul in 1851. Operating the store with his brother Joseph, he also sold groceries at wholesale. To the left is the stonecutters' shed in the "Amidon Marble Yards."

The Temperance House, commonly known as "Moffet's Castle," was built on a deep ravine crossed by the Jackson Street Bridge. Proprietor Lot Moffet, who refused to allow liquor on the property, kept adding stories to the hotel; by 1870 it had three basement floors and four above ground.

The bookstore of William G. Le Duc and Daniel Rohrer adjoined Le Duc's home, center. To the left was the office of the *Minnesota Pioneer.*

The Central House became Minnesota's first capitol when the territorial legislature convened there in 1849. A flagstaff in front of the weatherboarded log hotel signified that it was government headquarters. The building to the right was a private dwelling.

La Belle Saloon, Sweeny wrote, was "a famous Gambling and drinking place . . . and was general Head Quarters for the sporting men of the river."

William H. Forbes conducted his business as head of the "St. Paul Outfit" of the American Fur Company in this stone trading post. He was also one of the proprietors of the St. Paul townsite, purchased from the United States government in 1848.

FIRST PRESBYTERIAN CHURCH

FOURTH STREET

CRAMSIE'S BLACKSMITH AND WAGON SHOP

WABASHA STREET

"One pleasant day in the summer of 1857," Edward A. Bromley wrote in 1901, "B. F. Upton, a photographer from St. Anthony, ascended to the roof of the old Court House . . . and made nine views of the embryo city of St. Paul, each one lapping over the other so that there might be no difficulty in arranging the set." The views are shown here, with additional photographs positioned above and below each panorama panel to feature points of particular interest. In the St. Paul sequence that continues on the next eight pages (and the St. Anthony panorama that follows it), Upton reveals the cities in booming times, just before the panic that struck in late summer slowed their growth. This section looks southwest over Wabasha Street (foreground) at its intersection with Fourth Street; the west-side river bluffs rise in the background.

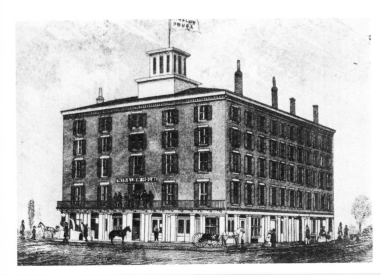

The Winslow House, built by James M. Winslow in 1854 and shown in an engraving made about that time, was one of several hotels in the city. In 1855 a booster commended the hotels for the "elegance with which they are fitted up" and tables "supplied with everything that tempts the palate of the epicure."

REV. J. G. RIHELDAFFER RESIDENCE

GEORGE GALLEY'S CHAIR FACTORY

The Methodist Episcopal Church on Market Street, known as the "Market Street Church," was built in 1849 and is pictured at right about twenty years later. It was said to be the first Protestant church erected in Minnesota. In 1850 the Minnesota Historical Society held its first annual meeting there, featuring a lecture by Edward D. Neill on the voyageurs and the music of the Fort Snelling band.

St. Paul's city hall, seen here about 1890, stood at the corner of Fifth and Washington streets. When the structure was finished in 1857, the trustees of the adjoining Baldwin School, a private institution organized by Neill and others in 1853, claimed that their building was "entirely ruined" for its original purposes. The former school was subsequently occupied by the post office, a public school, and city officials.

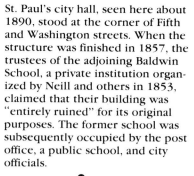

FIFTH STREET

WABASHA STREET

The Catholic cathedral, under construction, above, at Sixth and St. Peter streets, opened for services in 1858. The structure, shown at left about two years later with the bishop's residence, was reported to be "more remarkable for its massiveness and a certain imposing boldness than for any special architectural merit." It was the city's third cathedral, succeeding the Chapel of St. Paul and a building dedicated in 1851, visible at far right.

The peripatetic territorial government finally found its own home when the first capitol was built at Tenth and Wabasha streets in 1853. Governor Willis A. Gorman, addressing the legislature there the following January, urged that money be appropriated for a fire engine "to be kept for its special protection." The structure survived the perils of its pioneer years, only to burn in 1881.

MARKET
HOUSE

CENTRAL
PRESBYTERIAN
CHURCH

SEVENTH
STREET

Vendors sold products like meat, poultry, vegetables, and fruit from rented stalls of the public market at Seventh and Wabasha streets. The red brick structure was built in 1853 by Vital Guerin and leased to the city, which later purchased it. The municipal court occupied the second floor.

Louis Robert, a trader, steamboatman, and one of the proprietors of the St. Paul townsite, stood on the balcony of the family home on Robert Street near Ninth Street. Posing with him in about 1865 was his mother-in-law, Eulalie Turpin.

The Methodist Episcopal Church building at Jackson and Ninth streets retained in 1957 some of the architectural characteristics that distinguished it when it was built a century earlier. The congregation of the "Jackson Street Church," as it was called, moved to a new building at Minnesota and Twelfth streets about 1890. It was then called the "Central Park M. E. Church."

FULLER HOUSE

MINNESOTA STREET

Workmen laying stone on the walls of the new county jail at Cedar and Fifth streets completed construction of the building the following year. Law breakers then left the old log lockup for more secure imprisonment here or in the municipal jail, located in the new city hall.

Baptist Hill, named for the church built there in 1850-51, was a prominent St. Paul landmark. An artillery salute fired from its summit in the spring heralded the first steamboat arrival.

WASHINGTON SCHOOL   JAMES C. BURBANK RESIDENCE

The Ramsey County Courthouse was considered "an ornament to the town" after its construction in 1850-51 at Fourth and Wabasha streets on land donated by Vital Guerin. Upton photographed it in the same year he made the panorama from its roof.

The Merchants Hotel, shown at Third (later Kellogg Boulevard) and Jackson streets about 1866, had its beginnings in the St. Paul House (the frame structure on the corner), built in 1846-47.

LOUIS ROBERT'S
WORLD'S FAIR STORE

FOURTH STREET

This structure, called the first frame house in St. Paul, was built in 1844 of hand-hewn lumber by Charles Bazille for Louis Robert. It was moved from its original site on the Lower Levee to Fourth and Minnesota streets, where it appears in the panorama and in this photograph taken about 1890.

DAY AND JENKS
DRUGS •

MRS. GILL'S
SCHOOL •

FOURTH STREET •

Elfelt's clothing store stood at
Third and Cedar streets with Joel
E. Whitney's Sky Light Daguerrean
Gallery above it. This daguerreotype was made around 1855,
probably by Whitney. In the background are Christ Episcopal
Church (known as "the church of
the holy toothpick") and the
dome of the Ramsey County
Courthouse. The photographer's
skylights at the rear of the building
are visible in the panorama.

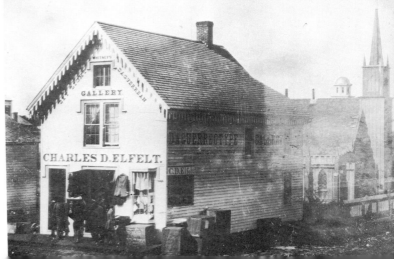

The St. Paul Bridge Company was spanning the Mississippi River at Wabasha Street when the panorama and this picture were made. Completed in 1859, the toll bridge eased communication with the developing farming communities across the river. The ferries used before the bridge was built had caused traffic congestion, and "when the wind was blowing, it [was] impossible to get across at all."

WILLIAM R. MARSHALL
RESIDENCE

WABASHA STREET

Choosing the "commanding height of the Winslow House roof" in St. Anthony as his vantage point, Upton swept vistas of St. Anthony and Minneapolis into the range of his camera in 1857. Although the combined communities had fewer residents than St. Paul, the well-defined industrial district at the falls intimated their growing strength. The series of photos continues over the next seven pages.

The First Congregational Church of Minnesota completed its building (shown here in a latter-day sketch) at present Fourth Street near East Hennepin Avenue in 1854. The congregation met in the university's building before moving into the new structure.

The University of Minnesota opened in 1851 in a building under the shadow of the Winslow House. Twenty students studied under the tutelage of Elijah W. Merrill, a Congregational minister.

PARSONAGE

FIRST
METHODIST
CHURCH

UNIVERSITY
AVENUE

The Winslow House was built near the falls in 1856-57 by James M. Winslow, who also erected the St. Paul hotel that bore his name. Thousands of southern visitors frequented the luxurious hotel before it closed in 1861. The Minnesota College Hospital occupied the building when this picture was taken in the early 1880s.

"WIDOW HUSE" RESIDENCE

Prominent buildings lined the St. Anthony shore in 1861 across from the old government mills (right foreground, near camera) and a sash, door, and blind factory (left foreground). Across the river, to the right of the Winslow House, are the Chute Building, the Upton Building, and the Tremont House.

William A. Cheever platted "St. Anthony City" in 1849 on land he owned on the east bank below the falls and built there a tower and hotel named for himself. Cheever invited the curious to "Pay your dime and climb" the one-hundred-foot tower, which tapered from a base about forty feet square to about six feet at the top. Before the tower blew down in 1865 or 1866, the proprietor kept a saloon, where he advertised

Good ale and good beer
At the tower I keep here.

HENNEPIN
ISLAND

MAIN
STREET

The house of Ard Godfrey, a Maine millwright who built Steele's dam and sawmill, stood behind Main Street in St. Anthony. The white frame structure was moved in 1909 to Richard Chute Square at University and Central avenues and now is operated as a historic house by the Woman's Club of Minneapolis. The Hennepin County Territorial Pioneers Association met at the house in about 1910 and posed for this picture.

29

"Sour angry feelings" attended the construction in 1856-57 of the Hennepin County Courthouse at Fourth and Ames (later Chicago Avenue) streets in Minneapolis, because the location was considered far from the business center. The county jail was in the basement of the cream-colored brick structure, pictured here about 1875.

FARNHAM AND LOVEJOY SAWMILL

MILL HANDS' BOARDING HOUSE

GOVERNMENT MILLS

R. C. ROGERS' GRISTMILL

The Hennepin Island paper mill began making wrapping and printing paper in about 1860, ten years before this picture was taken. When Upton made the panorama, the structure was being erected as a sash, door, and blind factory.

Godfrey, Steele's partner in the St. Anthony Mill Company until 1853, carried out duties as a businessman and a postmaster in this office, sketched about 1893, on the eastern bank facing Main Street. In the panorama, the building adjoins the new office built by the St. Anthony Falls Water Power Company after its incorporation in 1856.

A photographer on Hennepin Island about 1865 viewed the east-side row from downriver. Lumber was piled on a platform in front of the mills. The panorama shows the upriver side of the row, where logs were drawn from the pond into the mills.

In 1856 men lounged on the one-year-old porch of Snyder and McFarlane (Simon P. Snyder and William K. McFarlane), who opened their real-estate office on Bridge Square, at the foot of the Suspension Bridge, Minneapolis. Snyder platted an addition to Minneapolis, and the firm actively promoted development of the town.

JOHN H. STEVENS
RESIDENCE

MAIN
STREET

In 1854 the Mississippi Bridge Company, incorporated by Steele, Sibley, Stevens, Smith, and others, completed a suspension bridge from Nicollet Island to Minneapolis. The bridge, pictured about 1868, was the first to span the Mississippi anywhere, and it strengthened the bonds between St. Anthony and Minneapolis. On January 23, 1855, St. Paulites joined residents of the two communities in a celebration touched off by cannon fire and a mile-long parade of sleighs across the beautiful structure.

Roswell P. Russell, who in 1847 opened a store in St. Anthony, built a house on Main Street the following year from lumber sawed in Steele's mill. About thirteen years later, Benjamin Upton photographed the building, said to be the first frame house in St. Anthony.

CENTRAL (HENNEPIN) AVENUE

The Universalist Church was dedicated in the year the panorama was made and was renamed "Our Lady of Lourdes" when a French Catholic congregation acquired it twenty years later. This 1948 photograph shows alterations that changed its appearance. The oldest continuously used church in the city, it is considered "a landmark of French-Canadian culture in Minnesota"; the church was being restored in the early 1980s.

Minneapolis' industrial district demonstrated the energy with which manufacturing was being developed in about 1860. The town's dominant industries grew as the sawmill row extended along the dam and the new Cataract mill was built at the canal. The *Minnesota State News* commented in 1860 that "Minnesota flour, though generally of a darker color than that made from winter wheat, is sweet and is gaining a high reputation."

Bridge Square, located above the industrial district at the falls and shown here in 1863-65, was the business hub of Minneapolis. These vignettes of the square show: (A) John I. Black's dry-goods store; (B) the south side of the square with a goose pond in the foreground; (C) the post office; (D) the north side of the square, with Chalmer Bros. hardware store; (E) Oswald's Corner.

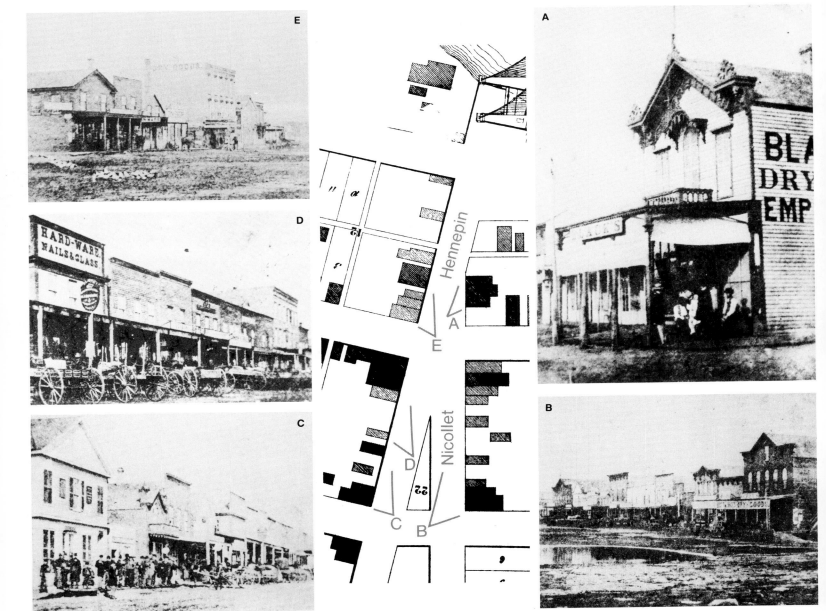

The town of Minneapolis, viewed distantly in Upton's St. Anthony panorama, moved toward cityhood and dominance at the falls in the scenes from 1857 shown here and across the top of the following three pages.

An 1857 view toward Bridge Square from Second Avenue South shows A. B. Kingsbury's livery stable (left center), which had a billiard saloon on the upper story. To the right of the distant bridge towers were the Crane jewelry store (with cupola) and the Bagley confectionery (with large windows).

This structure at Marquette Avenue and First Street, bearing the construction date of 1856 on the cupola, is the Crane building (see photo above). In about 1919 both the Charles W. Joy barbershop and the Tri-State Employment Company were its neighbors.

In the mid-1860s the east side of Nicollet Avenue from First Street showed Black's Corner at the extreme left and the store of Anthony Kelly and Bro. next to it.

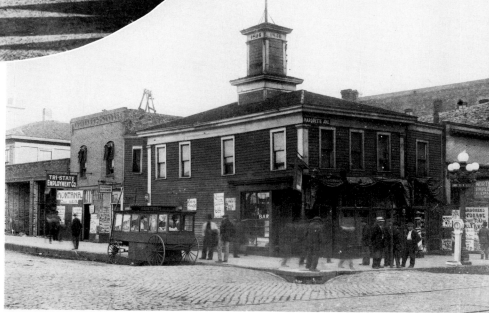

The *Minnesota Democrat,* formerly the *North-Western Democrat,* was published in the Barber Block at Second Avenue South and Washington Avenue. In 1854, three years before this photograph was made, the journal moved from St. Anthony to Minneapolis and became that town's first newspaper.

From the Barber Block, partially visible on the extreme left, to the Cataract House in left background, Washington Avenue was difficult terrain to travel. Appearing along the avenue to the right in 1857 were a furniture warehouse, a meat market housed with a harness and carriage trimmer, a blacksmith's shop, and a large frame home later occupied by William W. Eastman, one of the owners of the Cataract mill.

When the Cataract House opened in 1857 at Washington Avenue and Cataract Street (later Portland Avenue), it occupied a "commanding location overlooking the city and its environs." But by about 1900, surrounded by many buildings that obscured the view, it had become the Sixth Avenue Hotel.

Construction had begun on the second Woodman Block (left foreground) in 1857, when this view was made looking south from Washington Avenue along Second Avenue South. The photographer was probably standing in Ivory Woodman's first block, a brick structure with a hall on the third floor. The lumber piles in the foreground, like others seen in the panoramas, testified to local markets for the products of the sawmills at the falls.

Classes began in 1858 in the Union School at Oregon Street (later Third Avenue) and Fourth and Fifth streets; by the end of the year 450 students and 10 teachers occupied the building. The walls of the new school are rising in the center background of the above photo.

A primitive Washington Avenue extended from Helen Street (later Second Avenue South) west or northwest in 1857. The large building in the foreground was Mrs. Judith Walsh's boarding-house; in the right background was the Freewill Baptist Church near Utah Street (later First Avenue North); and left of the church were the foundations of the Nicollet House.

The Nicollet House, a cream-colored brick hotel at Washington and Hennepin avenues, opened in 1858. The businesses occupying the first floor in about 1865 included a millinery shop, a drug-store, and the First National Bank. With a later addition, the hotel was a home to travelers until a new Nicollet Hotel opened on the same site in 1924.

Omnibuses like this one carried passengers around the three communities. Lines serving mainly hotels and depots continued to operate long after streetcars appeared on the cities' streets.

On April 14, 1861, two days after the firing on Fort Sumter opened the Civil War, Minnesota became the first state in the Union to offer men for military service. A century later, an artist painted Governor Alexander Ramsey (right), who has handed the offer of a thousand men for service in the Union Army to Secretary of War Simon Cameron (left). Cameron reads the governor's message as he leaves his office for a cabinet meeting in the White House.

Volunteer groups in St. Paul, St. Anthony, and Minneapolis assembled clothing, bedding, food, and other gifts for the troops in depots like this unidentified office of a soldiers' aid society. Organizations like the Minneapolis Soldiers' Aid Society sometimes provided music, tableaux, and other entertainments at their meetings.

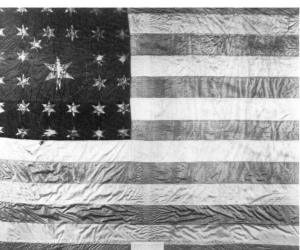

On May 21, 1861, the First Minnesota Volunteer Regiment marched from Fort Snelling to the falls at the invitation of the ladies of St. Anthony and Minneapolis. At a banquet on Nicollet Island the regiment received a flag sewn by the St. Anthony women. The flag, shown here, is now in the collections of the Minnesota Historical Society.

This group of Minnesota volunteers was probably Company B of the Sixth Regiment photographed in 1862 at Fort Snelling. The company served in the Dakota War during the summer of that year.

Members of the First Minnesota were presumably among the sick and wounded at Savage's Station, Virginia. James Gibson took the photograph on June 29, 1862, the day the regiment participated in an action nearby.

A few surviving members of the First Minnesota met in 1926 at the home of Mr. and Mrs. L. B. Bassett on Dudley Avenue in St. Paul. The old soldiers, "grayhaired and shaking of step," recalled the hot day in Virginia sixty-five years earlier when with "perspiration streaming from their faces they marched into the Battle of Bull Run."

Ossian E. Dodge (left) and his traveling troupe of entertainers, the twins Emma and Clara Macomber and Bernard Covert, sat for this daguerreotype in about 1846. After settling in St. Paul in 1862, Dodge managed Ingersoll Hall at Third and Wabasha streets, operated a music store, and dealt in real estate.

Mazourka Hall at Third and Exchange streets in St. Paul was on the second floor of another of Elfelt's dry-goods stores. The hall, shown here in 1852, was the scene the previous year of the first professional theatrical performances in St. Paul: *Maid of Munster* and *A Day at the Fair* by Placide's Varieties.

Sweeny, who made this ink sketch of "Monks Hall" in 1852, noted that it was "inhabited by some of the young lawyers of St. Paul who live in the style called 'Keeping Ba[t]ch' and judging from appearances they live very happily at least merrily." The site was later occupied by the Winslow House and then by the St. Paul Hotel.

Minnehaha Falls, in present-day Minnehaha Park, Minneapolis, attracted many tourists. Artist George Catlin publicized the falls after his 1835 visit, as did Henry Wadsworth Longfellow's *Song of Hiawatha,* published twenty years later. To create this view in 1857, Upton persuaded some Dakota Indians who lived in the area to pose in their "picturesque costumes."

The residents of Monks Hall, reputed to tipple upon occasion, were not the only drinkers in St. Paul. This daguerreotype, made about 1860, is a study of unidentified participants in the merrymaking that took place in hotels, saloons, and homes. The saloon was particularly popular as a social center, despite public agitation for prohibition.

In 1854 the *St. Anthony Express* advertised an entertainment common in the 1850s and 1860s. Artists painted the panoramas on huge canvases, some of them over a thousand feet long and twelve feet high. When on exhibition, a rolled canvas was mounted in a frame. As the panorama unrolled, panel by panel, a narrator commented on the scenes of faraway places moving before the audience.

"Spooner's Building" at Main Street and Fifth Avenue in St. Anthony was "surpassed by no wooden building in town" when it was completed in 1854. This view, about 1862, shows W. W. Wales's bookstore, left, W. F. Cahill's drugstore, center, and D. A. Secombe's law office on the second story, right. Cataract Hall occupied the upper story, like other halls at the time, and helped satisfy what a local newspaper called "the great, yearning, crying necessity of the soul — *amusement.*"

Wales Book Store placed several notices in the *St. Anthony Express* on December 1, 1855, to advertise its goods, which included gold pens, lawyers' seals, crochet needles, ivory combs, and shaving brushes.

Cahill, who claimed seven years' experience in the drug business and connections with firms in St. Louis and New York, offered customers "all prescriptions accurately compounded at his store, thereby saving the expense and trouble of sending to St. Paul." His advertisement ran in the *St. Anthony Express* on June 17, 1854.

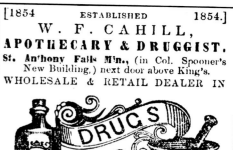

Cotillion parties featured local bands that encouraged dancers to "trip the light fantastic toe." This series was advertised in the *St. Anthony Express* on December 15, 1855; in another notice, a dancing master sponsored a party at St. Anthony's Stanchfield Hall for his eighty students and invited others to buy tickets.

41

Not everyone was satisfied with the speed of Davidson's boats when water in the Mississippi River was low.

The "Itasca" and the "War Eagle," frequent visitors, moored at St. Paul's Lower Levee in 1859. The "War Eagle" attracted particular attention on June 22, 1861, when it carried five companies of the First Minnesota Regiment to war via a railroad connection at La Crosse, Wisconsin. William F. Davidson, whose business is advertised on the wharf boat in the foreground, became so important a figure in steamboating that he was called "The Commodore."

The "Enterprise," built in St. Anthony in 1857, navigated the river above the falls for only seven years. It was then moved along St. Anthony's Main Street around the falls and launched on the lower river.

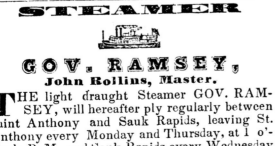

STEAMER

GOV. RAMSEY,
John Rollins, Master.

THE light draught Steamer GOV. RAM-SEY, will hereafter ply regularly between Saint Anthony and Sauk Rapids, leaving St. Anthony every Monday and Thursday, at 1 o'-clock, P. M., and Sauk Rapids every Wednesday and Saturday, at 8 o'clock, A. M.

☞ For freight or passage apply on board.
June 24, 1850.

Steamboat navigation on the Mississippi above the Falls of St. Anthony was much more difficult than on the lower river, but the "Governor Ramsey" inaugurated service there with its first trip in 1850. Despite the use of craft designed for shallow water and many attempts to improve the river for navigation, the steamboats played a very small role in the cities' trade with northern Minnesota.

Stagecoaches, wagons, and other vehicles connected the three communities to many points in Minnesota and the surrounding states. Sometime before 1863, a few of the conveyances appeared in front of the American House at Third and Exchange streets, St. Paul, was originally called the Rice House. The Red Coach Line, which used vehicles noted for their "elegance of finish," carried mail and passengers to towns on the Mississippi River above the falls.

RED COACH LINE.
ALLEN & CHASE, PROPRIETORS.
OFFICE NEXT DOOR BELOW THE AMERICAN HOUSE.

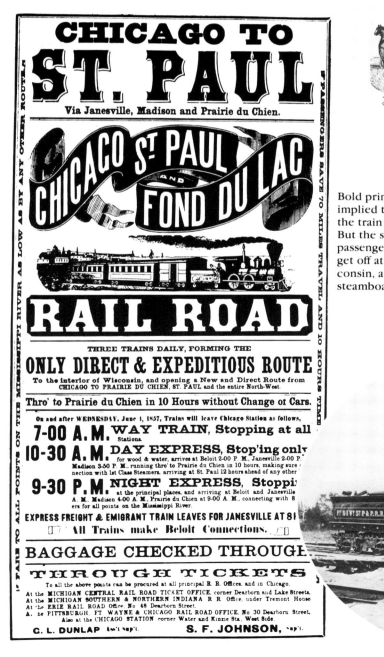

Bold print in this 1857 broadside implied that travelers might ride the train from Chicago to St. Paul. But the small print revealed that passengers bound upriver had to get off at Prairie du Chien, Wisconsin, and finish the trip by steamboat.

Francis R. Delano, general superintendent of the St. Paul and Pacific railroad, stood in the cab of the first locomotive in Minnesota, the "William Crooks," in the mid-1860s. Beside him is J. C. Morrison, probably a company clerk. Delano donated this picture to the Minnesota Historical Society in 1866, noting that it "may be of value to our successors, as they will have occasion, and time, to criticise the work and machines of the present day, as we do those of days long gone by." The "Crooks" is now in the Lake Superior Museum of Transportation in Duluth.

In 1866 the "Shakopee" began carrying passengers and their baggage between the Minnesota Central railroad's Minneapolis depot and the Minnesota Valley railroad's West St. Paul station.

1865-80
The Railroad Age

THE "WILLIAM CROOKS" steamed over the tracks from St. Paul to St. Anthony in 1862, finally connecting three communities that had long clamored for railroads. Although they depended on the Mississippi and overland stages for most of their transportation, the cities born on the river were also born into the railroad age. From the early years, visions of railroads inspired their most imaginative concepts of what the future might hold for them. Lines crisscrossing the state would tap the Great Lakes, connect with roads from the East, South, and Canada, and penetrate the West. The prospect of a route to the Pacific Ocean set off particular flights of fancy. "Then indeed will we be the half way house" between the East and the West, the *St. Anthony Express* commented in 1853, and "quietness will give place to the roar and bustle of business."[1]

The communities' enthusiasm for railroads persisted through false starts in the 1850s and through the stagnation of the Civil War years. Although the panic of 1873 further slowed development, many ambitious designs were realized. Crews of Scandinavian and Irish immigrants laid almost 3,000 miles of track in Minnesota between 1865 and 1880 and pushed additional rails beyond the state's boundaries. Lines connected the cities with the East, with Lake Superior at Duluth, and with Winnipeg, through St. Vincent in the Red River Valley. Especially exciting was the progress of the Northern Pacific's tracks across Dakota Territory, moving to meet rails heading east from the Pacific Coast.[2]

The railroads carried thousands of farmers and other settlers into the region that the cities claimed as their trade area: Minnesota and Dakota and Montana territories. Minnesota's population swelled to 780,773 by 1880, as a new agricultural frontier opened in the Red River Valley and farming families spread northwestward from their early concentration in the southeast. The populations of Dakota and Montana territories increased to 135,177 and 39,159, respectively, as new immigrants expanded the economies from fur trading and mining to agriculture and grazing. The cities' trade interests were not limited to this core area, nor did they have exclusive economic dominion over the region. But during these years of railroad

building, a strong link was forged between the urban center and the agricultural hinterland vital to the cities' development.[3]

Railroad development in some respects strengthened the bonds between St. Paul and the falls communities. At times they co-operated to block incursions into their intended empire by Chicago — the giant "devilfish" — and other cities; at times they joined forces to thwart the power of "monopolistic" railroads that threatened to engulf them "like a constrictor enfolds a victim." But when left to face each other, the cities quarreled over issues like the locations of tracks, terminals, shops, and depots, and they competed for the trade of the area they were so ready to defend together against invaders. The capital city advocated a "St. Paul system" of railroads, while the rival center countered by sponsoring "home roads" such as the Minneapolis and St. Louis.[4]

The community of interests between waxing Minneapolis and waning St. Anthony, as evident in the railroad age as it had been earlier, led to a merger in 1872. Residents of St. Paul, watching this development, must not have appreciated the *Minneapolis Daily Tribune*'s sly prediction that a future metropolis might include the capital city, renamed "South Minneapolis." After the merger, however, new terms expressing a metropolitan identity gradually crept into the language — the "Dual Cities," and, with increasing frequency, the "Twin Cities."[5]

"CITIES, like men, have golden opportunities sometimes afforded them, which once neglected, never occur again," the *Minneapolis Daily Tribune* commented as the city boomed in the late 1860s. The co-existence of water power, an abundant supply of wheat, and a railroad network that penetrated the wheat-growing regions presented Minneapolis with a truly golden opportunity. Mill after mill sprang up, until by 1880, 24 of them crowded the small industrial district within reach of the water power. The millers, using new grinding and purifying processes, produced a nutritious, fine white flour from hard spring wheat and found widespread markets for their product. When production of this popular flour reached over two million barrels in 1880, Minneapolis displaced St. Louis as the nation's leading flour-milling center.[6]

Other industries also prospered. Although sawmilling fell behind flour milling as the city's leading industry, the lumbermen almost doubled their production during the 1870s. From immense quantities of logs harvested in the northern pineries and driven down the Mississippi to their mills, they turned out 179,585,182 board feet of lumber in 1880. The products of sash, door, and blind factories, foundries, and wool, cotton, and paper mills added to the output. The city's desire to use raw materials from its trade empire for manufacturing at times seemed boundless. For example, the *Tribune* claimed in 1870 that with the completion of the railroad to Duluth there was no reason why Minneapolis, like cities in Pennsylvania, should not "manipulate the fine iron ores of Lake Superior."[7]

Two disasters menaced the industrial progress of the "Mill City" in this period. The most serious was a threat to the cataract that powered its most important industries. Held in place only by a thin layer of limestone, the falls had been receding for many years; the process accelerated when they were harnessed for power production. A scheme hatched by William W. Eastman and his partners for developing power on Nicollet Island brought a more immediate threat. On October 5, 1869, the tunnel they had been digging under the limestone sheath collapsed, and the river rushed into the hole. Hundreds of residents crowded up to the falls as an eddying current in the shattered area tore away chunks of limestone. The citizens labored for many days to fill in the chasms and build protective dams; then they enlisted support for more permanent measures. The city, the two water-power companies, private citizens, and the federal government rallied to save the falls. Over the next fifteen years preservation projects swallowed almost a million dollars.[8]

The mills rumbled on throughout the years that workmen fastened the falls securely in place. Then on May 2, 1878, disaster struck again. The Washburn A, the finest flour mill at the falls, exploded with a force resembling an earthquake. The blast and fire that leveled the "A" killed 18 men and destroyed five other flour mills, as well as planing mills, a railroad roundhouse, a machine shop, and additional structures. The owners responded by building new, more modern mills, and the flour millers quickly resumed their course toward supremacy in the nation.[9]

Minneapolis, while crediting industry for its prosperity, also attempted to overcome St. Paul's primacy in wholesaling. Strengthened by the railroad network, Minneapolis strove throughout the 1870s to "secure a foothold in the great Northwest." At the decade's close the volume of trade was still far short of the business done by St. Paul, but it was clear that the city was making progress toward diversification. Together the Twins claimed a $51,000,000 wholesale trade in 1879, distributing varied products like groceries, liquor, boots, shoes, farm machinery, drugs, hardware, wagons, and notions. They also marketed raw materials, among them furs, hides, wool, and grain.[10]

THE TUG-OF-WAR between the Twins was producing two cities with overlapping commercial and manufacturing functions. As Minneapolis built up its wholesale trade, St. Paul played its part by developing its varied industries. The capital city tried to acquire water power in the 1860s and early 1870s through a trade off: a lock and dam built below the falls near the Minneapolis city limits would give St. Paul water power and extend navigation into Minneapolis. After a spirited controversy that created dissension among Minneapolis businessmen as well as between the cities, the project failed. Nevertheless, St. Paul made some progress toward catching up with its neighbor's industrial output. By 1880 the value of its manufactured products totaled a little more than a third of that for Minneapolis — a marked increase over the tally recorded a decade earlier.[11]

St. Paul's industries were characterized in a revealing comment by a St. Paulite who, on a visit to the East in the early 1890s, found that his hosts assumed he was from Minneapolis. He concluded that the explanation for this mistake — an error that would be familiar to later residents of the cities — was the "wide advertising given to Minneapolis by the sale of its flour," while St. Paul had "no special product to make it famous." The capital city's growing manufacturing output was indeed miscellaneous. In 1880 there were 593 establishments, most of them small and labor intensive. Their products, like those of smaller Mill City firms, included clothing, machinery, patent medicine, mirrors, and harnesses. St. Paul also lacked a concentrated industrial district that could command the same attention as the solid core at the falls.[12]

In some respects the communities drew closer together as transportation and communications improved. Passengers traveled in omnibuses, carriages, and wagons as well as in trains that shuttled between the cities. More significant for the future of interurban transit, however, was the horsecar service begun by the St. Paul Street Railway Company in 1872 and the Minneapolis Street Railway Company three years later. By 1880 horses were pulling forty-seven cars at the rate of about six miles an hour over twenty miles of track — although rails spinning out from the cities' central business districts were not yet joined.[13]

The tiny cars, sometimes called "cracker boxes on

wheels," measured ten feet long between bulkheads and were painted colors like vermilion and green to distinguish the lines. Their interiors were lighted by dim oil lamps and heated by sheet-iron stoves; hay covered the floor to help keep the passengers' feet warm. The streetcars grew more popular as Twin Citians moved to residential districts farther and farther away from the downtowns. In 1880 almost two million passengers put their nickels into the fare boxes. Supplementing the horsecars at the end of the decade was a steam motor line to Lakes Calhoun and Harriet, opened by the Minneapolis, Lyndale and Lake Calhoun Railway.

Communications between the cities improved, too, when engineers laid out University Avenue — a route that was more direct than the "dozen or two meandering and labyrinthian cowpaths" residents had been traveling. First proposed in 1873, the parkway was to be a 600-foot-wide "grand boulevard" with a streetcar line, parks, and avenues; it would both link the cities and offer them an opportunity for great development. At a meeting to discuss plans for "Union Avenue," one of the proponents "launched into an eloquent and enthusiastic rhapsody over the prospective glory of 'Mississippi City.'" This new metropolis, to grow from the two cities, would have the state capitol and fairgrounds midway between the two old downtowns. Although the street that the cities built fell short of the "gorgeous ligatnent *[sic]*, the bond of union and the assurance of commercial thrift" that its planners envisioned, it did become a major artery of traffic later lined with businesses and houses.[14]

Communications were strengthened in other ways. The communities gained a telegraph service in 1860. In 1877 a new marvel — the telephone — was added when Richard H. Hankinson, general manager of the Northwestern Telegraph Company, installed homemade instruments that carried voices over an iron wire between his Minneapolis home and office. Two years later workmen connected the systems of the two cities, and by 1880 residents manipulated almost six hundred of the strange instruments.[15]

Telephoning was so simple, the *Minneapolis Tribune* assured its readers, that "any child able to speak distinctly can hold communication over the wires quite as readily as the most learned in the electrical sciences." The instructions the paper gave, however, might have been baffling even to an engineer. After describing how to make connections with "Mr. Jones," the following admonitions were given: "During the sending of the signal to Mr. Jones and the receipt of his answer, allow the speaking tube to REMAIN ON THE SWITCH hook. Having received the three answering taps from Mr. Jones, you take the speaking tube from the hook and turn the hook to the right or left, as you have been directed. Then proceed to talk, *the person making the call beginning the conversation by announcing his name and stating his wishes.* Having done this, he takes the telephone from his lips and presses it closely enough over one of his ears to shut out outside sounds while he receives the reply — taking care that the hole in the center of the telephone is placed over the centre of the opening in the ear. In speaking through the telephone, observe this rule: Hold the telephone as close to the lips as you can *without muffling your own voice . . . .* Having said your say, conclude with the words 'Good-bye,' after having received his answer that he understands you perfectly, and then replace the speaking tube on the hook. This is, in brief, the mode of communication."[16]

AS THE CITIES put their pioneer years behind them, their attitudes toward some urban services changed. For example, when the St. Paul Water Company was incorporated in 1856, Mayor George L. Becker observed that private enterprise had "happily relieved" city government of a responsibility. But it took the dilatory firm more than a dozen years to provide service. By that time an irritated Mayor Daniel A. Robertson declared that "you might as well . . . farm out the construction of your streets, your Levees, and even the business of the City Government to a private corporation, as the construction of Water Works." St. Paul's government delayed assuming responsibility for the water supply until 1882, but Minneapolis promptly established a municipal system when it was incorporated as a city in 1867.[17]

City governments also took charge of the bridges at the falls and at St. Paul's Wabasha Street, but private corporations still provided street lighting. In 1870 the newly organized Minneapolis Gas Light Company illuminated the lamps on the Mill City's streets; private enterprise had lighted St. Paul since 1856. The lamps of both cities glowed on streets still largely unpaved.[18]

Volunteer fire departments were disbanded in another move toward municipal assumption of urban services. Proud of their companies and the role they had played in community service, some volunteers were loath to give way to progress in the form of paid fire departments. The St. Paul companies reluctantly disbanded in 1877. Two years later the Minneapolis volunteers paraded with gaily decorated engines and hose carts to mark the end of their service. "They have [been] the pride of the city," Mayor Alonzo Rand said, and "the debt we owe them can never be paid."[19]

Both cities expanded their peace-keeping forces and togged out their policemen in brass-buttoned uniforms. The natty officers carried out sentences putting many male lawbreakers to work — some Minneapolis prisoners labored in a stoneyard while their St. Paul counterparts joined the "ball and chain gang" that improved streets, filled in swamps, and graded hills. Both cities tolerated some forms of vice, imposing regular fines on houses of prostitution, but not eradicating the red-light districts. Penalties paid by errant women were invested in their redemption. Half of the fines collected in Minneapolis brothels supported the Bethany Home, opened in 1876 as a branch of the Minnesota Magdalen Society and dedicated to saving "fallen women" who wanted to change their ways. St. Paul's female prisoners were boarded at the House of the Good Shepherd, a Catholic home for "wayward girls" of all creeds, and the city's fines were divided among this institution, the Magdalen Society, and the city hospital.[20]

The institutions receiving such support were part of a growing social welfare network spread by private and public agencies. The Christian Aid Society in Minneapolis, the Home for the Friendless in St. Paul, and the St. Paul Society for Improving the Condition of the Poor were among several groups established after the Civil War. Government also assumed a stronger role in providing care for the indigent. Ramsey County had opened a poor farm in 1854. After the state legislature required that other counties do the same, Hennepin County followed suit in 1865. Although a poorhouse was regarded "as a sort of community woodpile where vagrants could work out their board and keep," public responsibility for the indigent had at least been given greater recognition. State institutions in other Minnesota cities offered care for the deaf, mute, blind, and insane.[21]

St. Paul extended public responsibility for health care with the establishment of a city-county hospital in 1873. Minneapolis and Hennepin County were without a public hospital (other than a pesthouse) until the following decade, but their governments paid the expenses of many patients admitted to the Cottage Hospital of the Brotherhood of Gethsemane (later St. Barnabas), founded in 1871. Both cities had boards of public health, required by an 1873 state law to make inspections of sanitary conditions (still deplorable) and ensure adherence to regulations regarding infectious diseases. By 1879 St. Joseph's and St. Luke's, private hospitals founded earlier in St. Paul, and 136 individual physicians or partnerships added to the health-care services in the Twin Cities. The physicians indicated something of the variety of treatment by identifying themselves in city directories as homeopathic, physio-medical, magnetic, botanic, eclectic, or "hygenic."[22]

Combined public and private efforts also expanded the educational system from the firm base laid down in earlier years. By 1880 each of the cities had thirteen public schools, as well as a number of private institutions. As the University of Minnesota continued to grow and church-sponsored Augsburg, Macalester,

and Hamline put down their roots, the Twins began to win a reputation as cities of colleges.[23]

And the churches seemed to be everywhere, both in their community involvement and in their many buildings dotting the urban landscape. By 1880 St. Paul had forty-nine congregations and Minneapolis had fifty-eight, most of which had buildings. The churches reflected the Twins' ethnic mix. For example, in addition to Jewish synagogues, there were congregations of German, French, Polish, and Bohemian Catholics, German, Norwegian, Swedish, and Danish Lutherans, and German, Scandinavian, and African Methodists. St. Paul had special prominence for Catholics as the administrative headquarters of a diocese extending westward to the Missouri River.[24]

A strong Scandinavian influx beginning in the late 1860s added variety to the ethnic mix, although the ratios of foreign-born to native-born residents remained about the same. By 1880 the Swedes formed the largest foreign-born group in Minneapolis, and the Norwegians were in third place following the British Americans; in St. Paul the Swedes ranked third after the dominant Germans and Irish. Many poorer Swedes and Norwegians clustered in such ethnic pockets as St. Paul's Swede Hollow and a large apartment building in Minneapolis called "Noah's Ark." As the influx continued, Minneapolis acquired the image of a Scandinavian city that it bears today.[25]

The Scandinavian wave did not wash away German and Irish influences. The Germans, with their "affinity for beer," were well-known brewers and saloonkeepers and remained prominent in the cities' cultural life. The Irish were exceptionally visible in St. Paul. One historian suggests that this community, predominantly German, acquired an Irish image because of the Irish domination of St. Paul politics and the city's strongly promoted observances of St. Patrick's Day.[26]

FADS, FASHIONS, AND ENTERTAINMENT were the trappings of city life that came with diversity and growth. A visitor commented as early as 1866 that Minneapolis was "doffing the simplicity of a country town for the more pretentious dignity of a city. . . . Ladies ape the latest styles of dress, such as the tiniest little hats and the biggest tilting hoops. Men go about sporting monkey coats and plug-hats. Fast young men sport fancy turn-outs, drive fast horses, and talk race-course slang. 'Brandysmashes,' 'mint julips [sic],' are imbibed with the most inimitable *sang froid,* and fifteen cent cigars, or meerschaums are puffed with a gusto truly interesting."[27]

The admiration of fast horses was not limited to fast young men. Notable citizens could be counted among the Twin Citians who flocked to driving parks and the state fair, where they watched horses in tests of "speed, blood and bottom." The contenders, racing "under the saddle" or pulling sulkies, buggies, or wagons, vied for a variety of prizes. The St. Paul Driving Association, which sponsored its events in the midway area, tried to ensure respectability by enforcing racing rules and barring drunks and persons of "known bad character." Nevertheless, some critics censured racing as an inducement to gambling, which in turn led to "demoralization."[28]

Baseball, like racing, was a popular sport in the Twin Cities and the rest of the state. The Minnesota State Association of Base Ball Players, formed in 1867, reflected the widespread interest. In the 1860s and 1870s players in the Twin Cities formed many clubs, including the Saxons, Unions, Olympics, North Stars, Blue Stars, Silver Stars, White Shirts, Red Caps, Red Stockings, Blue Stockings, and Brown Stockings; there was also at least one all-black team. Wearing their bright uniforms, the teams played clubs from Milwaukee and Chicago as well as from several Minnesota towns. Heckling by the fans sometimes enlivened the numerous contests between St. Paul and Minneapolis. But baseball, like racing, had its detractors. For example, the *St. Anthony Falls Democrat* commented on May 6, 1870, that "One of the advantages of winter over summer is that the people are not afflicted with base ball club doings. . . . Of what possible account is it to any human being whether one club or another beats?"[29]

A velocipede mania in 1869 brought crowds into halls to see riders of the "untamable" machines cavort on sawdust courses. Additional hundreds found amusement in William S. King's Lake Calhoun Pavilion. When the three-story pleasure palace opened on June 28, 1877, nearly six hundred Twin Citians toured the building. A band played on the veranda and guests savored a banquet prepared by the pavilion's new chef from Washington, D.C., and danced the night away in the grand ballroom.[30]

Visiting musicians, stock companies, variety artists, and other performers flocked to the cities' stages, at times competing for public attention. Musical groups of the two cities sometimes played together, in counterpoint to civic disharmonies. For example, in

1867 musicians from both cities helped dedicate the St. Paul Opera House and the Pence Opera House in Minneapolis. These elaborate new playhouses offered fancy settings for performances. The Pence featured excellent acoustics, a drop curtain depicting "Beautiful Venice, Bride of the Sea," a bust of Shakespeare supported by two angels over the proscenium arch, and upholstered settees for patrons.

But while Mill Citians had turned out in force to dedicate the St. Paul Opera House, the *Minneapolis Tribune* reported that only eleven St. Paulites were among the 1,300 celebrating the Pence's opening night. The *St. Paul Pioneer* retorted: "Well, what of it? Nobody expects the denizens of a metropolis to go into the country to witness musical or dramatic entertainments."[31]

By 1880 even chauvinistic St. Paulites would have to admit that their neighbor was no longer out in the country. The census revealed that Minneapolis had passed the "metropolis" in population, 46,887 to 41,473. The triumphant *Tribune* expected St. Paul newspapers "to be seized with gripes and conniptions," and its expectation was fulfilled. The journals worried the subject in many inches of print, warming up for the greater census war that would be waged at the end of the next decade.[32]

In many ways the years from 1865 to 1880 were a crucial period in the development of Minneapolis and St. Paul. Their character had been cast as twin cities, performing duplicate social, cultural, urban, and economic functions. Although they were alike in many respects, they were also acquiring distinctive images — Minneapolis as Scandinavian, Protestant, and Republican, and St. Paul as Irish, Catholic, and Democratic. In population Minneapolis had grown larger than St. Paul, and would remain so, and yet the capital city would remain a large, growing, and vital neighbor. Together the cities had been nurtured by the river; together they had been strengthened by the railroad network. Equaled by no other urban center west of Chicago and Milwaukee in the northern reaches of the nation, they were in 1880 poised on the edge of a remarkable era that would carry them into the ranks of major American cities.[31]

"God speed the coming of the Northern Pacific railroad!" exclaimed the *Minneapolis Tribune* in August, 1869, as explorers examining the route headed back to the city from the western plains. This section of the returning expedition paused in front of Alonzo H. Beal's Washington Avenue gallery, located beyond the camera's range near the tea and coffee sign to the right. Construction of the railroad began the next year.

Railroad and water transportation met at St. Paul's Lower Levee in this photograph from the middle or late 1860s. James J. Hill's business enterprises symbolized the intersection that was so important to the city's development. Hill, who was the freight and ticket agent for the Northwestern Union Packet Company, in 1866 became general transportation agent for the St. Paul and Pacific railroad. He transferred shipments between rails and water through the warehouse that stood in front of the railroad's huge elevator.

In about 1873, trains, freight, and people passed through the St. Paul and Pacific's elevator and depots at Washington Avenue and Fourth Avenue North in Minneapolis. When a train first "thundered over the new bridge" in 1867, Minneapolitans, who up to then had to catch trains in St. Anthony, greeted it with "loud huzzas" and a salute from the German Turners' band.

St. Paul and Pacific coaches, below, took passengers to destinations as far north and west as Breckenridge on the boundary of Dakota Territory. The 1872 timetable at left advertised services that had been greatly expanded since the company issued its first schedule a decade earlier.

THE FIRST DIVISION
OF THE
ST. PAUL AND PACIFIC
RAILROAD.

1872. SUMMER TIME TABLE. 1872.

MAIN LINE.

GOING WEST.					GOING EAST.		
7.50	A. M.	Leave,	ST. PAUL,	6.15	P. M.	Arrive,
8.23	"	"	ST. ANTHONY,	5.42	"	Leave,
8.35	"	"	MINNEAPOLIS,	5.35	"	"
10.05	"	"	DELANO,	4.08	"	"
11.56	"	"	LITCHFIELD,	2.09	"	"
1.25	P. M.	"	WILLMAR,	1.00	"	"
2.50	"	"	BENSON,	11.16	A. M.	"
4.00	"	"	MORRIS,	10.00	"	"
7.30	"	Arrive,	BRECKENRIDGE,	6.15	"	Leave,

ST. PAUL & LITCHFIELD TRAIN.

3.45	P. M.	Leave,	ST. PAUL,	10.35	A. M.	Arrive,
4.20	"	"	ST. ANTHONY,	10.02	"	"
4.32	"	"	MINNEAPOLIS,	9.55	"	"
6.10	"	"	DELANO,	8.30	"	"
8.05	"	Arrive,	LITCHFIELD,	6.30	"	Leave,

ST. PAUL & MINNEAPOLIS TRAIN.

11.30 A. M.	6.15	Leave,	ST. PAUL,	7.50 A. M.	2.40 P. M.	Arrive,
12.05 P. M.	6.50	"	ST. ANTHONY,	7.17 "	2.07 "	"
12.15 "	7.00	"	MINNEAPOLIS,	7.10 "	2.00 "	Leave,

BRANCH LINE.

GOING NORTH.					GOING SOUTH.		
8.30 A. M.	4.45 P. M.	Leave,	ST. PAUL,	11.05 A. M.	7.15 P. M.	Arrive,
9.00	5.15	"	JUNCTION,	10.35	6.45	"
9.50	6.00	"	ANOKA,	9.50	6.00	"
10.40	6.45	"	ELK RIVER,	9.02	5.10	"
12.50 P. M.	8.25	"	ST. CLOUD,	7.28	3.00	"
12.56 "	8.30	Arrive,	SAUK RAPIDS,	7.20	2.45	Leave,

☞ PURCHASE TICKETS at the Stations before entering the Cars, at a Discount from the regular Train Rates.

☞ Passengers must get their Baggage Checked before it will be carried over the road, and on the arrival of the Train at place of destination, must present the check and take possession of their Baggage.

The Company will not be responsible for the Safety of any Baggage after its arrival at Station for which it is checked—it being no part of the business of this Company to receive and store baggage unless a special contract is made to that effect.

J. H. RANDALL,   E. Q. SEWALL,
Superintendent.

Although rails connected the three cities with Chicago in 1867, the Milwaukee and St. Paul railroad (later the Chicago, Milwaukee and St. Paul) provided a more direct link some five years later. At about that time a Milwaukee and St. Paul train halted on St. Paul's Lower Levee in the shadow of the city's business district.

The railroads were not popular with everyone. At the meeting this handbill advertised, Ignatius Donnelly assailed them for creating monopolies, raising freight rates, manipulating wheat markets, and corrupting legislators. When the audience at Ingersoll Hall, St. Paul, laughed, cheered, and stamped their feet in response, the *St. Paul Pioneer* remarked that "Mr. Donnelly had evidently struck the nail on the head, and the point was appreciated by his hearers."

The Chicago, Milwaukee and St. Paul railroad's Italianate passenger depot (left) and freight station in Minneapolis reflected the road's importance as a major tie between the Twin Cities and the East. Carriages and other horse-drawn vehicles pulled up to the depot in 1878, two years after its construction on Washington Avenue between South Third and Fourth avenues.

Four miles separated the cities' boundaries in 1875 when this map was published. Already there were almost two thousand miles of railroad tracks in Minnesota. The legend on the map boasted that twelve "important" railroads were bringing to the "Dual City" the "Commerce of an Empire."

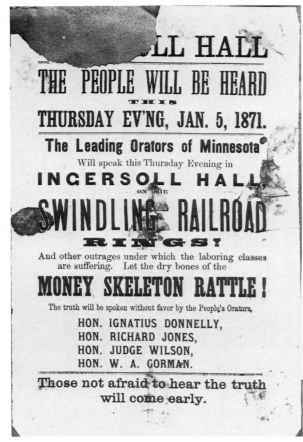

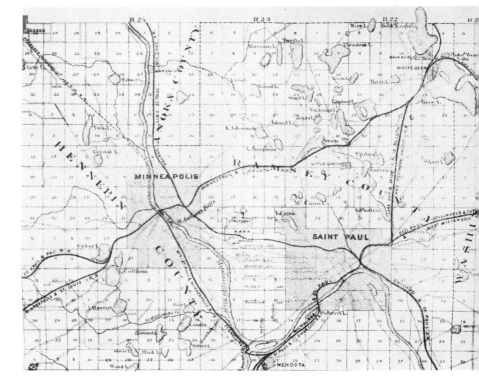

St. Paul's commercial district still centered at the river when this panoramic view was made from Dayton's Bluff about 1866. The city's population of over 12,000, however, was spreading from the riverbank over the amphitheater of hills. The dome of the state capitol is visible at far right and the Wabasha Street Bridge is at the left.

Although steamboat traffic at St. Paul had declined by the mid-1870s, cargo like these chairs could still be shipped by water. The large building to the right is the depot of the Chicago, Milwaukee and St. Paul railroad at the foot of Jackson Street. The Wabasha Street Bridge is in the background.

The "Minnesota," the "City of St. Paul," and forty-three other steamboats made 792 trips to St. Paul in 1869, the year this photograph of the Lower Levee was made. Many of them towed barges that contributed to the volume of freight handled at the levees. In the background, from the left, are the St. Paul Fire and Marine Insurance Company's building at 84 Third Street; the Merchants Hotel at Third and Jackson streets; and Henry Eames's flour and feed store at 105 Jackson.

Outward-bound passengers at the corner of Third and Jackson streets in the early 1870s could buy a railroad ticket in Prince's Block and travel down the slope to the depot — or take the steamboat waiting at the foot of Jackson Street. They could also send messages from the telegraph offices located nearby on Third Street.

In the early 1870s William Illingworth photographed St. Paul's main business thoroughfares. Scenes from the warehouse district and from Third Street (later Kellogg Boulevard), the commercial heart of the city and a trade center for thousands of people in the Northwest, are reproduced on these pages.

Beaupre and Kelly, a wholesale grocery firm, moved into a new building on the southeast corner of Third and Sibley streets in 1873. In saluting the event, the *St. Paul Daily Press* claimed that the partners "control a trade whose ramifications extend over hundreds of miles in every direction, from the interior of Iowa to Lake Winnipeg, and from central Wisconsin to the Rocky Mountains."

The structure housing the rival grocery firm of P. F. McQuillan and Company stood on the northeast corner of Third and Sibley. A vehicle of the St. Paul Omnibus Line paused in front of the building in about 1874.

At Sibley and Fourth streets, one block from the busy Third Street intersection, stood the Sherman House. Its billiard hall, advertised in a first-floor window, was one of six in the city when this view was made in about 1873. The grain elevator at the right reaches up from the Lower Levee.

The four-story building of Auerbach, Finch, Culbertson and Company, a dry-goods wholesaling and retailing firm on the northeast corner of Fourth and Jackson streets, was new when this photograph was made about 1876. Prominently displayed over the Jackson Street boardwalk was an advertising symbol — the mortar and pestle of A. J. Wampler, druggist.

(A) As prospective customers strolled west on Third Street from Sibley Street, they passed a row of wholesaling firms that offered goods to St. Paul and the Northwest. Visible from right to left were Nicols and Dean, iron and heavy hardware (62 Third), John H. Camp, dry goods and notions (64 Third), and Forepaugh and Tarbox, boots and shoes (66 Third).

(B) Across the street were, left to right, Noyes Bros. and Cutler, drugs, paints, oils, and glass (67 Third), Comstock, Castle and Company, stove manufacturer (69 Third, above), and Strong, Hackett and Chapin, stoves, hardware, and tinners' stock (69 Third, below).

(C) In the next block of Third Street, between Jackson and Robert, Anson H. Rose kept a drugstore on the corner (118 Jackson) and, in the distance, R. A. Lanpher and Company sold hats, caps, and "gents furnishing goods" (94 Third). Prince's Block (see p. 53) was across the street from the Rose store.

(D) The St. Paul Fire and Marine Insurance Company shared its building at Third and Jackson, across from the Rose drugstore and Prince's Block, with the Spread Eagle Bar (left, lower floor) and the St. Paul Commercial College and Telegraphic Institute (right, upper floor). The institute offered "Rare Facilities . . . to Young Ladies for a Valuable Course of Training."

(E) West on Third from Cedar Street, left to right, businesses included Le Bon Ton dining room (177 Third), E. B. Tenney, merchant tailor (179 Third), Willius Bros. and Dunbar, bankers (183 Third), and the Pacific and Atlantic Telegraph Company (191 Third). Detail is at left, (F).

(G) On Third west from Minnesota Street, left to right, other merchants sold their wares: Prendergast Bros., stoves and tinware (161 Third), Kalmon Lion and Son, gents' furnishings and clothing (165 Third), and Henri Rochat, watchmaker and jeweler (167 Third). The Young Men's Christian Association Reading Room was on the north side of the street. The delivery van of the Farmers and Mechanics Grocery Association, headquartered at Seventh and Robert streets, visited the block. Detail is at left, (H).

The St. Paul Roller Mill Company at 34 West Third Street near the Wabasha Street Bridge advertised itself in 1881. The company probably succeeded the Capital Mills, which operated at the same location in the previous year, when it was one of seven flour mills in the city.

The crew posing for this group portrait in 1882 manufactured "Orange Blossom" flour and other brands. "Strangers visiting St. Paul always remark the superior quality of the bread found at the hotels," a business directory commented. "This is due, in a great degree, to the fact that they all use the Orange Blossom flour."

By 1867 Theodore Hamm's Excelsior Brewery operated at Phalen Creek on the East Side near Swede Hollow. In 1880 St. Paul's eleven breweries, many run and patronized by German immigrants, gave the industry a prominent position in the city's business life.

Phalen Creek attracted other industries as well. Water from the creek and steam powered Schaber and Wendt's flour and feed mill (foreground), which had been in operation for many years when this view was made about 1885.

Blodgett and Osgood, photographed in about 1875, made wooden boxes and planed lumber at Cedar and Sixth streets. The firm benefited from a St. Paul Chamber of Commerce scheme to encourage industrial development. In 1867 the chamber had organized the St. Paul Manufacturing Company, which constructed the building and offered its rooms and power at low rents to a variety of small industries.

The Keller family had been wholesale and retail lumber dealers at Seventh and Minnesota streets under several firm names for many years before these men posed in the 1880s. At various times the family also had mills at Phalen Creek and Como Avenue, St. Paul, as well as in South Stillwater.

The Syllabi, first publication of John B. West and Company, was printed on a hand press in a small shop at 60 West Third Street. In the early 1880s, when the company was on its way to becoming the largest law book publisher in the world, compositors set type by hand in the firm's new quarters at 313 Wabasha Street.

ST. PAUL HARVESTER WORKS

The thousands of farmers who followed the railroads westward and settled the prairies encouraged the manufacture of farm machinery in the Twin Cities. Among the plants was the St. Paul Harvester Works, depicted in 1874, when it was just northeast of the city limits near the line of the Lake Superior and Mississippi railroad. Over two hundred men worked in the plant, turning out machines that were "gorgeous in vermillion, gold and black."

The railroads created their own demands for manufacturing and repairing equipment. The Jackson Street shops (also known as the Mississippi Street shops) and roundhouse of the St. Paul and Pacific, photographed in about 1875, helped keep that road running.

Building demands became intense as the Twin Cities' population more than quadrupled between 1865 and 1880. The enormous need for construction materials fostered many new companies, including that of M. H. Crittenden, a St. Paul manufacturer at Eighth and Wabasha streets who sold paving cement and concrete walks as well as the products advertised here in 1871.

The United States Army's Department of Dakota had its headquarters in St. Paul from the 1860s until 1881, when it occupied this new building at Fort Snelling. The department encompassed Minnesota, Dakota Territory, and Montana Territory during this critical period of white expansion into Indian country. The headquarters administered forts in the district and dispatched troops to protect crews building the Northern Pacific railroad across the western plains.

The United States Customs House at Fifth and Wabasha streets took six years and $350,000 to build. Two years into construction in 1869, below, the Kasota limestone walls are flanked by the Cathedral of St. Paul at right and the tower of the Market Street Methodist Episcopal Church facing Rice Park. The building housed the federal courts and the post office in the 1870s and 1880s; streetcar wires frame the view at right, about 1900.

St. Paul's police department in 1874 consisted of a chief, a captain, a sergeant, and twenty-four patrolmen. A historian of the department observed that the force struggled to keep peace in the "low river dives and dance halls, and groggeries" on Bench or Second Street, into which "no respectable man, much less a woman, dared enter" after dark.

Students and teachers lined up in front of the new Franklin School on Broadway between Ninth and Tenth streets in 1865. The cost of $16,969.13 included the site, structure, furniture, fence, and outbuildings.

More than fine manners were taught at the St. Paul Female Seminary. The course of study included English literature, drawing, painting, music, penmanship, French, Italian, German, mathematics, natural philosophy, astronomy, botany, and natural, mental, and moral science. St. Paul pupils sometimes entertained boarders in their homes. *"We did have a glorious time,"* wrote one such partygoing student from Vermont in 1867, about the time this view was made.

"THAT OUR DAUGHTERS MAY BE AS CORNER STONES, POLISHED AFTER THE SIMILITUDE OF A PALACE."

The Minnesota State Reform School opened in 1868 at St. Anthony Avenue and Griggs Street, near the St. Paul city limits, to provide training for wayward children. It housed more boys than girls when this photograph was made in the 1880s. Superintendent John G. Riheldaffer, who also operated the St. Paul Female Seminary, reasoned that the "bad conduct of boys is more open and annoying to the community, and hence officials are more ready to seek their restraint and reformation."

In 1875 the reform school opened a carpentry and notion shop to manufacture "all kinds of wheelbarrows, boys' sleds, wagons and carts, and a variety of things in plain furniture as we may find a market for them." School administrators emphasized teaching trades to the boys before their release.

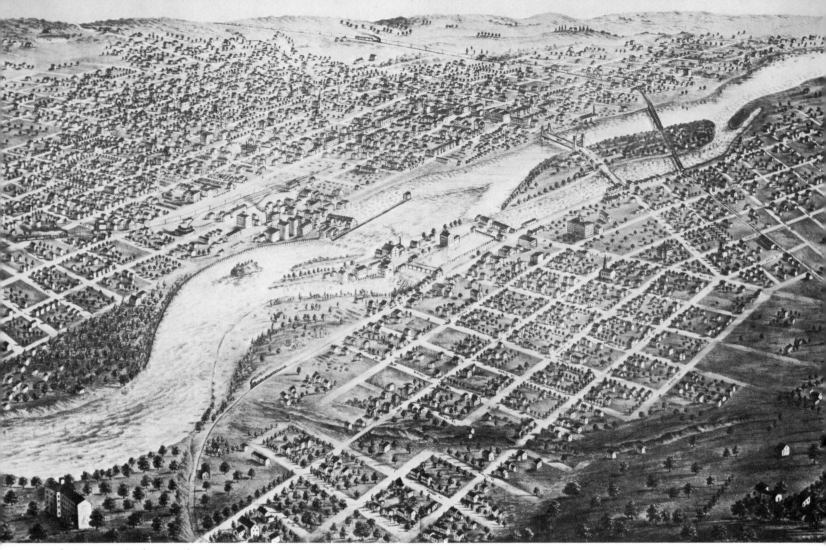

By 1867 Minneapolis (across the river in this bird's-eye view) had made great strides to eclipse St. Anthony. Already the number of mills on the Minneapolis water front exceeded those on the opposite riverbank, and a substantial business complex extended from the end of the Suspension Bridge across Bridge Square to Washington Avenue. The St. Paul and Pacific reached over the horizon toward the northwest, while other tracks led south and east toward connections with Chicago.

Minneapolitans chose Bridge Square as the site of their first city hall, constructed in 1873, one year after the merger with St. Anthony (and long after St. Paul had built one). The blue limestone structure, pictured here about 1875, housed the post office, the *Minneapolis Tribune,* and the Northwestern Telegraph Company as well as city offices. The main entrances were on Nicollet (left) and Hennepin (right) avenues. It had a steam-powered elevator, reported by the *Tribune* to be "the first . . . erected in the State for carrying passengers."

Minneapolis caught up with St. Paul in another respect when Harlow Gale, a real-estate dealer, built this new market house in 1876 on Bridge Square at Hennepin Avenue and First Street under an agreement with the city. A visitor impressed by the picturesque structure commented that "it appeared to have been transported bodily from some Spanish or Italian city."

(B) A mass of stores, banks, offices, halls, and other buildings crowded onto Bridge Square in the 1860s and 1870s to form the business district of Minneapolis. An unknown photographer stood atop the Nicollet Hotel in 1869 to shoot this view of Hennepin Avenue from the corner of Washington Avenue toward the river.

Brick and stone had begun to replace frame construction at the square. D. R. Wagner's tea, coffee, and spice store, at left, marks the intersection with Washington; the large building to the right is the Pence Opera House at Hennepin and Second Street. The St. Paul and Pacific railroad's bridge spans the river in the background.

(C) Washington Avenue is in the foreground and Hennepin Avenue intersects it to the left in this 1871 view. On the corner is the Johnston Block, which Savory and Johnston, druggists, shared with several other businesses.

(A) In about 1870 Wagner's store anchored this view along Washington Avenue North toward Fourth Avenue North, where the St. Paul and Pacific's elevator rose at top left.

Posters on the wall of Greely, Loye and Company's harness rooms (see page 69) announced performances by Professor Anderson, "The Great Magician," as well as other entertainments offered in the early 1870s.

(D) Nicollet Avenue from Washington Avenue to the river is seen in a view made about 1873. The First National Bank is at the corner in the left foreground; the new city hall was soon to rise on Bridge Square, in the background.

(E) The Northwestern National Bank of Minneapolis, doing business in the mid-1870s at the corner of Washington Avenue and First Avenue South, was organized by millers, merchants, railroad men, and other businessmen. Like the First National Bank, it became an enduring and influential financial institution.

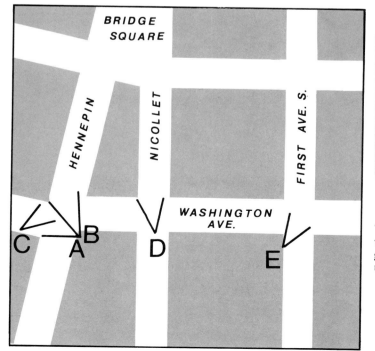

This map shows the locations and viewing angles used by the photographers who took the pictures on these two pages.

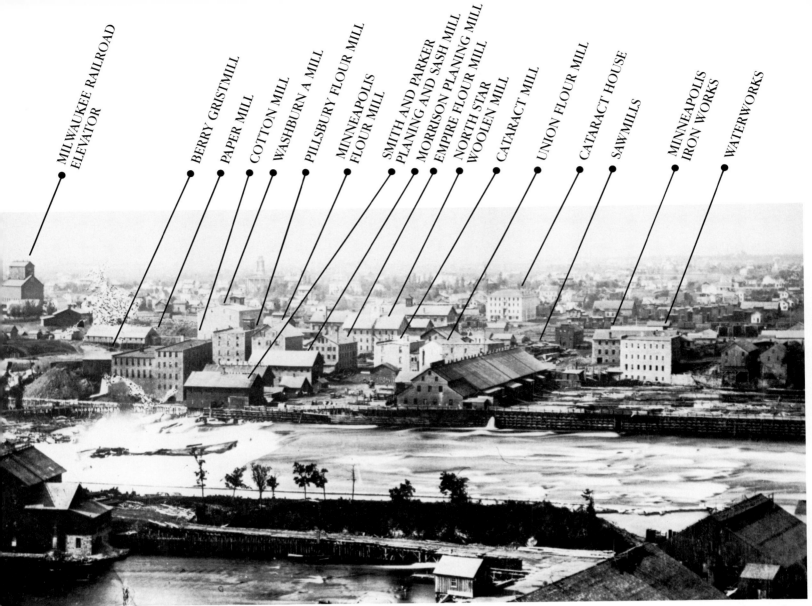

MILWAUKEE RAILROAD ELEVATOR

BERRY GRISTMILL

PAPER MILL

COTTON MILL

WASHBURN A MILL

PILLSBURY FLOUR MILL

MINNEAPOLIS FLOUR MILL

SMITH AND PARKER PLANING AND SASH MILL

MORRISON PLANING MILL

EMPIRE FLOUR MILL

NORTH STAR WOOLEN MILL

CATARACT MILL

UNION FLOUR MILL

CATARACT HOUSE

SAWMILLS

MINNEAPOLIS IRON WORKS

WATERWORKS

Logs and lumber destined for markets downriver traveled around the falls through these sluices along the west bank, shown here about 1868. To adventurous boys, the sluices were slippery slides. According to one observer, they would "undress at the mills, get into the chute, and go with the strong current, feet foremost, away down the decline and drop out at the lower end."

Minneapolis industries clustered close to the water power in about 1872. The Board of Trade estimated in 1872 that ninety-five water wheels at the falls provided 6,000 horsepower to the industries.

Continuing dangers menaced the falls after the collapse of Eastman's tunnel in 1869. Breaks in the limestone sheath and spring floods through the early 1870s damaged the falls and impeded stablization efforts. Major breaks, at points A, B, and C, are keyed to photographs on the opposite page.

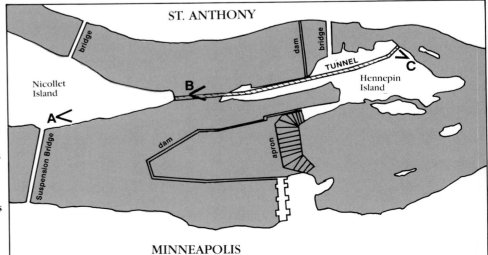

ST. ANTHONY

bridge

dam

bridge

TUNNEL

C

Nicollet Island

B

Hennepin Island

A

Suspension Bridge

dam

apron

MINNEAPOLIS

(A) Observers feared that Hennepin Island would wash away when they saw the destructive force of the water unleashed as the tunnel collapsed. But workmen's heroic efforts saved the day. Here they are building a coffer dam of timber cribs filled with rocks, probably around the area shattered by the first break on October 5, 1869.

(C) High water and ice masses once more imperiled Hennepin Island mills during the spring of 1870, while falls preservation work was still in progress. In mid-April the weakened limestone base on the lower island sank, and the Summit flour mill, Moulton's planing mill, and a wheat warehouse adjoining the Island mill tumbled into the river.

(B) The river again rushed into the tunnel on October 20, 1869, through a new break between the foot of Nicollet Island and the head of Hennepin Island. The force was so great that water spouted thirty to forty feet into the air. Again workmen quickly rallied to save the falls by plugging the hole and building coffer dams. The Farnham and Lovejoy sawmill on Hennepin Island (background) withstood the shock, as it had the earlier catastrophe.

Apron construction was a major engineering project. Over a foundation of huge pine logs and fragmented rock, workmen placed tiers of thick timbers. When the apron was completed, the water flowed over the falls on "an easy inclined plane." The *Minneapolis Tribune* printed the cataract's obituary in 1870: "The great Falls of St. Anthony, as a work of nature, have passed away. They exhibit now the wonderful genius and power of man, and are shorn of their power for destruction to property and capital."

A committee of citizens and industrialists undertook a long-term preservation project in 1866 to halt the recession of the falls caused by erosion of the sandstone under the hard limestone sheath. A flood in 1867 and the 1869 tunnel breaks defeated their early attempts to build the permanent protective shield, called an apron. These workmen were probably laboring on the falls in 1870, when the project succeeded.

The Washburn A on the west bank was the largest flour mill at the falls when it was completed in 1874. Built of limestone, it measured about 90 feet high and 100 by 138 feet at ground level. Some of its machinery was manufactured in Austria, and its workmen were trained in European milling techniques. These exterior and interior photographs were made about 1875.

THE MINNEAPOLIS
MILL DISASTER

Words and Music by M. L. RENTFROW.

Illustrated by Permission of W. H. Jacoby, Minneapolis, Minn.

PUBLISHED BY
A. M. HALL & C?
MINNEAPOLIS, MINN.

The explosion on May 2, 1878, that killed eighteen men and destroyed the Washburn A and five other flour mills was commemorated in sheet music published in the same year. Milton L. Rentfrow's verses included:
All that was left next morn to tell,
Of how those mighty Mills had fell,
Was a smoking mass of crumbled walls,
Which lay beneath our feet.

The shattered walls and twisted machinery of the Washburn A testified to the force of the blast. A Minneapolis woman reported soon after the 1878 disaster that most of the windows on Washington Avenue and some on Nicollet Avenue were broken, debris was carried as far as St. Paul, and the "jar was felt in Stillwater."

The Monitor Plow Works, established at the falls in 1860, switched to steam power and moved in 1875 to a twenty-acre tract on the west side of Minneapolis. The plant, photographed a year later across the line of the St. Paul and Pacific railroad, manufactured "brush breaking" plows, gang plows, and other machinery.

From the 1850s, some manufacturers in Minneapolis and St. Anthony had built plants powered by steam. In the 1870s and 1880s more businesses joined them as the falls area became crowded, the flour mills absorbed much of the available water power, and businessmen recognized that the limit of the cataract's potential power would soon be reached. The industries that developed away from the falls were much like those in St. Paul.

Catering to the needs of the horse-using public in about 1870, Greely, Loye and Company handled whips, collars, and blankets as well as making harnesses and saddles. The company shared the building at Nicollet Avenue at Second Street with well-advertised firms.

Workmen in this 1874 engraving are moving wheels along a ramp connecting the second floor of the Minnehaha Carriage Works with the storage yard. The factory was located on Second Street between South First and Second avenues.

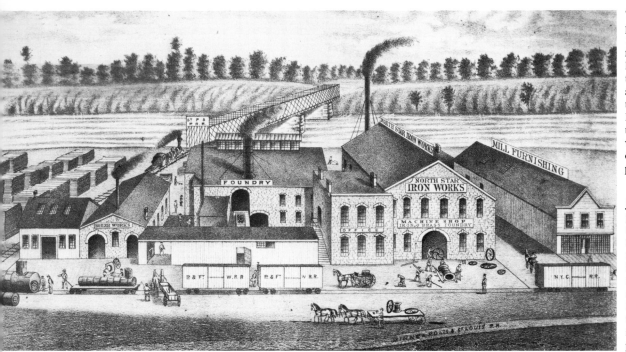

The North Star Iron Works, depicted in 1874, left the falls about 1870 when its proprietors could find no land for expansion. Its new location was the entire block between North Second and Third avenues, on the river and adjacent to the tracks of the St. Paul and Pacific railroad. The firm manufactured steam engines, water wheels, flour and sawmill machinery, hot air furnaces, and other products.

Joseph Dean, who built his steam-powered Pacific Mills in 1866 above the Suspension Bridge on the west bank of the river, was in the vanguard of lumbermen establishing a new center for the industry in North Minneapolis. In their more spacious location, mills like Dean's, seen here in 1874, retained access to the log supply arriving by river from the northern pineries.

HOLBROOK & Co.,
PORK & BEEF PACKERS.
WHOLESALE DEALERS IN
Pickled, Smoked and Dried Meats
OFFICE AND PACKING HOUSE:
300—315 First Avenue South,
MINNEAPOLIS.

OUR BRAND

WILLARD·STURTEVANT

☞ CAUTION.—*Please notice that all our Goods bear our Trade-Mark, as above,* BRANDED *on the meat or package. None other are genuine.* ☜

Our meats are highly recommended both for Quality and Economy, and are already in very great demand.

SWEET PICKLED HAMS—Mild Sugar Cured—Superior Quality.
"   "   SHOULDERS—Same Quality as our Hams.
DRIED OR SMOKED BEEF—Extra Quality—For Family Use.
ENGLISH BREAKFAST BACON—Very Superior—For Family Use.
PICKLED OR SMOKED BEEF and PORK TONGUES—Very Choice.
"   "   "   PORK HOCKS a Specialty.—"English Cut."
SMOKED AND FRESH SAUSAGE—of all kinds.

Minneapolis, like St. Paul, hoped to become a major meat-packing center. Several small plants were operating in both cities by 1877, when Holbrook and Company placed this advertisement.

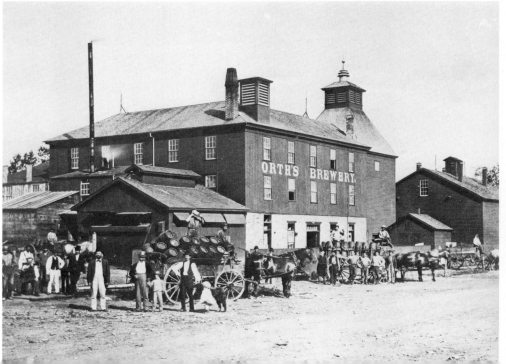

Orth's Brewery, shown here about 1880 at Marshall Street and Thirteenth Avenue Northeast, was established in St. Anthony in 1850. John Orth, like Theodore Hamm of St. Paul, was a German immigrant who helped make brewing into a major Twin Cities industry. By 1880 there were four breweries in Minneapolis.

70

Augsburg Seminary's class of 1878 was trained in a Minneapolis building completed in 1872 at Seventh Street Southeast and Twenty-first Avenue South. The Norwegian Lutheran institution evolved into the present-day Augsburg College.

After a slow beginning, the University of Minnesota in Minneapolis was on its way by 1880, about the time this picture was made of "Old Main." Enrollment that year totaled 308, and seventeen students graduated. Old Main, however, was an uncomfortable headquarters for a flourishing university. It had no ventilation system, plumbing, or gas, and wood stoves did not adequately warm what one writer called the "Siberian stretches of the recitation rooms."

Winthrop School at Mill and Third streets in Southeast Minneapolis, shown about 1875, was known as Central School until 1878. It housed a primary department, an intermediate department, a grammar school, and a high school when it opened in 1867. The grammar school was divided into three grades that indicated the scholarship of the pupils. "Under this rigid classification age has no claims to place," a newspaper noted. "Small boys journey with large ones, and little girls with those nearly out of their short dresses on the road to learning."

Minneapolis' new Central High School was constructed in 1877-78 between Third and Fourth avenues south and Eleventh and Twelfth streets. Students could use laboratories, a gymnasium, an art room, a "literary society room," a hall with a recessed stage, and water closets.

During the horsecar era that began in the 1870s, barns were scattered throughout the Twin Cities. This one at Ramsey and Forbes streets in St. Paul, pictured about 1885, also housed the offices of the St. Paul City Railway Company.

In about 1876 this Minneapolis horsecar on Washington Avenue at Twelfth Avenue traveled the "R.R. Depot and Riverside Ave." route. The tracks ran down Washington Avenue from Hennepin, past the Milwaukee depot to Seven Corners, and then down Cedar and Riverside. The cars ran on wooden rails capped with iron plates.

Car number 43 of the Minneapolis Street Railway Company passed the Hennepin Avenue Methodist Episcopal Church on Hennepin at Tenth Street in about 1882. Four years earlier the average streetcar horse traveled twelve miles a day and a driver sixty-five miles.

The Tenth Avenue Bridge, also called the Lower Bridge, was one of the structures built in the 1870s to cement the union between Minneapolis and St. Anthony. Completed in 1874, it connected Tenth Avenue in the city's West Division and Sixth Avenue in its East Division. The photographers stood on the west bank to record its construction and completion.

The Upper Bridge crossed the river from Thirteenth Avenue North (later Plymouth Avenue) in the West Division to Eighth Avenue North in the East Division. Known later as the Plymouth Avenue Bridge, the structure had an eighteen-foot roadway flanked by ample sidewalks. The cart of Michael Nowack, who made the stereopticon view in about 1876, is at the entrance to the bridge.

St. Paul also gained a new bridge. After many years of protest against dependence on the ferry, the federal government in 1880 built this connection from Fort Snelling to the eastern bank. The buildings of the old fort crown the far ridge.

Traffic passed through the wooden towers of the old Suspension Bridge while the limestone towers of the new bridge rose beside it. By the early 1870s the old roadway was rotting, and, since it had no sidewalks, pedestrians mingled with hogs, cattle, and vehicles in a "strange jumble." Its successor, completed in 1875, had pedestrian walks as well as a wider roadway.

"The Ticker's striking."

With great efficiency Twin Cities fire fighters back up the horses to the steam pumper. Then, by manipulating the overhead rigging, they drop the harnesses in place for buckling and uncap the boiler stack.

A raging fire in the International Hotel at Seventh and Jackson streets challenged St. Paul's volunteer companies. The blaze, fanned by a high wind, engulfed the structure in the early morning hours of February 3, 1869, and threatened to spread. Although the hotel was in ruins and some nearby buildings burned, the firemen rescued the occupants and controlled the blaze.

Minneapolis Hook and Ladder Company No. 1 posed in 1869, a year after the volunteer group was organized. The city purchased the hook and ladder truck for the company's use.

The St. Paul Pleasure Park was probably located in the Quonset-type building to the right of the International Hotel in 1867. The architectural style, which much later became common, was unusual for this period.

The Academy of Music, located in Minneapolis at Washington and Hennepin avenues, hosted the city's major theatrical events for more than a decade after it opened in 1872. The building, photographed under construction in 1871 and again about seven years later, had a third-floor auditorium with 1,300 seats, "all upholstered, with elevating bottoms to allow free passages."

St. Paul's Opera House opened in 1867 on Wabasha Street between Third and Fourth streets. Over a thousand people could sit in the auditorium. For a short time patrons were entertained by a drop curtain flamboyantly decorated with paintings of Indians, the local artist himself, nudes, and horses.

Marietta Ravel received top billing for her performances in the Opera House. Reviewers complained that a poor supporting cast weakened the drama.

Twin Citians celebrated the nation's centennial on July 4, 1876, with firecrackers, speeches, parades, and other festivities. The *St. Paul Dispatch* and St. Paul Type Foundry unit carried an old-fashioned printing press in the capital city's procession. The printers, seen here at Fourth and Wabasha streets, turned out facsimiles of the Declaration of Independence and distributed them to the spectators.

President Rutherford B. Hayes played no favorites when he visited the Twin Cities in 1878; he spoke in both cities at fairs running simultaneously on October 3-6. The first U.S. president to visit the state while in office, he reviewed prize cattle at the Minneapolis fair, sponsored by the Minnesota Agricultural and Mechanical Association.

THE GREATEST EQUESTRIENNE CONTEST OF THE WORLD

Miss BELLE COOK, of California, and Miss EMMA JEWETT, of Minnesota, in their Great TWENTY MILE RACE for $5,000.

The Knights of Pythias of Minnesota held its first state parade in Minneapolis on July 20, 1876. Twin Cities contingents of the fraternal lodge marched along Washington Avenue past the Nicollet House, the four-story building with cupolas in the background. Several other fraternal lodges, or "secret societies," had chapters in the Twin Cities, among them the Masons, the Odd Fellows, and the United and Ancient Order of Druids.

P. T. Barnum's circus entertained Twin Citians in several visits during the 1870s. These tents were pitched on St. Paul's west-side flats, within sight of the Wabasha Street Bridge. The large tent may be the one Barnum advertised as capable of accommodating 13,000 people. The circus traveled by rail and at a fast pace — often a hundred miles a night in order "to hit good-sized towns every day."

The 1880 Minneapolis fair ran for six days and featured a "galaxy" of well-known "turf performers" in the popular horse races.

The Lake Calhoun Pavilion, built in 1877, still stood in an isolated country setting about three years later. Like other resort hotels on nearby lakes, it was accessible to party-goers and vacationers via the Minneapolis, Lyndale and Lake Calhoun railroad. Later called the Hotel Lyndale, it was located high on the bluff on the east shore of the lake.

17th DECEMBER
STEAMBOAT
EXCURSION!

The Ladies of the HOME FOR THE FRIENDLESS invite the Citizens of St. Paul to a Steamboat Excursion on

SATURDAY, DECEMBER 17, 1870,

at 12 o'clock, noon.

The Steamer NELLIE KENT has been tendered for the occasion. A Hot Lunch will be served on the boat to all holding tickets. GOOD MUSIC to enliven the entertainment.

COME ONE! COME ALL!

For further particulars read all the papers.

Lake Minnetonka attracted many southerners and other tourists who flocked to the Twin Cities after the Civil War. Among the popular resorts was the Lake Park Hotel, built in 1879 at Excelsior and designed by LeRoy S. Buffington with verandas surrounding the entire structure.

The "Nellie Kent" sailed on schedule from St. Paul on an excursion planned to raise funds for charity. The sun shone, the air was "pure and bracing," and the river was free of ice — "comparatively speaking." A number of strangers on board expressed "astonishment at a steamboat excursion in Minnesota in midwinter," but such events were apparently common in the Twin Cities.

1880-95

Telephone and electric power lines threaded the intersection of Nicollet Avenue and Third Street South in Minneapolis in 1886. Technological progress in the golden age brought these improvements to many areas of the Twin Cities.

1880-95
The Golden Age

ST. PAUL AND MINNEAPOLIS, their key pieces in place on the chessboard, stood ready to seize the opportunities that opened in the 1880s — the golden age of western cities. In these exhilarating years, the *Northwest Magazine* commented, "Every village believed it was bound to become a city . . . and every city dreamed of becoming a new Chicago." No new Chicago was born in the Northwest, but by the end of the decade, cities on the Pacific slope and south of the Twins' coveted hinterland were commanding attention. Seattle, Tacoma, and Portland — Omaha, Kansas City, and Denver — these urban centers in the trans-Mississippi West shared with the Twins in the growth of the golden age. Despite the slowdown the Twins suffered when the boom subsided, only one city within their trade area challenged them. This was Duluth, the "Chicago of Lake Superior," which in the 1880s grew from a village of 838 people to a city of 33,115.[1]

With only one nearby city threatening a checkmate, the Twins played a good game. The cities' continued growth marked their success: the population of Minneapolis more than quadrupled from 1880 to 1895, reaching 192,833; St. Paul's population more than tripled to 140,292 in the same years. By 1890 Minneapolis was the nation's eighteenth largest city, and St. Paul ranked twenty-third. None of the cities rimming the hinterland equaled Minneapolis in size, and the combined Twin Cities urban center seemed invincible.[2]

Railroad improvements between 1880 and 1895 strengthened the Twins' competitive position. New rail lines almost doubled the miles of track within Minnesota, the Northern Pacific and Great Northern completed their transcontinental lines, and the Minneapolis, Sault Ste. Marie and Atlantic (later the Minneapolis, St. Paul and Sault Ste. Marie) opened a direct route to the Soo, linking up with the Canadian Pacific. An observer noted, with some justification, that the "railroad map of the Northwest has been shaped largely with reference to St. Paul and Minneapolis." So great was the congestion of freight traffic at Twin Cities terminals that in 1883 several railroads organized the Minnesota Transfer Railway Company to operate yards in St. Paul midway between the two downtowns.

The railroads also built new downtown depots, bridges, and other facilities to handle the business.[3]

In 1888 Minneapolis millers dramatized the opening of traffic on the new line to Lake Michigan by sending eighty-two carloads of flour in gaily decorated trains to the Soo. This enormous single shipment also emphasized the city's pre-eminence as the nation's milling capital. The manufacturers, expanding production capacity without increasing the number of mills, had raised the output from over two million barrels in 1880 to five times that volume fifteen years later. Powerful corporations gained control of many of the mills. The giant among them was the Pillsbury-Washburn Flour Mills Company, Ltd., followed at some distance by the Washburn-Crosby Company and the Northwestern Consolidated Milling Company. A regional business magazine boasted that "the position of Minneapolis as the leading milling city of the continent is too strong to be shaken by any new competition." Nevertheless, the millers kept a wary eye on fast-rising Duluth and Superior, which by 1895 were producing almost a third as much flour as Minneapolis.[4]

As Minneapolis milling expanded and wheat supplies exceeded even the industry's huge requirements, the city in the 1880s became the nation's largest primary wheat market. Across the wheat-growing region lines of elevators "stand[ing] everywhere along the horizon like ships at sea" gathered the harvest for shipment to terminal markets. The Minneapolis Millers Association, formed in 1867, reduced competition among the local manufacturers and thwarted Milwaukee and Chicago dealers' incursions into the wheat-growing area. In 1881, with the establishment of the Minneapolis Chamber of Commerce as a grain exchange, the millers began buying their wheat on the exchange rather than through the association, and Minneapolis also became an important shipping market. Grain merchants like Frank H. Peavey and William and Samuel Cargill strengthened the Minneapolis business, and several local dealers also entered the Duluth-Superior trade. Wheat receipts at the Lake Superior twin ports rose sharply, but the Mill City's volume in 1895 almost equaled the combined total of its northern rival and Chicago. The

Minneapolis Chamber of Commerce, like the earlier association, became a symbol of economic power, the target for farmers' protest movements that swept through the hinterland.[5]

In the North Minneapolis sawmilling district lumbermen were slicing up white pine logs as if there were no tomorrow. Michiganders, leaving their own demolished forests for Minnesota's fresh supplies, accelerated the industry's growth; in the banner year of 1899 the city became the world's leading lumber market. In 1895 one mill alone sawed over 81,000,000 board feet of lumber of the city's total production of 479,102,193. There were signs, however, that tomorrow was coming and that it might not be a fair day. Growing production in Duluth, where Michiganders also joined the lumbermen's ranks, indicated that the industry was moving northward to the pine. And realists acknowledged that Minnesota's forests, too, were fast falling before the onslaught.[6]

ST. PAUL, which shared little of the flour-wheat-lumber economy that was making Minneapolis boom, attempted in the 1880s to claim livestock marketing and meat packing as its own great business. Both cities recognized the opportunities awaiting them as Minnesota became a surplus livestock producer. In the Twins' trade area of the Dakotas, Montana, and Wyoming, grasslands that once had nourished massive buffalo herds now fattened both sheep and cattle. Although Twin Citians had long operated small stockyards and packing plants, much of this growing livestock business went to Chicago.[7]

Businessmen's interest quickened in the early 1880s when stockyards and packing plants were established at Minnesota Transfer. Ignoring the Mill City's stake in the Transfer, the St. Paul Chamber of Commerce predicted in 1884 that the yards would make its city "one of the most important cattle markets in the country." This time St. Paul matched its familiar bold statements with unaccustomed deeds. A chamber delegation spearheaded by tall, red-bearded Alpheus B. Stickney traveled in 1886 to Miles City to discuss marketing with the Montana Stockgrowers' Association. On a return visit a committee from the association inspected property Stickney had bought in what would become South St. Paul and then recommended opening a market in the vicinity of the Twin Cities.[8]

Stickney immediately announced plans to develop his property. He quickly joined with other St. Paul businessmen and a representative of the newly organized Montana Livestock Company to incorporate the St. Paul Union Stockyards Company. The firm developed trading, packing, and stockyards facilities and even acquired land on New York's Staten Island for cattle-feeding grounds and steamship wharves. The *Northwest Magazine,* noting the swift progress, com-

mented that "With one hand on the vast cattle ranges of the West and the other on Eastern and European markets, the new St. Paul corporation is evidently destined to play a large part in the cattle and beef movement of the future."[9]

Minneapolis grumbled as St. Paul pressed forward to build its great industry. In 1886, for example, the *Minneapolis Tribune* branded the chosen site as "grotesquely unsuitable." One year later William D. Washburn and other Mill City businessmen incorporated the Minneapolis Stockyards and Packing Company. Locating its facilities at New Brighton in northern Ramsey County, the firm began to compete with the South St. Paul center. The companies contested hotly for business during the years that followed. South St. Paul — incorporated in 1887 and strengthened in 1897 by Swift and Company's major new packing plant — emerged the winner.[10]

St. Paul businessmen and politicians also organized the Manufacturers' Loan and Investment Company to promote enterprises within St. Paul and its "tributary suburbs." These suburbs included West St. Paul, South St. Paul, and St. Paul Park south and east of the central city; North St. Paul on Silver Lake; and Gladstone on Lake Phalen. A great deal of puffery attended the promotion both of these communities and of the residential parks that pushed the city's limits westward toward Minneapolis. Bound to the central city by streetcar lines and commuter trains, they offered the dual advantages of urban and small-town living, claimed the promoters.[11]

Although Mill City industries were extending into West Minneapolis (later Hopkins) and St. Louis Park, the strong manufacturing development within Minneapolis made the suburban contributions less critical to that city's economic welfare than it was to St. Paul's progress. No reliable statistics, however, measured the contributions of St. Paul's suburban businesses. Reports on the value of meat-packing products illustrate the statistical perils. The United States census in 1890 credited the meat industry with $783,370 of St. Paul's total manufactured product value of $33,035,073. In the same year the St. Paul Chamber of Commerce put the meat-product value at $3,285,000, which probably included suburban production and may have been overly generous. Minneapolis did not need to claim suburban production to demonstrate its manufacturing superiority; in 1890 the United States census reported the city's product value at a whopping $82,922,974.[12]

Minneapolis was also the victor in a close race for primacy in the wholesale trade, although the issue was clouded by statistics that were incomplete and incompatible. As had become their custom, each city claimed dominance in the trade area, either ignoring the other or exchanging petty insults. For example, the *Minneapolis Tribune* reasoned that its city would prevail in the trade contest because the local retail business was larger — larger because "the average population is of a more intelligent character and maintains a higher standard of living." As usual, too, the Twins joined forces in what the *Tribune* called a "not too easy fight to hold all the territory that rightfully belongs to this general center of trade, as against Chicago and more eastern cities." Merchants did not limit their sphere to the core northwestern trade area, nor even to the continental United States. World trade, a siren's call that had always made the Twins a bit giddy, became a reality with exports as varied as flour, furs, and ginseng and imports like tea and silk.[13]

From the Twins' great wholesale houses went "knight[s] of the grip," traveling men who competed for sales in the Northwest with drummers from Chicago, Omaha, and other cities. The Minneapolis millers, campaigning to win new markets, also deployed salesmen, some of whom used imaginative techniques. "One will go into a town," it was reported, "advertise freely in the local papers, and place a small bag, containing enough flour for an ordinary baking, in every house, with circulars giving full directions for handling the flour. Another will advertise a 'grand baking exhibition,' hire a *chef,* and for weeks distribute to all who call, free samples of bread, cakes, etc., made from his flour."[14]

FAIRS, EXPOSITIONS, and exhibitions brought crowds from the hinterland to witness evidence of the Northwest's progress and to have fun. The Minnesota State Fair, which had originated in the 1850s, was the most enduring event. For many years it was a peripatetic celebration, traveling to Minneapolis, St. Paul, and other Minnesota communities. Minneapolis, playing the spoiler's role, sometimes put on its own fair when the event was held in St. Paul. The fair found a permanent home in 1885 when Ramsey County donated its 200-acre poor farm, located in the Midway area north of Minnesota Transfer. St. Paul had captured the state fair.[15]

Minneapolis, not to be outdone, organized an industrial exposition that featured industry and the arts. Although the event was held for only a few years, its inauguration in September, 1886 (state-fair time), was impressive. A Mexican band played on an upper floor of a splendid building erected for the exposition. "While the listeners hear the melodies of many lands rendered with smoothness and spirit by the dark-skinned players from the far South," commented the *Northwest Magazine,* "they can look down upon the flashing waters of the fountain and hear, like a subdued bass, the rumble of the machinery on the lower floor" demonstrating processes such as milling, barrelmaking, and printing. To illustrate that "Fine art

is the flowering of human growth," a gallery displayed reproductions of such masterpieces as the "Milo Venus" and paintings from Munich, New York, Chicago, and the Twin Cities. The *Pioneer Press* reported that the exposition was an "offspring of a jealous brain"; not so, the *Tribune* responded. "For we said from the first that Minneapolis will support the St. Paul fair —otherwise called the state fair — and she will. . . . We said Minneapolis will never take part in this fair as exhibitors, and she never will, not even if St. Paul, by some legedermain *[sic],* annexes Minneapolis to Ramsey County."[16]

St. Paul, as quick to kindle dissension as its rival, answered the Industrial Exposition with the Winter Carnival, launched in the same year. Featuring mammoth ice palaces with turrets, towers, and battlements, the carnivals held from 1886 to 1888 were celebrations of winter, intended to counteract bad reports about the climate and dramatize the city. Although Minneapolis was said to have given "a cold shoulder" to the event (because the capital city had slighted the Industrial Exposition), thousands of St. Paulites and visitors from neighboring towns turned out. Attired in colorful carnival suits, many of them paraded, participated in winter sports, and helped the forces of the Fire King storm the Ice King's palace.[17]

Enthusiasm for the carnival, however, soon waned. When January, 1889, did not produce the usual supplies of ice and snow, the event was canceled. The city should turn to celebrations of summer and autumn, intelligence and culture, advised the *Northwest Magazine,* for although those who attended the event might be convinced that the climate was moderate, "the multitude who did not come . . . are apt to shiver at the mention of a city where towering structures of ice are a regular thing every year."[18]

The great census war of 1890 followed these controversies over civic festivals. A United States deputy marshal from St. Paul touched off the conflict by arresting seven Minneapolis enumerators suspected of falsifying the count. Charges that the Mill City rolls were padded, followed by allegations that St. Paul's enumerators had also been quite imaginative, led to a recount that decreased the cities' figures by 18,229 and 9,425, respectively. The *St. Paul Pioneer Press* was incensed that its city was included in the recount with "Pad City" — a "Jezebel, whose dallying with sin is the jest or the scorn of a whole people." The *Northwest Magazine* predicted that the resulting bitterness would linger a long time, for "cities, like individuals, remember their quarrels and often nurse their wrath to keep it warm."[19]

Regret was particularly keen because the Twins were forging new bonds. Both cities extended their limits to absorb the territory that separated them, speeding toward the day when a traveler might pass from one to another without noticing a division. The street railway firms operating the newly electrified systems became part of a holding company called the Twin City Rapid Transit Company in 1891. And by 1894 the four-year-old intercity line "whirled" passengers between the two downtowns in only forty-five minutes. Still other signs of growing unity were the formation of the Twin City Commercial Club and the Twin City Bankers Association, as well as agitation for metropolitan water and park boards.[20]

More visionary enthusiasts suggested the ultimate in co-operation: complete merger in a center that might be called Paulapolis, Minnepaul, Twin City, Twincit, or Federal City. The arguments had by then become familiar. The united cities could compete with others as a "single powerful center of trade, transportation, population and civilization." The outcome was also familiar. In 1891 the Minneapolis Board of Trade, in a reference typical of the abortive negotiations, cited the census war and other grievances in rejecting the St. Paul Chamber of Commerce's offer to merge.[21]

SEPARATE the Twins remained, but together they took on the texture of big cities during the golden age. Downtown buildings — massive, vaulted, arched, towered, and profusely ornamented — reflected the cities' prosperity, civic pride, and exuberance, as well as new architectural styles. LeRoy S. Buffington, an architect who designed many notable edifices in the Twin Cities, captured the spirit of the era. His introduction of the cast-iron column, a structural innovation, was not without mishaps. A 3,000-pound column intended for the Boston Block in Minneapolis was left on the ground one fall Friday and had disappeared by Monday. Builders could not imagine who would steal it, or how. The mystery was solved the following spring when a wagon wheel struck it as it emerged from the mud.[22]

Visitors to the downtowns could enjoy their cities' growing maturity. Minneapolitans might drop in at the new public library, shop at Donaldson's Glass Block Store, and ascend on "fantastic bird cage elevators" to the twelfth floor of the Guaranty Loan Building (later the Metropolitan) for dining in the "sky room" restaurant, a stroll through the roof garden, and a climb to the lookout tower. From the tower they could watch workmen putting up the new city hall-courthouse known as the Municipal Building, a massive, red granite "stone pile" completed in 1905.[23]

St. Paulites visiting the downtown might shop at Mannheimer Brothers; buy Oriental fabrics, curios, and Chinese fireworks at the store of Quong, Gin, Lung and Company; transact business at the new city hall-courthouse; attend events at the auditorium; and dine at the Ryan Hotel, the "most conspicuous build-

ing in the city." In streets crowded at times with carts, delivery wagons, carriages, and streetcars, they also might watch the "fashionables" who would "leave liveried coachmen in charge of their fine turn-outs" while shopping. In winter, drivers exchanged their vehicles' wheels for "four little steel-shod sleds," and "the streets [were] musical with sleigh bells."[24]

The "fashionables," who had become rich as the cities grew, began to show their wealth in their houses, institutions, and attitudes. James J. Hill of St. Paul erected a great house with an art gallery that exhibited works by Corot, Millet, Delacroix, and other artists; William D. Washburn of Minneapolis furnished "Fair Oaks" with choice items from many lands. The Minnesota Club, organized in 1874, erected a building eleven years later. Visitors from the East commended the club for the "comfort of its building, its social characteristics and for the superiority of its restaurant." Its counterpart, the Minneapolis Club, became the "determining factor in practically all of the important movements" in the city after its founding in 1883. The *Dual City Blue Book,* which listed "the most prominent householders" of the cities, showed the subscribers' keen awareness of social status, although its publishers denied the intent to produce "a local and republican substitute for a book of the peerage." Some of the private schools shared the preoccupation with status. For example, St. Catherine's, an Episcopal school in St. Paul, was said to admit "only pupils from the best families, so that parents may be assured that the daughters entrusted to their care will have only fit associations."[25]

Although social lines may have been hardening, many people enjoyed the wealth of the golden age through cultural institutions that became an enduring part of Twin Cities life. The present-day Walker Art Center originated with the collection that Minneapolis lumberman Thomas B. Walker gathered in an annex to his home, where the "man in overalls [was] just as welcome as the man in broadcloth." Hill, William H. Dunwoody, Clinton Morrison, and others contributed to the new Minneapolis Society of Fine Arts. Many Mill Citians supported the musical groups that would soon evolve into the Minneapolis Symphony Orchestra, while in St. Paul the Schubert Club, originally called the Ladies' Musicale, brought fine artists to the city and fostered careers of young musicians.[26]

Many other amenities enriched urban life. Theaters new and old provided a wide variety of plays and other productions, while Twin Citians amused themselves with tennis, golf, baseball, roller skating, skiing, tobogganing, curling, dancing, ice skating, bicycling, horse racing, and boating. Institutions of higher learning now included St. Thomas College as well as Hamline, Macalester, Augsburg, and the University of Minnesota. City improvements included cedar-block and asphalt paving that eased travel on some streets, improved sanitation and hospital facilities, and hundreds of acres of parklands. Private power companies began to generate electricity, lighting more streets and buildings and providing industry with a new source of energy.

The growth of city parks was especially important in the golden age. Some residents had recognized the need for parks early in the communities' history; in 1851, for example, the *St. Anthony Express* urged that a "Public Green" be reserved "before the land becomes so valuable that the all engrossing spirit of avarice shall have sacrificed the whole to Mammon." Small parks were established in the 1850s and 1860s, but the movement gained real momentum in 1872. That year the St. Paul Common Council invited Horace W. S. Cleveland, a Chicago landscape architect, to visit the city and propose a plan. He called for a city-wide park system (including Como, Phalen, and St. Anthony parks) and suggested that St. Paul and Minneapolis be connected by a grand boulevard along the Mississippi River.[27]

The movement shifted into high gear with the creation of a Minneapolis board of park commissioners in 1883 and a St. Paul board four years later. Spirited opposition came from some citizens, notably the Knights of Labor, who declared that the projected Minneapolis system might "rob the working classes of their homes and make driveways for the rich at the expense of the poor." Both cities, however, began to establish major parks that became gems in the system. By 1895 St. Paul was improving Como Park, acquired in the 1870s, and buying land at Lake Phalen. Minneapolis, led by miller Charles M. Loring and also counseled by Cleveland, included among its acquisitions Central (now Loring), Lake Harriet, Lake Calhoun, Lake of the Isles, Powderhorn, Columbia, and Glenwood (later Theodore Wirth). While the parks remained undeveloped as playgrounds for many years, these critical acquisitions were fortunately made before population expansion made them difficult or impossible.[28]

THE PROSPERITY of the golden age that added these amenities to urban life was not shared equally. Many of the foreign-born residents, who in 1890 reached their highest proportion in the cities' population, were far removed from the circles of affluence. Throughout society, in fact, inequalities were often striking. For example, some women enjoyed opulence in the Victorian manner, allotting time to social rituals like making calls and planning proper seating arrangements at formal dinners, while others sat at sewing machines in factories for long hours, turning out clothing sold by dry-goods firms. Children's lives varied widely, too, from gentle rearing in the great

houses to the lot of the homeless — "the Arabs of the city, newsboys, boot-blacks and others, ill-born, ill-bred, left early in life to shift for themselves, educated only in the rough schooling of the street."[29]

Concerns for the homeless, poor, aged, orphaned, and other disadvantaged persons increased the number of social welfare agencies. Recognizing their need for co-ordination, the agencies formed Associated Charities of Minneapolis in 1884 and Associated Charities of St. Paul in 1892. Both organizations attempted to serve as clearing houses for requests, prevent welfare abuses, and professionalize social work. Wealthy Twin Cities families contributed heavily to the social welfare agencies, as they had to cultural organizations. Yet, reviewing in 1909 events of the past quarter century, Associated Charities of Minneapolis observed, "it is unfortunately true that with increase of population and development of industry comes an increase in misery and sorry poverty for large numbers of people. This fact should make business men ponder."[30]

Laborers in the Twin Cities had been pondering the question for quite some time. Unionization, begun in the 1850s, had grown spasmodically throughout the 1860s and 1870s, then quickened in the 1880s under the influence of the Noble Order of the Knights of Labor. By the time the Knights' influence declined, workers formed other Twin Cities organizations to give cohesion to the movement — the St. Paul Trades and Labor Assembly in 1882, the Minneapolis Trades Assembly in 1883, and the Minnesota State Federation of Labor in 1890. These central organizations and their constituent unions fought for higher wages, arbitration of labor disputes, the eight-hour work day, regulation of child labor, compulsory education, free textbooks, safety regulations, and the observance of Labor Day.[31]

Many strikes darkened relations between employers and employees, sometimes with outcomes that pleased neither. For example, when women manufacturing shirts and overalls in Shotwell, Clerihew and Lothmann's Minneapolis factory struck in 1888, the firm, already in financial trouble, went out of business. The employer seemed to have won when a strike by the St. Paul and Minneapolis Street Railway Employees' Union was broken in 1889 and the union dissolved, but organized labor then became "an outspoken enemy" of the company.[32]

A severe nationwide depression in 1893 dulled the already tarnished glitter of the golden age and slowed the Twins' growth. Vacant houses, failed businesses, and unemployment testified to the severity of the "great financial storm." In the face of high unemployment, the urbanization process itself was questioned. Alpheus B. Stickney, maintaining that the population movement from farms to cities had caused the "hard times," advocated a reversal of the process. The *St. Paul Pioneer Press* shared his sentiments, counseling that "the best possible chance for the unemployed is to find a home and farm somewhere in the vast area of unoccupied lands awaiting settlement in Minnesota and the Dakotas." While such advice did not seem to spur an exodus from the cities, population growth from 1890 to 1895 was small compared with earlier years, and — ominously for the Twins — prosperous Duluth had a greater relative population increase than either of them. Sobered after their dizzying spin through the 1880s, the Twins now entered an age that would test their strength to hold the position they had won.[33]

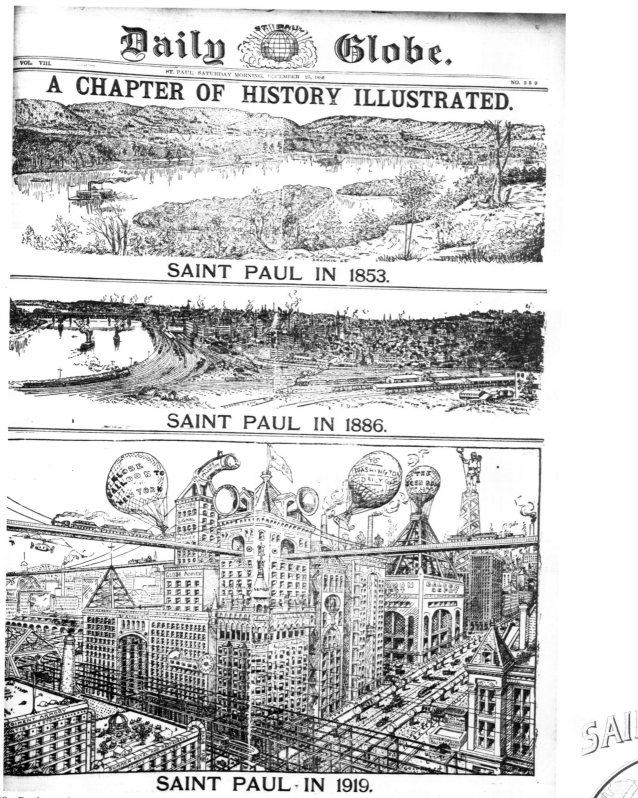

Daily Globe.

VOL. VIII. ST. PAUL, SATURDAY MORNING, DECEMBER 25, 1886. NO. 359

A CHAPTER OF HISTORY ILLUSTRATED.

SAINT PAUL IN 1853.

SAINT PAUL IN 1886.

SAINT PAUL IN 1919.

St. Paul may have lost the population race to Minneapolis, but boosters still envisioned a great future for the city.

Ignoring Minneapolis, the St. Paul Chamber of Commerce's *Facts* placed the city at the center of North American and world trade.

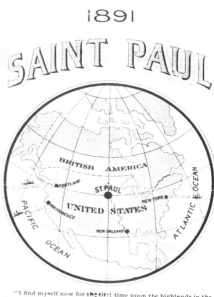

1891

SAINT PAUL

"I find myself now for the first time upon the highlands in the centre of the continent of North America, equidistant from the waters of Hudson's Bay and the Gulf of Mexico—from the Atlantic Ocean to the ocean in which the sun sets."—*Hon. Wm. H. Seward, St. Paul, 1860.*

FACTS

COMPILED BY
ALFRED S. TALLMADGE,
SECRETARY CHAMBER OF COMMERCE.

Charles A. Pillsbury of C. A. Pillsbury and Company worked in the 1880s in his Minneapolis office, which was equipped with an electric fan and a telephone. The Pillsbury mills were among the first subscribers to telephone service that began in Minneapolis in the late 1870s.

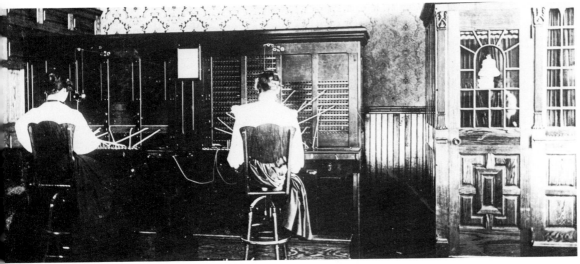

To handle the increasing volume of calls in the Twin Cities, the Northwestern Telephone Exchange Company added switchboards like this one, the Minneapolis South Branch at First Avenue South and Twenty-sixth Street. By the late 1890s, when this photograph was made, the company claimed that it was serving 250 towns and cities in Minnesota, North Dakota, and South Dakota.

Spectators witnessed an "indescribably beautiful" sight on February 28, 1883, when electric arc lamps on a 257-foot mast first illuminated Bridge Square in Minneapolis. Soon electricity competed with gas in the lighting of both cities.

Transit companies traded horse power for faster electric power when electricity came to the Twin Cities. Service began in St. Paul on February 22, 1890, with a trolley train trip on Grand Avenue. Among the passengers were Thomas Lowry, president of the St. Paul City Railway Company (front row, right) and Archbishop John Ireland, one of the promoters of the Grand Avenue line (second from right). Service in Minneapolis had begun two months earlier.

Several steam and water-powered plants generated electricity to operate Twin Cities streetcars. In 1893 the steam station at Third Avenue North and Second Street in Minneapolis delivered current to the streetcar system by overhead insulated wires.

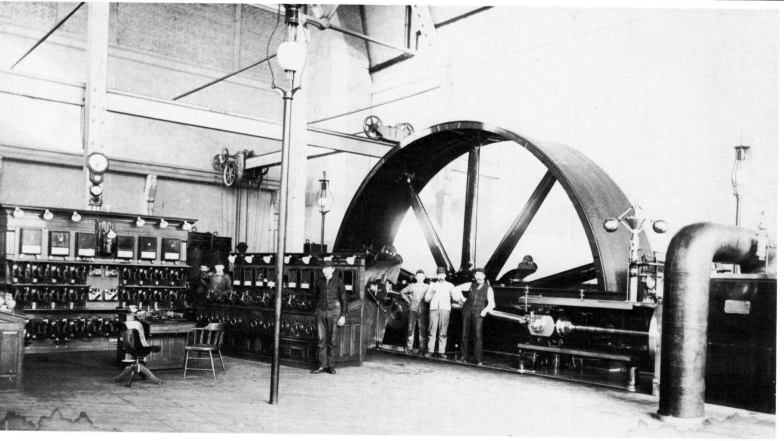

Many new Twin Cities firms sold electrical supplies and equipment, manufactured electrical machinery, and built and repaired electrical systems.

Although streetcar companies assured Twin Cities residents that the transmission of electricity through insulated wires was safe, fear of the current's destructive power was common.

THE ELECTRIC TERROR.
He's only dangerous when he combines with a conductor.

"The completion of the Northern Pacific was celebrated as no other work in this century has been," wrote an observer in describing the festivities. Minneapolitans celebrated the linking of the Twin Cities with the Pacific Coast in 1883 with a parade along Washington Avenue.

The arch built across St. Paul's Wabasha Street between Ninth and Tenth streets expressed the continuing hope for fulfillment of the Twins' long-held dream of trade with the Orient. The inscription on the reverse side of the arch read, "ST. PAUL GREETS JAPAN THROUGH THE N.P.R.R."

The Stone Arch Bridge spanned the Mississippi below the Falls of St. Anthony in 1883. Once called "Jim Hill's Folly," it provided a crossing for his St. Paul, Minneapolis and Manitoba railroad. The oldest mainline railroad bridge in the Northwest, it is now a National Historic Engineering Landmark.

During the early 1880s pedestrians on the Washington Avenue boardwalk in Minneapolis passed between the horse car line, soon to be electrified, and the yards of the Chicago, Milwaukee and St. Paul railroad. The milling district was to the left of the yards.

In the 1880s this driver and team traveled over a covered canal that distributed water to a long row of mills on the west side of the Falls of St. Anthony. The wagon passed the pioneer Cataract mill, built in 1859 and dwarfed by its newer neighbors.

Cadwallader C. Washburn and John Crosby incorporated Washburn-Crosby Company in 1879. The firm produced flours with brand names like "Snow Drop," "Iron Duke," and the famous "Gold Medal."

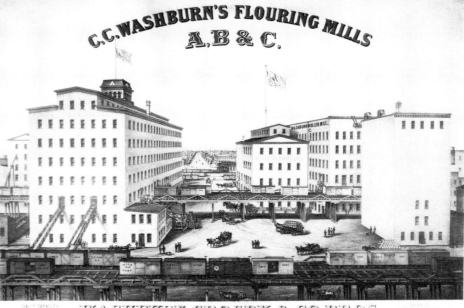

"Pillsbury's Best," manufactured by C. A. Pillsbury and Company, became a brand of the Pillsbury-Washburn Flour Mills Company, Ltd., in 1889 through a merger of the firm with the Washburn Mill Company of William D. Washburn, Cadwallader's brother. The Minneapolis millers worked hard to develop foreign markets for their flour, and by 1894, when this trade-mark was registered, the business was flourishing.

C. A. Pillsbury and Company brought the finest mill in Minneapolis — the Pillsbury A — into the new corporation. Designed by LeRoy Buffington, the mill was built on the east riverbank five years before this photograph was taken in 1886. It became the world's largest mill of its type. The structure is now a National Historic Landmark.

The sawmill of the C. A. Smith Lumber Company, photographed about 1895 at the foot of Forty-fourth Avenue North in Minneapolis, was a major contributor to the city's production. From its construction in 1893 to its closing in 1912, the mill sawed over 1.6 billion board feet of lumber.

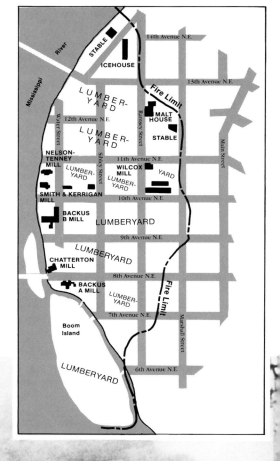

Fires constantly menaced North Minneapolis' sawmills and lumberyards. On August 13, 1893, the east-side district from Sixth to Fourteenth avenues (see map) caught fire and became "one blazing pile." The heat was so intense that water from firemen's hoses "turned to steam and went sailing skyward."

Traders inspected samples in about 1895 at the grain exchange of the Minneapolis Chamber of Commerce on Third Street and Fourth Avenue South. They bought and sold millions of bushels of wheat and other grains here annually.

In a run that began on May 15, 1893, depositors frightened by news of economic crises stormed the Farmers and Mechanics Bank at 115 South Fourth Street, Minneapolis. Although this and other strong Twin Cities banks survived the panic years, several financial institutions failed.

In 1881 the railroad companies serving St. Paul built a union depot at the foot of Sibley Street for all their passenger traffic. Six years later these omnibuses awaited travelers in front of the brick building.

Clothing wholesalers in the 1880s and 1890s often manufactured the merchandise they distributed. Myers and Scholle, a St. Paul firm at Fifth and Robert streets, hired women as well as men to sew garments from furs gathered in China and other parts of the world.

Nicols and Dean, a prominent hardware wholesaling firm at 365 and 369 Sibley Street in St. Paul, handled iron, steel, and hardware supplies for wagon makers, carriage makers, and lumbermen. In this view of the company's office made about 1891, Louis T. Herrmann, the firm's stenographer, sits at the right. The other persons have not been identified.

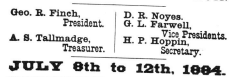

EXCURSION
OF THE
St. Paul Jobbers' Union.

Geo. R. Finch,
President.

A. S. Tallmadge,
Treasurer.

D. R. Noyes.
G. L. Farwell,
Vice Presidents.
H. P. Hoppin,
Secretary.

JULY 8th to 12th, 1884.

COMPLIMENTS OF

FIRST QUALITY GOODS
A SPECIALTY.

On July 8, 1884, members of the St. Paul Jobbers' Union and their guests set out on a 1,000-mile trip into southern Minnesota and Dakota Territory to develop trade. The jobbers, or wholesalers, traveled with the Great Western Band and a "double quartet" of vocalists in seven decorated railroad cars. Twin Cities wholesalers often made such promotional tours, and sometimes representatives of the two cities traveled together.

The St. Paul Union Stockyards Company displayed impressive growth in 1896, ten years after it began to develop the packing business in South St. Paul. The slaughtering capacity at the yards, which occupied a 150-acre tract, was reported to be 5,000 hogs and 800 cattle a day.

In about 1890 buyers cast practiced eyes over some of the thousands of cattle shipped to the South St. Paul yards from Minnesota, Wisconsin, the Dakotas, Montana, and other points.

The golden age brought imposing public buildings, hotels, and stores to the downtown districts. Among them was the West Hotel at Hennepin Avenue and Fifth Street in Minneapolis. Designed by LeRoy Buffington, the West, pictured above left about 1895, was called the "ne plus ultra of hotels." Four hundred Twin Citians celebrated the opening of the hotel in 1884 with a seven-course feast.

The Columbia Marching Society of Indianapolis paraded in front of the hotel in 1892, the year the Republican party made the West its headquarters and renominated Benjamin Harrison for the presidency. People flocked to the convention city, and the hotel housed "five times the number of human beings that can be comfortable in it."

The Guaranty Loan Building (later the Metropolitan) at Third Street and Second Avenue South in Minneapolis was said to be the tallest structure west of Chicago when it was dedicated in 1890. Elegant wrought iron elevator cages and a central court described as a "fantasia in glass and iron" graced the building, which was designed by Edward Townsend Mix. Both pictures were taken in about 1900.

The Donaldson name became well known in the Minneapolis retail trade in the early 1880s, when the brothers William and Lawrence moved into a store at Nicollet Avenue and Sixth Street. The building, pictured here in 1883, was known as the "Glass Block Store" because of its unusual expanse of windows.

The new Minneapolis Public Library opened its doors at Hennepin Avenue and Tenth Street in 1889. These patrons using the reading room in about 1895 could also visit an art gallery, the Minneapolis School of Fine Arts, and the museum of the Minnesota Academy of Natural Sciences, all housed in the building.

The monumental and "strikingly mundane" St. Paul City Hall and Ramsey County Courthouse at Wabasha between Fourth and Fifth streets was under construction for five years after ground-breaking ceremonies on October 9, 1884. A cable car passed the building in 1887, the year cable lines were established to cope with some of the steep grades in St. Paul, likened to the hills of Rome.

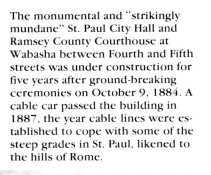

The rear wall of the building housing Mannheimer Bros. store and the offices of the *Northwest Magazine* overlook St. Paul's Lower Levee in this 1890 sketch from that publication. Inside the dry-goods retailing firm (shown here in 1888) clerks sold such merchandise as fine underwear, cloaks, shawls, kid gloves, dress goods, household linens, notions, toilet articles, and clothing from its large dressmaking department.

The Ryan Hotel in St. Paul, with its ornate exterior (about 1900) and well-appointed dining room (about 1890), was a popular social center after it opened in 1885 at Sixth and Robert streets. Here wealthy young ladies were introduced to society, the prosperous attended balls, and state legislators, who favored the hotel with their patronage, continued their deliberations at day's end.

This class divided its attention between the teacher and the photographer in 1887. The view was probably made at the Elizabeth Peabody Primary School at Nineteenth Avenue South and Two-and-a-half Street, Minneapolis. Many of the children in the school's grades one through four lived in Bohemian Flats, an immigrant community on the riverbank below the Washington Avenue Bridge.

Minnie McLeod, at the railing, third from top, was twelve years old in 1886 when a photographer captured these students and teachers of Humboldt School, Colorado Street and Eaton Avenue, St. Paul.

The Judson Female Institute in Minneapolis was established in 1880 by Abby A. Judson, who is wearing a light-colored dress and standing at center left. Four years later, about the time this picture was made, the school was at Harmon Place between Tenth and Eleventh streets.

By the mid-1880s, Macalester College had moved from its quarters in the Winslow House, Minneapolis, into its first building near Snelling and Grand avenues in St. Paul. Edward D. Neill, who had founded the Presbyterian institution as Baldwin School many years earlier, gave the principal dedication address for the building later known as "Old Main." He assured his audience that the religious teaching at Macalester "would not offend Baptists, Lutherans, Methodists, or Episcopalians."

In the 1890s these scholars at Hamline University in St. Paul worked in the library rooms on the second floor of University Hall. The Methodist school, which had opened in St. Paul in 1880 after an earlier sojourn in Red Wing, had an enrollment of 113 in its first year.

The University of Minnesota began to fulfill its mission in agricultural education by establishing a new farm campus near the St. Paul city limits. The experimental farm, which had not prospered on a site adjoining the Minneapolis campus, moved to the beautiful new location in the early 1880s. These were two of around twenty buildings on the St. Paul campus about 1895.

Minneapolis sidewalk scenes in the golden age: (A) the Northwestern Stove Works, 204 Hennepin Avenue, about 1881; (B) Casper Himmelsback's furniture and undertaking shop, 115 First Street North, 1875, before it burned in 1883; (C) his new building at the same site, about 1885; (D) The Fair, Zuckerman and Company's dry-goods store, shared with tailor John J. Finn, 521 Washington Avenue South, about 1881.

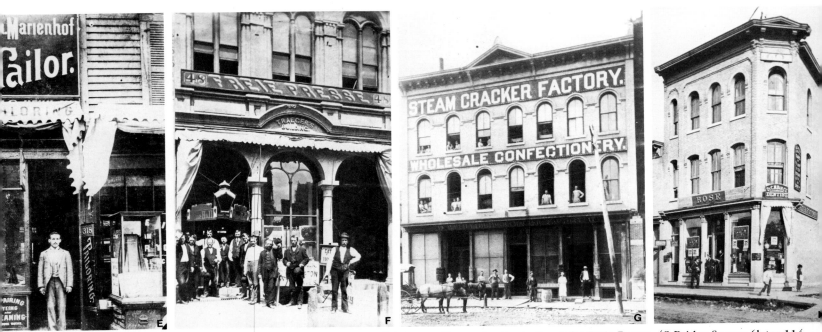

(E) Benjamin Marienhof, tailor, 318 Hennepin Avenue, about 1890; (F) August Traeger's wine hall and the Freie Presse, 48 Bridge Square (later 114 Hennepin Avenue), about 1881; (G) H. F. Lillibridge's cracker factory and wholesale confectionary, 17-19 Third Street South, 1885; (H) Anson Rose, druggist, and C. M. Bailey, dentist, 208 Central Ave., about 1881.

(I) John J. Bruce, clothier, 627 Washington Avenue South, about 1881; (J) Ball and Naylor, mill and railway supply dealers, 250 First Avenue South, about 1879; (K) Albert O. Buck, photographer, 27 Central Avenue (Nicollet Island), about 1881; (L) unidentified billiard hall, about 1881.

St. Paul sidewalk scenes in the golden age: (A) Frederick Jerrard (fifth from left) and Jack De Camp (seventh from left), wholesale fruit dealers, 353 Robert Street, about 1886; (B) Georg Pabst, meat marketer, 790 Margaret Street, about 1891.

(C) August Mueller (pictured), "zephyr worsteds" (clothing), toys, and fancy goods, 133 East Seventh Street, about 1880; (D) Sebastiano Pellegrini, confectioner, 91 East Seventh Street, 1889; (E) Philip Fabel (second from left), shoes, 123 West Third Street, about 1885.

(F) James H. Demarest, locksmith and trunk repairer, 385 Wabasha Street, 1880s; (G) Charles C. Miles, locksmith, bellhanger, and dealer in safes, 91 Jackson Street, about 1881; (H) Yanz, Griggs and Howes, wholesale grocers, 242-252 East Third Street, 1886; (I) St. Paul Pioneer Press printing plant, 78-80 East Third Street, about 1890.

St. Paul's wealthy businessmen built their mansions along the graceful curve of Summit Avenue, high above the downtown district. At right in this 1890 drawing is the James J. Hill House, characterized as "costly, elegant, unique, rich," and yet "quiet and dignified."

Albert Scheffer, a German immigrant and St. Paul banker, lived with his family in a great house at 52 Bates Avenue on Dayton's Bluff, seen here about 1890.

Minneapolitan Thomas Lowry, street-railway owner and real-estate developer, raised his mansion on "the Devil's Backbone," later known as Lowry Hill. In 1878 the house at the corner of Hennepin and Groveland avenues commanded a fine view of the city; Lowry's streetcar system would soon spread far out from the downtown district.

"Fair Oaks," William D. Washburn's house at Stevens Avenue and Twenty-second Street, was a Minneapolis landmark by 1910. Twenty-five years earlier an observer commented that the residence "fills almost as large a space in the public eye as the Grand Opera House or the Chamber of Commerce building; and, to hear it spoken of[,] one would think it were as much a piece of public property as Central Park or Nicollet Avenue."

102

Many middle-class Twin Citians displayed Victorian elegance in their homes. In 1888 Dennis B. Nye, a Minneapolis photographer, posed the members of his family in the parlor of their home at 114 Eleventh Street South. Mrs. Nye holds Marguerite; to the right are Bess, Jay, Etta, and Nye, who probably tripped the shutter with a remote air-bulb release.

Substantial frame houses like the residence of Charles M. Jordan at 615 East Eighteenth Street, Minneapolis, were common in the Twin Cities in the golden age. Jordan, superintendent of the Minneapolis public schools, his wife, and a woman identified only as "mother" relax on the porch in about 1890.

The "Warman Flats" (John A. Warman Block) at Sixth Avenue South and Eighth Street, Minneapolis, were among the growing number of multiple-family dwellings appearing in the Twin Cities. In 1885, about five years before this view was made, an observer noted that the apartment houses were economical in land use, plumbing, and sewage disposal. In winter they also had marked advantages "over the isolated frame house, exposed on all sides to the wind."

St. Paul's Western Avenue, on the western fringe of the platted city in the 1850s, was lined with substantial houses by 1888. Sleighing provided Twin Citians with entertainment as well as transportation during the long winters.

Many immigrants lived on the low-lands bordering the Mississippi River. A photographer standing on the University of Minnesota campus (east bank) in the mid-1880s recorded Bohemian Flats, which attracted Slovaks, Scandinavians, Irish, and other groups. The Northern Pacific railroad bridge, then under construction, is in the foreground; the Stone Arch Bridge spans the river upstream. Residents of the Flats ascended the bluff to the city on stairs like these, photographed about 1890.

Advertisements from the *Minneapolis Tribune* of April 7, 1890, show opportunities that were available to skilled and unskilled workers. Ethnicity was an issue for some employers.

WANTED—All lathers to meet at hall 22 Labor Temple, Tuesday, April 8, at 7 p. m. Important business.

WANTED—500 boys to sell the Tribune-Star every night. One boy sold $2.76 worth in one day.

WANTED—Young man with some experience in wall-paper store. Middlemist & Taylor, 408 Nicollet av.

WANTED—Practical bookkeeper to give lady a few lessons evenings. Address M. T., Tribune.

WANTED—To engage a housepainter for a week or more. Call 227 Fifth st N.

WANTED—Man competent to take full charge of books, accounts and collections for wholesale house. No other need apply. Address, giving experience, etc., J 6, Tribune.

WANTED—A canvasser; horse and wagon furnished. Board guaranteed. Call Morely, 716 Sixth st S.

WANTED—To go to Montana an A No. 1 yardman and salesman, strong and active, who thoroughly understands the lumber business and can take estimates from plans; one not afraid to work. O 95, Tribune.

WANTED—Man who understands hand laundry work. Good solicitor, willing worker; state wages. Address J 4, Tribune.

WANTED—A good honest German, young man for hauling in the city, steady work the year round. Call 3035 Nineteenth av S. No other need apply.

WANTED—Six or eight salesmen to sample the city and sell goods after the sampling is done. Thomas Wray, 516 Second av S.

WANTED—A neat and competent girl for general housework in small family, $4 per week. Address M. letter box 458, Minneapolis.

WANTED—Girl for general housework, small family. 410 East Fifteenth st.

WANTED—Good girl at 816 Tenth st S.

WANTED—A woman to do house cleaning at 812 Eighteenth st S.

WANTED—Girl for general housework; two in family; must be a good cook, and come well recommended. Apply 1515 Chicago av.

WANTED—Girls or women to take work at their homes; steady employment. 709 Hennepin.

WANTED—A girl about 15 years old to look after children from 9 till 5 o'clock; sleep at home; references required. 2208 Grand av.

WANTED—Good sewing girl to do cutting and fitting; wages 75 cents per day. 207 Second av NE.

WANTED—Lady cook. 212 Nicollet av. D. C. Fisher.

WANTED—Girl for general housework; small family; good wages. 2518 Portland av.

WANTED—One or two good stout willing girls for kitchen work. 20J Thirteenth st S.

WANTED—A girl to take care of children. 822 Hennepin av.

WANTED—A good girl for general housework. family of two. Apply this afternoon. 13 Maple place, Nicollet Island.

WANTED—Competent girl, German or American. 1727 Eleventh av S.

WANTED—A good girl for general housework.

SITUATION WANTED—By a temperate young man as bookkeeper, assistant or clerk; experienced in office work. Address G 65, Tribune.

SITUATION WANTED—Good tea and coffee salesman. F 59, Tribune.

SITUATION WANTED—By a lady stenographer, good reference, operates the Remington; nothing under $12 per week will be accepted. Address 1564 Hennepin av.

SITUATION WANTED—A good girl wants a place in a small family. Call at 2540 Seventeenth av S.

SITUATION WANTED—By refined, educated lady, as companion or nurse to invalid; no objections to traveling; references. Address X 34, Tribune.

SITUATION WANTED—By a refined, intelligent lady, as housekeeper; would leave the city; references. Address X 33, Tribune.

SITUATION WANTED—A good business firm to collect for. Address H 84, Tribune.

SITUATION WANTED—By a young man in real estate office. A 14, Tribune.

SITUATION WANTED—By an educated young lady, a position as governess. Address E 57, Tribune.

SITUATION WANTED—Lady stenographer and typewriter with some experience; unquestionable references. Address A 38, Tribune.

SITUATION WANTED—As collector in every kind of business; can furnish bond if necessary, and the best of city references. A 21, Tribune.

SITUATION WANTED—A Canadian lady would like a position as housekeeper; understands cooking and not afraid of work. Address or call at

Italians joined Germans and Poles on St. Paul's Upper Levee flats in the shadow of the High Bridge, which was completed in 1889. Houses of tarpaper, tin, and lumber were often built on piles for protection from floods. Some Italians later built more substantial houses there and planted gardens and grape arbors; the neighborhood long maintained its ethnic identity.

Swedes, Irish, and other immigrant groups who settled on Phalen Creek in St. Paul's Swede Hollow expanded their houses as their families grew. They climbed from the valley on a stairway or on a narrow road that passed Hamm's brewery (see page 56). The Sixth Street Bridge crosses the background of this photograph, made about 1900; to the right are railroad tracks — a dangerous playground for Swede Hollow children who caught rides on slow-moving cars.

In 1888 these Norwegian women observed *Syttende Mai* (May 17), their homeland's independence day, by posing in Minneapolis for a portrait in front of a Norwegian flag.

Germans in St. Paul in 1889 frequented Grote's Tivoli, a pavilion and concert hall overlooking the Mississippi River at Wabasha and Second Streets. There, listening to the orchestra, eating "Frankfurter Wurst mit Kren," and drinking imported and locally brewed beer, they could imagine themselves "in some popular resort on the Rhine or the Elbe."

Street railways and commuter train service encouraged residential developments in the area between the Twin Cities, including Groveland Park and Merriam Park in St. Paul by 1890. Summit Avenue, with the College of St. Thomas to the left and Merriam Park to the right, runs behind the Groveland Park station on the Grand Avenue streetcar line.

The development of West Minneapolis (later called Hopkins) was part of the Mill City's suburban movement. The Minneapolis Threshing Machine Company established its plant there in 1887. About thirteen years later, when the population had reached 1,648, these people walked on a road probably leading from the plant toward Excelsior Avenue. Daniel E. Dow, real-estate dealer, lived in the turreted house at left.

North St. Paul, organized in 1887 as a manufacturing town, was on the shore of Silver Lake, about a mile from the limits of the capital city. A development company offered cottages for sale on the installment plan to workers and others of modest means. This sketch was made in 1892.

In about 1899 these people relaxed at Lake Harriet, part of the Minneapolis park system. The Twin City Rapid Transit Company, under an agreement with the city of Minneapolis, built the shoreside pavilion that provided refreshments, bathing facilities, and a band shell.

St. Paul's Rice Park, donated in 1849 by Henry M. Rice and John R. Irvine, was one of the small public greens reserved early in the Twin Cities' history. By 1886 park users enjoyed electric lighting, an elaborate fountain, and twice-weekly concerts.

Thousands of people jammed the Washington Roller Rink on January 18, 1887, to watch Patrick "Patsy" Cardiff of Minneapolis fight John L. Sullivan to a draw. A haze of tobacco smoke hung over the spectators, who packed the main floor, the balconies, and the bandstand to cheer the local hero and admire the famous John L. "Great slabs of muscle line his [Sullivan's] shoulders and back, but they are symmetrically laid as on a Grecian statue," the *Minneapolis Tribune* reported. Famed singer Adelina Patti and her opera company performed at the rink on March 2 of the same year. The *Tribune* commented that those claiming "'Nothing draws like a prize fight,' are compelled to admit that nothing draws like Patti." Both artists are depicted in 1885.

The roller rink, at Washington Avenue and Tenth Avenue North, was one of thirteen rinks in Minneapolis by 1885. With spectator balconies, a bandstand suspended from the center of the roof, and a large skating floor, it was called "as complete . . . an asylum as the most exacting rinkomaniac could desire."

Fruit-flavored concentrates from Chicago were used in sodas dispensed at this unidentified fountain about 1890. Dozens of soda fountains and confectionaries in the Twin Cities did a flourishing business in satisfying the public's taste for sweets.

Bicycles reached such heights of popularity during the 1890s that Twin Cities streetcar revenues declined for a time and parking space for the machines became a problem. The ladies spinning along Park Avenue in Minneapolis in about 1891 had not adopted the "short skirts reaching down only to the tops of high boots and leggings" that became fashionable for cyclists during the decade.

Cyclists could buy machines from Frederick Roach at 519 Hennepin Avenue, Minneapolis, pictured here in 1896.

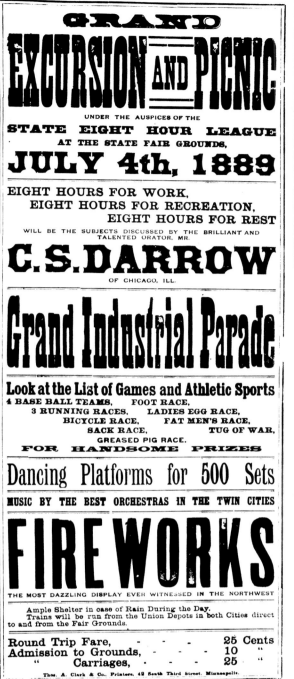

GRAND
EXCURSION AND PICNIC

UNDER THE AUSPICES OF THE

STATE EIGHT HOUR LEAGUE
AT THE STATE FAIR GROUNDS,

JULY 4th, 1889

EIGHT HOURS FOR WORK,
EIGHT HOURS FOR RECREATION,
EIGHT HOURS FOR REST

WILL BE THE SUBJECTS DISCUSSED BY THE BRILLIANT AND TALENTED ORATOR, MR.

C. S. DARROW
OF CHICAGO, ILL.

Grand Industrial Parade

Look at the List of Games and Athletic Sports

4 BASE BALL TEAMS,   FOOT RACE,
3 RUNNING RACES.   LADIES EGG RACE,
BICYCLE RACE,   FAT MEN'S RACE,
SACK RACE,   TUG OF WAR,
GREASED PIG RACE.

FOR HANDSOME PRIZES

Dancing Platforms for 500 Sets

MUSIC BY THE BEST ORCHESTRAS IN THE TWIN CITIES

FIREWORKS

THE MOST DAZZLING DISPLAY EVER WITNESSED IN THE NORTHWEST

Ample Shelter in case of Rain During the Day.
Trains will be run from the Union Depots in both Cities direct to and from the Fair Grounds.

Round Trip Fare,	-	-	25 Cents
Admission to Grounds,	-	-	10 "
" Carriages,	-	-	25 "

Thos. A. Clark & Co., Printers, 42 South Third Street, Minneapolis.

Wildwood Park on the south shore of White Bear Lake attracted these picnickers in 1894.

Fourth of July festivities at the state fairgrounds drew 2,500 people, among them labor-union members who were active in the State Eight Hour League. They listened to attorney Clarence S. Darrow, who had become identified with the issue after the Haymarket Riot in Chicago.

The Minneapolis Millers played the St. Paul Saints and other members of the Western Association in their home park, pictured in the 1890s, at First Avenue North and Fifth Street, behind the West Hotel. Over the scoreboard is an advertisement for Hach S. Griffin's bicycle school in the Panorama (Cyclorama) Building.

The Twin Cities acquired two new theaters in 1883, both called the Grand Opera House. The Minneapolis Grand, shown the year it opened at 60-62 South Sixth Street, seated 1,345 and was the first "downstairs" theater in the city. On opening night, the *Minneapolis Journal* reported, people from many parts of the state gathered in the audience "beneath the blaze of the gas jets. . . . Evening dress was worn, and the toilets of the ladies were magnificent." Like its St. Paul counterpart, the theater had a lavish interior, seen here about 1889 after it was redecorated in an exotic Moorish motif.

Edwin Booth, at right, and members of his company visited Minnehaha Falls while performing in the Twin Cities in 1886. Booth played Othello, Hamlet, and other Shakespearean roles during his Minneapolis and St. Paul visits.

Amateur theatrical groups like this Minneapolis troupe, posing in about 1885, performed in Twin Cities theaters, halls, and churches.

Panoramas, like roller skates and bicycles, were in vogue in the Twin Cities. The red brick, octagonal Cyclorama Building at Fifth Street near Nicollet Avenue in Minneapolis opened in 1886 with the "Battle of Atlanta." The panorama — 368 feet long and 50 feet high — drew large crowds during the twenty-one months it was exhibited in the building. Painted in 1885-86, it has now been restored and is on display in Grant Park, Atlanta, Georgia. The view depicted here is the "Slaughter of DeGress' Horses."

Members of the Nushka Club of St. Paul, organized in 1885, enjoyed winter sports, gave balls, and attended tennis tournaments, races, and regattas. In 1890 these members boarded a train in St. Paul for a regatta in Duluth, where the sailboat "Nushka" was the winner.

Frederick Schiek's restaurant at 45 South Third Street, Minneapolis, began attracting many notable visitors as well as Twin Citians in the golden age. It is shown here in the early twentieth century, with its impressive bar, tiled floor, and "chaste nudes" painted on the ceiling.

When the Twin Cities quarreled over the location of fairs in the late 1870s and early 1880s, Minneapolitan William S. King sponsored the Mill City's "Great Northwestern Exposition." A major attraction was horse racing at this track, located at present-day Franklin Avenue and Twenty-fourth Avenue South.

King's exposition in 1881 featured the flight of "The Great Northwest," a balloon brought to Minneapolis by noted aeronaut Samuel Archer King. The balloon, launched from a field close to the race track, ascended to about 4,200 feet and drifted to a landing in a cow pasture near present-day Randolph Street and Mississippi River Boulevard, St. Paul.

Exhibitors showed fruit from Oregon at the state fair in 1888. The *Northwest Magazine* hoped that the event would "invite the attention of the whole country to resources of the entire region tributary to St. Paul and Minneapolis. We want an exhibition in which Minnesota, Wisconsin, Dakota, Montana, Idaho, Washington, Oregon, and perhaps also the Canadian Northwestern provinces shall join."

The permanent state fairgrounds were established in 1885 in the Midway area. The domed Main Building, a race track, a grandstand, and other buildings were all built for the fair that year; about five years later, this photograph was taken.

The Exposition Building at First Avenue Southeast and Main Street, Minneapolis, was "not a marvel of chaste architectural beauty," but a "vast room with admirable acoustics." In 1892 it accommodated sessions of the Republican National Convention, depicted in this drawing from *Harper's Weekly.*

On August 23, 1886, crowds paraded through Minneapolis streets past buildings decorated with bunting, streamers, and mottoes to celebrate the opening of the Industrial Exposition. Special gaslights gave Nicollet Avenue, pictured here, a "Blaze of Glory" when people returned for nighttime festivities. A bicyclist on a high-wheeler also took in the scene. The Exposition Building towered over Joseph Cousineau's saloon in 1887. Called "the most conspicuous object in the city," it remained a Minneapolis landmark long after its significance in the rivalry between the Twin Cities faded.

Montreal men, experienced in ice construction, designed the ice palace for St. Paul's first Winter Carnival in 1886, pictured here on a sheet-music cover. Located in Central Park on Central Avenue (later part of the capitol approach), the "crystal building" glowed at night with the brilliance cast by fifty large electric lights.

The second palace, designed in the shape of a Latin cross and built in Central Park in 1887, was even grander than the first. The Winter Carnival flag bearing an image of a polar bear on a field of azure blue flew from its turret. During the carnival's finale, when the forces of the Fire King stormed the palace, the scene was brightened by 20,000 Roman candles.

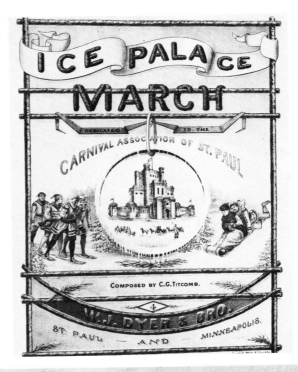

A parade touting St. Paul's industry and commerce highlighted the 1888 carnival. "It was a great industrial exposition out for a sleigh ride," the Chamber of Commerce observed with unconcealed delight. William R. Burkhard's shop was located at 128 East Third Street.

Twin Citians held conflicting views during the census war of 1890. Expressing them were the *St. Paul News,* June 28, 1890, right, and the *Minneapolis Tribune,* August 1, 1890, below.

FOR HER HONOR'S SAKE.
There are cases where a brother must interfere in his sister's affairs.

—St. Paul Graphic.

HOW IT WORKS.
JUST WHAT MINNEAPOLIS WANTED, BUT THE SAME MEDICINE MAKES ST. PAUL SICK.   HONEST PEOPLE DON'T OBJECT TO INVESTIGATION.

The generating room of the Minneapolis General Electric Company's Main Street Station symbolized the industrial age in about 1910. Built on the east side of the falls in 1894-95, the plant generated electricity from steam and from the extra water power that became available after sawmills moved from the falls district.

1895-1920
Passage to the Twentieth Century

THE TWIN CITIES began their passage to the twentieth century by climbing from the "ruts of hard times" furrowed deep by the panic of 1893. Like many other northwestern cities, they found that their postpanic world was quite different from the one they had known. A significant change for the cities was the end of the population boom. Now, rather than doubling or tripling in size every ten years, the Twins would have more modest growth rates. Minneapolis increased during each decade from 1890 to 1920 by an average rate of one-third, while St. Paul averaged only one-fifth.[1]

But other cities in the nation were also slowing in growth. Although St. Paul slid in size from twenty-third largest in 1890 to thirtieth in 1920 among the nation's cities, Minneapolis held its status as number eighteen. The cities showed up to an even better advantage after 1910, when the United States census bureau established statistical units called "metropolitan districts" — a concept that sometimes suited the Twins' way of looking at themselves. In 1920 the Minneapolis-St. Paul Metropolitan District, with a few suburbs swept into its population of 629,216, ranked twelfth largest in the nation and supreme in the Northwest.[2]

Distant northwestern cities like Seattle, Spokane, and Portland did not directly threaten this supremacy, but Duluth still did. "In these days of rivalry," the *Northwest Magazine* commented in 1896, "no territory belongs to a market center except by right of conquest." The Zenith City, as a center for sawmilling, flour milling, grain trade, shipping, and business generated by the new northern Minnesota iron mines, was ready for conquest. Its wholesalers reportedly believed that people selling grain in Duluth should buy goods there, and such trade penetration into the spring-wheat country threatened to diminish the Twins' business.[3]

Duluth and the Twins shared an interest in northern Minnesota's cutover lands, left by the lumber companies that had felled the pine. Many people believed that farming was a natural successor to forests in the cutovers. For example, a Minneapolis businessman — as mistaken in the nature of northern Minnesota soils as he was in botany — boasted that "leaves which have fallen for centuries from the trees of vanished pine forests have made of the land a rich, black loam, which cannot be excelled within the borders of the United States." Although much of the region would not support the type of agriculture Minnesotans knew, a great deal of land was sold for farming. The farming frontier was also a trading frontier, and the rival centers exerted efforts to swing the business into their respective orbits.[4]

Duluth, with strong ties to the cutovers and other parts of the northland, took on a role as the region's champion. Sometimes it used that role to marshal opinion against the Twin Cities. For example, in 1905-06 it supported the protests of northern Minnesotans who argued that reservoirs built on the headwaters of the Mississippi River were operated to benefit Twin Cities water-power and navigation interests, causing floods in the north. A Duluth newspaper, capping its arguments against selfish Twin Citians, stated that the fate of "any community within the territory of which Duluth is the chief receiving and distributing point, has a bearing upon the welfare of this city."[5]

Protests from the north country during the reservoir crisis were part of a widespread resentment of the Twin Cities in their trade area. The Twins often claimed that urban and rural interests were locked together in an indivisible union, but one country spokesman angrily wrote that the interests were as compatible as "those of the Wolf and lamb." Protesters had long scored the inequities in a system that fattened Twin Citians, who controlled terminal markets and other economic factors, at the expense of agricultural producers. In the nineteenth century they expressed their grievances in political movements like the Farmers' Alliance and the Peoples party. Succeeding these movements was the National Nonpartisan League, which in 1915 set a "political prairie fire" that blazed across states marketing wheat in Minneapolis and Duluth.[6]

Prime generators of these urban-rural tensions were the grain-marketing practices of the Minneapolis Chamber of Commerce and the Duluth Board of Trade. Several investigations in the early twentieth century focused on problems relating to the power concentrated at terminal markets. Bitter relations between opposing forces disrupted meetings and heated up testimony in hearing rooms. Both sides published emotion-packed literature, either branding the grain exchanges as monopolistic, greedy, and corrupt, or labeling the reformers as agitators, radicals, socialists, Bolsheviks, and economic innocents ignorant of the complexities of the grain trade.[7]

In 1908, in the midst of the fray, arose the Equity Cooperative Exchange, headquartered in Minneapolis where it took on the powerful Chamber of Commerce. Although the Equity was chiefly a commission firm, selling grain through members of the Chamber of Commerce, it soon tried to assume trading functions by organizing the Independent Grain Exchange. Attitudes in Minneapolis toward the Equity were hostile, to say the least. St. Paul businessmen, who saw an opportunity to establish a rival grain-trading center, supported the organization, which moved to the capital city in 1914, built a terminal elevator, and opened an exchange. The *Commercial West,* a conservative journal that was close to the Minneapolis chamber throughout the controversy, feigned amusement at St. Paul's inheritance of the troublesome Equity and the magical appearance of an exchange. It also deplored the Equity's role in fomenting discord between the Twins — "a popular pastime a generation ago, but . . . certainly out of date now."[8]

The position of the Twin Cities as strongholds of economic power was not the only contributor to urban-rural tensions. Their size also counted against them. Minneapolis and St. Paul were big cities, constituting an urban center of over half a million people, and their proportion of the state's total population had been growing. About one-tenth of the people lived there in 1880, but the proportion soared to almost one-fourth in the next decade, and even with the subsequent slowdown stood at 26 per cent in 1920.[9]

Knud Wefald, state legislator from Hawley and later a United States congressman, eloquently expressed the unease of a small-town man visiting the big city in 1913. "We farmers and villagers," he wrote, "are a lot of uncivilized savages compared with the city people. No matter how we dress and tog up when we come to the cities, they see we don't belong there." He felt estranged while attending sessions in St. Paul, where the "noise, hum and clatter almost drives a person crazy," where "a steady stream of human beings goes surging and seething up and down the narrow streets," and where urbanites were alienated from nature. "Now that I am a legislator . . . ," he observed, "it dawns upon me that if we are to make men happy and virtuous, we should legislate against letting people build big cities."[10]

Some Twin Citians also expressed concerns about urban growth that were common among reformers of the time, echoing comments made during the earlier depression years. Even spokesmen for business were eloquent on the subject. "City life stands, on the whole, for mental, moral and physical deterioration," arguments ran, while returning to the farm means "back to sanity, back to health, back to efficiency, back to life." Business journals supported groups working to increase the rural population, cited amenities like telephones, electricity, free mail delivery, cars, and farm mechanization that were "making rural life less objectionable to the best elements of our society," and advocated changes in an educational system that had turned children away from farms into cities. "All our children are being educated one way . . . for the professions which already are overcrowded," observed Joseph Chapman, a Minneapolis banker. He believed that the situation was serious, for in addition to the farm exodus "millions of Italians, Poles, Huns and Jews who flock to America in droves every year concentrate in the cities, creating unspeakable conditions."[11]

URBAN PROBLEMS such as these were concerns of the Progressive movement, from the turn of the century a strong force in American life that attracted persons of various political beliefs and economic interests. During their rush to become big cities, the Twins were also beset by other problems the Progressives cited, among them labor strife, monopolistic public utilities that were granted franchises when the cities were eager for the services offered, cumbersome city governments, corruption, and political machines.

The cities made some progress toward achieving reforms. Labor unrest was common, particularly in Minneapolis where an employers' group called the Citizens Alliance fought for the open shop. But labor attained one important objective in 1913 when the state legislature provided for workmen's compensation. The next year St. Paul established a commission form of government recommended by Progressives. And in 1920 — twenty years after the capital city had done so — Minneapolis finally adopted a home rule charter that freed its government from domination by the legislature.[12]

Both cities, too, threw out some rascals during the age of reform. In the Mill City the genial Dr. Albert Alonzo Ames, elected in 1900 as mayor for the fourth time, presided over a vice-riddled administration that Lincoln Steffens publicized in *McClure's Magazine* as "The Shame of Minneapolis." A grand jury investigation brought down Ames and his cohorts. The scandal, labor strife, an embroglio over the renewal of the street railway franchise in Minneapolis, and other concerns helped put the city in a mood for reform, and one sign of a change was the election of socialist and laborite Thomas Van Lear as mayor in 1916. Two years later the voters rejected Van Lear in a close contest, but the influence of a labor-socialist-reform coalition for a time remained strong in the traditionally Republican city.[13]

Bossism in St. Paul was epitomized in the power of Richard T. O'Connor, called "The Cardinal," who was one of the masters of the Democratic political machine. Reaction came in 1910 when Republican Herbert P. Keller was elected mayor on a pledge to clean house. O'Connor's day was not over, however, and reformers waged several subsequent campaigns to break the tenacious grip of the machine. A 1918 grand jury investigation revealed fraudulent voting in a city election, further staining the municipal record. The *St. Paul Pioneer Press* commented that "elements of vice and political cunning" had invaded "the mansion of our liberties."[14]

This turbulent age also saw the reform that outlawed alcohol in 1919 with the ratification of the Eighteenth Amendment to the United States Constitution. Temperance groups, including the Woman's Christian Temperance Union and the Anti-Saloon League, had battled for a long time against the "vile seductions of the cup." When prohibition began in 1920, the WCTU in St. Paul observed the event with prayers, music, and speeches, while Anti-Saloon Leaguers held a dinner in Minneapolis and heard addresses on "Sunshine vs. Moonshine" and "Where Do We Go From Here?" There were also mourners who watched the "total eclipse of alcoholic hope," some of them at the Ambassador Restaurant in St. Paul where "the orchestra sounded a dirge and the venerable alliance between the United States and Barleycorn was officially severed."[15]

In the memorable year that the prohibition amendment was ratified, women won the right to vote through adoption of the Nineteenth Amendment. Suffragists had waged their campaign for many years, often in an inhospitable atmosphere. For example, in 1867 the *Minneapolis Daily Chronicle* argued that women "have greater privileges now than men. Are treated better; honored, loved and obeyed to a greater degree now than they would if they doffed the robe of modesty and with brazen faces urged their measures in public political gatherings." In the nineteenth century women had gained power in the arena of school and library affairs — the rights to vote on issues and candidates for offices, and to hold these offices. The continuing effort to achieve full suffrage brought into the crusade notable Twin Cities women. Among them were Dr. Martha Ripley, founder of Maternity Hospital in Minneapolis; Clara Ueland, civic leader; and Mrs. Cordenio A. Severance, member of the women's advisory group of the Republican National Committee.[16]

When the Minnesota legislature ratified the amendment on September 8, 1919, noted one historian, the "ordinary decorum of the houses was abandoned for long-continued demonstrations of flag-waving, cheering, and the singing of the 'Battle Hymn of the Republic.'" Emily Grace Kay, a St. Paul member of the National Woman's party, sewed a star on the suffragists' banner to signify that Minnesota had joined the states that had voted for ratification. Mrs. Severance, also of St. Paul, declared, "For forty years, we have wandered in the wilderness, and now we have come into our own. I feel like General Pershing must have when he stood at the statue of Lafayette and remarked 'we are here.' I want to say, Susan B. Anthony, we are here."[17]

The United States government introduced another reform in 1913-14 by establishing the Federal Reserve System to bring stability and elasticity to banking. The system functioned through twelve districts, each defined with consideration for the "convenience and customary course of business," and each centered in a bank in a headquarters city. Included in the Ninth District were Minnesota, North Dakota, South Dakota, Montana, the Upper Peninsula of Michigan, and northern Wisconsin. The national banks in this area voted for the Twin Cities as district headquarters, despite a pull toward Chicago in South Dakota, the Upper Peninsula, and northern Wisconsin.[18]

In the banks' vote, Minneapolis outpolled St. Paul 365 to 93 as a choice for the location of the bank. An elaborate brief submitted to the Reserve Bank Organization Committee buttressed the Mill City's case. This masterpiece of cogent argument not only cataloged the city's strengths, but also stressed its influence in the Duluth grain trade and in Minnesota Transfer (which was actually within St. Paul's city limits). In contrast, St. Paul seemed to have conceded the election by offering only a short and weak argument. Its brief concluded with the affirmation that the Northwest looked to St. Paul "as its capital in a commercial and financial sense as truly it is the political capital of Minnesota." The committee could only conclude that the city was no match for its rival, although the *Commercial West* observed that the "combined business of the two cities doubtless was a powerful factor in bringing the [Ninth District's] bank to the Northwest."[19]

Although Minneapolis may have seemed shameless in its self-promotional claims, there was no doubt about its growing ascendancy over St. Paul. Minneapolis far outranked its twin in clearing-house totals, one measure of banking activity. The population difference by 1920 was 380,582 to 234,698. The Mill City may have widened the margin of its leadership in wholesaling; it certainly did so in manufacturing. Its pre-eminence in manufacturing persisted despite the loss of one of its basic industries. In 1899 Minneapolis was the leading lumber market in the world. But sawmilling declined sharply after the early years of the twentieth century and vanished in 1919 when the last mill cut the last logs pulled out of the river. Offsetting the loss were the prosperous flour-milling industry, linseed oil mills, and the array of miscellaneous manufactures that had long varied the economic base.[20]

St. Paul, although outdistanced, developed its industries substantially. Armour and Company opened a large meat-packing plant in South St. Paul in 1919, after dallying with the New Brighton site sponsored by Minneapolis. St. Paul continued to turn out large quantities of other products like boots, shoes, fur goods, butter, and beer; it also made a strong bid for flour mills. Commenting on the nascent flour business, the *Northwestern Miller* reported an unidentified St. Paul miller's parody of Minneapolis' reaction thus: " 'Whasamater wit youse? Haven't you got all the business on shoes and booze? Yes, an' cattle, an' hogs, an' even sheep? For Heaven's sake, go on back to sleep.' "[21]

WHILE MANY ISSUES divided the Twins, including an abortive effort by Minneapolis in 1895 to fix the site of the new state capitol at Loring Park, they united in support of the Spanish-American War. The conflict started in 1898 after the battleship "Maine" was sunk in Havana harbor. Archbishop John Ireland of St. Paul, the Pope's emissary in Washington, D.C., during the critical days preceding hostilities, stated that he had "labored for peace, but if the will of the nation is for war, I pray that victory alight on the banners of my country." The Third United States Infantry, long stationed at Fort Snelling, and four Minnesota volunteer regiments, which trained at Camp Ramsey established on the state fairgrounds, carried the banners to war from Minnesota. Twin Citians cheered the Thirteenth, their home regiment, when it departed. Groups that formed in St. Paul to aid the soldiers included the German-American Red Cross Society of Minnesota and the St. Paul Red Cross Aid Society. The Red Cross Society of Minneapolis, whose name was soon changed to the Red Cross Society of Minnesota, performed the usual relief work and provided nurses to care for wounded soldiers in Cuba, the Philippines, and several camps in the United States.[22]

At the close of the brief war, United States Senator Cushman K. Davis of St. Paul was named one of the commissioners to negotiate the peace with Spain that brought the Philippines, Puerto Rico, and Guam into the United States' possession. The imperial role that the nation assumed with its new Pacific territories stimulated the Twin Cities' long-held interest in the Orient. The *Northwest Magazine* asserted that the country wanted the Philippines "not only for the trade of their eight million inhabitants, but as a depot and commercial outpost from which we can reach forward for the immense business of China." The journal pre-

dicted that the Twins would share in the benefits of the trade, although Pacific Coast cities would reap the major advantages.[23]

Twin Citians' experiences were far more complex in World War I than during the Spanish-American conflict. Residents' humanitarian impulses were stirred even before the nation entered the war in April of 1917. In 1914-16 they contributed food, clothing, and bedding to Belgian relief as well as funds for German and Austrian relief. Welfare agencies mobilized humanitarian efforts during the war, which lasted until November 11, 1918, while businessmen contributed to a different kind of relief by marshaling volunteers to help harvest crops across the Northwest. Inspired by the "hum of myriads of great industries all centered on the one great business of the war," Twin Citians also traveled to Washington, D.C., to get the government contracts that stimulated their industries.[24]

Another effect of the war was the campaign unleashed in the name of Americanism and patriotism against the foreign born, particularly Germans, and various dissidents. The Minnesota Commission of Public Safety, local groups, newspapers, and journals carried attacks throughout the state. German Americans were accused of disloyalty, the use of the German language was castigated, and textbooks were censored. The attackers pictured socialism as a German export — "the trail of the Hun serpent" — that spread propaganda by means of the schools, the Nonpartisan League, and "all other movements aimed to break down the industrial and business structure of this country." They hailed defeats of socialist candidates for city offices as victories for loyalty. Fear of Bolshevism spread with the advent of the Russian revolution, and labor was tarred with the brush of radicalism.[25]

Accounts of the strike of Minneapolis newsboys in 1918 illustrated the tenor of the arguments. The *Commercial West* attributed the disorders accompanying the strike to Mayor Van Lear, whom it accused of exacting vengeance on newspapers that had opposed him. "Can you think of a more cowardly or contemptible act," the journal stated, "than to use the small newsies as a weapon of vengeance, to say nothing of the crime of teaching them anarchy? Here was a concrete example of what the modern radical socialistic creed means when put into practice. We need not go to Russia and inspect the Bolsheviki, because anarchy and mob rule in possession of the streets of Minneapolis has afforded us a lucid illustration of it."[26]

Some of these apprehensions about dissident views stemmed from deep concerns about the assimilation of the foreign born that transcended wartime fears. Although the proportion of the foreign born in the total population of the Twin Cities declined after

1890, emphasis on Americanization of the newcomers increased. This widespread movement focused on the growing number of immigrants from southern, eastern, and central Europe.

The conservative *Commercial West* voiced the fears of many, predicting in 1905 that the influx of ethnic groups like the Italians, Poles, Hungarians, and Russian Jews would create serious labor, political, educational, and "criminal" problems. As late as 1922, the journal observed that such people "do not readily assimilate American ideas, nor appreciate American ideals. It is among these classes that socialistic and radical reformers find the most fertile field for their work." Settlement houses, state and city Americanization committees, and the public schools performed many useful services for the immigrants, but a rejection of cultural diversity was implicit in their work. Dr. Carol Aronovici, an immigrant who worked in the movement, observed that "folks who used to be just human beings are being classified into American and unAmerican, according to their willingness to agree or disagree with Americanizers as to what their social, economic and political ideals should be." The time would come when more respect would be given to diversity, but some of the immigrants who became Twin Citians during the passage to the twentieth century would long remember those troubled years.[27]

OTHER CHANGES MARKED the passage to the new century for Twin Citians. The interest in fine music evident throughout the cities' history led to the founding of new symphony orchestras. Although some music-lovers suggested that the Twins join forces to support one orchestra, each city established its own. The Minneapolis Symphony Orchestra debuted in 1903 under the baton of Emil Oberhoffer, a European-trained maestro who for several years had directed the Apollo Club, a notable choral group, and played other roles in the cities' musical life. Three years later the St. Paul Symphony Orchestra, conducted by Chevalier Nathan B. Emanuel, gave its first concert. The *St. Paul Pioneer Press,* reviewing the concert, commented that "in one glorious bound" the city had "reached a plane of artistic achievement which places it in an entirely new light in the musical world." But the orchestra folded after eight seasons, and the Minneapolis organization began a regular concert schedule in St. Paul. The surviving orchestra rejected suggestions that it reflect its new status by substituting "Twin Cities" or "Minnesota" for "Minneapolis." Not until 1968 did the group adopt the name of the Minnesota Orchestra.[28]

Perhaps no form of entertainment was as pervasive in its impact as the movies, which crept into Twin Cities theaters at the turn of the century and soon exerted a strong influence on manners and customs —to no good, some inhabitants complained. Presented in

the same theaters that offered plays and vaudeville, the movies soon became a popular form of entertainment. Who could resist the call of the Metropolitan Opera House in Minneapolis in 1900 to see the "Biograph Motion Pictures" of the Jeffries-Sharkey fight, spun over 7¼ miles of film with "Positively no Flickers"? Or the terrors of the "San Francisco Earthquake and Fire," playing in 1906; the exotic pageantry of a British coronation in India depicted in "The Durbar," shown in 1911 in "Kinemacolor"; and the controversial excitement of "Birth of a Nation," running briefly in 1915 before both cities banned it for violence?[29]

In professional sports baseball led the way. Responding joyously to the popular new song, "Take Me Out to the Ball Game," Twin Citians trooped by the hundreds to Lexington Park, home of the St. Paul Saints, and to Nicollet Park, playing ground of the Minneapolis Millers. The two teams, members of the American Association organized in 1902, fought annually for this minor league's championship with nines from Milwaukee, Kansas City, Columbus, Toledo, Indianapolis, and Louisville— and with one another.[30]

A giant among managers was Michael Joseph Kelley, who piloted the Saints for most of the years from 1902 to 1923. The interruptions included his defection to Minneapolis in 1906 and his suspension for two seasons after he accused an umpire of crookedness. Petitioned by 36,000 fans, the Association readmitted the mighty Kelley; his return to the Saints was celebrated with a parody of "Casey at the Bat" that concluded:

> There may be places in this land where hope has
>   long been dead,
> Where joy has long departed and tears are often
>   shed;
> There may be places in this land where children
>   never play,
> But all is well with us, sir, for Kelley's home
>   to stay.

His "wonder teams" of Lexington Park won the championship six times between 1902 and 1924, the year he again defected to the Millers, who had "terrorized the league" in 1910, 1911, 1912, and 1915.[31]

An innovation that would have a dramatic effect on the way Twin Citians lived was the automobile, a vehicle that became a symbol for independence, coming of age, personal identification with power, and a pride in possession probably more universal than that felt by owners of fine horses. There were those, of course, who believed that the automobile would never replace the horse in the public's affections. "Dominion-loving man likes things receptive, and intelligently so," the *Northwest Magazine* commented in 1903. "A steel mechanism is neither receptive nor intelligent" — it does not have the "physical sympathy that exists between the right sort of man and the mettlesome horse."[32]

But the interest in automobiles was not a fad. The cars that were rarities on the streets of the Twin Cities at the turn of the century quickly took a firm hold on the public's fancy. Motorists swathed themselves in dusters, gloves, and goggles (for men) or billowing veils (for women); they drove machines that often resembled horse-drawn carriages in rallies, hill-climbing competitions, and reliability contests to distant points. Car owners in both cities formed automobile clubs with clubhouses where they dined, danced, played cards, and discussed their common interests. They might have to "get out and get under" to repair the strange machine, suffer injury from a kicking crank, or endure the humiliation of being towed home by a horse, but the automobile age had definitely come to stay.[33]

The automobile also brought a variety of new economic activities. From about 1910 to the mid-1920s it seemed that the Twins might become a major automobile production center. Local manufacturers turned out cars and trucks — the Wolfe and the Stickney Motorette among them — and engines for a racing car called the Duesenberg. More permanent businesses included the assembly plants of Willys-Overland in the Midway district and of Ford in Minneapolis; gas stations, which initially dispensed fuel from barrels with pails and funnels; repair shops that eventually supplanted the emergency services offered by blacksmiths; and sales organizations that penetrated the Northwest with dealerships, often taken on as adjuncts to farm-implement businesses. Automobile shows in the Twin Cities attracted dealers from the trade area as well as local residents eager to see the latest models. Dunwoody Institute, responsive to the need, added courses in automobile mechanics to its curriculum, and new products, such as ready-to-assemble garages, appeared on the market.[34]

While the automobile age brought new business to the Twin Cities, it also brought new woes. "Automobile crazy" people who mortgaged their homes to buy cars should be saved from their madness by cooler heads, the *Commercial West* warned in 1910, for the squandered money represented a serious economic loss. Manufacturers accentuated this loss, the journal claimed, by advertising a model "as if it represented the last word in automobile building" and then changing the design the next year, leaving the buyers in possession of "back-numbers." Cars created opportunities for a new class of criminals — automobile thieves — ranging from joy riders who snatched them for quick spins to a crime syndicate that shuttled them between the Twin Cities and Chicago. The machines were also dangerous, killing in 1920 half as many people in the United States as all industrial ac-

cidents combined and polluting the air with carbon monoxide. The roar of muffler "cut-outs" — exhaust systems that bypassed the muffler for added noise and power — assaulted the ears. And what about the inroads their voracious engines were making on the nation's petroleum supplies? Suggestions for solutions would sound uncannily familiar to drivers of a half-century later: more fuel-efficient motors, lower speed rates, improved petroleum-refining processes, and substitutes like alcohol and benzol.[35]

Motor buses and trucks also appeared on Twin Cities streets. Sometimes called "jitneys," a slang term for the nickel in-town fare, passenger buses in the metropolitan area may have been in operation as early as 1912, when the Twin City Motor Transit Company announced its intention to provide thirty-minute interurban service on vehicles dubbed "greyhounds." The street railway company, fearing competition from jitney buses, took measures to eliminate them and by 1926 had purchased several Twin Cities bus firms. Trucks gradually replaced dray wagons after the early years of the century. A Minneapolis pioneer was Floyd Raymond, who in 1910 cut away the rear part of a car and mounted a box on it. Trucks of less exotic design soon became common. In 1913, for example, one Minneapolis manufacturer claimed to have several hundred of its vehicles in use in the city.[36]

Motorized vehicles on the ground were prosaic compared to airplanes. Following the Wright brothers' flight at Kitty Hawk in 1903, Twin Citians became increasingly fascinated by the prospect of taking to the skies. Sometime in the future, the *Commercial West* observed in 1904, "every citizen of ordinary means will have his airship as now he has his bicycle, carriage or automobile, while the poorer classes will be carried on aerial lines of public transportation."[37]

Early local flyers were daring men. Hugh Robinson, for example, took off from Lake Calhoun for New Orleans in 1911, carrying mail in his pontoon airship — and aborted the flight at Rock Island, Illinois. Although a local writer shrugged off the venture with the comment that "men are but boys grown old," the number of daring pilots grew, particularly after World War I aviators quickened the interest in flying. Doing the loop-the-loops, barrel rolls, figure eights, nosedives, wing walks, and parachute jumps, opening flying schools and landing fields and offering charter service, flyers promoted the cause of aviation from its birth into the 1920s by preachment and their own élan. Among them were Walter Bullock, the "daredevil" exhibition performer who introduced young Charles "Speed" Holman, motorcycle racer, to the wonders of flying; barnstormer Clarence Hinck, who traveled with his Flying Circus; and William Kidder, who sold rides at the State Fair. Among them, too, was Charles A. Lindbergh, Jr., from Little Falls, who flew into the cities or roared in on his motorcycle before his remarkable trans-Atlantic flight in 1927 brought him local acclaim as "our own intrepid knight of the air" and world wide adulation.[38]

The tempo of life quickened in other ways. Revolving doors spun so fast that they were subdued with speed governors. Whirling around the tracks at the state fair was Dan Patch, king of the pacers — a big mahogany-bay stallion from Savage who set new records for running the mile. The Duesenberg and other racing cars roared around the speedway at Fort Snelling. "Make It Snappy" was the motto of *Capt. Billy's Whiz Bang,* a magazine published in Robbinsdale. Twin Citians heard the beat of ragtime; and to the beat of jazz they danced their way into a new age that would bear the name of the music.[39]

Church spires, the towers of public buildings, smokestacks, and bridges crossing the Mississippi River accented the St. Paul skyline in 1908 from the new state capitol on the hill, left, to the lowlands of the west side, right. Harriet Island, foreground, was developed in the early twentieth century into a recreation area with pavilions, public baths, picnic grounds, tennis courts, and a zoo.

On the Minneapolis skyline in 1908, behind the west-side mills and elevators, left, stood the new city hall and courthouse. To the right of the falls, in the east-side industrial district, were the rising walls of the Hennepin Island hydroelectric plant, the Exposition Building framed by smokestacks, and the Pillsbury A mill.

Huge piles of lumber filled the yards of North Minneapolis' booming sawmills in about 1904, when this photograph was made from the New York Life Building at Fifth Street and Second Avenue South. Fifteen years later, after a precipitous decline, the industry would be gone from the city.

A growing linseed oil business centered in an industrial district in Southeast Minneapolis and St. Anthony Park in St. Paul. The Midland Linseed Products Company, whose elevators stand here on Malcolm Avenue, Minneapolis, in about 1912, later became part of the Archer-Daniels-Midland Company.

In 1897 the Northwestern Knitting Company (later Munsingwear, Inc.), at 213 Lyndale Avenue North advertised George Munsing's new garments — underwear without the itch. Munsing also patented the union suit, a one-piece garment that would "change the apparel habits of the nation."

Wholesale and commission houses near the Butler Building in Minneapolis dealt in fruit and other produce. The firms were concentrated in a row between North Second and Third avenues on Sixth Street North, by the Central City Market, where they created traffic jams in the early twentieth century.

The Butler Brothers, general merchandise wholesalers, built their Minneapolis warehouse on the corner of Sixth Street North and First Avenue North in 1906, four years before this view was made. Harry Wild Jones's design for the structure has been called "magnificent." The building, renovated as Butler Square, is on the National Register of Historic Places.

Brickmakers practiced their trade in Frank A. Johnson's yard at 5008 Lyndale Avenue North, Minneapolis, in about 1905.

Cars from many railroad lines crowded into the St. Paul Union Depot yards in 1918, buttressing the Twin Cities' position as the dominant metropolis in the Northwest. On the skyline, center background, were the Merchants National Bank, the Pioneer Building, and the Northern Pacific-Great Northern general office building.

Coal barges near St. Paul's Upper Levee in 1918 demonstrate some success in the Twin Cities' attempts to revive Mississippi River navigation. In 1917 coal docks were built both at the foot of Chestnut Street in St. Paul and, when completion of the High Dam (Ford Dam) made navigation feasible, at the Washington Avenue Bridge in Minneapolis.

A special Minneapolis and St. Louis train advertised "Log Cabin Syrup," blended of maple and cane syrups, on its way to Omaha. Patrick J. Towle, who began his St. Paul business career as a wholesaler in the late 1880s, headed the Towle Syrup Company in 1895, the year this photograph was made.

Nels T. Nelson (center) stands with two other coal haulers in 1906 near St. Paul's Seven Corners. Like the brickmakers, teamsters and draymen were important in the Twin Cities' work force well into the twentieth century.

"3,000 Tons of Steel Shapes in Stock," boasted the St. Paul Foundry Company, located at Como Avenue and Mackubin Street and shown here about 1920. The firm, established in the 1880s and still in business a century later, produced railroad equipment, machine castings, and structural steel and iron.

Craftsmen labored in about 1917 at Foot, Schulze and Company's factory on Robert Street between Ninth and Tenth streets. The firm, which had operated in St. Paul since the 1880s, at first specialized in footwear for lumbermen and miners. In the twentieth century its shoemakers also produced shoes, slippers, rubbers, and other types of boots.

The Merchants National Bank of St. Paul, strengthened in 1912 by a merger with the National German American Bank, built a new home at Robert and Fourth streets in 1914-15. The tall structure (visible on the skyline on page 128), faced with enameled brick and terra cotta, was hailed as "a distinct addition . . . to the architectural beauty of St. Paul's business district."

Many brokerage firms added to Twin Cities commerce by the turn of the century. Quotations for pork, lard, ribs, and the New York Stock Market appear in about 1900 on the board of this office, probably that of C. H. F. Smith and Company, 102 Pioneer Building, St. Paul. Ticker-tape machines are in front of the board.

Wistful Minne received the valentine a little late. It was presented on April 2, 1914, when Minneapolis was named headquarters of the Ninth Federal Reserve District. With the new bank the city gained prestige and strengthened its influence in Minnesota, North Dakota, South Dakota, Montana, Wisconsin, and Michigan.

In the early 1890s proposals for a new state capitol brought renewed efforts to remove the seat of government from St. Paul. A *Minneapolis Tribune* article on March 26, 1895, described "The Mighty Movement Looking Toward the Location of Minnesota's Government in the Flour City," but legal difficulties involved in donating Loring Park, the proposed site, deflected the campaign.

IN SORE AFFLICTION.

St. Paul—"Come back, come back! Will you follow all the rest and run off with her too?"

Fortunately for St. Paul, high ground overlooking its downtown was chosen as the new capitol site. "Once remove the capital from this city," a legislator commented, "and there will not be enough of it left to hold a tallow dip for Minneapolis and Duluth to grow by." The photographer took this picture looking across Wabasha Street before construction began in 1896.

The Italian Renaissance design by Cass Gilbert, a St. Paul architect, was selected from forty-one plans submitted to a state commission. Gilbert (seated) posed with his staff about 1900, when construction was in progress. The capitol project launched the architect on a career of national importance.

The capitol's walls of Georgia marble were rising as the century turned.

A crowd gathered at the "gigantic Renaissance palace" on June 14, 1905, to witness the transfer of the flags of Minnesota's Civil and Spanish-American war regiments from the old capitol to the new. Archbishop John Ireland gave the main address on this festive day.

Ireland presided over another important ceremony in 1915, when he celebrated the first Mass in the new Cathedral of St. Paul, pictured here about 1920. Designed by Emmanuel L. Masqueray, the cathedral stands high on St. Anthony Hill, a short distance from the capitol. The archbishop evenhandedly employed the same architect to design an imposing church for Minneapolis, which was opened in 1914 and is now called the Basilica of St. Mary.

Minneapolis' new city hall and courthouse, a "granite palace," opened a year after this photograph was taken in 1905. A soaring tower, rising 345 feet from the sidewalk level, distinguishes the structure, which was designed by Long and Kees in the age of monumental public buildings. The structure is listed on the National Register of Historic Places.

A four-faced clock was the "jewel" of the tower. With minute hands over fourteen feet long, it was "the largest working tower clock in the world" at the time of its installation in 1898. New clock faces were substituted for the originals in 1949, after the glass in them cracked.

These gentlemen gathered in about 1906 in the Minneapolis city council's third-floor chamber, which was decorated with oil panels depicting scenes from the city's history.

New bridges in Minneapolis added to the Mississippi River landscape and helped to relieve traffic congestion. Workers took six years to build the Third Avenue Bridge, which was opened for traffic in 1918. The forms for the concrete arches rise from the river in this view of the construction scene taken in about 1917 from the Exposition Building. The beautiful bridge, designed by Kristoffer Olsen Oustad and Frederick W. Cappelen and built in a distinctive "S" curve, was restored in 1980. The restoration, which included a new bridge deck and columns, won a national design award for historical preservation from the Federal Highway Administration.

Construction on the Franklin Avenue or Cappelen Memorial Bridge, also designed by Cappelen and Oustad, began in 1919. Hailed as a notable engineering achievement, its four-hundred-foot center span was called the longest of its type in the world when it was built. The concrete arch bridge was still in use in the 1980s.

A tornado with winds exceeding 180 miles an hour tore away part of St. Paul's High Bridge in 1904. The damage was repaired, and the bridge was still in use in 1983, when plans were under way to replace it.

The regimental band of the Thirteenth Minnesota Volunteer Infantry paraded in Manila in 1898. Many Twin Citians served during the Spanish-American War in the Thirteenth Minnesota, whose band played concerts popular with the Philippine people.

The Thirteenth Minnesota returned from service and took a place of honor in Minneapolis on October 12, 1899, in a huge parade reviewed by President William McKinley. The regiment dined well that day. The soldiers breakfasted at the St. Paul Auditorium following a parade through that city and feasted at a banquet in the Exposition Building after the Minneapolis ceremony.

Great crowds lined East Sixth Street in St. Paul on April 4, 1903, when President Theodore Roosevelt visited the Twin Cities. Units of the United States Army, the Grand Army of the Republic, Spanish-American War veterans, and the Minnesota National Guard marched in the parade. Roosevelt, hailed as the "nation's idol" by the *St. Paul Pioneer Press,* waves his hat from the first carriage.

McClure's Magazine

VOL. XX   *JANUARY, 1903*   NO. 3

THE SHAME OF MINNEAPOLIS

The Rescue and Redemption of a City that was Sold Out

BY LINCOLN STEFFENS

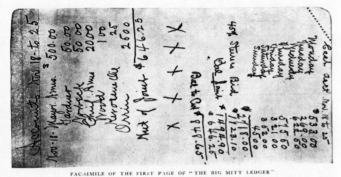

FAC-SIMILE OF THE FIRST PAGE OF "THE BIG MITT LEDGER"

An account kept by a swindler of the dealings of his "Joint" with City Officials, showing first payments made to Mayor Ames, his brother, the Chief of Police and Detectives. This book figured in trials and newspaper reports of the exposure, but was "lost"; and its whereabouts was the mystery of the proceedings. This is the first glimpse that any one, except "Cheerful Charlie" Howard, who kept it, and members of the grand jury, has had of the book

WHENEVER anything extraordinary is done in American municipal politics, whether for good or for evil, you can trace it almost invariably to one man. The people do not do it. Neither do the "gangs," "combines," or political parties. These are but instruments by which bosses (not leaders; we Americans are not led, but driven) rule the people, and commonly sell them out. But there are at least two forms of the autocracy which has supplanted the democracy here as it has everywhere it has been tried. One is that of the organized majority by which, as in Tammany Hall in New York and the Republican machine in Philadelphia, the boss has normal control of more than half the voters. The other is that of the adroitly managed minority. The "good people" are herded into parties and stupefied with convictions and a name, Republican or Democrat; while the "bad people" are so organized or interested by the boss that he can wield their votes to enforce terms with party managers and decide elections. St. Louis is a conspicuous example of this form. Minneapolis is another. Colonel Ed. Butler is the unscrupulous opportunist who handled the non-partisan minority which turned St. Louis into a "boodle town." In Minneapolis "Doc" Ames was the man.

The front page of *McClure's Magazine* of January, 1903, bannered the story of corruption in Minneapolis. The account featured a reproduction of the "Big Mitt Ledger," a record of pay-offs to Mayor Albert Alonzo Ames and other city officials.

Richard T. O'Connor, the mastermind of St. Paul's politics and every inch a boss, was a United States marshal in the 1890s. In 1898, while serving warrants at Leech Lake, "The Cardinal" had his picture taken in Walker.

St. Paul did not have all of the Irish politicians. Michael W. Nash, a Hennepin County commissioner in 1888-96 and 1900-04, campaigned on Nicollet Avenue in Minneapolis, probably early in the twentieth century.

The South Minneapolis and Folkets Vel (The People's Welfare) temperance societies contributed this swan to a temperance parade held in the Mill City on May 14, 1910. Delegations from churches, temperance societies, schools, charitable organizations, and businesses gathered after their march at The Parade. There they heard the Reverend Dr. Ervin S. Chapman of Los Angeles speak on "The Stainless Flag." Comic songs bewailed the passing of favorite drinks with prohibition. "Oh my darling old frappé, they will soon take you away . . . No more saying: 'Let me buy,' no more coming through the Rye," mourned this dirge.

EVERY DAY WILL BE SUNDAY WHEN THE TOWN GOES DRY

GOOD BYE HUNTER, SO LONG SCOTCH
FAREWELL HAIG AND HAIG

WORDS AND MUSIC BY WM. JEROME AND JACK MAHONEY

LEO. FEIST — NEW YORK

In 1909 visitors from across the Northwest inspected new Fords, Packards, Reos, Overlands, and many other models in Minneapolis' second automobile show at the National Guard Armory on Kenwood Parkway, across from the parade ground.

Minneapolis drivers parked in the middle of the street in about 1918. This view of Seventh Street between Nicollet and Hennepin avenues foreshadowed traffic congestion in the Twin Cities' downtown districts. A St. Paul traffic study in 1918 cited motorists' "absolute disregard for the safety of pedestrian traffic" and recommended establishing "Isles of Safety" at important intersections.

J. George Smith, a St. Paulite who ran a popular candystore and soda fountain, bought the Waverley electric car in 1900, the year the photograph was made. A salesman had assured him that it would climb hills and "almost go from St. Paul to Minneapolis and back without being pushed." Frightened horses "climb[ed] up the sides of buildings" when he motored downtown, where he recharged the batteries through a wire strung from his store. The car is in the museum collections of the Minnesota Historical Society.

Aeronaut Charles Hamilton piloted Roy Knabenshue's airship or "aerodrome" in several flights over the Twin Cities during July and August, 1906. A gasoline motor drove the ship's propeller; the gas bag was made of Japanese silk inflated with hydrogen. Crowds attracted by the novel sight dashed for open spaces, cars tried to follow its course, and streetcars made unscheduled stops. The airship here flies over the falls area in Minneapolis, with the west-side milling district to the right and the Exposition Building to the left.

Wireless transmission was still a novelty when Governor John A. Johnson sent a message to Minneapolis Mayor James C. Haynes, sometime between 1906 and 1909.

This "suitcase" Edison phonograph, developed in the late 1890s, played two-minute recordings for its St. Paul owners. Although Thomas A. Edison patented the phonograph in 1877, the machines and the recording industry developed somewhat later.

A cigar maker displayed the product of an unidentified tenement factory in Minneapolis in about 1912. The industry was widely dispersed in the Twin Cities: 109 establishments and 1,142 persons produced tobacco products in 1910.

Many Jews from eastern Europe settled in North Minneapolis. A tenement building at Sixth Avenue North and Third Street, seen here in 1909, was home to families who could buy groceries from a store at Sixth Avenue North and Lyndale Avenue (below). Many newcomers started their own businesses in their homes or in small shops nearby. Because most of the neighborhood observed kosher dietary laws, butchers had an especially good trade.

This notice, posted in railroad depots throughout the state, prompted many letters from women seeking employment in 1910. Mary Starkweather, known for her pioneering efforts to help working women, observed that trains and depots "have always been infested with vicious and depraved persons who prey upon the unsuspicious and innocent."

Frieda (Mrs. Frederick) Groechel invited women job-seekers into the "parlor" in her agency at 257 Twelfth Avenue North, Minneapolis, about 1904. She had been in the "intelligence" and employment business for two decades by then, and operated an agency at the same address for many years thereafter.

These women worked in 1911 for the Western Freight Traffic Association at Raymond and University avenues in St. Paul. There were over 4,000 female workers in Twin Cities offices.

The "singles" employed by the Minneapolis Dry Goods Company, a department store at 501-507 Nicollet Avenue, proclaimed their status at the firm's picnic in 1910.

The Minneapolis "newsie" at Washington and Hennepin avenues in 1904 was one of hundreds of Twin Cities boys — many of them orphaned or poor — who sold newspapers on the streets and made home deliveries. The *Minneapolis Tribune* advised the boys who hawked newspapers in the streets: "Do not stand around with your papers under your arm and let people ask you what paper you are selling, but keep moving and calling The Minneapolis Tribune so that every person in town knows that The Tribune is sold there morning, noon and night and that you are after the business."

On November 28, 1917, about 2,500 workers marched to St. Paul's city hall-courthouse to support union employees of the Twin City Rapid Transit Company in their dispute with the firm. Those who could not get into the city council chamber gathered in Rice Park to hear an account of the proceedings. "There was no yelling, no loud talk, and no rowdyism," the *St. Paul Daily News* reported. "The extra platoons of policemen that had been thrown about the courthouse, and the blue-coats scattered through the crowds, had nothing to do."

Charismatic Arthur C. Townley enlisted farmers in the National Nonpartisan League's assault on powerful Twin Cities economic interests. "Will you stick?" Townley asked from many platforms across the wheat-growing region. "We'll stick!" shouted audiences in a response that became a battle cry.

THERE SHALL BE NO ABRIDGEMENT OF THE FRANCHISE BECAUSE OF SEX

LOU ROGERS

He: "But, madam, you cannot bear arms."
She: "Nor can you, sir, bear armies."

A poster published in St. Paul in 1914 argued eloquently for woman suffrage.

The gravity of war came to a porch
in St. Paul.

An editorial writer in the *Commercial West,* a Twin Cities journal, asserted in 1918 that "No sketch artist has yet been clever enough to indicate by pictures . . . the barbaric savagery of kaiserism." Barron G. Collier, Inc., an advertising firm with offices in both cities, seems to have done so in this poster.

Parades and rallies reached "spectacular proportions" in the Twin Cities as involvement in the war deepened. The Hutchinson Hun Hunters marched with other delegations from Minnesota communities in a loyalty parade in St. Paul on November 16, 1917. Their banner "set the crowd wild," reported the *Hutchinson Leader.* "The camera and movie men all took pictures of it." The reverse side read "30 HUTCHIN-SONS in France NOW."

Germania Life Insurance Company removed the figure of Germania from the front of its building at Fourth and Minnesota streets, St. Paul, in 1918. The company, which changed its name to Guardian Life, followed the practice of other firms in removing the "Hun word."

Women making tractor parts at the Minneapolis Steel and Machinery Company at 2854 Minnehaha Avenue were probably hired during World War I. In 1918 the firm announced that its women employees would be trained at Dunwoody Institute and would earn "the same wage as we pay to men performing the same work."

Red Cross nurses who had volunteered for active service helped open the organization's second war-fund drive in a parade held in St. Paul on May 18, 1918. The 20,000 marchers included Red Cross auxiliaries, government officials, military units from Fort Snelling and training camps, floats, automobiles, trucks, and a "small bi-plane moving on its own power."

In 1918 the William Hood Dunwoody Industrial Institute in Minneapolis trained these "outside wiremen" for war service, along with technicians, mechanics, carpenters, and others.

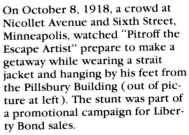

On October 8, 1918, a crowd at Nicollet Avenue and Sixth Street, Minneapolis, watched "Pitroff the Escape Artist" prepare to make a getaway while wearing a strait jacket and hanging by his feet from the Pillsbury Building (out of picture at left). The stunt was part of a promotional campaign for Liberty Bond sales.

Some 200,000 people in St. Paul welcomed home the 151st U.S. Field Artillery on May 8, 1919. The parade was routed through a triumphal arch erected at Sixth and Wabasha streets. After the festivities in St. Paul, the soldiers moved on to Minneapolis, where another celebration awaited them.

Soldiers throughout the nation who had lost hands, feet, arms, and legs received replacements from the Minneapolis Artificial Limb Company at 240 South Fourth Street. In 1918, the year this picture was made, the firm contracted with the federal government to supply artificial limbs to men injured in World War I.

Through depression, war, and the ferment of reform movements, many Twin Citians enjoyed festivals, sports, music, theater, the movies, art, the parks, and other pleasures of urban life. Louis W. Hill, the bearded man at the center table, led a revival of the St. Paul Winter Carnival in 1916 and was honored with a banquet at the St. Paul Auditorium.

During the carnival of 1896, the first since 1888, pioneer jurist Charles E. Flandrau, left, acted the part of Boreas Rex. Beside him stands Samuel R. Van Sant, a future Minnesota governor, masquerading as the Lord High Chancellor.

The Christian T. Hedlund family of 410 Baker Street in St. Paul celebrated July 4, 1911, with appropriate firepower.

Twin Cities groups often chartered the steamboat "Hiawatha" for river outings early in the century.

Bert Parson mixed elaborate concoctions at the soda fountain in the drugstore of A. T. Guernsey and Son, 171 North Dale, St. Paul, in 1896.

Ladies played cards at a meeting of the Minnesota Garden Flower Society in St. Paul about 1898.

This young man recorded the class of 1910 at St. Paul's Central High School, on Tenth Street at Minnesota, whose magazine published a friendly benediction: "May you find that sometimes elusive little fellow, happiness." Casual photography had become popular after hand-held, roll-film camera was introduced in 1888.

The Town and Country Club on Marshall Avenue in St. Paul held this lawn party in 1905 at its beautiful site overlooking the Mississippi River. Organized in 1887, the club drew its membership from the "upper stratum of the social world" in both cities.

Sportsmen about 1900 rolled bowling balls down the long alley in Schade's Park at 891 West Seventh Street, St. Paul. Fred H. Schade, a St. Paul pioneer, operated the park for a number of years.

The lily pond (seen here in 1903), lake, band concerts, and pavilion at St. Paul's Como Park drew many visitors. At times, an observer noted in 1900, the city seemed to empty itself into "this cool and beautiful retreat."

The Twin City Wonderland Park at Lake Street and Thirty-first Avenue South, Minneapolis, operated from 1905 to 1912. The 120-foot-high electric tower had 7,000 incandescent bulbs and a powerful searchlight, providing "a blaze of light that can be seen for miles around." Among the amusements offered were a rifle range, a carousel, a "House of Nonsense," a scenic railway, and a pavilion for dancing.

Skating in Van Cleve Park in southeast Minneapolis helped satisfy Twin Citians' taste for winter sports in 1912.

Seals performed for Robert "Fish" Jones sometime after 1906 at his Longfellow Gardens Zoo near Minnehaha Falls in Minneapolis. Jones kept a wide variety of birds and animals in his zoo, which operated into the 1920s. Other trained animals performed in the Arena Building in the background. The statue in front of the building is of Henry Wadsworth Longfellow, after whom the gardens were named and whose home in Cambridge, Mass., was the model for Jones's own home on Minnehaha Parkway.

A skier takes flight from the steel slide of the Twin City Ski Club in Minneapolis. This slide may have been the Glenwood Park ski jump, built in 1908.

Iceboats on lakes in the Twin Cities area, like this one on Lake Calhoun, Minneapolis, about 1901, provided pleasures when summer craft were beached. Among the groups promoting iceboating was the Calhoun Yacht Club, organized in 1901.

A sculling crew from the Minnesota Boat Club passed the St. Paul river front in 1897. The organization dated from the 1870s and had its clubhouse on Raspberry Island nearby; John A. Kennedy (back to camera), the club's long-time trainer, was coxswain. Sculling retained its popularity despite the inroads made by golf, bicycling, and what one wit called "milder games which permitted the uninterrupted use of the cigarette and the cocktail and afforded one all the comforts of home in their pursuit."

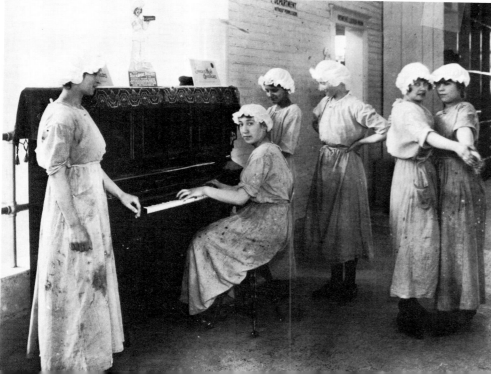

Employees of the Sanitary Food Manufacturing Company at University and Fairview avenues, St. Paul, took a noontime break about 1916.

149

On a Saturday afternoon in about 1904 the usual crowd gathered to watch the *Minneapolis Journal's* play-by-play account of a University of Minnesota football game. A "gridiron" showing the position of the ball stretched from the *Journal* building across Fourth Street between Nicollet, foreground, and Marquette avenues.

The baseball park (upper right) behind the West Hotel in Minneapolis provided a poor playing field for the university's football team in about 1898. From the mid-1880s, however, a very good yell cheered the teams — "Rah. Rah. Rah. Sik-U-Mah. Minn-e-so-ta!"

Spectators in about 1902 watched from the railroad viaduct near the university campus as the team played on Northrop Field. Thomas A. Lowry's carriage is on the left.

In 1896 the Minneapolis Millers, led by outfielder-manager Walter Wilmot (center, front row) and Perry "The Moose" Werden (back row, second from left), won the Western League championship. Werden hit forty-nine home runs during the season, setting a record for organized baseball that Babe Ruth would break twenty-five years later. When the team was on the road, fans at home could follow the games at saloons and other places where scores received by telegraph were recorded on blackboards.

Michael J. Kelley, later called "one of the most colorful, smartest and resourceful men in the long history of baseball," was manager of the St. Paul Saints when this picture was made in 1904. He was associated with Twin Cities teams for forty-five years.

"Calamity Jane" (Martha Jane Canary) appeared in 1896 at the Palace Museum, Washington Avenue and First Avenue South, Minneapolis. Wearing "immaculate buckskins with two highly polished guns on her hip," she toured dime museums in the 1890s to exploit her legendary career.

The Palace Museum, seen here in the 1890s, offered other attractions to capture the public's fancy. Among them were the Crawling Fat Woman, the Elastic Man, the Dancing Four-Legged Girl, the Two-Headed Wild Giant, an Edison phonograph recording of a murderer's last words, and a "cineograph" of a heavyweight fight.

Dan Patch (right), the remarkable horse who set the world's mile record for pacers, pulled Marion W. Savage, his owner, around their home track at Savage about 1910. Harry Hersey drove Minor Heir, at left. The name and image of Dan Patch were used in advertisements for the International Stock Food Company, located in the Exposition Building, Minneapolis, and for an electric railway line linking Minneapolis with southern Minnesota towns.

Performers who visited the Twin Cities in the late nineteenth and early twentieth centuries included, left to right, Ignace Paderewski, the "idolized" young pianist; Sylvia Lynder, actress; Julia Arthur, actress; and Otis Skinner, actor.

The Cable Piano Company, which operated stores in both cities, sold pianos, pianolas, organs, and sheet music. The Minneapolis store at 729 Nicollet Avenue carried tall racks of music in 1909.

Several songs using local themes were issued in sheet music, including "The Twin City Summer Song," published in 1906, "Minneapolis Mill Disaster" (see page 68), "Ice Palace March" (see page 114), "Old Betz," "The Minnesota Boat Club," "Minneapolis Makes Good," and "I Want to Go to Lake Como."

Talented Frederick T. Swanson of St. Paul composed "Minnesota Street Rag" and other pieces, taught guitar and mandolin, and managed the Twin City Mandolin Orchestra. He posed (third from the left) with the orchestra about 1900.

The Miles Theater at Nicollet Avenue and Seventh Street South, Minneapolis, offered four "advanced vaudeville" shows a day when it opened in 1908, about two years before this photo was made. Its appointments, as lavish as theaters offering more pretentious fare, included gold plush seats, rose, ivory, and gold decorations, a marble lobby, and marble stairs leading to the gallery. In 1915 it became the "New Garrick," advertised as "A Revelation in Photo Play Theatres."

About 1910 a smartly uniformed band led by Frank Danz, Jr., played a regular gig at the Como Park pavilion in St. Paul. Danz also led a band at the Lake Harriet pavilion in Minneapolis, conducted the Metropolitan Theater Orchestra in Minneapolis and the Danz Orchestra, and toward the end of his career was concertmaster of the new Minneapolis Symphony Orchestra.

The Apollo Club, which was organized in 1895 and still sang in the 1980s, celebrated an anniversary on October 2, 1915, at a concert in the Minneapolis Auditorium. Director Hal Woodruff, seated second from the left, had joined Twin Cities musical circles in 1886 when he played the organ at the opening of the Exposition Building.

R. H. Adams (left), curator of Thomas B. Walker's art collection, and Carl L. Boeckmann, Minneapolis artist who restored many paintings in the notable collection, conferred about 1915 in the gallery at Hennepin Avenue and Eighth Street South. A visitor to the gallery in 1912 wrote: "I met the old lumberman strolling among his treasures, glad in the pleasure they gave his guests, the public."

153

Delights of the new decade, compactly advertised on a theater curtain, tempt motion-picture patrons at the Bijou, 18 Washington Avenue North, Minneapolis, in about 1921. Such commercialism drew fire as early as 1900 when a critic complained that people went to the theater "to be pleased — not to have the eye disgusted with a lot of advertisements on an otherwise artistic canvas."

1920-29
The Jazz Age

It was called the Jazz Age and the Roaring Twenties, this decade when Twin Citians with the rest of the nation experienced an urge for a return to normalcy after the troubled passage to the new century and the upheaval of World War I. The crusades of the past years had been rigorous, and the *Minneapolis Journal* complained, "We have earned a rest and we need it." In an economy that seemed to promise more wealth for more people than ever before, many Twin Citians turned to the pursuit of pleasure. The pursuit itself became big business. Minneapolitans in one year at mid-decade, for example, spent an estimated $53 million on sports, movies, cars, radios, dancing, and other forms of amusement.[1]

Baseball was the reigning sport, but Twin Citians found excitement in other arenas as well. Boxing had come out from the shadows in 1915 when the Minnesota legislature lifted the ban it had imposed in 1892. Great St. Paul fighters then joined the ranks of sports heroes: Mike O'Dowd, who won the middleweight title in 1917; Billy Miske, who challenged heavyweight Jack Dempsey in 1918 and again in 1920; Tommy Gibbons, who went fifteen rounds with the great champion in 1923; and his brother Mike, the "St. Paul Phantom" whom Gene Tunney called "the perfect boxer." Then Americans discovered ice hockey —"the fastest game in the world" — and fans thrilled to the exploits of the Minneapolis Millers and the St. Paul Saints. Frank "Moose" Goheen, a powerful member of the St. Paul club, starred in the 1920 Olympic games at Antwerp and later joined the sport's immortals in the Hockey Hall of Fame.[2]

A more sedate sport was golf, played since the late-nineteenth and early-twentieth centuries at private clubs like the Town and Country in St. Paul and the Minikahda in Minneapolis. The "rich man's game" gained in popularity after 1916 when the cities opened public courses. Proliferating organizations and tournaments fostered remarkable golfers, among them Harry Legg of Minneapolis, state champion many times, and his successor to fame, Harrison "Jimmy" Johnston of St. Paul, winner of the national amateur championship at the close of the 1920s. Exciting moments for golf fans came when Twin Cities courses hosted national tournaments; perhaps the most memorable was the sizzling July day in 1930 when Bobby Jones, idol of golfers on two continents, won the National Open at Interlachen in suburban Edina.[3]

Stars of the screen tightened their hold on the public's imagination. Many of those popular in the 1920s were long remembered for their roles: Charlie Chaplin in "The Kid," Pola Negri in "Passion," Mary Pickford in "The Love Light," Constance Talmadge and the Ziegfeld beauties in "Polly of the Follies," and Rudolph Valentino, Latin lover of a million dreams, dissembling as "The Young Rajah" and "The Sheik." Clara Bow with her cupid lips personified "It," a word given a new meaning by novelist Elinor Glyn. "Either you *had* It or you didn't," wrote a social historian describing the phenomenon, "but, look, you simply *had* to or all life went punk." At the decade's close there was a new star — Greta Garbo, a mystic beauty who inspired photographers long after her Hollywood reign was over. And St. Paulite F. Scott Fitzgerald, whose novels became movies, was himself an idol. When "The Beautiful and The Damned" played in the capital city, his elegant profile adorned the show programs.[4]

Three-dimensional movies made a brief splash in Twin Cities theaters. Viewing "Plastigrams" through special glasses at St. Paul's Capitol Theatre in 1924, patrons discovered "an entirely new set of thrills when objects were seemingly thrust in their faces from the screen" — a monkey on a trapeze swinging over their heads, a girl proffering a foaming drink, and a "thrilling and dangerous ride in a speeding automobile." A more enduring change was the talking picture produced by Vitaphone, a device that synchronized sound and picture more successfully than earlier systems. In 1927 Twin Citians marvelled at Al Jolson in "The Jazz Singer," a production that profoundly affected the industry. "Now all movie actors had to sing," a historian commented, "or at least talk. Strangely enough, not all of them could."[5]

Local publications were quick to capitalize on the culture and trends spawned by the movies. *Greater Amusements,* advertised as the nation's first regional motion picture trade magazine, originated in Minneapolis in 1914. Fawcett Publications of Robbinsdale, creator of *Capt. Billy's Whiz Bang,* issued four new magazines in the 1920s: *Screen Secrets,* which professed to be factual in articles like "The Romantic Story of John Gilbert's Life"; *True Confessions,* with intimate tales like "Experiences of a Dope Slave" that seemed more fiction than fact; *Fawcett's Triple-X Magazine,* outright fiction that featured not only "bang-up" tales of the West, but also adventure and detective stories, and *Fawcett's Battle Stories,* "Dedicated to the fighting forces of the United States and Canada, whose gallant daring and deathless courage has always distinguished their deeds on land, sea or sky."[6]

Flamboyant covers on Fawcett publications were matched by those on sheet music like "The Flapper Girl" that rolled off Twin Cities presses during the peak of production from 1900 to 1929. Tinkling pianos in department and ten-cent stores advertised music published locally and elsewhere. It was music to hum and whistle, music inviting listeners to the dance floors. "During the 1920s . . . ," one historian observed, "America went dance mad, and Tin Pan Alley had a field day catering to this craze." Pleasure seekers did the fox trot, shimmy, Charleston, and black bottom at ballrooms like the Coliseum Pavilion in St. Paul, where the rubber-lined floor — "resilient" and "rhythmic" — gave "dancing a new and delightful charm," and at the Black Cat Club, a roadhouse overlooking the Minnesota River Valley "10 Little Miles from Town" where the Chat Noir orchestra played nightly.[7]

Music, sports, drama, and news reached thousands in the Northwest when commercial radio came to the Twin Cities. "Radio fever" began in 1922 with the licensing of WLB, the University of Minnesota's station, which was quickly followed by others. Receiving the programs at first with crystal sets and earphones, then soon with more sophisticated radios using tubes, listeners tuned in on Twin Cities stations with call letters that are still familiar — WCCO, named for the Washburn-Crosby Company, KSTP, called the "mouthpiece for Saint Paul," and WDGY. The new craze opened avenues for business in the manufacture, sale, and servicing of radios. It also created a powerful new advertising medium when commercials succeeded the original delicate sponsorship credits.[8]

"For the intelligent listener," a Minneapolis journalist wrote in 1928, "it is possible to round out such a life as the cosmopolites of old were noted for, though he lives in the backwoods and gives most of his hours of life to grinding toil." Something for everyone seemed to be the goal of broadcasters — for farmers concerned with market and weather reports; for housewives enthusiastic about Betty Crocker, Washburn-Crosby's name for a succession of cooking experts; for sports fans who tuned in on events like the Dempsey-Tunney fight, the World Series, and

football games at the University's Memorial Stadium, reported blow-by-blow in a chatter that became the hallmark of sports announcers.[9]

Strains of the Minneapolis Symphony went out over the air waves, played by musicians in shirt sleeves performing in an empty theater for a distant audience. A little girl in Montana wrote to WCCO that she had not expected to hear the orchestra until she was old enough to come to the city; the music, she added, "sounded like wind blowing through the trees. It made me all shivery." Stars of the Metropolitan Opera singing in New York could be heard in the Northwest. Candidates for political office declared where they stood, presidents were inaugurated, and mystery thrillers riveted attention on the set. Aviator Charles "Speed" Holman, ever a man to try something new, carried aloft musicians who played the merry notes of "Breezin' Along with the Breeze." All went well except that the saxophonist lost his wind power as the plane dipped, and sound faded on the turns.

Radio personalities won fame and fans throughout the trade area. Blues singer and pianist Corine Jordan moved from a Chicago station and gained many new followers during her long career in the Twin Cities. And John Wilfahrt of New Ulm, leader of a concertina orchestra, played immensely popular polkas, waltzes, and schottisches while issuing the beguiling invitation to "dance on and on with Whoopee John."

But the programming did not please everyone. "Too much jazz," some WCCO listeners complained. "Even on the dance programs," the station's news bulletin reported, the listeners "want something besides mere rhythm; they no longer get much pleasure out of drum solos with saxophone accompaniment, and they are weary of tunes which have no tunefulness." Although the station recognized that thousands of listeners wanted jazz as part of every entertainment program, it promised to eliminate "the kind of music which is nothing but a riot of noise, in which the melody is so trivial as to be practically not there at all, and in which the dissonances are the result of nothing more than the desire to make a racket."[10]

Jazz Age radio stations had to share Twin Cities airways with commercial aviation. Although a critic of the previous decade's daredevils had ventured that stunts performed to thrill the public "might better be left to the chimney-swallow and the night hawk in their quest for flies," Twin Citians were quick to capitalize on the aviation vogue these pioneers helped inspire. One of the benefits they sought was the establishment of air-mail service between the Twins and Chicago. Nor did the cities neglect the importance of airports as they made their bid to become an aviation center. Acting in rare accord, they selected as an airport site the Twin City Motor Speedway, which opened with much fanfare in 1915 when Eddie Rickenbacker, Barney Oldfield, Ralph DePalma, and others zoomed around the course in a great race, but was soon abandoned. In 1920 they formed the Twin City Aero Corporation, raised money to lease the speedway, and developed the Twin City Flying Field.[11]

Later that year the government authorized the air-mail route, and on August 10, 1920, aerial acrobats and 5,000 people saluted the first plane from Chicago. After four pilots were killed and eight planes lost within a few months, service on the route was discontinued. It was revived in 1926, however, when a contract was awarded first to Charles Dickinson and then to Northwest Airways, Inc., organized in that year.[12]

Securing the air-mail contract was an important motive in the organization of Northwest Airways. Intent on winning the contract but lacking an airline, Colonel Lewis H. Brittin, vice-president of the Saint Paul Association, and William Kidder, an aircraft dealer and charter-service operator, enlisted the support of the Ford Motor Company. Detroit and St. Paul stockholders provided capital for the firm, which was incorporated in Michigan but passed to Twin Citians' control three years later. Speed Holman flew the company's first mail plane. Passenger and freight express business was quickly added to air-mail service. Before the decade closed, pilots, wearing navy blue uniforms adorned with air-mail wings designed by Brittin, were flying planes like the Ford Trimotor "Tin Goose" on routes to Rochester (Minnesota), Chicago, and several points in Wisconsin. Holman became the firm's operations manager, a position he held until he plummeted to his death in 1931 at the Omaha air races.

Other companies joined Northwest in carrying the Twin Cities into the air age. From mergers of several small firms came the Universal Aviation Corporation, headquartered in Minneapolis and operating lines from the Mill City to points in Minnesota, Illinois, Ohio, Missouri, and Kentucky. Supplemented by Mamer Air Transport, which flew into St. Paul from Spokane and Seattle, and by transfer agreements with railroads, the lines enmeshed the Twins in a spreading transportation network.[13]

In the midst of this aviation boom, St. Paul had a change of heart about the flying field, renamed Wold-Chamberlain in honor of two Minneapolis aviators killed during World War I. Complaining that it was farther from St. Paul's business district than from Minneapolis' and that the Mill City had refused to consider a joint midway facility, St. Paul built its own field. Opened in 1926 across the river from the downtown district, the airport was renamed Holman Field in 1932 to honor the fallen ace.[14]

Although air transportation clearly held promise, motorized ground vehicles had a greater impact on

the Twins during the 1920s. From the base established in the century's early years, buses, trucks, and cars began to influence the shape of the metropolitan area, the nature of interurban transportation, and the efficiency of communication with the hinterland. The good-roads movement gained momentum as motorists who battled crude surfaces, mud, and snow pressed for a highway system that would maximize their new mobility.

Bus transportation, foreshadowed by the interurban service of the Twin City Motor Transit Company and a pioneering line from Hibbing to Alice in northern Minnesota, mushroomed during the 1920s. In 1926, twenty-one operators claimed to have carried 12,000,000 passengers, 4,750,000 of whom rode intercity or overland buses outside urban areas. By the end of the decade routes from the Twin Cities extended into Minnesota, Wisconsin, Iowa, North Dakota, South Dakota, and to distant Kansas City, St. Louis, and Chicago. Many of the firms that blazed these routes were consolidated later into large corporations. A notable example was the small northern Minnesota enterprise that evolved into the Greyhound Corporation, a nationwide company with regional subsidiaries, identified from 1930 by the sign of the running dog.[15]

Buses rumbling over the highways carried their passengers in varying degrees of style. C. H. Will Motors, Inc., of Minneapolis, for example, manufactured parlor cars equipped with lavatories, toilets, reading lamps, vanity mirrors, drinking fountains, and sometimes radios. These sumptuous cars, however, must not have been common; a driver for Greyhound, one of the firm's customers, remembered the buses of the 1930s as "ramshackle beasts."[16]

Like bus transportation, trucking became a big business during the decade. By 1930 the Minnesota Railroad and Warehouse Commission had certified seventy-five operators, twenty-seven of them with Twin Cities connections. Although as early as 1912 a truck was observed traveling to Duluth through bitter December weather, the business was mainly a short-haul one concentrated within a one-hundred-mile radius. Trucks bearing familiar names like Murphy and Raymond hauled milk, cream, butter, eggs, poultry, and other products into the cities; on return trips they carried cargo like groceries, fruits, and hardware to country merchants. As the industry grew, traffic in the Twin Cities was increasingly centralized at terminals located in the wholesale districts near railroad terminals, with transfer service between the two cities.[17]

Most observers in the 1920s believed that trucking would remain a short-haul business because long-haul costs exceeded those of railroads, highways far from the cities were usually poor, and carrying bulky products like livestock, potatoes, and grain was not economical. One prophet, however, saw a different future. Elihu Church, transportation engineer of the port of New York, predicted in 1925 that within ten years private corporations would build trunk toll roads between the nation's cities, and tractors hauling trailers would speed across the country. "When the trunk line comes to a city," he wrote, "it will go around it and if the city is large enough to justify it, there will be a belt line around it, and the trailers will be dropped off and handled by a smaller tractor."[18]

While the full potential of truck transportation lay in the future, there was no doubt about the place of cars in the new age of mobility. The increasing number of motorists who took to the roads faced many challenges as they ventured farther and farther from home. Among them were the maps that required the dexterity of "a Houdini" to handle and skill enough to follow geographic labyrinths coded in five colors. *Sparks* magazine offered some advice to the bewildered: Stop at the crossroads to look at the map. Allow each passenger thirty minutes for study. Ask each of them to write his verdict and put it into a hat. Dump the verdicts onto the road without looking at them. Then, "trusting to Providence and familiar sign posts," proceed on your way.[19]

Serious omens attended the increased use of cars, buses, and trucks. The vehicles made parking a "bug-bear" and traffic control a concern in the Twins' downtown districts. The fortunes of the Twin City Rapid Transit Company declined after patronage peaked in 1922. Railroads were apprehensive about the impact on their business. And suburbanization — the movement that would change the shape of the metropolitan district — began to exert its pull.[20]

Observing a national suburban trend, an automobile manufacturer commented in 1923 that cars were "largely responsible for the disintegration of urban residential life and the development of suburban life." Although no such phenomonen occurred in the Twin Cities during the decade, the suburbs did grow. In 1920, only 13,936 of the 629,216 persons in the Minneapolis-St. Paul Metropolitan District lived outside the Twin Cities. In 1930 the district's population was 832,258, and 96,296 lived beyond the cities' limits.[21]

More than a statistical unit, the Twin Cities Metropolitan District was viewed in terms of interests shared by its residents. A city plan for Minneapolis published in 1917, for example, considered linkages with St. Paul and future relations with the suburbs. Among its recommendations was the creation of a suburban planning commission empowered "to secure the harmonious development of this entire territory, in order to insure access for years to come to undeveloped land, as the population of Minneapolis is forced to live beyond its present borders."[22]

The metropolitan movement gained momentum during the 1920s. Many groups, including planning boards of the two cities and counties, urged that a commission be formed to develop common programs to deal with common concerns. One result was the Metropolitan and Regional Planning Association of Minneapolis, St. Paul and Environs, organized in 1923 to deal with questions like parks, zoning, airfields, water supply, drainage, and sewage.[23]

By 1926 a group called the Metropolitan District Planning Association was studying sewage and industrial waste disposal problems, a responsibility assumed a year later by the newly appointed Metropolitan Drainage Commission. The commission laid the groundwork for the Minneapolis-St. Paul Sanitary District which in the 1930s built a sewage disposal plant at Pigs Eye Lake in Ramsey County. Reviewing the progress made, a historian commented that those "who delight in pointing out the fierce rivalry and lack of co-operation between the two cities usually neglect to mention the Minneapolis-St. Paul Sanitary District, one of the finest examples of municipal co-operation in the United States."[24]

The Minneapolis-St. Paul Metropolitan District ranked thirteenth in population in the nation in 1930, trailing districts on both coasts, as well as Pittsburgh, Cleveland, Chicago, St. Louis, and Detroit. No area in the Northwest, however, outranked it, and a precipitous drop in Duluth's growth rate blunted the challenge from the north. Individually the Twins also fared quite well— Minneapolis better than St. Paul. Although the Mill City's growth rate fell from 26.3 per cent in 1920 to 22 in 1930, its position among the nation's cities climbed from eighteenth to fifteenth. St. Paul's rate rose from 9.3 per cent to 15.7, but its national status slipped from thirtieth to thirty-first.[25]

With a population lead of 464,356 to 271,606 by 1930, Minneapolis was increasingly the dominant twin. As the *Minneapolis Journal* claimed in 1923, the city may well have owed its vitality to the "yield of living gold" mined from the soil of Minnesota, North Dakota, South Dakota, and Montana — the golden grain that in turn stimulated other sectors of the economy. For whatever reason, Minneapolis led by a wide margin not only in population, but in bank clearings, retail trade, wholesaling, and manufacturing. One writer declared in 1928 that St. Paul "has become the bedfellow of defeat, weary of the incessant babbling of the Minneapolis boosters." St. Paul's predictions for greater development, native son Harold E. Wood observed a year later, were akin to Disraeli's comment on remarriage as the "triumph of hope over experience."[26]

Yet, as in all the years since 1880 when Minneapolis broke into the lead, St. Paul grew enough to sustain a strong, independent role in the metropolis. And sometimes hope for new enterprises triumphed. In 1917 the federal government completed the High

Dam to extend Mississippi River navigation into Minneapolis; St. Paul's candidate won the ensuing competition for hydroelectric power. The candidate's name was Henry Ford, and in the early 1920s his company built an assembly plant at the dam within the St. Paul city limits. Among other important enterprises were two small organizations with big futures. In 1910 Minnesota Mining and Manufacturing Company (3M), which had moved from Two Harbors to Duluth in 1905, relocated in St. Paul, and the Farmers Union Terminal Association (succeeded by the Grain Terminal Association and later by Harvest States Cooperatives), became the nation's largest grain co-operative during the decade.[27]

While thousands of small businesses succeeded in the Twin Cities during the Roaring Twenties, the late-nineteenth-century trend toward "big business" gained momentum. Typifying the "urge to merge" was the Minneapolis-Honeywell Regulator Company, a fusion of the Minneapolis Heat Regulator Company and the Honeywell Heating Specialties Company of Wabash, Indiana. Other now familiar firm names appeared during the decade: General Mills, Inc., sprang from the historic Washburn-Crosby Company; powerful Twin Cities banks spawned the Northwest Bancorporation (later Norwest Corporation) and First Bank Stock Corporation (later First Bank System, Inc.). Gamble-Skogmo evolved from an automobile dealership into a network retailing hardware and other products. National chains like J. C. Penney opened local stores, local department stores became parts of national chains, and public-utility firms fused into complex holding companies.[28]

Wilbur B. Foshay, a daring king of the holding-company movement, epitomized the optimism of the age. Foshay, a businessman widely experienced in public utilities, arrived in Minneapolis in 1914, where he soon formed a company bearing his name. During the 1920s he put together an empire by acquiring firms in many parts of the nation. Long an admirer of the Washington Monument, he built a tower modeled on it for his Minneapolis headquarters. John Philip Sousa composed "The Foshay Tower Washington Memorial March" and led his band during the dedication festivities that began on August 30, 1929. Scores of guests invited from afar joined local enthusiasts in saluting the tower that symbolized the heights reached by its creator.[29]

It was an age of euphoria, these years characterized nationally by high production, high employment, and stable prices. As John Kenneth Galbraith wrote: "Although many people were still very poor, more people were comfortably well-off, well-to-do, or rich than ever before." But beneath the facade of euphoria in the Twin Cities was not only poverty in the midst of plenty, but crime born of moonshining and bootlegging, the continued struggle of organized labor, intolerance fostered by the Ku Klux Klan, and lingering shadows of the great Red Scare.[30]

There were other signs that all was not well in the Roaring Twenties. Flour production in Minneapolis, which had peaked in 1916 at 18,541,650 barrels, declined to 10,797,194 by 1930, when the city lost to Buffalo the milling crown it had worn for fifty years. Agriculture, the bedrock of the Twins' prosperity, was shaken as markets contracted following wartime expansion, prices fell, and costs rose. Sensitive to the implications of the farmers' distress, Twin Cities businessmen participated in efforts to provide credit, stabilize banking in the region, encourage diversification in wheat-growing country, and restore optimism.[31]

While farmers might have lacked the optimism needed to cure their blues, stock-market investors had an overabundance of it. The *Commercial West* observed in 1928 that "persons of all types of our democratic civilization" had been added to the professional trading class — "jacks of all trades, including clerks, salesmen, plumbers, chauffeurs, and many others, who seem to find the stock market more alluring than their ordinary work." The journal cautioned its readers, "The present market has reached the stage of being very unsafe for democracy." Other warnings cited the perils of the "wild orgy of speculative activity," the possibility that the "greatest speculative era of all ages" might collapse, and the loss of control of the market to "stock exchange operators."[32]

The grim prophecies were fulfilled. In October, 1929, came waves of reports from New York City about a stock debacle. "Like the mysterious but certain dissemination of 'news' through the uncivilized areas of a savage land," the *Commercial West* observed, "these rumors of the stockmarket flew between the two suns from town to town and state to state. Wherever they touched they wrought havoc." On streetcars, on street corners, in offices, homes, and factories, wherever people gathered, whisperings about great business failures were heard. More than a whisper was the collapse of Foshay's empire that left the lofty tower standing bleak against the Minneapolis skyline as a reminder of the decade's aspirations. The great American joy ride was over, and the nation began an ordeal so prolonged and so acute that ever after it was known as the Great Depression.[33].

Leona Wood Kilbourn, a pianist and blues singer, entertained night owls in 1929 on KSTP's "Northland Airman's Frivolities" — a midnight broadcast — and other late programs.

Church services and religious music were standard Sunday radio fare by mid-decade. In addition to local services, one from New York City, and a studio program, WCCO boasted in 1927 of its Sunday "civic asset" — the weekly concerts of Hugo P. Goodwin, St. Paul's municipal organist, broadcast from the city's auditorium.

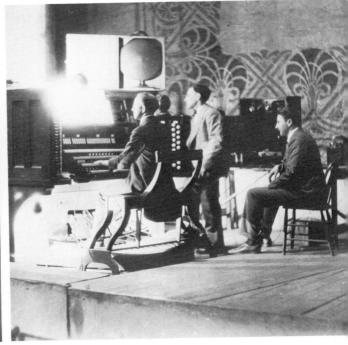

Part of a generation that grew up with radio, students in 1922 at Horace Mann School, Chicago Avenue and East Thirty-fourth Street, Minneapolis, began to unravel some of its mysteries.

By 1929 there were seventy-four motion-picture theaters in the Twin Cities, many sporting elaborate marquees. Among those brightening downtown St. Paul by night were the Riviera at Wabasha and Seventh streets, pictured in 1929, the Strand on Wabasha and Eighth streets, and the Capitol at 22 West Seventh Street, both pictured in 1926. The Capitol proudly promoted its cooling system, based on artesian well water that chilled and cleaned the circulating air every five minutes.

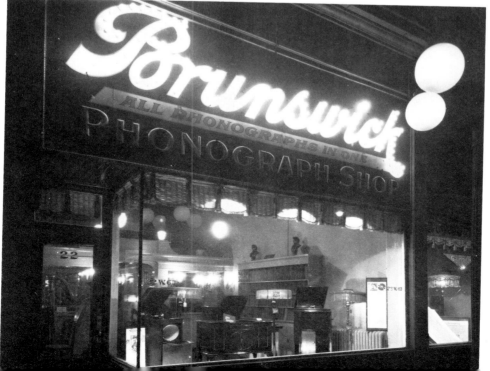

In the early 1920s the Brunswick, 22 West Sixth Street, St. Paul, was one of the Twin Cities stores that catered to a growing demand for phonographs and records. The shop sold the products of the Brunswick-Balke-Collender Company of Dubuque, Iowa, a leading producer of phonographs that had handsome cabinets, a capability for playing lateral- and vertical-cut records, and, at mid-decade, electric power. Brunswick recorded the Minneapolis Symphony, among other orchestras.

The "Queens of Syncopation," billed as the "only Ladies' Jazz Band in all the world," prepared to swing into a number in 1929. St. Paulite Arma Milch, trained with her sisters Adeline and Margaret as a classical musician, led the way.

The Arcadia Palace at 315 South Fifth Street, Minneapolis, in 1918 offered Jazz Age patrons a place to dance at low prices. Operated by J. C. Conway, the Palace was also called the Arcadia Dancing Academy and, in the 1930s, Conway's Arcadia Dance Palace.

Bystanders watched a demonstration of the fox trot at mid-decade in the Lake Street Auditorium, 5 East Lake Street, Minneapolis. The onlookers were probably students of Anna M. Scott, who operated a dancing academy there.

Wally Erickson's Coliseum Orchestra, about 1928, entertained fans at the Coliseum ballroom, 453 North Lexington Avenue, as well as at home. Like other Twin Cities dance bands, the St. Paul group broadcast over WCCO. The pioneer in remote-control broadcasting, however, was reputedly Dick Long's orchestra, which played at the Nankin Cafe, Minneapolis.

Capt. Billy's Whiz Bang, the first in a series of successes for Fawcett Publications of Robbinsdale, featured Nancy Nash of Fox Films as its January, 1928, cover girl. Among the jokes for the month was the observation that "Petting comes to every man in due season, but the average flapper favors an epidemic."

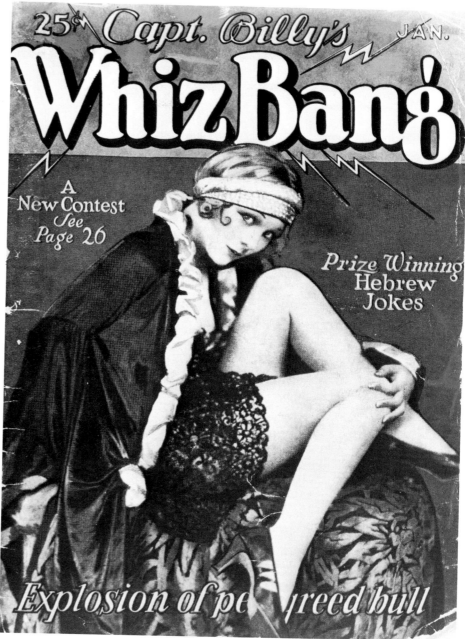

A newsstand in Minneapolis offered entertainment in many forms about 1920. Colorful magazines, treating everything from scandal to sports, helped fans follow the lives of their favorite public figures.

Dayton's department store on Nicollet Avenue, Minneapolis, in 1923 presented its ideal of fashion for the "Bride at Home."

Behind the scenes at Dayton's about 1925 an artist "made up" a wax model.

Twin Cities women could choose among almost 380 beauty shops in 1929, the year this woman relaxed under a hair dryer.

Home cooks in the 1920s used some new, innovatively packaged products, but the interest of the little spectator was familiar. Swans Down cake flour, originally manufactured in Indiana, was acquired by Postum Cereal Company of Battle Creek, Michigan, in mid-decade.

Foreshadowing the fast-food age, the Auteria Company, a cafeteria-equipment firm in downtown St. Paul, displayed a model automat designed by its president, Woodland H. Gilbert, about 1924.

The Fort Worth, Texas, band played as the American Legion paraded in downtown St. Paul during its national convention, September 15-19, 1924.

Swedish immigrant Hjalmar Peterson of Minneapolis, called "Olle i Skratthult" (Olle from Laughtersville), toured the country with his troupe of actors, singers, and dancers. Besides acting in plays like this 1927 rendition of "Käringa Mi's Kusin" (My Old Lady's Cousin), Peterson also recorded many songs, the most popular of which was "Nikolina."

"Laurello, The Man with the Revolving Head" and other marvels awaited St. Paulites when the Ringling Bros. and Barnum and Bailey Circus pitched its tents near University and Lexington avenues on August 5, 1925, after playing two days in Minneapolis. Twin Citians' only complaint was the lack of a circus parade.

Motorists who took to the road with their camping gear found a haven in the Cherokee Tourist Camp at Southwest Chippewa Avenue between Winona and Annapolis streets on St. Paul's West Side in 1923. About a hundred camps were operating in Minnesota in that year, most of them outside the Twin Cities.

Viewed from a Northwest Airways plane about 1926 was Lexington Park, Lexington and University avenues, home of the St. Paul Saints. Some hard-hit balls sailed out of the park and landed on the roof of the Coliseum ballroom, to the right.

Sand-lot aces about 1925 stole a look through a knothole into Nicollet Park, home of the Minneapolis Millers at Nicollet Avenue and West Thirty-first Street.

Excitement ran high in Nicollet Park about 1925 when the Millers mixed it up with a visiting team.

Frank "Moose" Goheen and other great St. Paul hockey players called the Hippodrome on the state fairgrounds their home rink. The Millers, with the fabulous Ivan "Ching" Johnson as their star, were formidable opponents.

OFFICIAL SCHEDULE AND PROGRAM
St. Paul Hockey Club
AMERICAN HOCKEY ASSOCIATION

ST. PAUL SAINTS

MINNEAPOLIS MILLERS

DULUTH HORNETS

KANSAS CITY PLA-MORS

WINNIPEG MAROONS

Season 1927-1928
HIPPODROME ICE RINK

Minneapolis fireman Lewis Rober sewed a kittenball in 1899 in his station workshop, four years after making the first one by stitching leather over the station-house cat's ball of string. He continued to produce and sell handmade "Official Kitten League" balls for years, and by the 1920s the game he invented (later called softball) was spreading nationwide.

Crowds turned out in downtown St. Paul on September 18, 1929, to welcome Jimmy Johnston home from Pebble Beach, California, where he won the National Amateur Golf Tournament. A city-wide committee that arranged the royal reception asked industrial plants to blow their whistles in salute to the hero.

These marble shooters photographed by the *St. Paul Daily News* in March, 1925, were probably training for the paper's annual tournament. Winners from seven district contests in the city were to play for the championship in April, but the picture had another significance for winter-weary Twin Citians. The caption asked — "Has Spring Arrived?"

By mid-decade motorized vehicles had replaced all of the Twin Cities fire horses. In St. Paul the historic last run left in 1924 from Engine House No. 13 at Raymond and Bayless avenues.

Cars rolled off the assembly line in the Ford Motor Company's new St. Paul plant on Mississippi River Boulevard near the Ford (or High) Dam as operations began in 1925. By the close of its first year, the plant was turning out sedans, touring cars, and roadsters.

A shiny Willys-Overland waiting at the curb about 1920 provided new mobility for Anna Blair, 711 St. Anthony Avenue, St. Paul. Automobiles quickly became favorite backdrops in photographs of proud owners or excited passengers.

Twin Citians, like these Northern States Power Company employees in 1923, were no longer dependent on streetcars and carriages to tote their feasts to the picnic grounds.

A crew paving "Richfield Road" in Hennepin County in 1912 symbolized the good-roads movement that gained momentum in the 1920s. Motorists, like bicyclists before them, were strong supporters of the campaign to lift the state out of the mud.

One-stop service awaited patrons of Coleman's Greasing Station at Sixth Street and Marquette Avenue, Minneapolis, in 1928, where motorists could fill up with Red Crown, buy Iso Vis oil, and steam clean their vehicles. The station was one of four in the city operated by Carl J. Coleman.

Beneath a sign urging them to travel by bus, passengers, about 1925, could board coaches at the Union Bus Depot, Seventh Street and First Avenue North, Minneapolis.

Crowded stockyards at South St. Paul about 1930 testified to the growing importance of trucking. Over 100,000 livestock shipments arrived at the market in that year; improved roads allowed for increased load sizes and year-round transport.

A crowd gathered at Wold-Chamberlain Field on August 23, 1927, to greet Charles A. Lindbergh, Jr., who was touring the nation after his flight across the Atlantic. Artillery fire saluted the arrival of the "Spirit of St. Louis" and about 20,000 people surged onto the field. Lindbergh then rode in a parade with Minneapolis Mayor George Leach and St. Paul Mayor Laurence C. Hodgson. In the background of this picture is the Twin City Motor Speedway, site of the cities' first airfield.

In 1926 the post office delivered letters to St. Paul's airport (later Holman Field) where they were weighed and quickly dispatched. St. Paulites enthusiastically predicted great benefits from airmail service based at an airport less than a mile and a half from the downtown district.

Northwest Airways demonstrated the ease with which passengers could board the new Hamilton "Metalplane" about 1928, under the watchful eyes of Charles "Speed" Holman. A marked improvement over earlier airplanes, the Hamiltons had heated cabins and toilets.

Falling from the sky "like a bird with a broken wing," an army plane and its pilot, W. A. Butters, crashed into the plate-glass window of the McNulty and Dafoe Company, automobile dealers at 1528 Hennepin Avenue, Minneapolis, on April 28, 1919. Workers here hoist the engine from the wreckage. Butters was not injured, but crashes and the menace of low-flying planes inspired Twin Citians to recommend the regulation of flight heights over cities.

Twin Citians at work in the 1920s included (A) a seed bagger at Northrup King and Company, Jackson Street Northeast, Minneapolis; (B) a shoe vamper at Foot, Schulze and Company, Robert Street, St. Paul; (C) riveters at the Crown Iron Works Company, Tyler Street Northeast, Minneapolis;

(D) a textile worker at the Munsingwear Corporation, Western Avenue, Minneapolis; (E) a clergyman at baptismal festivities; (F) a daring steeple-jack atop the clothing store of Maurice L. Rothschild and Company, Nicollet Avenue, Minneapolis; (G) a streetcar conductor collecting fares;

(H) welders at the Minneapolis Bedding Company, East Hennepin Avenue; (I) clerks at the Andrew Schoch Grocery Company, East Seventh Street, St. Paul; (J) Louis Nassig (right) at a cash-and-carry ice store, probably the Cedar Lake Ice Company, Minneapolis;

(K) laundresses in the Minneapolis General Hospital, Fifth Street South; (L) Captain Harry Nelson at the second precinct police station, Central Avenue, Minneapolis; (M) head baker at the Nicollet Hotel, Minneapolis;

(N) James W. Love shoveling coal in the boiler room of the Nevens Company's laundry, dry-cleaning, and hat plant, Marquette Avenue, Minneapolis; (O) Bernice Babler, chief operator for Finkelstein and Ruben, Northwest Theatre Circuit, Inc., Sixth Street North, Minneapolis; (P) ushers at a Finkelstein and Ruben theater in St. Paul;

(Q) a clerk showing fashions in the ladies' dress department of the L. S. Donaldson Company, Minneapolis; (R) William H. Sieloff delivering milk, cream, and butter in downtown St. Paul; (S) a workman checking generators in the powerhouse of the Ford Motor Company assembly plant, Mississippi River Boulevard, St. Paul; (T) "Frankie" Heath slinging hash at a Hennepin Avenue restaurant, Minneapolis.

Conducting its seventh annual community fund campaign in 1924, the Minneapolis Council of Social Agencies placarded the streets on behalf of charity in a prosperous decade. Both cities solicited through a united appeal system.

Members of the Junior League of St. Paul found treasures in attics and storerooms for a benefit sale in the city's auditorium on March 12, 1925. Preparing for the event, left to right, were Elizabeth Catlin, Theodora Hamm, Marie Hamm, and Peggy Kalman. The league supported the Red Cross, the Community Chest, child welfare, convalescent care, and other charitable efforts.

A "Better Baby Contest" in the parish of the Cathedral of St. Paul brought out some robust contenders. Mrs. A. J. Gillette, who sponsored the event, sat in the center.

The Children's Protective Society of Hennepin County, which brought a battered child to court about 1925, handled hundreds of cases of abuse, neglect, desertion, and nonsupport each year.

Children looked on during their mothers' backyard conversation, about 1925.

Willie Gertrude Brown, who directed the Phyllis Wheatley Settlement House from its beginnings in 1924 to 1936, helped create recreational activities in a blighted neighborhood. The organization moved in 1929 from 808 Bassett Place, Minneapolis, into a new building at 809 Aldrich Avenue North, where it operated a day nursery, an employment service, a clinic, and expanded activities to alleviate the trauma of the unemployed trying to cope with enforced leisure.

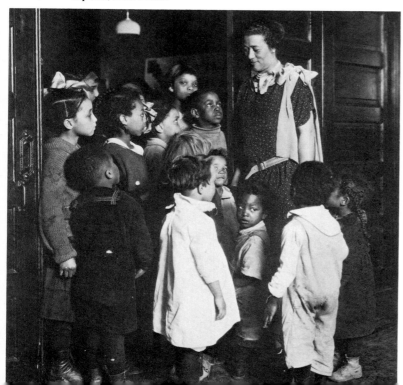

Transient laborers were among those who found help at the Union City Mission, 124 and 124 1/2 Hennepin Avenue, Minneapolis. The *Community Fund News* published this picture in 1925, commenting, "homeless men, veterans of many a harvest field and lumber camp, have done much for the progress of the northwest, for which they will never receive credit."

In all eras of Twin Cities' history, private social agencies eased the pain of old age with many services. An elder posed in about 1925, left, at the Jewish Home for the Aged (later Sholom Home), which served the communities of both cities from its new building at Midway Parkway and North Snelling Avenue, St. Paul. Residents gathered in the lobby of the Ebenezer Home, center, a Norwegian Lutheran establishment located since 1919 at 2545 Portland Avenue, Minneapolis. For many years aged people like this woman, right, have shared in activities at the Hallie Q. Brown Community Center, established in 1929 in St. Paul.

The mall for the University of Minnesota's Minneapolis campus, planned early in the twentieth century by Cass Gilbert, finally took shape in the 1920s. In 1925 the administration building (later Morrill Hall), center foreground, neared completion; the library (later Walter Library), to the left, was two years old. Before the close of the decade the pillars of Northrop Auditorium marked the north end of the mall just beyond the administration building.

The chemistry building, located near the library and expanded during the decade, housed classrooms and laboratories. In the physical chemistry lab faculty and students in 1926 investigated subjects like radioactivity and the extraction of radium from carnotite.

The Minnesota-Wisconsin football game drew a crowd to the university's new Memorial Stadium in 1925. The stadium, used for track as well as football, included a broadcasting booth.

Panoramic photography, once dependent on tall buildings, rose to greater heights during the air age. Buildings stretch from the crowded river front north to the state capitol in this 1923 view of St. Paul's downtown district shot from a Curtiss Northwest Airplane Company craft. The Wabasha Street Bridge (right), Harriet Island (foreground), and moored barges completed the urban scene.

Passenger trains bound for many parts of the nation prepared to steam out of St. Paul's Union Depot yard one early morning in May, 1925. The *St. Paul Daily News* commented how well its photograph "illustrates the importance of St. Paul as a railroad and transportation center."

Festoons of streetcar cables accentuated the contours of Seven Corners, the downtown hub of an old St. Paul neighborhood, about 1920. The streets are, from left to right, Fourth, Main, West Seventh, Fourth, Third, and Eagle.

Lined with modest houses, businesses, and billboards, University Avenue in about 1926 was not the grand parkway Twin Citians had envisioned in the nineteenth century. Offices in the Midway in this view looking east and north included the state highway building (center) at 1246 University Avenue, St. Paul, and, set back between Hamline Avenue and Syndicate Street, Brown and Bigelow, manufacturers of remembrance advertising, pencils, and novelties.

St. Paul Mayor Laurence C. Hodgson cut a silver cord to mark the opening on August 6, 1926, of the new Robert Street Bridge. Representatives from many nearby communities, bringing with them bands and decorations, paraded with St. Paulites across the structure with its distinctive rainbow arch, designed by Toltz, King and Day.

Like their neighbors, Minneapolitans took a new look at their city from the air. In 1929 the newly built Foshay Tower, right, dominated the downtown skyline. The city hall-courthouse looms at upper left, behind the First National Bank Building, the light-colored Rand (later Dain) Tower and the sketched-in contours of the projected Northwestern National Bank Building; at center left are Donaldson's and Dayton's department stores.

An aerial photographer about 1921 looked downriver from the railroad yards and warehouses in North Minneapolis, past the west-side milling district (right) and Nicollet Island (left). The Hennepin Avenue, Third Avenue, and Stone Arch bridges linked the city's old east and west divisions.

A corridor of mills and elevators on Hiawatha Avenue south of downtown Minneapolis, seen in an aerial view about 1921, followed the railroad tracks through a residential district far from the falls where milling began.

By 1930 Bridge Square, once the core of Minneapolis, wore a new look. The old city hall had been razed, automobiles had replaced the horses that had crowded the approach to the Suspension Bridge, a new Nicollet Hotel (left center) stood where the Nicollet House once was, and Gateway Park, in front of the hotel, had been developed to help halt the blight creeping through the district. The inscription on the Gateway Building, which served as a visitors' information center, read: "More than her gates, the city opens her heart to you."

A block of flats with a corner grocery store, like this one about 1920 at Fifth Street South and Seventh Avenue South, Minneapolis, was a familiar sight in both cities.

The Soo Line Terminal Elevator stood adjacent to cornfields at North Forty-eighth and Penn avenues in about 1920. Like elevators along the rail lines in Southeast Minneapolis and on the Hiawatha strip, it was part of the trend to store grain near transportation facilities and away from the city's core.

Powderhorn Park in Minneapolis, pictured about 1919, developed into an important recreational center as population density increased south of the central business district. The park, located between East Thirty-first and South Thirty-fifth streets and Tenth and Fifteenth avenues, encompassed about sixty-five acres by that time.

The Minneapolis Board of Park Commissioners ordered extensive improvements at Lake Nokomis, south of Minnehaha Parkway and north of East Fifty-seventh Street. In 1921 workmen cleared and graded land once covered with willow and poplar trees. A year earlier they had constructed a bathhouse.

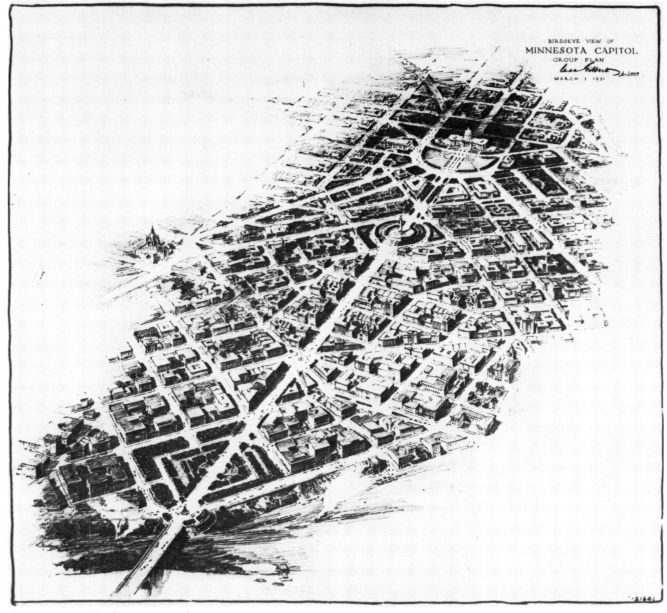

Planners during the first quarter of the twentieth century were ambitious in their designs for the Twin Cities. From early in the century until 1931 when he made this sketch, architect Cass Gilbert inspired other St. Paul planners with proposals that prominently featured the state capitol.

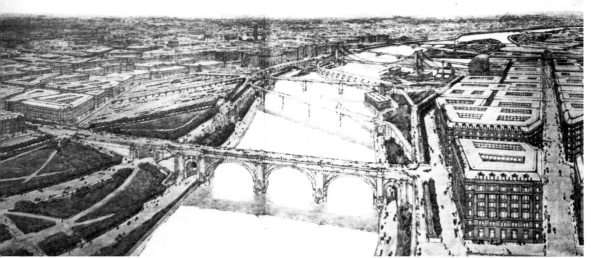

Designs for Minneapolis published in 1917 echoed the spirit of architect Daniel H. Burnham's admonition: "Make no little plans; they have no magic to stir men's blood and probably themselves will not be realized." The plan, which envisioned Minneapolis as a magnificent economic and cultural center, included Jules Guerin's sketch of low-level roadways along the waterfront and high-level routes linking the bridges.

Two politicians with buoyant spirits met in 1920 when St. Paul's Mayor Laurence C. Hodgson, Democratic candidate for governor, welcomed vice-presidential candidate Franklin D. Roosevelt at St. Paul's Union Depot. Neither won in the election year that ushered in a Republican decade.

Republican Calvin Coolidge's quest for the presidency in 1924 was promoted in campaign headquarters at Eighth Street and Nicollet Avenue, Minneapolis, where many women also registered to vote. Both Hennepin and Ramsey counties gave more votes to Coolidge than to any other candidate. In the 1928 election, Hennepin went for Republican Herbert Hoover and Ramsey, by a narrow margin, for Alfred E. Smith, the Democratic opponent.

The Norse-American Centennial brought Calvin and Grace Coolidge to the state fairgrounds in St. Paul on June 8, 1925. People stormed the gates and climbed fences to join the huge crowd assembled at the grandstand to hear the president speak.

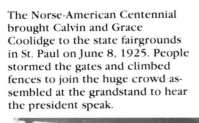

"Law — Not War" was a slogan of the Minnesota League of Women Voters in 1923 when members collected a "Mile of Signatures" in support of the nation's entrance into the World Court. The league delegation that carried the petition to Washington, D.C., included, left to right, Mrs. Sumner T. McKnight, Mrs. N. C. Peterson, Mrs. Richard T. Hargreaves, Mrs. Arthur J. McGuire, and Mrs. Milton D. Purdy.

On the eve of prohibition in 1919, a liquor store offered Twin Citians an opportunity to stock up for a long dry spell.

Federal agents operating out of St. Paul on July 26, 1922, raided the "most complete moonshine distillery ever found in Minnesota" on a farm near Gladstone in Ramsey County. Although the agents found little moonshine, they destroyed 2,600 gallons of mash and all the distillery equipment.

185

Save Sacco and Vanzetti
from the ELECTRIC CHAIR
Mass Meeting
In protest against the attempt to railroad these
two innocent Labor Organizers to death.

Sunday, May 10th, 8 p.m.
CITY HALL ASSEMBLY ROOM

SPEAKERS:

LOUIS ENGDAHL,
of Chicago, well-known lecturer and editor, formerly of Minneapolis

S. A. STOCKWELL,
Farmer-Labor Representative, Chairman

DAN STEVENS,
representing Painters' Union

ERNEST LUNDEEN,
"in-famous anti-war ex-Congressman

L. A. ROSELAND,
representing Carpenters' Union

And Others

The Sacco-Vanzetti Defense was endorsed by
the last A. F. of L. Convention

Auspices Labor Defense Council of Minneapolis
ADMISSION FREE

Many people believed that Nicola Sacco and Bartolomeo Vanzetti, executed in 1927 for the murder of a paymaster and guard in Massachusetts seven years earlier, were innocent men being penalized for radicalism. Supporters rallied at a mass meeting in Minneapolis on May 10, 1925, to protest their conviction.

Governor Jacob Preus called out the National Guard in December, 1921, to break the picket lines of striking packinghouse workers at South St. Paul's plants. The *Commercial West* echoed "Red Scare" attitudes toward labor, commenting that the strikers "came as near as they dared to a Soviet control of the packing industry at South St. Paul."

Published by the North Star Klan No. 2 with the assistance of other Minneapolis and suburban Klans, this newspaper campaigned against Catholic and Jewish influences in the city.

The flaming symbol of the Ku Klux Klan blazed on the bluff at Mounds Park, St. Paul, on the night of May 25, 1926. The Klansmen vanished after lighting the cross, but the spectacle attracted a crowd.

Two years after the famous Scopes trial, the Reverend William B. Riley of Minneapolis in 1927 carried his crusade against teaching the theory of evolution in tax-supported schools to the Minnesota legislature. T. H. Foley's cartoon, entitled "Monkey Business Before the House," appeared in the *Minneapolis Daily Star,* January 5, 1927.

Americanization, religion, and recreation were major emphases of the YMCA's regular noontime meetings like the one held on December 14, 1921, at the Great Northern railroad's Jackson Street shops in St. Paul.

As dramatic as Wilbur Foshay's immense utilities empire was an artist's image of the Foshay Tower, under construction from 1927 to 1929 on Ninth Street in the heart of Minneapolis.

Called "an achievement no less outstanding than the company it represents," the tower in 1930 dwarfed all neighboring buildings.

During dedication ceremonies on August 30, 1929, the Rainbow Nymphs danced to the music of Sousa's band at the unveiling of "Scherzo," the fountain figure in the tower's garden court. Sculpted by Harriet Frishmuth to depict youth in "gay, joyous abandon," it later graced Charlie's Cafe Exceptionale and the Hotel Leamington, both in the shadow of the Foshay.

On May 26, 1930, less than a year after the dedication festivities, Joseph Chapman as receiver (seated) offered the tower at an auction held at the foot of the "Father of Waters" in the city hall-courthouse lobby. No one bid on the symbol of Foshay's ruined empire.

1929-45

Floyd B. Olson, the newly elected
Farmer-Labor governor, addressed
a joint session of the House and
Senate on January 7, 1931, in the
capitol's house chamber. The audience was eager to hear how he
planned to meet depression crises.

1929-45
Depression and War

The buoyant optimism of the 1920s faded slowly as the nation's economy slipped inexorably into the depression. Although the *Commercial West* observed a year after the crash that the depression "seemed determined to lie down and make its bed among us for all time," most people believed the affliction was temporary. But prosperity was not "just around the corner." The depression was tenacious, resisting efforts to end it until the onset of war production for World War II revitalized the economy. And the troubles were pervasive, altering the lives of millions of people throughout the nation and affecting them more profoundly than any of the nineteenth-century depressions. Fundamental changes in concepts of personal financial security, the nation's economic system, and the responsibilities of government took root in the rubble and endured long after the crisis years had passed.[1]

The depression hit the Twin Cities hard but Minneapolis suffered more than St. Paul. The Mill City's manufacturing output declined more precipitously than that of its twin and unemployment was more widespread. The Minneapolis population growth rate decreased to a greater extent, falling from 22 per cent in the 1920s to 6 per cent in the succeeding decade. St. Paul, with less distance to tumble, declined from 15.7 to 5.9 during the same years. The Twins' population rank among the nation's cities slipped between 1930 and 1940 — Minneapolis from fifteenth to sixteenth, and St. Paul from thirty-first to thirty-third. Their share of the total population of Minnesota also shrank slightly, while the state's population increased at a faster rate than did either city's. But growth in the metropolitan district outside the two central cities moderated the relative loss of population; this increase helped raise the district's rank among other metropolitan areas in the nation from thirteenth to twelfth.[2]

Nothing in the Twins' experience had prepared them for the storm that swept over them as thousands of formerly self-supporting men and women sought relief. "It has been said that one half of the world doesn't know how the other half lives," a Minneapolis welfare official observed. "This is truer than fiction. The tragedy of the present situation is that the half is now learning about the other half through the bitter cup of experience." Social workers sadly identified the groups that converged in the cities' crowded relief offices. The habitual dependents were there, as were the "marginal people" who even in good times did not earn enough to be completely self-sufficient. But newcomers to relief lines far outnumbered those accustomed to dependency. Devastated by unemployment, they exhausted their savings and often lost their homes before applying for relief. To some, the psychological impact was powerful, permeating whole families with a sense of "discouragement and despondency."[3]

Agency employees wrote eloquently about the new poor swelling the relief lines. "To many," one official wrote, "it [the crash] came like a thief in the night — unannounced and unheralded. As if by the stroke of the pen, jobs and savings were wiped out leaving people dazed and confused." Taking a larger view, another official urgently recommended national planning for an economic order that would ensure "some measure of security in employment to the millions that are today battered about from pillar to post in a vicious and recurrent cyclic insecurity." Although statistics do not indicate the full dimensions of the ordeal, those for 1937 — by no means the depression's worst year — are revealing. At that time 43,750 Minneapolitans and 26,047 St. Paulites declared that they were either wholly or partially unemployed. Multiplied by the numbers of people affected by the loss of the workers' earnings, such figures help explain the crises in relief funding the cities experienced.[4]

Traditionally poor relief was a local and private matter rather than a state or federal government responsibility. For months after the depression began, Twin Citians believed that the problem of caring for the poor could be managed on a local level. "Saint Paul . . . has assured President Hoover that this city will care for its own," the Association of Commerce announced in 1931 at the beginning of a "Give Double!" million-dollar Community Chest drive; later that year public officials of each city expressed the same conviction at a meeting called by Governor Floyd B. Olson.[5]

The cities, ignorant of what the depression had in

store for them, placed their faith in their strong networks of private charitable organizations and their long-established boards of public welfare. Early responses to the crisis reassured them. Private charities industriously raised funds to provide assistance. Many groups of businessmen organized relief efforts. The *St. Paul Pioneer Press* and *Dispatch* campaigned to obtain local firms' pledges guaranteeing employment through the winter months of 1930-31; the Minnesota Mining and Manufacturing Company offered an unemployment benefit plan to its employees; and the Citizens Alliance in Minneapolis operated an employment bureau.[6]

The Organized Unemployed, Inc., founded in Minneapolis in 1932, demonstrated the slow-waning belief that voluntary efforts could play a major role in coping with the emergency. A key figure in the group, the Reverend George H. Mecklenburg, decided to take action when his congregation discovered that it could no longer provide relief for the growing number of needy families. Implementing the motto "Work, Not Dole," the Organized Unemployed leased a farm, processed and canned food, cut wood, made clothes, operated a cafeteria, and performed other self-help functions using scrip as a medium of exchange. A defeated "rear guard of an outmoded individualism," it was soon forced to seek aid from private donors and federal agencies.[7]

When the burden of providing relief proved too heavy for local public agencies, as well, Twin Citians turned to the national government. Beginning in 1933 President Franklin D. Roosevelt's New Deal released federal funds through agencies like the Federal Emergency Relief Administration, the National Recovery Administration, the Civil Works Administration, the Civilian Conservation Corps, the Public Works Administration, and the Works Progress Administration. These programs, however, did not provide all of the assistance needed. Buffeted by winds that shifted with the focus of federal-state programs, the demand for increasing local funding of direct relief, and the intensity of the depression, the Twins dug deep into local treasuries to provide food and shelter for the hungry and homeless.

Each city issued millions of dollars in relief bonds to pay the bills, and both feared that deficit financing would lead to bankruptcy. Minneapolis by 1939 had almost $29 million in relief bonds outstanding and a shrinking tax base. The city had come "to the end of its rope," claimed a citizens' committee, and more than 20 per cent of the city's population depended upon government for sustenance — a number equal to the total population of Duluth. Furthermore, the committee saw in the growing public welfare agencies a monster that was wreaking havoc on the average citizen and taxpayer.[8]

St. Paul's Board of Public Welfare co-operated closely and generally in harmony with private agencies to administer relief. In contrast, political intrigue and internal crises wracked the Minneapolis Board of Public Welfare, which set policy, and the Division of Public Relief, which executed it. Nevertheless the agencies in both cities responded with a great deal of humanity to the needs of people impoverished by the depression.[9]

Relief workers made serious efforts to provide assistance more generous than mere rescue from starvation. They tried to sustain the morale of their clients, get them on the rolls of public works projects, send young men to CCC camps, help families move from the cities to farms where they might have a better chance to weather the storm, distribute surplus commodities the federal government provided, and provide health care, fuel, and clothing.[10]

Particularly when dealing with transients, relief workers' humanity and practicality came into conflict. Minneapolis suffered the more severe transient problem, for its decaying Gateway district harbored numerous unemployed seasonal laborers, alcoholics, and other distressed persons. Some of those down-and-outers drifted into St. Paul, which was already burdened with costs of caring for its own. The welfare board in St. Paul protested that Ramsey County was being "used as a 'dumping ground' by other communities" and affirmed that it would have to be more "hard boiled." Nevertheless, denying relief to nonresidents whose own communities would not assume responsibility for them proved to be impossible. The situation improved somewhat after 1933 when the states received federal funds for transient camps. From then on, transients registered in the Twin Cities for assignment to camps located at various points in the state.[11]

The WPA and other work projects produced substantial benefits despite their detractors' cartoons that showed a man lazily leaning on a shovel and rendered the agency's initials as "We Plod Along." Twin Cities projects included construction of airports, public buildings, park facilities, playgrounds, waterworks, sewers, streets, and sidewalks. Other workers performed functions in public institutions — assisting in hospitals and libraries, helping needy sick persons, and redecorating school buildings. Workers also inventoried public records, and artists, musicians, and writers honed their talents in projects that paved the way for a greater government role in fostering cultural life. The movement would again flower in the 1960s when President Lyndon B. Johnson, who had entered public service during depression years, created cultural and antipoverty programs to build a "Great Society."[12]

Although government programs gave life-sustain-ing support to depression victims, the recipients had mixed feelings about being on relief. The public welfare board in St. Paul observed that while some people accepted the situation philosophically, many "become ardent opponents of an economic system which permits such inroads upon normally employed individuals." Through the ballot box in municipal, state, and federal elections they registered their protests against the system and the type of relief it provided. They demonstrated on the streets, at the Minneapolis city hall, and at the state capitol — the state's storm center. The *Commercial West* expressed the fears of many when it declared that embittered workers "will be easily led into the shadow of the red flag." And through the turmoil and dissent many, either hopeful or alarmed, saw the bright flash of the Communist banner.[13]

The depression exacerbated an already tense labor union situation. For over fifty years unions had struggled for the right to organize, but the Trotskyite affiliations of a few union leaders, particularly Vincent and Miles Dunne and Farrell Dobbs, further inflamed business opposition to organized labor. In Minneapolis the conflict sharply polarized opposing political ideologies, much more so than in St. Paul. The Citizens Alliance, the Minneapolis employers' group which had struggled fiercely to maintain open shops and limit union effectiveness, was anathema to labor. The most dramatic encounter came during the truckers' strike of 1934 after the General Drivers and Helpers Union's Local 574, led by the Dunnes and Dobbs, struck on May 15. Before the issues were resolved in August, four men had died in street combat, many others were injured, Governor Olson had declared martial law, and the ugliness and violence of the conflict had drawn national attention to the city.[14]

The conservative recoil from organized labor and Communist influence stung protesters in the Twin Cities who were employed in the WPA work relief program. When in 1939 the federal Emergency Relief Appropriation Act cut hourly wages, added to the number of hours required, and provided for layoffs, around 10,000 Twin Citians joined workers in thirty-seven states who went out on strike. The Twins again attracted national attention when encounters in Minneapolis involving the police, pickets, and nonstrikers resulted in one death and many injuries. The strike was settled after two weeks, but retribution followed swiftly. In addition to the dismissal of workers, a federal grand jury indicted 162 WPA strikers for intimidation, use of physical force, and conspiracy. In the subsequent trials, fifteen of the defendants were sentenced to terms ranging from thirty days to eight months, while seventeen others were given suspended sentences and probation.[15]

The singling out of Twin Citians for indictment in

a nationwide strike remains a mystery. Contributing factors included a conservative reaction to never-ending demands to provide relief, President Roosevelt's ebbing commitment to the WPA program, and the scheme of using prosecutions of a few to encourage many workers elsewhere to accept the new federal regulations. The underlying causes involved a concern about Communist subversion of WPA workers, fears of the Trotskyite leadership in the General Drivers and Helpers Union Local 544 that had organized the Minneapolis unemployed, and general apprehension of "red" influence in the Mill City. The latter point was certainly underscored when prosecutor Victor E. Anderson asserted that "Minneapolis is not going to become the Moscow of America as long as I am district attorney."

Increased organization of crime was another aspect of the depression that put the Twins in the national spotlight. Although according to police department statistics there was no major crime wave during the years of prohibition and depression, lawbreaking certainly was dramatic and frequently well organized. Bootlegging, rum running, and hijacking spiced up the chronicles of crime. Spinning through the cities and countryside in their high-powered cars, bandits armed with machine guns hit banks, sometimes gunned down police and citizens, grabbed the loot, and sped away. To strengthen local law enforcement, volunteer groups organized themselves as "Rangers," and citizens urged the establishment of a state constabulary.[16]

The *Saturday Press*, a scandal sheet published in Minneapolis in the 1920s, put the spotlight on the Mill City when it contended that "Jewish gangsters were controlling gambling and bootlegging" there. But St. Paul, too, took its turn in the spotlight's glare. The city had long been a favorite haunt of gangsters from Chicago and other areas who enjoyed asylum there as long as they committed their crimes elsewhere. Although the extent of collusion between the criminals and municipal government has never been determined, the roster of lawless visitors was certainly impressive. It included the notorious John Dillinger, "Baby Face Nelson" (Lester Gillis), Alvin "Creepy" Karpis, Roger Touhy, George "Machine Gun" Kelly, and Kate "Ma" Barker and her two sons. Enjoying the good life in local entertainment spots and renting spacious houses and lake cottages, the desperados went on crime sprees in Minneapolis and other communities in Minnesota and the Upper Midwest. The agreement must have broken down in the early 1930s, for the gangsters took to kidnaping St. Paulites. Held for ransom and released after hefty payments were Leon Gleckman, a political boss; Haskell Bohn, son of a wealthy refrigeration company founder; William Hamm, a brewer; and Edward Bremer, a banker.[17]

St. Paul had often exerted great efforts to garner favorable publicity; it did not welcome the attention it now received. The United States Attorney General labeled the city the "poison spot of the nation," *Today* magazine branded it a "gangster's paradise," and *Fortune* commented maliciously on its sinful ways. Spurred by the crusading *St. Paul Daily News,* the city inaugurated a clean-up. Although a 1934 grand jury investigation of crime ended in a whitewash of the police department, the gangsters fell upon hard days. Dillinger fled after a shootout with law enforcement officials at his St. Paul apartment and died a few months later in Chicago. Members of the Barker-Karpis gang went to jail after being convicted in the city's federal courts building on kidnaping charges; and Dillinger gang members Homer Van Meter and Eugene "Eddie" Green died of gunshot wounds in St. Paul. As prison or the grave claimed the gangsters that had once haunted Minnesota's capital, crime reporter Nate Bomberg observed, "St. Paul returned to being the safe and sane city free of organized crime it once had been."[18]

One source of crime dried up in 1933 when legal liquor began to flow again. Congress legalized 3.2 per cent beer in March — a prelude to the repeal of the Eighteenth Amendment a few months later. During the months before and after April 7, the date scheduled for the first deliveries, Twin Cities breweries were laying in supplies of malt and hops, hiring workers, overhauling machinery, burnishing the great copper kettles, and scouring the wooden aging vats. Crowds in downtown hotels and cafes blew the foam off the first schooners after the trucks rolled out from the breweries at one minute past midnight.[19]

INTERNATIONAL INCIDENTS foreshadowing a war that would end the depression began to capture the attention of Twin Citians by the mid-1930s. The whirlpool of events sucked in isolationists, internationalists, pacifists, and the proponents of national defense and, after war came to Europe in September, 1939, of aid to the Allies. Into the maelstrom, too, went humanitarians outraged by the Nazi persecution of the Jews and by the Silver Shirts. The latter, headed by William Dudley Pelley and headquartered in Asheville, North Carolina, preached a virulent anti-Semitism identifying Jews with the Communist menace. The complexity of the issues produced ideological dilemmas for the large numbers of isolationists and pacifists in the Twin Cities and the rest of the state. Like many other organizations, the Farmer-Labor party split on the war issue, with some leaders continuing to support isolationism and pacifism while others felt that collective security had become the only way to preserve peace.[20]

Speaking at a Peace Day student demonstration at the University of Minnesota in 1937, Governor Elmer A. Benson argued for limiting neutrality in order to support causes like the Spanish defense of the republican government against Francisco Franco's fascists. Benson, like other opponents of war, experienced the ideological dilemmas of the era as Soviet Communists supported the Spanish republicans, the German and Italian dictators supported Franco, and the bloody confrontation in Spain shook isolationist citadels.[21]

The interventionists organized the Committee to Defend America by Aiding the Allies to give support primarily to Great Britain while keeping the United States out of the war. The local chapter in Minneapolis, which became virtually a state organization, from 1940 opposed isolationist campaigns like those of the America First Committee and championed a variety of measures to aid the Allies. Among them were the Lend-Lease program, increased weapons production, naval escorts for convoys carrying arms to Great Britain, extension of the term of service of drafted men, and unwavering opposition to Japanese aggrandizement.[22]

When war came with the Japanese bombing of Pearl Harbor on December 7, 1941, it was "With all its ghastly consequences," with "no turning back, no evasion, no procrastination, no isolation," the *Commercial West* editoralized. The Twin Cities metropolitan area, encompassing about a third of the state's population and many of its industries, felt the conflict deeply. Minnesotans fought and died at Pearl Harbor, Kasserine Pass, Bataan, Anzio, Salerno, Guadalcanal, and other battlefields whose names would be as well remembered as Verdun. Fort Snelling once again became a training, induction, and discharge center. At Wold-Chamberlain airfield the navy conducted a flight-training program, filling the air with open-cockpit biplanes nicknamed the "yellow perils." English-speaking Nisei (children of Japanese immigrants) studied Japanese at Camp Savage and Fort Snelling to prepare for intelligence work with the Pacific forces, and women went into uniform as WAACs, WAVEs, and nurses.[23]

War was present, too, in the crowded train depots where resonant and haunting train calls alerted family groups as they greeted or said good-bye to members of the armed forces. Many social service groups organized to ease the lives of the thousands who passed through the depots or were stationed in the cities. At the St. Paul Union Depot, the Red Cross operated a canteen, a sick bay, and a dormitory where servicemen could sleep, take a shower, shave, and polish their shoes.[24]

For others, stranded in St. Paul on long layovers between trains or buses, there was Mickey's Diner, open twenty-four hours a day. "In the wee hours of the morning," a resident recalled, there was "no place to go, just roam the streets — or find a Mickey's."

There were "maybe two girls on duty at this time of the morning," he continued, "so they had their work cut out for them. But, joking, laughing and sometimes singing along with the songs from the nickelodeon, they made it through the night. With 'Paper Doll,' 'I'll Get By,' 'Good Night, Irene,' 'Chattanooga Choo-Choo,' 'Don't Sit Under the Apple Tree,' and so on."[25]

Rationing, victory gardens, civilian defense activities, and bond drives became part of the home-front experience of Twin Citians. There were both sparkles of glamor, as Cary Grant and about thirty other movie stars toured to raise funds for army and navy relief, and grim, undiscussed research, as University of Minnesota physicists traveled to Oak Ridge and Los Alamos to develop the atomic bomb. Others served in different ways: F. Peavey Heffelfinger, Mill City wheat merchant, became regional director of the War Production Board; Carl R. Gray, Jr., of St. Paul, a railroad executive, served as director general of the United States Military Railway Service; and Professor Ancel Keys of the University of Minnesota worked with conscientious objectors who volunteered for experiments with partial human starvation to develop the emergency combat K ration.[26]

Defense work touched the lives of other Twin Citians as the government awarded contracts to local firms. Minnesotans, in competing with more heavily industrialized regions in the nation, campaigned hard to win the contracts. Into new and old plants trooped thousands of men and women who manufactured artillery in the Midway district, munitions at New Brighton, and navy blankets in Minneapolis' North Star Woolen Mill. Some firms branched into new fields. Cargill, Inc., built tankers and submarine chasers at Port Savage; General Mills, Inc., manufactured gun sights and torpedoes; Minneapolis-Honeywell Regulator Company developed bombs as well as precision instruments like airplane controls; and Northwest Airlines, Inc., added final modifications to bombers at the St. Paul airport.[27]

Out of the plant of the Minneapolis-Moline Power Implement Company rolled a vehicle destined to become famous around the world. The company's engineers, beginning as early as 1938, produced a machine that was "not a tractor, not a truck, but a super-powerful combination of both a farm tractor and a truck." To Minnesota National Guardsmen who used it during maneuvers at Camp Ripley in 1940 the hybrid suggested a creature from the Popeye cartoon strip which was "neither fowl nor beast, but knew all the answers and could do almost anything" — the JEEP. Although vehicles later produced by other companies were also called JEEP and controversy over rights to the name ensued, Minneapolis-Moline claimed credit for creating the original vehicle.[28]

Large numbers of women who entered the labor force served not only as factory workers — celebrated in song as "Rosie the Riveter"— but also in other jobs like taxi driving that traditionally had been male occupations. When a Minneapolis brokerage house had two "natty young women" instead of the usual male board markers chalking up the quotations, "Old-time chair-warmers in the board room could hardly believe their eyes." In general, however, home-front women employees created no more stir than their sisters in military service in carving out new roles for women.[29]

Although the years seemed long on the home front and longer still to those under fire in battle arenas, the war finally ended on August 14, 1945, with Japan's unconditional surrender. In the Twin Cities ticker tapes, streamers, and paper scraps floated down from tall buildings, whistles screeched, car horns blared, and the downtown blocks became "a riotous scene of wild and unrestrained celebration." On that cool, clear August evening, "Men slapped each other on the shoulders, cheered and shouted, laughed and cried. Mothers who now could hope soon to have their boys back home, wept openly, their tears mingling with those of other mothers whose sons never would come home."[30]

A NUMBER OF DIVERSIONS testified to the resiliency of the human spirit during the depression and the war. The antic splendors of the St. Paul Winter Carnival, lapsed since its brief revival in 1916-17, reappeared in 1937 when civic leaders decided that the festival would help chase away the blues and generate much-needed business. It was abandoned in 1943 for the duration of the war, to be resumed with a Victory Carnival in 1946. Sheriff Thomas "Tommy" Gibbons, reigning over the Victory Carnival as Boreas Rex IX, ordered his subjects to "Go forth and have all the fun you want" and crowned Shirley Peterson Queen of the Snows in a regal court. Hastily planned after the war ended, the event lacked an ice palace. High enthusiasm was evident, however, when about 250,000 spectators from many parts of the state cheered veterans marching in the "Big Parade."[31]

Minneapolis, choosing to celebrate summer rather than winter, launched its civic festival in 1940. It called the elaborate pageant led by its Commodore and Queen of the Lakes the Aquatennial — a suitable name, some thought, for a festival featuring a city with "more water within its city limits than any other metropolis in the world — with the possible exception of Venice." Coronations, concerts, parades, and water sports brought out crowds of visitors as well as Minneapolitans. The organizers viewed the event as one way to improve a city image that had been tarnished by labor conflicts, crime, and depression. Moreover, it proved to be a vehicle for expressing wartime spirit and bringing business to the city.[32]

Among other Twin Cities festivities were ice carnivals, in which skaters embellished the sport with elements of the theater. When the Hippodrome Skating Club of the Twin Cities put on its sixteenth annual carnival in 1925, featured performers included St. Paulites Roy Shipstad, pirouetting to the music of "Daughter of Love," and Eddie Shipstad and Oscar Johnson in an "Apache Dance-Comedy" set to the strains of "Me and My Boy Friend." The Shipstads and Johnson rose to national prominence when their skating routines evolved into the "Ice Follies." Combining features of ballet, the circus, and vaudeville, the brilliantly costumed productions toured the nation in the 1930s and 1940s.[33]

Inspired by the popularity of ice shows, St. Paul put on summertime "Pop Concerts," which were a "unique combination of summer ice skating and symphony music" and featured themes like "A Night in Old Vienna" and "A Night of Rhapsodies." The St. Paul Figure Skating Club, the St. Paul Civic Opera, musicians from the Minneapolis Symphony Orchestra, visiting performers, and others participated in the events held in the St. Paul Auditorium. Among the "Pop Concert" skaters was Robin Lee, member of the St. Paul club and national figure skating champion, who also represented his home city when the United States Figure Skating Association held its championship competiton there in 1939.[34]

Other sports tested the talent and endurance of local athletes. Professional hockey languished, but skiers tried their skills on high jumps that from 1939 included the "towering 'monster' of steel and wood" built by the WPA in Battle Creek Park. Guided by Mike Kelley, the Minneapolis Millers baseball team won the American Association championship in 1932 and 1935, an honor that had gone to the Saints in 1931. Basketball mania swept the cities for three days each March, when winning teams from district and regional contests trooped into the University of Minnesota Field House, the Minneapolis Auditorium, or the St. Paul Auditorium to vie for the state championship in tournaments played before thousands of home-town fans.[35]

The Golden Gophers football team of the University of Minnesota probably kindled the most excitement during the 1930s and early 1940s. Coached by Bernard "Bernie" Bierman, the Gophers played such great football that the "shirts that they wore in honor of their university's maroon and gold colors seemed to become the wear of demigods from some ideal world of sport." Four times voted national champions and six times winners of the Big Ten Conference title between 1934 and 1941, the Gophers placed a number of players on All-American teams. Stars like Francis "Pug" Lund and Bruce Smith — Minnesota's only Heisman Trophy winner — joined earlier Minnesota heroes like Bronko Nagurski and Herb Joesting in that select company.[36]

While the Golden Gophers were creating their legend, a Minneapolis teenager named Patricia "Patty" Berg began her notable golfing career. In 1936 a sports writer declared that "another Bobby Jones, this time a blue-eyed, redheaded, freckled-face girl with a super-celestial nose, and as fine a fighting heart as ever palpitated under a golfer's jersey, is on the way to the hall of fame." He was right. In a career of more than forty years, she won over eighty amateur and professional tournaments, was named three times the Associated Press Woman Athlete of the Year, became a member of state, national, and world halls of fame, and through founding the Ladies' Professional Golfers Association contributed substantially to the development of women's golf.[37]

Twin Citians' attention turned skyward when Jean and Jeanette Piccard ballooned into the stratosphere. In 1937 — three years after their record-breaking eleven-mile-high ascent from Dearborn, Michigan — Jean joined the department of aeronautics at the University of Minnesota. Their ventures, which may have seemed futuristic at the time, later won them notable recognition. The National Aeronautics and Space Administration appointed Jeanette as a consultant in the 1960s and honored her with the Gilruth Award in 1970 for her contributions to manned space flight.[38]

In addition to festivals and sports contests, musical entertainment in its myriad forms reached throughout the Twin Cities. Dimitri Mitropoulos, a conductor whose fame became so widespread that an Easterner referred to Minneapolis as "Mitropoulos, Minnesota," took over the baton of the Minneapolis Symphony Orchestra from Eugene Ormandy in 1937. Ormandy, gifted and gregarious, had successfully guided the symphony from 1931 through the depression years when other orchestras in the nation were experiencing troubled times. As his successor, Mitropoulos, characterized as a "mystic and missionary," further enhanced the orchestra's reputation and enriched Twin Cities musical life before leaving in 1949 to become conductor of the New York Philharmonic. His interests ranged beyond classical music to popular compositions such as those performed by Benny Goodman and "Fats" Waller, but he was displeased by "Beat Me, Dimitri," a boogie-woogie number composed in his honor.[39]

Twin Citians listened to lighter forms of music including old-time polkas, western ballads, jazz, swing, boogie-woogie, and late in the war years, the bebop of Dizzy Gillespie. Visiting jazz musicians, Duke Ellington's band among them, jammed with local groups at after-hours clubs. Big bands played in big ballrooms like the Coliseum in St. Paul and the Marigold Gardens in Minneapolis; there and on other floors dancers moved through the steps of the Big Apple, the Lambeth Walk, and similar fashionable dances. Although "Brother Can You Spare a Dime?" and other songs carried the lament of the depression and lyrics such as those of "I'll Be Seeing You" expressed wartime poignancy, light-hearted themes enjoyed great popularity. The Andrews Sisters of Minneapolis tapped the market for music with a happy sound when their recordings of "Rum and Coca-Cola," "Bei Mir Bist Du Schoen," "Don't Sit Under the Apple Tree," and other songs became national favorites.[40]

The production of talking pictures that began in the 1920s boomed in the succeeding decade; the growing movie industry was "depression-proof" and "war-proof" as people bought escape for the price of a theater ticket. The rippling marquees of Twin Cities theaters drew crowds to see westerns, mysteries, musicals, comedies, cartoons, dramas, horror stories, historical epics, and sagas of gangsters, convicts, and war. Edward G. Robinson's intent and brooding face appeared in "Little Caesar," Laurel and Hardy cavorted in "Pack Up Your Troubles," the Marx Brothers were up to monkeyshines in "Monkey Business," and Spencer Tracy starred during wartime in "A Guy Named Joe." Minneapolis-born Lew Ayres performed in the disquieting "All Quiet on the Western Front" before becoming young Dr. Kildare, while in "The Wizard of Oz" Minnesota-born Judy Garland made immortal the

wistful strains of "Over the Rainbow." Ginger Rogers and Fred Astaire danced, Jeanette MacDonald and Nelson Eddy sang, and dimpled Shirley Temple tap-danced, sang, tossed her curls, and smiled even through her tears. George Raft managed to look both sinister and romantic; more remarkably, musical cowboys like Gene Autry succeeded in riding a horse and singing at the same time.[41]

And so in joy and sorrow, playing, working, and suffering, Twin Citians had passed through the Great Depression and World War II. Some of their losses were irretrievable. Proud people who had been reduced to dependency carried the memory of it with them for the rest of their lives. Family circles had been broken by deaths in the war. Strong men had been maimed in body or mind. But in ordeals of the human spirit more prolonged than any in the nation's history, many people had found something of value. They had survived their troubles with courage, a sense of humor, an ability to make-do, a resiliency that often made possible the pursuit of ordinary activities in unusual times — and hope. Even while the war raged they looked to the future. They hoped that the depression was really over and that they would not again know the bitterness of those years. They hoped that in the United Nations the people might find a collective security that would prevent another war. And Twin Cities civic leaders hoped that the metropolitan center of Minnesota would fare well in the postwar world.

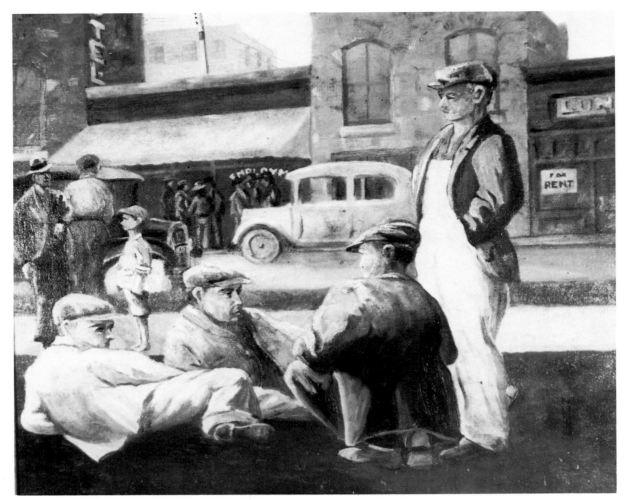

Unemployed men in 1933 lingered near a Minneapolis employment office besieged by job applicants.

On a January day in 1938 job seekers lined up on Robert Street by the St. Paul office of the Minnesota State Employment Service. The Minnesota State Unemployment Compensation office was located nearby on Wabasha Street.

A Farmer-Labor headquarters during the 1932 campaign posted reminders that in July of that year President Herbert Hoover, a Republican, had used United States troops to disperse World War I veterans who were petitioning Congress for bonus payments. In the subsequent election Franklin D. Roosevelt won the presidency and Floyd B. Olson a second term as governor.

On April 6, 1934, a booing crowd of about 3,000 at the Minneapolis City Hall-Courthouse hurled bottles, rocks, and tin cans and tossed tear gas bombs back at the police who had launched them. The unemployed men and women demanded increased relief, continuation of the Civil Works Administration, and abolition of discrimination against single persons, the foreign born, and blacks.

On March 22, 1933, Farmers' Holiday Association members from central Minnesota led by, left to right, K. H. Marsh, Reuben Felt, and Peter Newman marched toward downtown St. Paul to the old state capitol for a meeting. Later they returned to capitol hill to join a crowd of about 20,000 farmers from all parts of the state in presenting relief demands to the legislature.

The St. Paul Committee for Unemployment Insurance announced a rally to be held on May 1, 1935. More than a year later the state legislature enacted the Minnesota unemployment compensation law. The May Day demonstration was chilled by the Minnesota weather; nine inches of wind-driven snow, ice, and rain fell on the Twin Cities that day.

WORKERS!
EMPLOYED AND UNEMPLOYED
ALL OUT MAY FIRST

UNITE in the struggle for genuine Unemployment Insurance, for the Workers Bill, H. F. 120 in the State House; H. R. 2827 in the National Congress.

UNITE in the struggle against relief cuts and wage cuts; for a decent Standard of Living.

MAY 1st is a traditional Labor Holiday of the American Workers. Growing out of the struggle of the American Workers for the 8 hour day, it was adopted by Workers everywhere and became International Labor Day. On May Day this year millions of workers throughout the world will join in united struggle against the rising threat of Fascism and Imperialist War and against the steady worsening of their conditions of Life.

WORKERS OF ST. PAUL!

The St. Paul Committee for Unemployment Insurance, representing forty-five Labor and Fraternal Organizations calls on all Workers to come out in masses on May 1st to demonstrate their Unity in the struggle for Unemployment and Social Insurance and for a decent Standard of Life.

GATHER AT STATE CAPITOL STEPS WED., MAY 1st
4:00 P. M.

PROMINENT LABOR SPEAKERS WILL ADDRESS MASS-MEETING.
WORKERS! Join your Trade Unions and Unemployment Organizations.
IN UNION LIES OUR STRENGTH.

St. Paul Committee for Unemployment Insurance: Delegates from
Carpenters Local No. 87 .... Building Trades Council .... Lathers Local No. 483
Cigar Makers Local No. 98.... Truck Drivers No. 120 .... Machinists & Mechanics No. 459
Plasterers & Cement Finishers No. 20 .... Painters No. 61 ...... Building Laborers No. 132
Sheet Metal Workers .... Cleaners & Dyers .... Operating Engineers No. 967.... Carmen No.4
Steel & Metal Workers Ind. Union .. Electrical Workers .... Iron Workers .... Roofers Local
Street Railwaymen.... Packinghouse Workers Ind. Union .... Unemployment Councils
Master Shoe Repairers Ass'n ...... Rondo Div. Farmbr Labor ...... Int. Workers Order
Scandinavian Workers Club ...... Communist Party .... International Labor Defense
So. St. Paul Workers Club ...... St. Paul Continuation Committe of Youth Conference
Young Communist League........ F. S. U. ...... American Building Trades Association
Minn. State Building Service Employees .... Russian Mutual Aid Society
Farmer-Labor Veterans...... Farmer-Labor Ward Clubs......Etc.......Etc.

M. D. Levine Printing Co., 148 No. Dale St., near Selby   7 6

Demonstrating for the passage of House File 120 to provide for unemployment insurance, about 5,000 urban workers and farmers marched to the capitol on March 11, 1935. While the crowd waited outside, the leaders entered the building to press their demands on the legislature.

199

Flour piled in Hopkins was one of
the commodities distributed to
the needy after the creation in
1933 of the Federal Surplus Relief
Corporation, which also distributed salt pork, canned beef, butter,
and cereal.

A WPA worker in 1936 made posters to announce events sponsored
by the Minneapolis Public Library.

Women participated in a 1936
WPA sewing project at the Phyllis
Wheatley Settlement House, 809
Aldrich Avenue North,
Minneapolis.

St. Paul banks and 4,300 other firms formed a parade of 50,000 marchers who moved along West Sixth Street on August 24, 1933. The parade signaled the beginning of a campaign to combat the depression by bringing the city's businesses "under the shadow of the blue eagle" — the emblem of the National Recovery Administration, a program to enforce fair competition codes.

Cheering and singing, Civilian Conservation Corps members of Company 701 left their training camp at Fort Snelling on May 7, 1933, like "soldiers starting off for the battlefield." They were on their way to the Superior National Forest near Ely. More than 84,000 Minnesota men planted trees, fought fires, and carried out other CCC projects in the state during the depression.

Typists prepared Social Security identification cards as the midnight deadline for employee registration neared on December 5, 1936. They worked in temporary quarters in the St. Paul Post Office, 180 East Kellogg Boulevard, under the watchful eyes of Postmaster Arthur A. Van Dyke, standing, left background.

Workers placed reinforcing steel in a St. Paul-Minneapolis sewer that was part of a system begun in 1934. Funds allocated by the Federal Emergency Administration of Public Works (PWA) helped build the sewers and a sewage treatment plant.

The sewage treatment plant, located in the Pigs Eye Lake area below downtown St. Paul, neared completion in 1937. On May 16, 1938, it was dedicated "to the citizens of Minneapolis and St. Paul and to their good health."

In 1936 the razing of buildings in the deteriorated North Minneapolis neighborhood (bounded by Dupont and Emerson avenues between Eleventh Avenue North and the present Olson Memorial Highway) began the Sumner Field Housing Project—the only PWA public housing development in the Twin Cities. Governor Floyd B. Olson, who claimed the area as his birthplace, was the principal speaker at ground-breaking ceremonies. The first families moved into their new homes two years later.

Data processing equipment in the late 1930s facilitated the task of analyzing the huge volume of relief records generated by the depression.

Gustave H. Barfuss, St. Paul's Commissioner of Public Safety, smashed a bottle of champagne to dedicate the city's new traffic signal system in 1937. Forty-seven corner installations, acquired with the help of PWA funds, replaced "bobby" signals at the centers of intersections and added new "Walk" signs to control pedestrian traffic.

The St. Paul City Hall-Ramsey County Courthouse on Kellogg Boulevard, funded by bonds fortuitously sold before the crash, offered a striking contrast to depression-era utilitarian construction. Pictured here in 1936 is Carl Milles's gleaming onyx "god of peace" housed in the building's three-story War Memorial Concourse.

In 1936 workmen assembled John K. Daniels' statue of a three-generation pioneer family on Pioneer Square at 100 South Second Avenue in Minneapolis. In words that may have appealed to depression-weary Twin Citians, Edward C. Gale dedicated the work to the "pioneers of the great Northwest" as a "monumental symbol of the true pioneer spirit — its faith, its achievements through great hardships, its foresightedness, its rugged honesty, and its kindness." The statue is now at Fifth Avenue Northeast and Marshall Street.

Roger "Terrible" Tuohy's gang was tried in St. Paul for the kidnaping of William Hamm, Jr., and acquitted in November, 1933. Tuohy is in the back row, center, flanked by defense attorneys Thomas W. McMeekin of St. Paul, left, and William Scott Stewart of Chicago, right. In the front row are Gustav "Gloomy Gus" Schaeffer, left, and Eddie "Father Tom" McFadden, right.

Alvin "Creepy" Karpis "folded up like the yellow rat he is," J. Edgar Hoover commented after the capture of "Public Enemy No. 1" in New Orleans in 1936. He was returned on a specially chartered plane to St. Paul, where a jury convicted him and other gang members of the Hamm kidnaping. Karpis, in straw hat and handcuffs, was escorted by Hoover, immediate left. Nate Bomberg, St. Paul police reporter, is in right foreground.

The long, dry, prohibition years ended when Twin Cities brewery whistles blew at midnight on April 6, 1933, to mark the legalization of beer with 3.2 per cent alcohol. Waiting trucks rolled out from the Glueck Brewing Company yard at 2021 Marshall Street Northeast, Minneapolis, a few seconds early when drivers mistook the blast of an automobile horn for the plant whistle. The next day "Kegs, cases, barrels and more kegs were still pouring from the brewery . . . in a steady stream as trucks, automobiles and railroad cars were loaded hurriedly and shot out through Minneapolis and into the surrounding country."

Crowds of drinkers in the saloons had only a short time to quaff beer after the midnight whistle blew, but on subsequent nights they came back for more.

Part of the "elemental economic struggle" that marked the Minneapolis truck drivers' strike in 1934 was played out in the streets on May 21. With fists and clubs the strikers battled the city police and citizens acting as special deputies. The battle resumed on the following day and ended with the death of two of the deputies.

After a troubled truce in the strike, violence again broke out when police escorting a truck in the market area shot a number of strikers and bystanders. One of two men who died was picket Henry B. Ness, whose funeral procession on July 24 moved through crowds on Eighth Street South near the strike headquarters.

Europe was already at war when Syd Fossum's drawing appeared on the cover of the Minnesota CIO's 1941 *Directory and Annual Convention Brochure.* In the brochure CIO state counsel Ralph Helstein advocated the safeguarding of civil liberties, raising the standard of living, and extending democratic processes while supporting national defense. "For such an America," he urged, "Labor must fight."

From the late 1930s the new Congress of Industrial Organizations gained strength in the Twin Cities. Joe Glazer, "labor's troubador" who was later co-compiler of *Songs of Work and Freedom,* discussed the CIO's Textile Workers Union of America during a visit to Minneapolis in 1946.

In the year of the crash, the First National Bank of Saint Paul made plans for a building that would add distinction to its city's downtown profile, while the Foshay Tower rose above the Minneapolis skyline as a reminder of the failed dreams of the 1920s. Completed in 1931 on Fourth Street between Minnesota and Robert streets, the thirty-two-story structure is pictured here about nine years later.

Scotch Brand cellophane tape helped make the depression years prosperous for the Minnesota Mining and Manufacturing Company, 791 Forest Street, St. Paul. In 1931, the first full year of production, sheets of tape passed through a slitting machine to be cut into standard widths and wound on spools.

St. Paul's ambitions to develop its grain trade gathered momentum in 1930 when the Farmers Union Terminal Association built a large elevator adjoining the municipal elevator at the foot of Chestnut Street. The terminal, pictured here about mid-decade, was said to be the "largest and best equipped plant on the river for loading grain on barges."

Butter packers in the plant of Land O'Lakes Creameries, Inc., 2201 Kennedy Street Northeast, Minneapolis, worked in 1941 for a cooperative that began in St. Paul and was wooed and won by the Mill City in 1925. The co-op developed into a flourishing organization with plants in several states that turn out a wide variety of products.

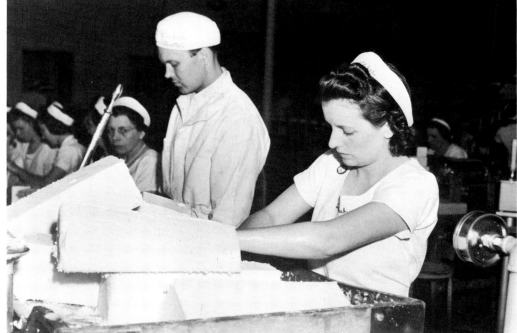

The Twin Cities remained an important lumber distribution point, although Minneapolis was no longer a lumber manufacturing center. In the 1930s the Twin Cities branch of the Weyerhaeuser Timber Company maintained a "unit package shed" in St. Paul's Midway district on Franklin Avenue.

The west-side industrial district in Minneapolis was still imposing in 1939, despite the decline of flour milling and the construction of manufacturing plants and elevators away from the falls. The elevators in the foreground contributed to the city's total grain storage capacity of over ninety-two million bushels, making it a national leader through the 1930s.

A neon display in 1937 brightened a new service station at Tenth Street and La Salle Avenue, Minneapolis. In publishing the picture, the *Minneapolis Star* commented that the station symbolized "the success of the Tidewater Oil Company and the Petroleum Service Company of Minneapolis, Twin Cities Tydol-Veedol distributors, in this area." A street crossing "bobby," lower right, regulated traffic flow at the busy intersection.

Fashions displayed about 1932 at Charles, 630 Nicollet Avenue, Minneapolis, temper the threadbare image of depression years. Many retail merchants cut prices drastically in order to reduce their inventories and avoid bankruptcy.

Shopping carts rolled toward the check-out counters in the Lexington Food Arcade at 1100 University Avenue, St. Paul, probably in the late 1930s. The Great Atlantic & Pacific Tea Company (A&P) remodeled the arcade and used it as a supermarket for a short time before moving to 1204 University Avenue about 1942. Increased use of automobiles and better refrigeration contributed to the boom in supermarket development.

Flashing the yellow, orange, maroon, and brown colors of the Milwaukee Road, the "Hiawatha No. 1" broke through a festive curtain at its christening on April 30, 1935, at the American Locomotive Company's works in Schenectady, N.Y. Bound for service on the Chicago-Twin Cities run, the steam-driven, oil-fueled engine had a top speed of 120 miles an hour.

While some travelers took furtive rides in boxcars during the depression, others relaxed in dining cars, lingering over fine meals served on silver-plated tableware from the Great Northern's commissary in the Mississippi Street yards, St. Paul.

Northwest Airlines' new fleet of twin-engine Lockheed "Electra" 10-As made the Twin Cities-Seattle flight in only thirteen hours. The airline bought the ten-passenger planes in 1934 for $36,000 each and was the first to place them in commercial service.

Ambulances coming to the rescue became familiar sights in the Twin Cities by 1944 when this photograph was made in Minneapolis. An increase in the number of car accidents in the 1930s forced state and local governments to set speed limits and test drivers before licensing them.

An auto show that opened on February 2, 1935, in the St. Paul Auditorium featured over 100 cars representing the "latest thing in motordom —smart new lines, more power, speedier motors." Governor Olson, introduced by Mayor Mark Gehan, dedicated the week-long show to "state prosperity." The Chrysler Airflow, center, was one of the first automobiles to boast a streamlined design.

A good-roads movement helped to strengthen the bonds between the Twin Cities and their trade area in the 1930s. But "improvements" made by depression agencies on the St. Paul end of the road leading to Hudson, Wisconsin, won no praise from the *St. Paul Daily News.* It commented on June 23, 1936, that "rutted barrenness" had replaced a good road used daily by thousands of people traveling to the city.

A drama of changing times took place in downtown St. Paul on September 15, 1942, when a car crossing the Robert Street Bridge hit the back of Sam Hartman's junk wagon. The wagon hit the horse; the horse bolted, threw the driver to the pavement, and then ran away, sideswiping three cars with the careening wagon. Stanley Hubbard, president of KSTP, saved the day when he stopped the horse, and a policeman then drove the frightened animal out of the downtown district.

The International Institute's folk festivals in St. Paul fostered pride in ethnic traditions. The 1934 festival held in the auditorium featured Armenian dancers, left to right, Arme Ousdigian, Togue Tufenk, Rebecca Bajakian, Aukinsé Bangotch, and Sossy Keljik.

The Northwest Division of the Union of Swedish Singers performed on July 17, 1938, before a crowd of about 30,000 people gathered at the state fairgrounds to honor Crown Prince Gustav Adolph and Crown Princess Louise of Sweden, who were visiting the Twin Cities to observe *Svenskarnas Dag*.

Mexican Americans held a parade on St. Paul's West Side to celebrate Mexican Independence Day, an annual event from 1937. To the right is the banner of the Comité de Reconstruccisón, an organization formed in 1939 to acquire and furnish a building for Our Lady of Guadalupe Catholic Church.

More than a thousand people attended the various festivities that included a banquet on August 12, 1933, held to salute the opening of a new building housing the Italia Club (Società Italia di Mutuo Soccorso) and the Christ Child Community Center at Bradley and Patridge streets, St. Paul. Mayor William Mahoney and other city officials joined the group in celebrating the event.

At the Jewish Educational Center, 743 Holly Avenue, St. Paul, teacher Dorothy Berman of Minneapolis guided Beverly Kauffman in blackboard work in 1931. The class in Hebrew met daily at 4:00 P.M.

The National Eucharistic Congress of the Catholic church brought an estimated 450,000 people to the four-day gathering that began on June 23, 1941. Crowds massed near the altar, center, at the race track on the state fairgrounds for one of the events.

The crowd at the Hennepin Avenue Methodist Episcopal Church, Hennepin and Groveland avenues, Minneapolis, enjoyed a spring thaw for Easter Sunday on April 12, 1936.

St. Mary's Russian Orthodox Greek Catholic Church, 1629 Fifth Street Northeast, Minneapolis, newly redecorated in preparation for the celebration of its Golden Jubilee, received the blessing of The Most Reverend Metropolitan Theophilus, head of the Russian Orthodox Church of North America and Canada, center, on May 3, 1936. Among other church officials present was The Most Reverend Leonty, Bishop of Chicago and Minneapolis, upper left, a former pastor of St. Mary's.

Evangelist Luke Rader, who established the River-Lake Gospel Tabernacle at 4610 East Lake Street, Minneapolis, turned his attention to the question of the day in 1939 — will it be peace or war? Rader broadcast services over WDGY as early as 1928, the year of the tabernacle's construction.

The Reverend Mr. Rader took advantage of fine weather on July 24, 1937, to baptize black-robed converts in Lake Nokomis, Minneapolis, instead of following the usual custom of using the tabernacle pool.

213

Aerial views and vignettes reveal something of the Twin Cities' character in the 1930s and early 1940s. By 1938 the boundary line between the cities is invisible from the air. From downtown Minneapolis the view sweeps across the Mississippi River northeastward into St. Paul. Elevators and mills along the railroad belt connecting the intercity industrial district are left-center, with the state fairgrounds in the background. The prominent structure in right-background is the Montgomery Ward building at 1400 University Avenue, St. Paul.

Branching elms in 1936 arched over Second Avenue South and Thirty-first Street in Minneapolis — one of the many tree-shaded residential areas in the Twin Cities.

Beyond this sign erected in 1925 by the Junior Pioneer Association at University Avenue and Emerald Street another beckoned — "Welcome to Minneapolis." The picture was made in 1936.

In 1931 Elsie Peterson operated a new pedestrian-controlled traffic signal at East Twenty-fourth Street and Portland Avenue, Minneapolis, with Hildur Peterson looking on.

An aerial view of St. Paul about 1934 strengthens the image of Twin Cities joined at the Midway. Holman Field is in the foreground. The grain elevators on the river at the foot of Chestnut Street are to the left of the high downtown buildings along the Mississippi River. Northwestward is the Montgomery Ward building; the intercity industrial area is in the background, center.

In 1941 the Ancker Hospital complex comprising the city and county hospital in St. Paul sprawled between West Seventh Street, which runs diagonally in the left foreground, and the rows of houses.

New houses on Capitol Avenue (now Englewood) near Griggs Street, St. Paul, in 1931 were part of the growing development of the Midway area. This bungalow-style architecture was popular in the 1930s.

The Cedarette Cafe and John Bassi's grocery store stood in 1932 on Cedar Street between Tenth and Eleventh streets near the state capitol, St. Paul. Lodging houses and private residences surrounded the little business center. The warehouse at far right after extensive remodeling became the Capitol Square Building.

Twin Citians pursued comfort and pleasure in fair and foul weather, and sometimes it was very foul. About 100,000 sufferers slept on the green expanses of parks, lake shores, boulevards, and church lawns as the temperature passed 106 degrees in mid-July, 1936. More than 200 Twin Citians died in the two-day heat wave that tied the all-time high temperature record. The long, hot spell followed the coldest winter that Minnesota had recorded.

Celebrators in 1938 toasted the fiftieth anniversary of the Town and Country Club, 2279 Marshall Avenue, St. Paul. Left to right are Mrs. A. A. Elvgren, Guy Chase, Elizabeth Reardon, Dr. W. C. Rutherford, Helen Reardon, A. A. Elvgren, and Mrs. Guy Chase.

Neighborhood children in August, 1930, sent up a basket of ice cream and candy to June Kelly on her perch in front of her home at 610 Jackson Street Northeast, Minneapolis. The seventeen-year-old tree sitter attempted to set a new record.

An advertising piece for displaying in drugstores gave assurance that Adler-I-Ka would relieve numerous discomforts. The Adlerika Company manufactured the medicine in St. Paul for many years.

Twin Citians were caught up in the national craze for marathon dancing in the 1920s and 1930s. In about 1928 these couples from both cities paused at the edge of a gleaming floor in St. Paul after completing a record-breaking 533 hours of dancing.

A warm February day in 1938 lured Rita Schwartzbauer and Jean Kittel — harbingers of spring — out of their houses on Edmund Street, St. Paul.

A radio-phonograph and a stack of records in the early 1940s brought music into this living room. Among the hundreds of artists who broadcast and made records were bands led by Glenn Miller, Paul Whiteman, and Wayne King.

KSTP demonstrated its new television equipment in Minneapolis on August 5, 1939, during an American Legion convention. The camera focused on announcer Rock Ulmer, who held a microphone for Elizabeth Lindstrom, left, and

Margaret Hagen, convention hostesses, in front of the Radisson Hotel, 33-35 Seventh Street South. The station showed the parade live on a television screen in the hotel.

More than 25,000 marchers paraded on Robert Street, St. Paul, during the convention of the Minnesota Department of the American Legion on August 12, 1941. One of the many bands from across the state made a great hit by dancing as it both marched and played a tune about Casey, who waltzed with a strawberry blonde ("The Band Played On").

At the Hotel Radisson, Minneapolis, on the New Year's Eve that ushered in 1936, merrymakers encouraged by signs of returning prosperity "let their back hair down" to join in the "wildest, noisiest, happiest celebration" Twin Citians had known since the crash.

Premiering at the Orpheum Theater at 19-21 West Seventh Street, St. Paul, on September 14, 1933, was "Lady For A Day," a movie directed by Frank Capra and boasting "more stars than in the heavens." The theater awning carried the NRA blue-eagle emblem and motto.

A young contender in the "Janet Gaynor Double Contest" sponsored on June 7, 1937, by the *St. Paul Daily News* arrived at the Paramount Theater, 22 West Seventh Street, St. Paul, where "A Star Is Born" starring Gaynor was playing. In imitation of a Hollywood premiere at Grauman's Chinese Theater, buglers saluted the contestants and newsreel cameras under brilliant lights filmed their dramatic entrance. The Boy Scouts provided the bugling, and Mayor Mark Gehan dignified the event by acting as a judge.

The Shipstads and Johnson took their Ice Follies company on the road in 1937. Roy Shipstad is thirteenth from the left, Oscar Johnson seventeenth, and Eddie Shipstad nineteenth. In this season they performed famous routines like "The Bullfighter," "The Human Top," "The Bloody Buccaneers," and "The Old Gray Mare."

218

The "cream of the skippers" from Minnesota and nearby states participated in an invitational regatta sponsored by the Lake Calhoun Yacht Club during the Minneapolis Aquatennial in 1940.

Cedric Adams, WCCO radio broadcaster and *Minneapolis Star-Journal* columnist, displayed the genial charm that made him a popular performer at the Aquatennial Queens' luncheon in 1940. Marion Campbell of Minneapolis adjusted the microphone for him.

"Zephyrus," a replica of the Chicago, Burlington and Quincy's gleaming streamliner called "Zephyr" for the west wind, rolled by the state capitol during the St. Paul Winter Carnival parade in 1938.

Passing the Cathedral of St. Paul on January 27, 1940, marchers moved along the Winter Carnival parade route to the auditorium downtown. "Here in St. Paul we have a festival of sport," the *Dispatch* observed. "Abroad . . . there is the grim tension, the tragedy and sorrow of war."

Twin Citians' heroes and heroines in the 1930s and early 1940s included (A) Governor Floyd B. Olson, center, with actor George Raft, right, young starlets, and Shriners at the Minneapolis Auditorium on June 19, 1934; (B) Thomas "Tommy" Gibbons, who fought Jack Dempsey and Gene Tunney in heavyweight prize fights in the 1920s, as Ramsey County sheriff in 1936; (C) Bernard "Bernie" Bierman, the Golden Gophers' football coach; (D) Franklin D. Roosevelt, charismatic president, speaking from a ramp at the St. Paul Union Depot yards on October 4, 1937; (E) balloonists Jeannette and Jean Piccard, of Minneapolis and the stratosphere, in 1936; (F) Frank "Bring 'Em Back Alive" Buck (with trowel), helping to lay the cornerstone for the WPA-built Zoo Building in Como Park, St. Paul, in 1936; (G) famed aviatrix Amelia Earhart in St. Paul in 1932, before taking off with Northwest Airways pilots on a flight to Seattle; (H) Dimitri Mitropoulos, Minneapolis Symphony Orchestra conductor, with pianist Artur Rubinstein, who ap-

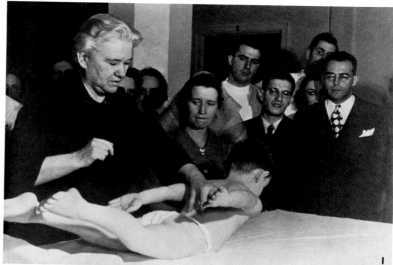

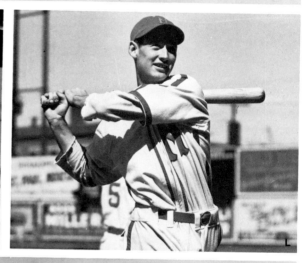

peared with the orchestra many times; (I) Sister Elizabeth Kenny, teaching and practicing her rehabilitative treatment for infantile paralysis in a Minneapolis clinic in 1943; (J) twenty-year-old Patricia "Patty" Berg playing in 1938 at Rochester, where she won her third women's state golf championship; (K) crusading Republican Harold E. Stassen of South St. Paul, who was elected governor of Minnesota in 1938 and joined the navy in 1943 —with Rose Spencer of Winona, far left, and Mrs. Stassen; (L) Ted Williams, home-run king of the American Association, going into his famous swing in Nicollet Park during his brief career as a Minneapolis Miller in 1938; (M) Minneapolis strike leaders William Brown, Miles Dunne, and Vincent Dunne (left to right), imprisoned briefly in a military stockade on the state fairgrounds after the 1934 truckers' strike; (N) pop singers the Andrews Sisters, Maxene, Patti, and LaVerne, in "Buck Privates" produced in 1941 by Universal Pictures Company, Inc.

Speaking under the auspices of the America First Committee, Colonel Charles A. Lindbergh warned the audience in the Minneapolis Auditorium on May 10, 1941, of the dangers of involvement in a European war. Crowds who had come to hear the famous flier filled the auditorium and overflowed into nearby streets.

—Drawing by Ellis, from "Daily Worker"

WE WANT NO A.E.F.!
Get Out and Stay Out of the War

Passage of the "Lease-Lend" Bill, H.R. 1776, will drag us farther into the imperialist war abroad **unless Labor and all friends of peace speak out NOW.** Roosevelt insists on the power to ship American boys to all corners of the world and to make us a belligerent in this war for colonies and markets. Only the people, united under the leadership of Labor, can block the war-mad assaults on their safety and well-being. The Communist Party continues to urge the people to act in their own defense, despite the abuse reaction heaps upon it for this reason. Raise your voice now—for preservation of civil liberties, for a decent standard of living, for the government to **get out and stay out of the imperialist war.**

Hear...

MOTHER
ELLA REEVE
BLOOR

Author of
"We Are Many"

Friday
March 21
8. P.M.

Seventh St. Hall
19 S. 7th St., Mpls.

Admission 20c

"She has traversed the broad bosom of our country and knows it well, as few professional patriots do. She has lived with the people, Negro and white, miners in their cabins, farmers in isolated rural places, textile workers in their fire-trap tenements, slum dwellers of great cities. She knows the needs of the people, native-born and immigrants. Strong workers have told her of their troubles, their dreams. 'Mother' she is in fact to them!"

Issued by: Hennepin County Committee, Communist Party, Helen Allison, Secretary, 10 S. 10th St., Minneapolis

Students gathered in front of Northrop Auditorium on the University of Minnesota campus and expressed their opposition to American intervention in a foreign war.

Ella Reeve Bloor, the "grand old lady" of the American Communist party and crusader for unpopular causes since the 1880s, supported American nonintervention in foreign wars. The Lend-Lease Act of 1941 provided for material aid to the Allies fighting Germany.

About 3,000 people assembled in the St. Paul Auditorium theater on January 16, 1938, to protest against civil and religious persecution in Nazi Germany. The Catholic-sponsored meeting adopted a resolution and forwarded it to Secretary of State Cordell Hull.

The committee published this appeal in newspapers in 1941 as part of its campaign to combat isolationist sentiment.

JAPS OPEN WAR ON U. S.!
Attack Hawaii, Guam, Singapore; U. S. Army, Navy Losses Heavy

Soldiers and sailors left the Twin Cities for war. Downtown Minneapolis took on a martial air as Mayor Marvin L. Kline stood by a cannon during a United States Navy recruiting campaign.

George Carlson kissed his wife good-bye from a bus carrying Washington County men from Stillwater to the induction center at Fort Snelling on April 18, 1942.

Captain Paul Sevareid, public relations officer for the state's Selective Service office, spoke to draftees in St. Paul in March, 1941. The Selective Training and Service Act, the nation's first peace-time compulsory service law, had been passed a few months earlier when the success of Germany's military operations spurred American defense efforts.

In Sansapor, Dutch New Guinea, naval gun crew members who had been together since Pearl Harbor displayed in 1944 a banner recording their victories. All but two of the men were from St. Paul.

The "Genesee," one of eighteen ocean-going vessels built by Cargill, Inc., in the shipyards near Savage, slipped sideways into the waters of the Minnesota River on September 4, 1943. Cargill also constructed many towboats and barges for use on the inland waterways — to the satisfaction of those who had fought long years to improve navigation on the Mississippi River.

Among the metropolitan area manufacturers to receive war production contracts was the Twin Cities Ordnance Plant in New Brighton, which made small arms ammunition. With housing short in 1942, many of the newly arrived plant employees lived in this nearby trailer camp.

Assemblers in the Minneapolis-Moline Power Implement Company's plant in Minneapolis, below, switched from manufacturing farm machinery to turning out steam cargo winches for the Maritime Commission in 1942.

The Minneapolis-Honeywell Regulator Company used experience gained in designing heating controls to produce the C-1 Autopilot in its Aeronautical Division. During the war the company produced more than 35,000 of the electronic devices, which guided bombers on instructions from the Norden bombsight.

A worker fitted a side gun in a B-24 bomber at Northwest Airlines' modification center at Holman Field, St. Paul. More than 5,000 women and men working at the center installed guns and other special equipment in the bombers during the war.

I'll give 'em HELL!

YOU GIVE ME THE *STUFF!*

A poster issued by the federal government in 1942 dramatized home-front obligations to support the war effort.

A test of the new air raid siren atop the St. Paul City Hall-Ramsey County Courthouse on December 18, 1941, pleased John McGrath, left, head of the firm that made the equipment, and Gustave Brissman, right, the city's superintendent of Fire and Police Alarm Telegraph.

Gasoline rationing drastically reduced automobile travel during the war. James C. Ferguson, a St. Paul physician, received these coupons in August, 1945, the month gasoline rationing ended. Cars, tires, fuel oil, bicycles, shoes, sugar, coffee, and meat were also rationed.

Customers lined up in front of the Capitol Meat Company, 515 Wabasha Street, St. Paul, in May, 1945, ready to buy "anything that was left." From their vantage point on the sidewalk, where the wait was as long as an hour, they could see the answer to the question "Where's the meat?" under the rows of canned Prem and Treet.

A soldier on leave received a warm welcome at a neighborhood grocery store.

Aluminum pots, pans, tea kettles, hair curlers, vacuum bottles, car parts, and other items were piled high on July 25, 1941, at Franklin School, Tenth and Temperance streets, St. Paul. This scrap drive brought out the Boy Scouts and fleets of trucks to collect metals for the Allies; more drives followed after the United States entered the war.

The Hollywood Victory Caravan, touring to raise relief funds for the army and navy, visited the Twin Cities in May, 1942. Appearing in St. Paul were, left to right, Merle Oberon, Risë Stevens, Charles Boyer, Claudette Colbert, James Cagney, Frances Langford, Cary Grant, Olivia de Havilland, Marie McDonald, Joan Blondell, Eleanor Powell, and Katherine Booth.

The Twin Cities went "Wild with VJ Joy" after President Harry S Truman on August 14, 1945, announced that Japan had surrendered. A crowd at Nicollet Avenue and Seventh Street, Minneapolis, celebrated the end of four years of "misery and waiting and expectation."

"We must not let hate consume us as we pass through the flames of the present world conflict," the Reverend Clarence T. R. Nelson, right, commented on August 16, 1942, at the Camphor Memorial Methodist Church, 585 Fuller Avenue, St. Paul, during services at which he accepted an Honor Roll from Mr. and Mrs. J. P. Williams. The roll listed sixteen men from the church who were in the armed services and one who was in a Civilian Public Service Camp.

Although the Minnesota State Fair in 1944 presented a Thrill Day with a simulated fight between a Japanese Zero and an American plane, plans for peace received much attention that year. At the booth of the Minnesota United Nations Committee fairgoers signed petitions urging the formation of the international organization. Marie (Mrs. Arthur J.) McGuire, the committee's executive secretary who had also worked on behalf of the World Court, designed the display featuring the Temple of Peace.

Transitions to peacetime and the beginning of a new era were evident as R. J. Raines, a member of Claire L. Chennault's famed Flying Tigers who served in China for four years, delivered the first air-shipped California fruit to Minneapolis Mayor Hubert H. Humphrey and Governor Edward J. Thye in the fall of 1945. Raines and other group members formed the peacetime Flying Tigers line to provide both passenger and freight service.

"We want Ike," a crowd of 12,000 chanted as Dwight D. Eisenhower, World War II hero, campaigned for the presidency on the Republican ticket on September 16, 1952, from a platform built on the state capitol steps, St. Paul. Democrat Adlai E. Stevenson carried Ramsey County in the subsequent election; Hennepin went for Ike, the winner. While Eisenhower spoke, the construction crews working on the capitol-approach, urban-renewal project silenced their bulldozers and stopped pouring concrete sidewalks.

On their long journey from frontier villages to major American cities, the Twin Cities experienced many changes that shaped their character. The postwar leg of the journey was no exception. They felt the impact of several trends that had been developing for some time within the central cities, in the suburbs, and in the hinterland, now commonly called the Upper Midwest. They were also swept by new movements, creating new urban tensions as severe as any they had yet experienced.

The Twins emerged as a widely praised, successful metropolitan center despite limitations in their responses to new and old challenges. One resident's comment in 1980 to a visiting writer indicated that the glory might have made once prickly Twin Citians a little blasé: "Promise me," he said, "you won't go back and write another one of those articles about 'the good life' in the Twin Cities. The whole country will be migrating here in droves."[1]

Past experience indicated that danger of a mass migration to the Twin Cities from more troubled urban areas was not imminent. The population growth rate declined precipitously after the 1880s, moderated for a number of years, took a sharp dip during the depression, and then leveled in the 1940s. The Twin Cities' combined population reached its highest point in 1950 at 833,047; Minneapolis was also at its zenith that year, with a population of 521,718. But the Mill City suffered a 7.4 per cent loss by 1960 — a figure that swelled to 10 per cent in 1970 and 14.6 in 1980. St. Paul's population, which peaked at 313,411 in 1960, declined less sharply, with a 1.1 per cent loss in 1970 and 12.8 in 1980. The cities' combined population in 1980 was 641,181 — 370,951 in Minneapolis and 270,230 in St. Paul.[2]

With declining population, the national status of both cities slipped, Minneapolis from its highest rank of number 15 in 1930 to 32 in 1970. St. Paul, which had reached its zenith rank of 23 in 1890 and was 31 in 1930, slipped to 46 in 1970. By 1970 the expansion outward had tilted the population balance from the two central cities to the five-county Standard Metropolitan Statistical Area (SMSA) beyond their limits — 744,380 to 1,069,267. Ten years later, only 641,181 people lived within the cities and 1,472,352 lived in a newly drawn ten-county SMSA. Despite substantial growth in the suburban districts, the area ranked only fifteenth nationally in 1980, in contrast to twelfth for the Metropolitan District in 1940. A modest rate of growth in the Upper Midwest, however, left the cities in their premier position regionally. In 1980 the metropolitan area encompassed over half of Minnesota's population, and the Twins remained by far the largest urban center in the Upper Midwest.

Economic diversification became increasingly significant in the postwar era as major industries based on agricultural, mineral, and timber production waned. In agriculture-based industry, flour milling continued the decline that had begun in 1916, and large meat-packing plants in South St. Paul closed. The great milling firms, which maintained headquarters in Minneapolis while producing most of their flour elsewhere, diversified extensively. General Mills, Inc., operated restaurants, developed products like Hamburger Helper and other convenience foods for the home, and bought Parker Brothers, manufacturers of "Monopoly" and other games. The Pillsbury Company also entered the restaurant business with chains like Steak and Ale, Burger King, and Bennigans. The Peavey Company, grain merchants and millers, expanded into retail merchandising and the manufacture of jams, jellies, and peanut butter; in 1982 — still headquartered in Minneapolis — it became a subsidiary of ConAgra, Inc., of Omaha, Nebraska, a firm that included Taco Plaza restaurants and Banquet Foods among its enterprises.[3]

Agribusiness conducted by giant organizations — including the milling companies, Cargill, Inc., Land O' Lakes, Inc., and Harvest State Cooperatives (formerly the Grain Terminal Association) — remained important in the cities' economy. Economic and political leaders who were concerned about diversification urged that the Twin Cities, as well as the state, actively foster fast-growth service and high-technology businesses based on human skills in addition to traditional industries. They often cited the success of two local companies in their arguments for expanding high-technology industries — Honeywell, Inc. (formerly Minneapolis-Honeywell Regulator Company), a firm that began making automatic thermostats late in the nineteenth century and grew to be a leader in the computer, defense, and space exploration industries, and St. Paul's 3M (Minnesota Mining and Manufacturing Company), which had evolved from a maker of sandpaper in the early twentieth century into a producer of tapes, computer discs, X-ray film, plain-paper copiers, and numerous other products based on sophisticated research.[4]

High-technology industries (electronics and science-related businesses) developed rapidly in the postwar era. The computer age in the Twin Cities began in earnest when Engineering Research Associates, Inc. — founded in 1946 — designed a system called "Atlas" in a St. Paul building that formerly had been used as a foundry, a warehouse, and a wartime glider plant. "The building had high ceilings with skylights which opened and closed by pulleys," one historian wrote, "but they operated very slowly, and when it rained the scientists and engineers could expect to get drenched before the skylights were closed." ERA was bought by Remington Rand, Inc., which merged with the Sperry Corporation; Sperry Rand centralized its computer operations in its Univac Division based in the St. Paul area. Honeywell's entrance into the computer business, the organization of Control Data Corporation, the proliferation of smaller firms making computer products, and the success of Medtronic, Inc. (a producer of cardiac pacemakers and other health products), attracted notable attention to the Twin Cities. Although the prophecy made in 1960 that the cities soon would be the world's electronics capital was not fulfilled, they did become a major center.[5]

Efficient, low-cost transportation offsetting the long distances from major markets continued to be central to the prosperity of St. Paul and Minneapolis. One of the ongoing battles was for the revival of Mississippi River navigation that had diminished with the onset of the railroad age. River-route supporters won a victory in 1917 when completion of the High (or Ford) Dam carried navigation into Minneapolis as far as the Washington Avenue Bridge below the falls. The Twins suffered a loss five years later, however. For many years the Interstate Commerce Commission's recognition of the Mississippi River as a competitive transportation route had moderated railroad freight rates. The commission eliminated this advantage when it ruled in 1922 that water competition on the river above St. Louis was no longer a significant factor in rate making. Faced with higher freight rates, the Twins campaigned with other communities in the valley to restore the consideration of competitive water transportation. They succeeded in 1932, and subsequently army engineers completed a nine-foot channel that floated craft through a series of locks from St. Louis to Minneapolis. The efforts of more than a century culminated in 1963 when locks and a canal built around the falls created a harbor in the heart of the Mill City.[6]

Air transportation underwent tremendous expansion in the new era. Carrying freight as well as passengers, an increasing number of airlines serving the Twin Cities made them a traffic center. Northwest Airlines, the pioneer, locally based line, in 1945 became the first northern transcontinental, flying between New York and Seattle via the Twin Cities on a route called the "Northwest Passage." In ceremonies reminiscent of those held in 1883 when the Northern Pacific drove the golden spike linking its east-west rails, Northwest carried a bottle of water from the Atlantic Ocean to the Pacific and another from the Pacific to the Atlantic. Two years later the airline saluted the international age by inaugurating service to the Orient. North Central Airlines, a major carrier based in the Twin Cities since 1952, exchanged its old name for a new one in 1979, when it merged with Southern Airways to become Republic Airlines, Inc.[7]

Railroading, too, underwent changes in the postwar era. The renewed boom in automobile ownership as well as the availability of air travel eroded railroad passenger traffic. In 1971 government-subsidized Amtrak took over rail passenger service and within the decade abandoned the great depots in the Twin Cities, once alive with the sounds of train calls, for a modest station. The railroad freight business prospered, but the historic names of Great Northern and Northern Pacific disappeared in 1970 when the companies became part of a merger producing Burlington Northern Inc. Eleven years later the principal corporate office moved from St. Paul to Seattle.[8]

As train travel declined, railroad buff Stephen Leuthold has written, nostalgia for the vanished Great Train Experience evoked a beguiling fantasy: "Order a chilled glass as the silver streak bisects the sun-brilliant countryside. Night falls. Sleep comes easily with the gentle sway, the rhythmic clicking of wheels on the tracks, the fading wail of the whistle. Awaken to a gentle knock, and, then, steaming coffee, bacon, eggs and fresh orange juice, immaculately served in the dining car, where the linen is crisp, and the flowers fresh."[8]

The increasing numbers of new automobile owners — now released from the limitations of wartime rationing — diminished travel on the interurban transit system and on overland buses as well as on trains. Cars also helped to speed the development of a suburban ring around the cities and population expansion into the countryside and towns beyond the suburbs.[9]

A dramatic example of the fast-rising suburbs was Bloomington, the "instant city" located south of Minneapolis. When the Twins were anchoring their communities on the banks of the Mississippi River in the mid-nineteenth century, the area that became Bloomington Township was the home of Chief Cloudman's Dakota people (who had moved there from Lake Calhoun), missionaries who offered white man's temporal salvation by teaching agriculture, and a few other settlers. A township of 3,647 in 1940, Bloomington experienced a postwar boom that brought the population count to 81,970 in 1970 before leveling off as the fourth largest city in the state in the following decade. Bulldozers ripped up soil that had once nurtured crops to clear the way for acres of houses, while businesses like Control Data Corporation and Toro Company relocated there from the Twin Cities. Office buildings, motels, restaurants, shopping and service centers, theaters, and a sports stadium mushroomed in the suburb, which was bound to the central cities by a freeway system and was near the Minneapolis-St. Paul International Airport (formerly Wold-Chamberlain Field).[10]

In the years between 1946 and 1970, 405 industrial firms left the central cities for the suburbs. Although Bloomington was a desirable location, many businesses moved to other outlying areas. Headlining the rush to the open land were General Mills, Inc., abandoning its headquarters in downtown Minneapolis for Golden Valley; 3M, building a headquarters and research center in Maplewood; and St. Paul's Univac, establishing a new plant in Eagan Township. Prominent downtown retailers also looked outward, among them the Dayton Company, which built Southdale in Edina while retaining its downtown Minneapolis store and building a new one in downtown St. Paul. Advertised at its opening in 1956 as "the largest shopping center in the world under one roof," Southdale — the first of several "Dales" shopping centers — enclosed seventy shops in a climate-controlled expanse centered on a garden court where flowers, trees, and birds provided a "summery motif throughout the entire year." Truck terminals in Roseville, touted in 1960 as the greatest concentration of its kind in the nation, typified the suburban trend as the industry expanded both short-haul and long-haul operations.[11]

Relationships among communities in the metropolitan area grew increasingly complex in the suburban age. These relationships evolved in a milieu of continued tensions between Minneapolis and St. Paul. Time and again, as they had earlier, spokesmen announcing postwar co-operative ventures commented that the days of divisiveness were past; and yet, time and again evidence of the cities' uneasy alliance percolated to the surface. The recognition accorded Minneapolis as the dominant and more aggressive twin often irritated St. Paul. When the *Minneapolis Tribune* observed in 1957 that the city "is now surrounded by suburbs (if you include St. Paul in that category)," the

St. Paul Pioneer Press responded that its city "is possibly a little too big to be classified as a suburb." In another instance a *St. Paul Dispatch* staff writer, piqued by the acquisition in 1976 of the city's Hilton Hotel by a Mill City corporation, cited it as one more example of the "Minneapolization" of St. Paul.[12]

The identification of communities within the metropolitan area as "St. Paul" or "Minneapolis" suburbs further reflected the Twins' continuing separatism. Migrating businesses tended to relocate within their home city's sphere; many residents viewed the metropolis as two distinct areas composed of the two cities, each with its own suburbs. The new titles of the commercial bodies were further indications of the dual hegemony. The Saint Paul Chamber of Commerce became the Saint Paul Area Chamber of Commerce, and the Minneapolis Chamber of Commerce changed to the Greater Minneapolis Chamber of Commerce. Conversely, both chambers promoted the cohesiveness of the two halves by sponsoring the Council of Twin Cities Metropolitan Area Chambers of Commerce as well as other organizations formed to foster common interests.[13]

The Twin Cities' ambivalent attitudes toward the suburbs further complicated community relations. While praising the values of suburban living, for example, a writer for the Minneapolis chamber's magazine described in 1973 what might happen to a taxicab passenger wandering in the suburbs in search of the "Ajax Building on Acme Avenue and Sarah Street." He observed, "After the cabbie has checked in two service stations, you'll find that once you were within 100 feet of the Ajax Building. But Acme Avenue is now Widget Way because the Acme Company decided not to rent some building, and Sarah Street is now Doris Drive because the developer quit going out with Sarah when he met Doris." More soberly the magazine in 1950 indicated mixed feelings about suburban development: it saluted Minneapolis as the center of a "magnificent urban Eden," but speculated that the city itself might become "a doughnut with a hole of blight."[14]

Hit hard by the flight to the suburbs and concerned about deterioration in the central cities, the Twins turned to regeneration with all of the energy that had been pent up during depression and war. A number of government agencies, citizens' organizations, and private enterprises participated in the urban redevelopment movements that began in the late 1940s; the intensity of the unfolding processes varied from decade to decade and from city to city. Despite the many plans flowing from the drawing boards, the efforts were often marred by confusion among multiple authorities with their fingers in the pie, conflicting citizen interests, and piecemeal projects not firmly embedded in an effective over-all scheme.

In the course of hectic redevelopment activities that crescendoed in the 1960s and 1970s, some developers demolished old buildings to make way for new ones, while preservationists adapted others for new uses and slowed the course of destruction. Often old neighborhoods carrying with them deep-rooted associations either disappeared forever under the bulldozer's onslaught or emerged revitalized by urban rehabilitaters. New neighborhoods coalesced in clusters of towers, townhouses, apartments, or condominiums built to meet the needs of the fast-increasing numbers of single people, senior citizens, and others seeking different life-styles. Freeways disrupted old patterns and created new ones, industrial parks carved within the cities' limits appeared, and the downtowns — blighted holes in the doughnuts — traveled their troubled routes to renascence.

Many Twin Citians experienced urban redevelopment most keenly on the level of neighborhoods, communities that St. Paul writer Kathryn Boardman has called "The Cities Within." Writing in 1969 about St. Paul's Fourteenth Street (east of the capitol and north of downtown), she described an old neighborhood that was "European and exciting," where "houses, duplexes and apartments were packed tight together so that women on one second story porch could talk easily with friends on the one next door" and small stores displayed kosher salami in their windows. She traced the changes in the community as the old residents moved out and others drifted into the deteriorating dwellings, and then through urban renewal that cleared the way for freeways and the new St. Paul-Ramsey Medical Center.[15]

Although former inhabitants may have considered Fourteenth Street "a good place to be from," other uprootings were more poignant. A resident of the Beltrami neighborhood in Northeast Minneapolis, once called "Dog Town," recalled that the freeway took "all the old-timers, all the old people who had been here for years. I had a brother lived on Lincoln Street, they took the house six years ago now and they still ain't doing nothing with it. They ruined this neighborhood as far as that goes — the freeways ruined this neighborhood. All the people have to go — they kicked them out of here."[16]

Controversy and dissent accompanied urban renewal in other neighborhoods, notably in the Cedar-Riverside area near the University of Minnesota's west-bank campus, where renovation began in the 1960s. No redevelopments, however, attracted more widespread interest than the two massive downtown projects. Punctuated by blighted blocks, empty store windows, darkened theater marquees, and deteriorating buildings, the downtowns seemed to lack the vigor that had once made them vital centers of their cities. "The disease might be called 'Death at The

Heart,'" Gene Struble of the Saint Paul Area Chamber of Commerce wrote in 1966. Spurred by warning signals flashing from Southdale and other retail and commercial developments in the suburbs, the Twins submitted their downtowns to radical remedial surgery.[17]

Minneapolis led the way in the long, erratic, and sometimes chaotic process of revitalizing its core into a complex hailed in 1979 as "a model of successful urban design." After a slow beginning, public and private redevelopers in the 1960s and 1970s made great progress in refashioning the downtown. Patterned with gleaming new buildings, a mall, plazas, gardens, fountains, and connecting skyways likened to "a modern-day version of the canals of Venice," the refurbished city might have delighted planners who in 1917 had envisioned a beautiful metropolis. Among milestones in renewal were the Gateway project to remove the "festering cancer" in the lower loop, the Nicollet Mall, and — superceding the Foshay Tower as the city's most prominent skyscraper — the 57-story IDS Center, called "one of the most icily elegant buildings in the world."[18]

St. Paul, which had been the focus of a modest renewal program even before the war ended, had expanded its vision by the early 1960s to a "downtown wonderland" encompassing many modern buildings, courts, flower beds, parks, and a network of skyways. The pace was slow in the 1960s and early 1970s, however, despite such evidence of rejuvenation as the new Civic Center, Dayton's department store, downtown luxury apartments, the St. Paul Hilton (later Radisson) Hotel, the Osborn Plaza, and beginnings of the skyway system. Lagging developments that left the downtown with a ragged look inspired mordant witticisms. One businessman commented that downtown was "a nice place to live — but no place to visit," while another declared that it was "the place to go if you wanted to be alone."[19]

In the late 1970s redevelopment momentum powered by Oxford Properties, Inc., of Canada, Curtis L. Carlson of Minneapolis, the St. Paul Port Authority, Mayor George Latimer, and many civic leaders brought stirring times to the city. Symbolic of the revival is the story of the site dubbed "Super Hole," a cavity that yawned as a reproach to civic pride for several years after razing had prepared the way for new construction. On the site of Super Hole rose Town Square, opened in 1980, with twin office towers, four levels of shops and restaurants, and a top-floor park larger than a football field. Located near the new Radisson Plaza and Northwest Crossing — a mall with shops modeled on turn-of-the-century buildings— Town Square inspired an observer to call it "a study in soaring granite and angular glass that marks the city's comeback."[20]

Such concentrated activity had not occurred since the 1880s growth explosion when construction began on many of the buildings that had given the downtowns their character. Ears assaulted by vibrating jackhammers and eyes drawn upward to towering cranes, sidewalk superintendents at the decade's turn wondered if the downtowns would ever be finished. Others seeking cohesion in the maze wondered where it was all leading. A local writer observed that while the buildings enhanced the urban design in both cities, "they fail in large part to achieve what the best architecture is capable of creating — excitement, drama, eloquence and delight." A visiting critic expanded on this negative view when he described some of the buildings as "almost identical" to those their architect had designed elsewhere and lamented the lack of a "totality that would permit residents to describe the physical look of their city in a few words."[21]

With downtown renascence came a flowering of the arts in the 1960s and 1970s, springing from deeply planted roots and from new growth. The rich cultural fare, St. Paul critic David Hawley commented, gave the Twin Cities "an artistic reputation of Florentine proportions." Several organizations founded in the nineteenth and early twentieth centuries remained important parts of the cultural scene, including the Schubert Club, the Apollo Club, the Science Museum of Minnesota (formerly the St. Paul Institute of Arts and Sciences), the Minnesota Orchestra (formerly the Minneapolis Symphony), the Minneapolis Institute of Arts, the Minnesota Museum of Art (formerly the St. Paul Art Center), and the Walker Art Center. A glittering array of new organizations also entered the field — prominent among them the Tyrone Guthrie Theater, described as "a dreadnought of the American regional-theater movement," and the St. Paul Chamber Orchestra, which under the direction of Dennis Russell Davies and Pinchas Zukerman, his successor, won a respected place in the world of music.[22]

Among others joining the crowded ranks of newcomers to the scene were the Actors Theatre of St. Paul, the Cricket, Children's, and Chimera theaters, the Minnesota Dance Theatre, and the Minnesota Opera Company. Touring companies of the Metropolitan Opera and the American Ballet Theatre provided additional opportunities to enjoy the performing arts. Minnesota Public Radio broadcast cultural programs; one of its most popular features was Garrison Keillor's "Prairie Home Companion," which made the fictional Lake Wobegon, Powdermilk Biscuits, and St. Paul's World Theater known across the country. And new buildings — Orchestra Hall, the Walker Art Center, the St. Paul Arts and Science Center, O'Shaughnessy Auditorium, and the Ordway Music Theater, under construction in 1983 — affirmed Twin Citians' dedication to art, music, and the theater.

The extensive cultural activities in the Twin Cities and the residents' enthusiasm for participating in them often aroused national interest. In the mid-1970s a Ford Foundation survey of individual exposures to the performing arts, including movies, "popular" music, and cultural fare more narrowly defined, revealed that, among the twelve metropolitan areas investigated, the Twins ranked second only to New York. Businesses, foundations, private donors, and government gave generous financial support to a wide variety of cultural groups, while hundreds of volunteers contributed their talents as performers, organizers, and behind-the-scenes workers. Some observers, however, viewed the cultural landscape as something less than Florentine. The reduction of government support from the early 1980s brought financial problems even to major institutions. At times less well-established groups faltered and the public's enthusiasm seemed limited to the tried and the true. Too, local artists and performers often expressed discontent, venting their feelings in such comments as "Schlock sells" and "Picasso would starve in this town," or labeling the Twins as "insular" and "provincial."[23]

The cities were in the mainstream in their enthusiasm for popular music. Although music from the past still had charms for those who had grown up with it, new generations turned from the big-band sounds, boogie, and bop to a rhythm-and-blues form called rock and roll. Beginning in the 1950s, the music of Elvis Presley, the Beatles, and others attracted fans as ardent as the bobby-soxers who earlier had made Frank Sinatra their idol. Some performers featured themes of protest — the protest of a "beat" generation and the hippies, a disenchanted youth fashioning their own culture outside the mainstream of the "establishment." They danced the twist, watusi, hully gully, monkey, dog, frug, go-go, and swim. They heard the music played on records, radio, and television, and in discotheques and the movies. Many of their elders joined them, danced in the discos, and despite perils to their spines and lingering nostalgia for the old music, carried the new music into more staid surroundings. With the civil rights movement and the antiwar feeling engendered by the war in Vietnam, the protest songs changed to reflect a more sober mood and encourage an active role in bringing about social and political reforms. Minnesota-born Bob Dylan wrote, recorded, and performed as the voice of those who worked to end discrimination and war.[24]

Television, the long-heralded new purveyor of popular culture, arrived in the nation's living rooms at the same time that the new music swept in. A local journal commenting in 1927 on the technology making television feasible had ventured to say that "it will some day be utilized in a commercial way and take its place among the wonders of radio and other modern marvels." Although home sets were still a rarity in the immediate postwar period, by 1948 there were an estimated 12,500 of them in the Twin Cities; two years later the number had jumped to 100,500. Popular performers like Jack Benny migrated from radio to television; the names of Arthur Godfrey, Milton Berle, and Ed Sullivan became household words across the nation, and everyone seemed to love "Lucy," enacted by zany movie comedienne Lucille Ball. Local stars known to audiences through other media gained new fans after appearing on television; among those making the transition were radio personality Arle Haeberle, newspaper columnist Cedric Adams, and — proving that his music did indeed go on and on — polka-band leader Whoopee John Wilfahrt.[25]

The popularity of television coincided with the advent of big-league sports in the Twin Cities. The parade began in 1947-48 with the Minneapolis Lakers, members of the National Basketball League (later Association). While winning several national and world championships, the team was the pride of the city. Players George Mikan, Jim Pollard, Whitey Skoog, Slater Martin, and Vern Mikkelsen were heroes in the mold of the Golden Gophers who had lighted up dark depression years. Mikan was the best of them. Selected by the Associated Press as the greatest player of the first half of the century, he commanded such respect that Madison Square Garden billed Laker games with the New York City team as "George Mikan vs. Knicks." Nevertheless, the team's years of glory were numbered. Its success and drawing power waned in the late 1950s as its aging stars retired; in 1960 the franchise moved to Los Angeles.[26]

The appearance of major-league baseball and football in the 1961 season may have eased regrets about losing the Lakers. Despite attachments to the Saints and the Millers, big-league baseball fever ran high in the cities during the 1950s. Learning that the support of both cities and an adequate stadium were prerequisites for getting a team, the cities co-operated for a time, but they parted company on the issue of stadium location. Predictably, each built its own.[27]

Overendowed with stadiums — Metropolitan built in Bloomington in 1956 and Midway completed in St. Paul the following year — the cities continued trying to attract a team. Success crowned their efforts when Calvin Griffith's Washington Senators transferred to Minnesota. Renamed the Minnesota Twins, the American League team took to the field in 1961 — at Metropolitan Stadium. While fans at the Met cheered new stars like Harmon "Killer" Killebrew and Camilo Pascual, Midway became an underused white elephant. It has now been razed, and the site is part of a housing and business complex called Energy Park.

Twin Citians, joined by Duluthian Oluf Haugsrud, pressed their campaign for a major-league football team to join the Twins at the Met. With the exception of the Duluth Eskimos, fielded by Haugsrud and others in the 1920s, Minnesota had never had a professional football team. The promoters won their bid for a National Football League franchise after complex maneuvers in the Machiavellian world of big-league sports. Incorporating as Minnesota Pro Football, Inc., the representatives of the three cities named their team the Vikings for the fearless Nordics who possessed "an aggressive desire and will to win." When the team began playing in 1961, Bert Rose was the manager and Norman Van Brocklin was the coach. One of their first moves was to draft Francis "Fran" Tarkenton, the now legendary quarterback who with other Viking warriors drew fans from far and wide into the bleachers at the Met and glued thousands of others to television sets.[28]

Their big-league appetites unsated, Twin Cities promoters pursued hockey and soccer teams. In 1967 they secured a franchise for the Minnesota North Stars from the National Hockey League. Playing at the newly built Metropolitan Sports Center near the Met Stadium in Bloomington, the North Stars had sole claim to local fans' loyalty until the Minnesota Fighting Saints took to the ice in 1972 at the St. Paul Civic Center as members of the rival World Hockey Association. Although the cities had many avid hockey fans, they were not numerous enough to support two major-league teams. In "an economic war of survival," the Saints went down in 1976, and another WHA team bearing the same name met an identical fate the following year.[29]

The luster of the sports shrine in Bloomington increased in 1976 when the Twin Cities acquired a soccer team called the Kicks. The North American Soccer League team's owners chose the turf trod by the Twins and Vikings after considering Midway Stadium in their search for a home. The Kicks' career ended in 1981, however, after foreign investors withdrew their support in the face of waning attendance.[30]

The days of Metropolitan Stadium were numbered by the time the Kicks took to the field. Spurred by the dissatisfaction of the Twins and the Vikings with the Met, the two cities' chambers of commerce by the mid-1970s had begun work on plans for a new stadium, preferably domed. The issues involved — need, financing, stadium type, and location — aroused heated controversy. Sports fans, taxpayers, civic leaders, and team owners leaped into the fray with notable rancor. To the Twins' claim that playing in an outdoor stadium exposed team and fans to Minnesota's whimsical weather and thereby reduced crowd size came the riposte that a winning team would do wonders for attendance; and to apprehensions expressed about the majors deserting the cities for more hospitable

236

homes came the accusation, "Blackmail!" Finally the struggle ended. The Twin Cities would have a new domed stadium, it would be located in downtown Minneapolis, and it would be called the Hubert H. Humphrey Metrodome. On October 2, 1981, powerful electric fans slowly lifted acres of fabric into a huge dome billowing over the new stadium, and Twin Citians continued a debate on its merits that may last through the decade.[31]

Sports fans did not expend all of their enthusiasm on the big leagues. Intercollegiate sports retained the popularity they had enjoyed for many years. And thousands of people still gathered annually in the Twin Cities to cheer their favorite teams during the state high school basketball tournament. From 1945 high school hockey teams playing a yearly championship tournament in the Twin Cities elevated the event to the level of a spectacle. Reporting on the tournament held in the St. Paul Civic Center in 1983, *USA Today* commented that the "arena's 15,706 seats are filled and the aisles overflowing, as they will be for each of 11 games over three days. Hotels are filled. Queues for standing-room tickets are the norm. The fans' fervor knows few bounds."[32]

Big-league sports, big-league culture, urban renewal, and high-technology businesses enhanced the Twins' traditional role as the commercial, financial, marketing, manufacturing, transportation, and entertainment center for the Upper Midwest and helped create cities that residents and visitors alike admired. In 1976 Wayne Thompson, the former city manager of Oakland, California, who moved to Minneapolis a decade earlier, observed, "This is the last outpost of urban paradise. The problems hit here last."[33]

Urban problems may have been less acute in the Twin Cities than they were in many other parts of the nation, but hit they did, affirming once more that national concerns had local repercussions. Women, American Indians, blacks, Mexican Americans, and other groups struggling for improved status — as well as those experiencing war, drug abuse, or poverty — knew that the Twin Cities were no paradise. Not since the Great Depression when the system had to answer for the economic debacle had there been greater alienation and militance. Once again in the 1960s and 1970s protesters marched on the state capitol, carrying signs, singing, chanting, and making speeches from its broad, high steps. Once again in scenes reminiscent of the depression there was turmoil in the streets as protesters decried the quality of their niche in Eden and antiwar demonstrators at the University of Minnesota clashed with police.[34]

In some ways the antiwar movement was more pervasive than any of the others. The Korean War, waged from 1950 to 1953, provoked protests. Nothing in the nation's history of peace movements, however, equaled the widespread vocal opposition to war during the Vietnam conflict, fought between 1957 and 1975. Chiefly at colleges and universities, groups such as the Minnesota Committee to End the War in Vietnam became active as the war escalated, sponsoring street demonstrations, supporting the cause of men prosecuted for refusing to fight, and publishing a newsletter called *Vietnam Crisis*. Antiwar protests did not end with the close of the Vietnam conflict. In 1982 and 1983, for example, demonstrators besieged Honeywell's Minneapolis office to protest the company's manufacture of weapons, evoking grim images of past wars and visions of a dangerous future.[35]

Conflicts in Southeast Asia during and following the Vietnam War brought large numbers of immigrants to the Twin Cities, much like the flood of Displaced Persons who settled there in the wake of World War II. One visitor in 1981 commented that the cities were "not nearly as exciting as a New Orleans or a New York, with their strong mix of ethnicities. It makes it [*the urban area*] much less vital in terms of language and culture and restaurants." If indeed the bold ethnic patterns once characterizing the Twins had faded into homogeneity, the new immigrants brightened the fabric. Between 1975 and 1981 newcomers settling in Minnesota — including Vietnamese, Lao, Cambodians, and Hmong — numbered 21,500 and a large majority of them were in the Twin Cities. On the streets, in the stores, in the churches, and in the businesses they operated, the immigrants contributed to a sense of international culture and kept green the memory of a war that had touched the conscience of many Twin Citians.[36]

The immigrants also inadvertently kindled new urban tensions. In St. Paul, where many of the Indochinese settled, tensions related to housing and jobs evolved between them and the blacks, and the Mexican Americans complained that the government was "overlooking the needs of the county's largest minority to cater to politically popular Asian refugees." In 1981, when an estimated 7,000 refugees depended on some kind of public assistance, the Ramsey County Board of Commissioners, citing waiting lists and strains on resources, called for a moratorium on "primary resettlement" in the area. The *St. Paul Pioneer Press* responded to the move in a stinging editorial, calling it "insulting to a people who are trying to become good American citizens, and it's insulting to the rest of Ramsey County as well."[37]

Many other concerns in the Twin Cities emerged as the metropolitan area sprawled over several counties, encompassing nearly three hundred local government units with interrelated problems that could not be resolved by any one of them. Sewage, air pollution, water supply, freeway locations, airport location and control, interurban transportation, and park development were issues that transcended the boundaries of municipalities, counties, townships, and other local political units. Moreover, proliferating federal government programs that addressed urban problems often required area-wide planning as a condition for funding.[38]

Twin Cities area leaders had long been active in promoting a metropolitan approach to metropolitan problems. Important steps along the way were the Minneapolis-St. Paul Sanitary District established in 1933, the Metropolitan Airports Commission founded ten years later, and in the postwar period the continuing process of creating special districts and authorities for particular functions. A long stride toward a broader approach occurred in 1957 with the inauguration of the Twin Cities Metropolitan Planning Commission, which not only did fundamental work in area-wide planning but further heightened metropolitan consciousness.[39]

In 1967 the state legislature created the Metropolitan Council as a decision-making as well as a planning organization to succeed the commission. The council, heralded as "the first of its kind in the U.S.," became less than an all-purpose metropolitan government and greater than the aggregate of the special-function commissions through which it operated. It also gave the area cohesion and direction without replacing the traditional governmental structure.[40]

Adding sinews to the economic, social, and cultural bonds forged over many decades, the council strengthened the identity of the Twins as part of a metropolitan complex. The identity is demonstrated in a symbol as homely as the *Minneapolis-St. Paul Metro Area Business to Business Directory* — an indexed guide to the yellow pages that lists products and services used by businesses in both cities. Its companion volumes, the general telephone directories, indicate the separateness of cities that is, nonetheless, temporized. Each city has its own "book" with white- and yellow-page listings for the central city and its "metropolitan area," and each book is studded with cross listings. The abolition in 1954 of tolls on calls between the cities as well as between the cities and most of the suburbs added to the sense of unity. Increasingly, the local media referred to "the metro area." The cities are indeed the core of a metropolis that in some ways is indivisible; they are also Twins. And they remain nonidentical Twins, each bearing the stamp of distinctive as well as common pasts and both marked by the scars of their long contention.

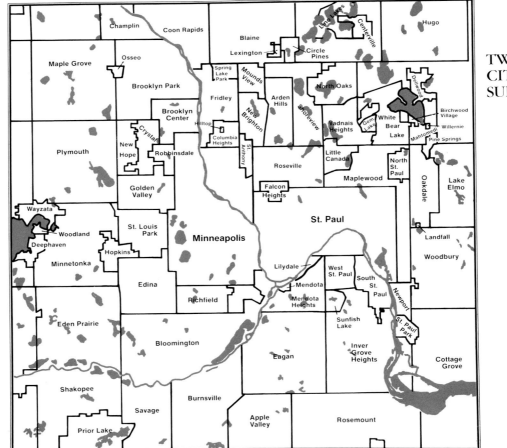

TWIN
CITIES
SUBURBS

Jitterbuggers competed in a dance contest in the Minneapolis Auditorium during the 1947 Aquatennial. The *Minneapolis Star* commented that "It takes a fly deuce to cover all spots with such boogity-boogity plank-pounding," translated as "It takes an alert pair to cope with such lively steps." The oldsters competed in rhumba, tango, fox trot, and Viennese waltz contests at the auditorium.

People gathered at Seventh and Wabasha streets, St. Paul, taking advantage of a downtown "family night" on September 4, 1952. The Twin City Rapid Transit Company offered free one-way rides and gave its riders chances on free admission to the movies. Patrons crowded some theater entrances to check their numbers against the posted list of winners. The transit company completed the conversion from streetcars to buses in St. Paul the next year, but some of the car tracks are still in place under a layer of asphalt.

With gold papier-mâché horses and a bathing beauty, the float of Brown and Bigelow, St. Paul, in the 1949 Minneapolis Aquatennial parade saluted the Minnesota Territorial Centennial. In this year St. Paul also marked the one hundredth anniversary of its incorporation as a town.

Beatrice "BeBe" Shopp of Hopkins, who became Miss America of 1948, demonstrated the talent on the vibraharp that helped her win the competition.

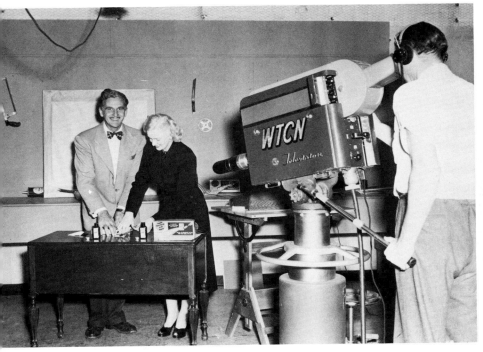

On this simple set, WTCN-TV produced a live local show called "The Idea House" in 1949. It featured Clifford John Rian, who used the name John Ford during his career at WTCN radio and television. "The man with the city slicker sort of mustache" and breezy manner drew varied assignments as an announcer, newscaster, and master of ceremonies.

This visitor to the home of the Raymond Horihan family, 732 Euclid Street, St. Paul, might be waiting to see a televised home game of the Millers *vs.* the Saints or one of the other popular features offered in the 1950s. Early owners of television sets, like early radio owners before them, often invited guests over to enjoy this new kind of entertainment.

Twin Cities families could find pleasures in their own back yards during fair weather. A home in the suburbs, with a large yard and a patio, was a popular dream in the postwar period.

"Why Worry? Come to A Friendly Place When in Distress," urged Joseph W. Smilow, advertising the services of his pawnshop at 28 Washington Avenue South, Minneapolis, seen here about 1950. By the late 1950s, as urban renewal claimed the Gateway District, the shop had been razed.

The Dayton Company on Nicollet Avenue between Seventh and Eighth streets, Minneapolis, displayed a new world of fashions and carefree fabrics for its 1957 Valentine's Day promotion.

School children studying the United Nations about 1950 were part of a generation that acquired a new international viewpoint. As they were pledging themselves to live "together in the same world at peace," the Korean War broke out.

Tan Ming Wang of Singapore, studying in 1951 for a graduate degree in journalism, conferred with Professor Mitchell V. Charnley of the University of Minnesota. The influx of foreign students as well as Displaced Persons in the postwar years added to the Twin Cities' international flavor.

Hungarian Freedom Fighters arriving in Minnesota in December, 1956, testified to the turmoil of the postwar world. Governor Orville Freeman (left) welcomed refugees who fled their homeland after an unsuccessful revolt against Soviet domination. During the following year about 300 more joined compatriots who had come to St. Paul and Minneapolis as Displaced Persons after World War II.

Tommy Heath (front row, second from left), manager of the Minneapolis Millers, and team members celebrated capturing the 1950 American Association pennant in the locker room at Nicollet Park after beating Kansas City. It was the eighth pennant win for the Millers in the associa-

tion's 49-year history — a record topped only by the St. Paul Saints, who had won the pennant nine times. Hoyt Wilhelm, who pitched the 8-4 victory game and went on to a notable major-league career, is the jubilant, trouserless figure to the right.

Rance Pless of the Minneapolis Millers instructed a Little Leaguer in the fine points of the game about 1955 in Nicollet Park. The Little League movement began in Williamsport, Pennsylvania, in 1939 and spread rapidly in the postwar era. Boys aged eight to twelve played games of six innings on diamonds two-thirds the size of a professional field.

The Minneapolis Lakers smiled during their championship days. Appearing, left to right, about 1950, are Slater Martin, Don

Carlson, Herman Schaefer, Vern Mikkelson, George Mikan, Jim Pollard, Arnie Ferrin, and Tony Jaros.

Skaters in 1949 in a warming house at Franklin Steele Square, Portland Avenue and Sixteenth Street East, Minneapolis, prepared to take to the rink. The Twin Cities were in the mainstream of the early twentieth-century movement that intensified the use of parks as playgrounds. Through the years the cities built a growing number of facilities for winter and summer sports.

The wreckers swept away many buildings as urban renewal progressed in a deteriorated area near the state capitol. The George Benz mansion at 5 Sherburne Avenue, razed in 1948, had been admired after its construction in 1888 for its "superb view over the entire city." In the 1980s the site was a parking lot.

A crane with an eighty-five-foot boom lowered a two-ton bell from the steeple of the Trinity Lutheran Church at Wabasha and Tilton streets, St. Paul, in 1952. Then the structure, built in 1885, was razed to make way for the new Capitol Approach. Since the congregation's new church did not have a steeple to house the bell, it was sold to the Emanuel Lutheran Church.

The Capitol Approach in 1953 took on some of its present contours. The State Office Building is to the left of the capitol and the Historical Building is to the right. The Central Presbyterian Church is in the foreground. Most of the structures between the Historical Building and the church were later removed to make way for the Centennial Building, the Armory, and Interstate 94.

Minneapolis in 1962 rented the areas cleared for redevelopment for large parking lots until construction could begin. The post office is in the foreground. The Third Avenue Bridge is to the left and the Hennepin Avenue Bridge to the right.

The Gateway Building, completed in 1915 at the convergence of Nicollet, Hennepin, and Washington avenues in Minneapolis, was part of an early attempt to counteract decay in the area. In 1953 it succumbed as the Gateway Center project undertook to renew the heart of the old city that had deteriorated into a skid row.

In 1962 — about the time this picture was made — the Minneapolis Housing and Redevelopment Authority reported that it had acquired 209 properties in the Lower Loop and had cleared away 176 structures. The building in the background is the main post office at First Street and Marquette Avenue.

Many of the buildings razed during redevelopment passed from the scene unmourned. Not so the Metropolitan Building, a heap of rubble that mocked its former grandeur in 1962. The superstructure of the new Sheraton-Ritz Hotel at 315 Nicollet Avenue is rising in the background.

Nicollet Mall, a key part of downtown revitalization, became "a pedestrian spine linking Gateway Center to the heart of the retail district." The strip, opened in 1967, was beautified with trees, flowers, fountains, and broad sidewalks. One of the heated shelters provided for bus passengers stands in the foreground.

In answer to growing numbers of students, the University of Minnesota campus spread across the river to the west bank by 1965. The towers of the new social science and business administration buildings are in the foreground, the Southeast Minneapolis industrial district and the east-bank campus are in the background, and the new Washington Avenue Bridge is under construction at left center. In 1965 daytime enrollment on the Twin Cities campuses reached 36,789, and the total enrollment on all campuses (42,178) was the highest in the university's history to that date.

A yawning hole in downtown St. Paul in 1962 awaited the construction of Dayton's new store on the block bounded by Wabasha Street, Cedar Street, and Sixth and Seventh streets.

Across from Dayton's, at Sixth and Wabasha streets, several small shops lost their homes during demolition in 1967. The Northern Federal Savings and Loan Association constructed a building on this site.

The eagle sculpture that once adorned the New York Life Insurance Building at Minnesota and Sixth streets, St. Paul, found a new home by a parking ramp at Fourth and Jackson streets when the building was razed in 1967. The eagle, created in 1891 by the New York studio of Augustus Saint-Gaudens, was the insignia of the life insurance company. By the mid-1960s preservationists were salvaging distinctive parts of old buildings.

247

A blighted dwelling at 508-510 Fremont Avenue North, Minneapolis, was ready in 1957 for removal as part of the Glenwood urban renewal project. A new housing development called Girard Terrace replaced the old house on the block.

St. Paul lost a former "stately house" when the old St. Luke's Catholic rectory at Lexington and Summit avenues went down in 1953. A portion of St. Luke's church appears to the left. The progress of razing is shown from the rear of the house; the site became a parking lot.

Homes in the old Upper Levee neighborhood in St. Paul were marooned by a flood in 1952. Cresting at 22.02 feet on April 16, the worst flood in the city since 1851 washed over the lowlands and into the downtown district. A destructive flood exceeded this unenviable record in 1965, when the river crested at 26.01 feet, and again in 1969, when it reached 24.52 feet. Long-term flood control measures undertaken after 1965 gradually provided the city with protection from such disasters.

New housing rose quickly in 1958 in the Mt. Airy Homes subsidized-housing project near the state capitol in St. Paul.

Much of the land for the Hi-Lo redevelopment project in Northeast Minneapolis, advertised in 1953, was tax delinquent when the city undertook the project. Builders graded down hills and filled in swamps to create suitable terrain for houses and apartment units.

On County Road F at U.S. Highway 10 and Minnesota Highway 51, workers in 1957 extended a natural gas pipeline from St. Paul to Arden Hills, New Brighton, and Shoreview. As the metropolitan population expanded into outlying suburbs, the demand increased for services such as power and sewer lines. A connection to a central city utility indicated the suburb's St. Paul or Minneapolis orientation.

New housing in 1950 at Twenty-eighth Avenue South and Fifty-fourth Street in Minneapolis helped expand development southeast of Lake Nokomis. Existing transit lines stood ready to handle the increased ridership as new homeowners began commuting to downtown jobs. Undeveloped residential lots were still abundant near the borders of both Twins, but they filled up quickly in the postwar building boom.

A new neighborhood took shape in 1952 on Belmont Lane near Hamline Avenue in Roseville, north of St. Paul. St. Rose of Lima Catholic School, left, overlooked the housing development.

Miracle Mile at Highway 100 and Excelsior Boulevard (viewed from the east above and from the west at right) was one of many shopping centers that sprouted in response to the suburban movement by 1955, the year these pictures were made. Opened in 1951, the center had twenty-six stores and parking space for six hundred cars. Its arrangement —the shops strung out in a line, with a parking lot in front — was typical of the early shopping centers.

In 1958 Lexington Plaza occupied a seven-acre tract at Lexington and Larpenteur avenues in booming Roseville. One of several shopping centers established in the northern suburbs early in the decade, it opened in 1951.

Southdale at France Avenue South and Sixty-sixth Street, seen here in 1958, was the giant among shopping centers at the time. It encompassed eighty-two acres, which included parking space for over five thousand cars. People came from near and far to experience the novelty of shopping there.

The road to Southdale was plainly marked on France Avenue South at Seventy-eighth Street in 1958, when the area was still open country. The Edina water tower appears on the horizon, center. Twenty-four years later, in 1982, the same location presented a suburban view of Edina. The camera looks north along France Avenue at its intersection with Interstate 494, which runs along the former Seventy-eighth Street. The water tower still stands near Sixty-ninth Street.

Lemon-yellow streetcars lined up on Hennepin Avenue, Minneapolis, for their last runs on June 18, 1954. Celebrators included Mayor Eric Hoyer, who won a streetcar in a raffle, Senator Hubert H. Humphrey, who piloted one of the cars, and over three hundred guests of the Twin City Rapid Transit Company. They all boarded eight cars, where they lunched on shrimp, salad, pie, and other delicacies while rumbling from the loop to the Snelling Avenue shops in St. Paul.

A parking ramp for 535 cars at Marquette Avenue and Fourth Street, Minneapolis, seen here in 1953, was built two years earlier when businessmen concerned about a lack of parking space in the loop organized Downtown Auto Park, Inc. Such facilities were part of a major effort by downtown interests to retain business in the face of suburban encroachments.

Students and teachers at Richfield High School, 7001 Harriet Avenue South, were part of the commuting world of the suburbs in 1958. Richfield's population had mushroomed to 37,350 by this year, and like other expanding suburbs it built new schools to keep pace with growth and the postwar baby boom.

This motorist at the First State Bank of St. Paul, 1000 Payne Avenue, in 1958 belonged to a generation growing accustomed to "drive-ins" for banking, movies, hamburgers, car washes, and dry cleaning.

Motorists in 1956 could also drive right up to the White House at present-day 4900 Olson Memorial Highway. To accommodate the auto, every new business tried to provide handy parking.

Express buses speeding along freeway routes furthered the integration of the Twin Cities and the suburbs into a metropolitan area. The Metropolitan Transit Commission, established in 1967, took over ownership of the Twin Cities lines three years later. Even with new riders patronizing buses because of the energy crisis and high downtown parking costs, the system continued to suffer financial woes in the 1980s.

The decade of the 1950s transformed Cottage Grove Township in Washington County, southeast of St. Paul, into a booming suburb. This tract housing development near Highway 61 reflected the area's population spurt from 883 in 1950 to 4,850 by 1960. Farm buildings like those near the water tower often remained part of the landscape in newly developed areas.

White Bear Township residents meeting at Gall School on March 1, 1963, voted to fight annexation of the unincorporated portion of the township to the towns of White Bear Lake and Vadnais Heights. This last unincorporated area in Ramsey County successfully fought the Minnesota Municipal Commission's annexation order.

During ceremonies in 1960 at the Town and Country Club in St. Paul, near the Mississippi River that divides the two cities, Joseph Maun (center), president of the St. Paul Area Chamber of Commerce, argued that Twin Cities rivalry must be ended and that businessmen should "concentrate joint efforts on the entire metropolitan area." Joining Maun in burying the hatchet in a flower bed at the club are Philip Harris (left), vice-president of the Minneapolis chamber, and St. Paul Mayor George Vavoulis. Such issues as the location of a stadium for major-league sports soon showed that the hatchet was still in active use.

A bridge under construction in 1962 across the Mississippi River near the Franklin Avenue Bridge (right) later carried traffic on Interstate 94 connecting the two cities. The aerial photograph looks eastward toward St. Paul. The solid lines on the photo show lands taken for freeway construction.

Resurfacing work on Kellogg Boulevard and other streets in downtown St. Paul resulted in a rush hour traffic jam on Fourth Street in 1967.

This concrete maze, often called "spaghetti junction," is east of downtown Minneapolis where Interstate 94 (foreground) and Interstate 35W meet. This 1983 view looks west. The Twins' two downtowns are only a few minutes apart on Interstate 94.

Concrete ribbons of Interstate 94 sweep under John Ireland Boulevard (foreground) and past downtown St. Paul to the interchange with Interstate 35E in this 1983 aerial view looking southeast toward the Mississippi River.

A new terminal building at the Minneapolis-Saint Paul International Airport was dedicated in 1962. With "'door-less' doors of air" and "a streamlined folded plate concrete roof," the building seemed futuristic to Twin Citians who flocked to see it. Governor Elmer L. Andersen cut the ribbon at the dedication ceremony, also attended by St. Paul Mayor Vavoulis, Minneapolis Mayor Arthur Naftalin, and Lawrence Hall, chairman of the Metropolitan Airports Commission.

More than 46,000 fans gathered at Metropolitan Stadium in Bloomington on July 13, 1965, to watch an All-Star game between the American and National leagues. The National League —assisted by the performance of Willie Mays — won the game 6 to 5. The "Say-Hey Kid," who had played briefly in 1951 with the Millers, led off with a homer, scored the go-ahead run in the seventh inning, and caught a line drive in the eighth to end an American League rally.

The Minnesota Twins, winners of the American League pennant in 1965, played the Los Angeles Dodgers of the National League in the World Series. Fans lined up at Metropolitan Stadium for tickets to the opening game on October 6. Although the Twins defeated the Dodgers 8 to 2 in the opener behind the great pitching of Jim "Mud Cat" Grant, they lost the seven-game series four games to three.

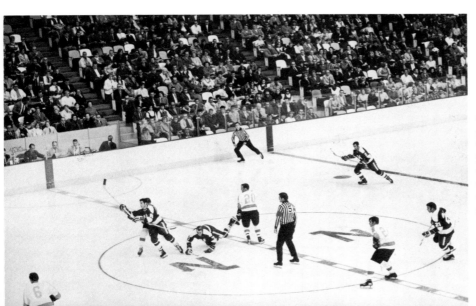

The Minnesota North Stars (dark uniforms) finished third in the Western Division of the National Hockey League in 1969-70 — the team's third season on the ice at the Metropolitan Sports Center. In that season an average of 14,351 fans attended each home game. In 1981 the North Stars reached the Stanley Cup finals, losing the trophy to the New York Islanders by four games to one.

The cloverleaf at Interstate 494 and Cedar Avenue near Metropolitan Stadium changed greatly between 1960 and 1983. The "Bloomington Strip," consisting of motels, restaurants, businesses, and other enterprises, formed along the freeway in those years.

Brown and Bigelow in St. Paul's Midway District, called "the world's largest producer of advertising playing cards," built a new, specially designed offset press for printing them. This firm — and others founded as small printing establishments in the nineteenth century —helped make the Twin Cities one of the nation's leading graphic arts centers.

Among those seated in 1949 at the new copy desk in the Minneapolis Star-Tribune building, Portland Avenue and Fifth Street, was Carl Rowan (at the upper right edge of horseshoe-shaped desk), an early black journalist. Rowan, who was a copy editor for the *Tribune* from 1948 to 1950, later won national fame as a reporter, columnist, author, and diplomat.

The First National Bank of Saint Paul, downtown, decorated the main banking floor to celebrate its centennial year in 1953. The institution began as Parker Paine and Company, a private banking firm.

In 1954, after more than a century of agitation for a harbor at the Falls of St. Anthony, work progressed on a lock below the cataract. In this view looking upstream, the hydro and steam electric plants at the Lower Dam are to the right, and the Stone Arch Bridge reaches across the river to the west-side milling district.

Delmonico's, a grocery store at 1112 Summer Street Northeast in an old Italian neighborhood in Northeast Minneapolis, featured trading stamps that had become popular in the postwar era. Curtis L. Carlson, a Minneapolitan who founded the Gold Bond Stamp Company in 1938 and later entered the hotel, restaurant, food wholesaling, and other businesses, was considered one of the state's "industrial titans" in the 1980s.

A Twin City Freight, Inc., truck left Interstate 35W near County Road C in Roseville in 1983. The TCF terminal was on nearby Long Lake Road; Cummins Diesel Sales, Inc., was conveniently located on Cleveland Avenue North. Trucking became increasingly important in the postwar era and Roseville was still one of the important terminals in the metropolitan area.

General Mills, Inc., moved its headquarters from downtown Minneapolis to Golden Valley in 1958. The new building at 9200 Wayzata Boulevard, seen here a year later, won praise as "one of the most beautifully proportioned structures built in Minnesota this century."

The search of Gamble-Skogmo, Inc., for space to build a major distribution warehouse ended in St. Louis Park. The two-million-dollar, six-and-a-half-acre structure at U.S. Highway 12 and Vernon Avenue is pictured at the time of its dedication in 1960. It then served 550 Gamble stores in the Upper Midwest and northern Michigan, and had docking facilities for a large fleet of trucks.

The Univac File Computer, Model O, was the first commercial computer designed as a general purpose electronic data processing system. Allen Yount, left, of the Remington Rand Univac Division of the Sperry Rand Corporation in 1956 pointed out its features. St. Paul continued as the base for Univac Defense Systems Division, the direct descendant of Engineering Research Associates (ERA).

A General Mills balloon carried a telescope and a television camera 81,800 feet aloft on July 11, 1959, to photograph the sun in one of several "Stratoscope" flights made that summer. The flight, here preparing for its 5:45 A.M. launch at the Lake Elmo airport, was sponsored by the Office of Naval Research and the National Science Foundation.

As a contractor for the National Aeronautics and Space Administration, Honeywell worked on the Mercury, Gemini, and Apollo projects, which in 1969 put two men on the moon. Among the Minneapolis firm's space-age contributions were guidance and control systems for space vehicles, a simulator "bringing the environment of space down to earth," and human-factors studies for the Apollo Project, shown here in 1966.

Women wired computer components about 1978 in Control Data's inner-city manufacturing plant at 277 Twelfth Avenue North, Minneapolis. The operation on the near north side was the company's earliest effort in a campaign to provide jobs for residents of depressed areas.

Medtronic, Inc., began developing the drug administration device pictured here in 1978; the first human implant was made four years later. The mechanism dispenses drugs such as insulin for diabetics in regulated, controlled doses. Other products of the company, headquartered in the suburb of St. Anthony at 3055 Old Highway 8, include heart pacemakers, mechanical heart valves, and instruments for heart monitoring.

The Minneapolis Gateway, the former skid row, had come a long way by 1982. To the left is the arched and columned portico of the Northwestern National Life Insurance Company's building at 20 Washington Avenue South, a distinguished structure designed by Minoru Yamasaki and Associates.

The buildings in the foreground of this 1983 aerial view, showing downtown Minneapolis from the southwest, are part of a major construction project of the 1980s, launched to provide convenient housing in the area between the upper Nicollet Mall and Loring Park. At lower left is Loring Green East, part of a condominium complex. On the edge of the picture at lower right is a corner of the Hyatt Regency Hotel. A "greenway" stretching from the mall to Loring Park lies between the hotel and two other units —1225 La Salle, front, and 1200 on the Mall.

262

"Downtown will never be the same," the *Minneapolis Tribune* observed soon after the completion of the Hubert H. Humphrey Metrodome that brought thousands of sports fans into the area. This 1982 panoramic photograph looks west from Interstate 35W. Symbols of the new and old city form the skyline from Control Data's Business and Technology Center, left, past the IDS Tower, the Hennepin County Government Center, and office and residential towers, to the familiar Gold Medal sign and elevators in the historic milling district, right. Grain cars await movement on the rails in front of the dome, while trucks hauling feed, new cars, and petroleum mingle with the passenger traffic on the freeway.

Part of St. Paul's extensive skyway system spans Sixth Street in this 1983 view looking east. Twenty-four walkways connected twenty-six St. Paul blocks by 1982, when Minneapolis had twenty-five linking thirty blocks. Rising in the background is the new Minnesota Mutual Life Center.

This 1983 view of downtown St. Paul looked west toward Minneapolis, whose towers are visible on the horizon. In the foreground, left to right, are the Wabasha Street Bridge, the Robert Street Bridge with its distinctive arch, the Lower Levee, and, above the levee, to the extreme right, the post office. The city hall-courthouse, facing Kellogg Boulevard (formerly Third Street), is left of the Wabasha Street Bridge, and the Radisson Hotel, also facing on Kellogg, is right of it. The domes of the Cathedral and the state capitol are in the left and right backgrounds, respectively.

A capacity audience of 1,437 people attended opening night at the Tyrone Guthrie Theater in Minneapolis on May 7, 1963. "Well done," Sir Tyrone commented to George Grizzard, who played Hamlet in a production of William Shakespeare's play staged in nineteenth-century dress. Also appearing in the play were Jessica Tandy as Queen Gertrude, Lee Richardson as King Claudius, and Ellen Geer as Ophelia. Critics hailed the Guthrie's commitment to bringing professional theater to audiences outside New York City.

The spotlight was on Scandinavian royalty seated in first-tier boxes at Orchestra Hall, Minneapolis, on September 11, 1982, for a gala "Tonight Scandinavia" concert. The hall, which opened in 1974 on Nicollet Mall at Eleventh Street, has been widely acclaimed for its fine acoustical qualities.

St. Paul's Ordway Music Theater took shape in 1983 facing Rice Park near Landmark Center. This view from the stage looks through the proscenium to the seating area and the rising concrete walls. The structure, designed to resemble "a traditional European opera house," will be the performing home for the Minnesota Opera Company and the St. Paul Chamber Orchestra; the Schubert Club and other organizations will also use the hall.

School children and their teacher watched a volunteer demonstrate spinning techniques at the Science Museum of Minnesota, Tenth and Wabasha streets, St. Paul. In 1983 the museum featured several demonstration groups for children and the general public. The new building, which opened in 1978, houses a "fabulous" Omnitheater that gives viewers the illusion of sitting inside the picture.

The Beatles met media representatives in a press conference at Metropolitan Stadium, Bloomington, on August 21, 1965. The famed performers from Liverpool were, left to right, Ringo Starr, John Lennon, Paul McCartney, and George Harrison.

About 30,000 fans attended the concert that followed the press conference. "Beatlemaniacs" screamed, wept "in hysterical happiness," and stared through binoculars and telescopes at the heroes from Britain performing on a platform erected at second base. The group sang and played a program that included "She's a Woman," "Ticket to Ride," "Everybody's Trying to Be My Baby," and "A Hard Day's Night."

Sorry Muthas — a Minneapolis group playing bluegrass, country, and folk blues —performed in concert in 1971. Left to right are Cal Hand, Bill Hinkley, Papa John Kolstad, Bob Stelnicki, and Judy Larson. Throughout the 1960s and into the 1970s long-haired singers and guitar players performed folk music and protest songs wherever young people congregated.

"Flower children and the children of flower children," hippies, "semi-hippies," rock fans, and the curious attended a "Be-in" at Loring Park, Minneapolis, on July 23, 1967. What was a "Be-in"? "Actually, a Be-in is just a free concert," commented the co-ordinator of the Sunday event. Performers included "The Family," "The Weeds," "The Jokers Wild," and other Twin Cities rock bands.

265

Antiwar speakers addressed a quiet crowd of about three hundred in Dinkytown near the University of Minnesota campus on April 11, 1967. The Minnesota Committee to End the War in Vietnam sponsored the demonstration — one of many —as part of an all-day protest at the university. It was followed by a weekend bus trip to New York City to participate in a "mass peace 'mobilization.'"

Senator Eugene J. McCarthy, who taught at the College of St. Thomas, St. Paul, before his election to Congress, campaigned in 1967-68 for ending the nation's involvement in the Vietnam War and for the Democratic presidential nomination; here he delivered one of many speeches in 1968 at St. John's University, Collegeville. McCarthy lost the nomination to Hubert H. Humphrey, vice-president in Lyndon B. Johnson's administration, who in 1968 lost the presidential election to Richard M. Nixon.

Minneapolis police and National Guardsmen patrolled the Plymouth Avenue neighborhood in North Minneapolis on July 21, 1967, during the second year of disturbances in the predominantly black area. Although black protests in the Twin Cities were mild compared to those in cities like Detroit, Newark, and Los Angeles, feelings ran deep. One visiting black leader commented that the "primary issue in Minneapolis is not the jobs, or the police, or housing, or anything like this, it's simply the hostility, the fear, frustration, and the feeling of powerlessness which black people feel in an alien white society." Blacks in the Selby-Dale area of St. Paul joined the protest the following night.

About 1,600 people, predominantly white, marched silently in the rain along Plymouth Avenue North on April 7, 1968, in one of several demonstrations in the Twin Cities that followed the assassination of civil rights leader Martin Luther King, Jr., in Memphis, Tennessee. The mourners on Plymouth Avenue assembled to show that "the entire white community shares in the guilt" for King's death.

Minneapolis Mayor Arthur Naftalin on May 13, 1963, used the power of the media to refute charges made by P. Kenneth Peterson, his opponent in the upcoming city election, that the "city's near north side had become a 'cesspool of crime'" under his administration. Naftalin was one of several Twin Cities mayors, as well as other politicians, who made an effective use of television in the postwar era.

Time stopped in 1978 at the Burlington Northern depot, Minneapolis, as a demolition crew prepared to raze the building. The Great Northern railroad completed the depot in 1914 at the foot of Hennepin Avenue. In 1970, when the Great Northern and Northern Pacific merged into a new corporation, it became the Burlington Northern depot, but it was abandoned for a newly constructed Amtrak station.

Hubert H. Humphrey — mayor of Minneapolis, United States senator, and vice-president of the United States — died on January 13, 1978. A great fighter, he carried his campaign for human rights from the local arena onto the national stage, particularly in the speech on civil rights he made at the 1948 Democratic National Convention in Philadelphia.

In 1977-78 a new Amtrak depot was built in the Midway district, St. Paul (730 Transfer Road). Passenger traffic in Minnesota had been declining since the 1920s, except for a resurgence during World War II. In 1983 the depot served only two Amtrak routes: the Chicago-Twin Cities-Seattle "Empire Builder" and the Twin Cities-Duluth "North Star."

Part of the Northern States Power Company's nuclear-powered generating plant at Prairie Island, near Red Wing, is shown in 1975. Established in 1973, it was preceded in the NSP system by a nuclear plant at Monticello in 1970. While many Twin Citians hailed nuclear power as a boon to an energy-poor state, others, particularly after a radioactive gas leak occurred at Prairie Island in 1979, protested against the health risks posed by the new power source.

Many Twin Citians still choose urban parks as the setting for Fourth of July picnics, family reunions, games, and fireworks. The group celebrating here in 1979 was in Powderhorn Park, Minneapolis.

Members of the Minnesota Chicano Federation, established in St. Paul in 1975 to foster co-ordination among the state's Mexican-American groups, met to discuss matters of mutual concern. St. Paul, which has a strong Mexican-American community, was headquarters for several of the affiliated organizations.

The Hmong pictured here in 1981 — following the route taken by many immigrants before them — studied to help adjust to a new culture. Individual volunteers, public schools, churches, and others contributed to the educational effort. The strongly motivated, resourceful immigrants also helped themselves through groups like the Lao Family Community, located in St. Paul.

Kindergarten and first grade students learned to play the hand game in 1980 at the Red School House, 643 Virginia Street, St. Paul. Keith Herman and Ron Leith sang the hand-game song to the accompaniment of the hand drum, while a parent, Kenny Jefferson, right, looked on. The school's programs sought to preserve Indian traditions as an important part of the students' lives. Minneapolis Indians, one of the largest concentrations of urban Indians in the United States, focused their cultural efforts in the Heart of the Earth Survival School and the Upper Midwest American Indian Center.

In 1969 a new generation was growing up on Goodrich Avenue in the Summit-Hill neighborhood, St. Paul, a district hospitable to "children, dogs, bikes and station wagons." Many neighborhoods in the Twin Cities aged gracefully, with well-maintained houses, stability in home ownerships, and — in the areas that escaped Dutch elm disease afflicting the cities in the 1970s — tree-lined streets.

Bibliophiles in 1982 found treasures at an annual book sale held in the Rosedale Shopping Center, Roseville, for the benefit of the Mount Sinai Hospital, Minneapolis. The interior malls of shopping centers lent themselves as display space for art and craft fairs and fund-raisers for nonprofit organizations.

The Minnesota Vikings (dark jerseys) battled the Los Angeles Rams at Metropolitan Stadium on December 29, 1974, to win the National Football Conference title. Jubilant fans tore down the goal posts and overran the field to celebrate the 14 to 10 victory. The team went on to play in the Super Bowl in New Orleans but lost to the Pittsburgh Steelers of the American Football Conference in the third of their four unsuccessful bids to be national champions.

The "tailgaters" cooking in the parking area at the stadium before the title game had a fair day for December — a temperature ranging into the high thirties. The cookout custom, which flourished at Metropolitan Stadium, vanished when the games moved downtown to the Metrodome — but not before the intrepid cooks had compiled a book of their recipes.

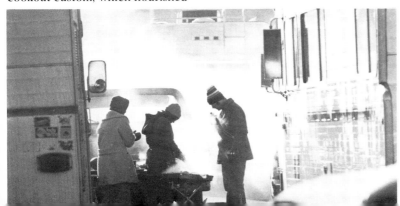

A 1983 night view of old and new buildings in Minneapolis spotlights the old — the Ard Godfrey House, built in 1848 and said to be the oldest extant frame dwelling in the city. As a Bicentennial project, the Woman's Club of Minneapolis restored the interior and exterior of the house, using some original Godfrey family belongings. The club opened it for tours in 1979.

Richard Chute Square, where the house stands, commemorates a man who, like Godfrey, was associated with Franklin Steele in water-power development at St. Anthony. The skyscrapers across the river are, from left, the IDS Tower, 100 Washington Square, the Multifoods Tower, and The Churchill apartment complex.

EPILOGUE
The Cities Remember

MANY MINNEAPOLITANS AND ST. PAULITES hailed the dramatic changes that transformed parts of the Twin Cities landscape during the heady years of redevelopment. *Action,* the newsletter of the Saint Paul Chamber of Commerce, reflected the viewpoint of enthusiasts when it commented in 1967: "With each new brick and girder we are slowly forgetting that only a few years ago better than two-thirds of the buildings in [downtown] Saint Paul had been built in the 1880's. By the end of this decade we will have forgotten it completely."[1]

Other Twin Citians were less eager to erase the trails leading from the present to the past. St. Paulite Georgia R. DeCoster, for example, urged in 1963 that urban renewal programs "should gradually develop the mixture of high-quality *old and new* buildings that best serves the diverse urban function and reflects the city's unique local history." Writing about redevelopment of the Mississippi River front, *Twin Citian* editor Roger E. Swardson observed in 1968 that "Perhaps this is one major chance for the progress cult to look beyond the bleak notions of a vapid new city and replace something of the charm and community that was lost in the demolition of the old."[2]

"It's not until you begin weighing the erasures of a decade against the new monoliths that you begin to wonder what happened to the flavor of the cities," Swardson commented. And no erasure triggered a greater outcry from preservationists than the razing in 1962 of the Metropolitan Building (formerly the Guaranty Loan Building) in Minneapolis. Despite the efforts of preservationists who recognized its importance to the city's fabric of life and architects who lauded its aesthetic qualities, the landmark fell victim to the forces of urban renewal. When wreckers had reduced the solid stone walls to rubble, a Minneapolitan wrote the building's epitaph: "May it rest in peace, and may its fate serve to alert our citizens to the need for early and more thoroughly organized efforts to safeguard other distinguished landmarks whenever they are threatened."[3]

The Metropolitan "went down 'like a Queen,'" and for a time it seemed that the Old Federal Courts Building in St. Paul would meet the same fate. The monumental building — "an exuberant collection of gables, turrets, and towers" constructed in 1894-1902 — was endangered when the United States government began erecting a new Federal Building in 1961. At the time, redevelopers in St. Paul, like those in Minneapolis, tended to view the renascence of the shabby downtown district in terms of new construction rather than restoration. The old building had a stay of execution, however, and many people rallied to its defense. Resolution of the complex preservation issues involved federal government agencies, the state legislature, the city of St. Paul, Ramsey County, the Ramsey County Historical Society, Minnesota congressmen, the Minnesota Historical Society, civic, cultural, and architectural organizations, and individual citizens. The efforts culminated in 1972 when the federal government transferred ownership of the building to the city of St. Paul; it was later conveyed to Ramsey County. Renamed Landmark Center and restored to more than its former splendor, it is now a community cultural center that enriches the architectural blend in the refurbished downtown.

There were many precedents in the Twin Cities for both the destruction and the preservation the two buildings reflected. Swept away during the cities' growth, long before the age of urban renewal, were landmarks like the Chapel of St. Paul, Franklin Steele's pioneer sawmill and the nation's first hydroelectric central station at the Falls of St. Anthony, the territorial capitol, early city halls and courthouses, and Fair Oaks, William D. Washburn's great mansion in Minneapolis.

But many buildings that evoked remembrance of the cities' evolution from separate settlements to a major urban center survived because preservationists reclaimed them or because they continued to be useful. Searchers for the past can visit such sites as Fort Snelling, the wilderness post that spawned the first settlements; the Mendota house of Henry H. Sibley, who protected the interests of St. Paul claimants at the 1848 land sale; the houses of Ard Godfrey and John H. Stevens, pioneer settlers at the Falls of St. Anthony; the Minneapolis City Hall-County Courthouse (Municipal Building), with its clocks high in the tower still measuring passing time; the St. Paul mansion of James J. Hill, a reminder of northwestern railroads that bound the Twin Cities to a trade empire; the Cathedral of St. Paul; and Cass Gilbert's state capitol — still the "renaissance palace" on the hill.

New recruits who enlisted in the cause of preservation during the years of urban renewal contributed further to retaining the texture of the past within modern cities. "It comes as no great surprise that in an age of upheaval such as this country has experienced during recent years Americans are increasingly aware of and interested in the past," Russell W. Fridley, director of the Minnesota Historical Society, wrote in 1972. Federal and state governments passed laws to protect and provide preservation funds for historic places. In one significant example, the legislature in 1971 established the Capitol Area Architectural Planning Commission as an effort to resurrect Cass Gilbert's impressive plan for the area's development and as a reaction against the inferior design of buildings constructed there during the 1950s. The cities responded by creating heritage preservation commissions — Minneapolis in 1972 and St. Paul in 1976. Each commission has responsibility for reviewing all building permits that affect the exterior of structures of a designated historic district or site; each must enforce adherence to historic design guidelines.[4]

Historical organizations also stepped up their preservation programs. Individuals choosing old houses as their homes invested talent, money, and sweat in restoring them to former beauty. In several notable instances — for example, Milwaukee Avenue in Minneapolis and the Historic Hill District (lower Summit Avenue) in St. Paul — restoration and preservation efforts encompassed a whole neighborhood. Adaptive reuse of old buildings became increasingly popular. Among the adaptations are restaurants and shops on Main Street in old St. Anthony including a building that once housed a mattress company; offices and stores in Butler Square, once a Minneapolis warehouse; and, most recently, Bandana Square in St. Paul's Energy Park, where restaurants and stores will do business by the mid-1980s in renovated railroad shops.

Other avenues to the past prompt Twin Citians to remember. On St. Patrick's Day in St. Paul the Irish (and friends) still parade as they have, off and on, for more than a century. Swedes still assemble in Minneapolis to celebrate Svenskarnas Dag. The "Josiah Snelling" and the "Jonathan Padelford," craft built by Captain William Bowell on the model of nineteenth-century steamboats, carry excursionists on the Mississippi River, while at Fort Snelling actor-troops and costumed guides replay scenes from the past. Hunters of the visible past haunt antique shops, estate sales, and museums. Practitioners of old crafts like spinning, weaving, quilting, and tatting transmit their skills to others. And hundreds of people become researchers as they study the records tracing the histories of their families, the structures they are restoring, the artifacts they are preserving, or the scale models they are building. In these and other ways Twin Citians find the dimensions of the past and give continuity to the story of St. Paul and Minneapolis that began long ago on the banks of the Mississippi River.

Three identical houses at 301-313 Laurel Avenue, St. Paul, nicknamed the "Three Sisters" and photographed in 1983, typify the stick style found in architects' pattern books and built by master carpenters in the 1880s. A century later the area, designated as the Historic Hill District, underwent extensive renovation according to strict design guidelines that governed construction materials, setbacks from the curb, and all changes to the buildings' exteriors.

At the Ramsey County Historical Society's Gibbs Farm Museum, children experienced life as their great-grandparents knew it. As part of a summer living-history program, elementary students attended classes in a one-room schoolhouse. These students played at recess time in 1973 in front of the farm's reconstructed barn as their teacher watched. The farmhouse, built as a one-room dwelling in 1854 and later expanded, is on the National Register of Historic Places. Located at Larpenteur and Cleveland avenues, it is operated as a museum by the society.

The sternwheeler "Jonathan Padelford" carried sightseers past the St. Paul waterfront. With its big, red paddlewheel and ornate curliques on the roof, and brass lanterns lighting the dining room, the boat gave its passengers a taste of life on the Mississippi. Captain Bowell heads the Padelford Packet Boat Company, with offices in a covered barge moored at Harriet Island, across the river from downtown St. Paul.

In 1983 old buildings blended with new structures in Energy Park, a housing, commercial, and office development in St. Paul's Midway area between Snelling Avenue and Lexington Parkway. The site was formerly a railroad yard that included the Northern Pacific railroad's Como Shops (left of the crane), built in 1885. The cream-colored brick structures once used for woodworking, painting, car building, storage, and offices became Bandana Square — a complex housing retail stores, restaurants, a health center, and a gymnasium.

Playwrights became researchers when they wrote for the Great North American History Theatre (formerly St. Paul History Theatre). In 1980-82 the theater produced "A Servant's Christmas," written by John Fenn. Presented at Landmark Center, the play was set in a Victorian mansion on Summit Avenue. Other subjects the playwrights explored included the lives of Nina Clifford, St. Paul's most famous madam; Eva McDonald Valesh, a Minnesota Populist and labor leader; and James J. Hill, railroad magnate.

Irvine Park, pictured in 1983, was one of St. Paul's early fine residential areas. The white house, center, and the two houses to the left of it were built in the early 1850s. Others, including the house of Alexander Ramsey, the territory's first governor, date from the 1870s and 1880s. The neighborhood was placed on the National Register of Historic Places in 1973 and made a city historic district in 1981. The park itself has been restored to its 1881 appearance.

Landmark Center, 75 West Fifth Street, St. Paul, offered a pleasing prospect to viewers seated in Rice Park in 1983. Cleaning had restored the dirty gray exterior to rosy beige, the window trim was painted brown, and terra-cotta tile on the roof replaced the asphalt shingles laid in 1937-40. Across the park, at 350 Market Street, the refurbished St. Paul Hotel, renamed The Saint Paul, was once again noted for the elegance it had when it first opened in 1910.

Butler Square, formerly the Butler Brothers warehouse, was the first large, old business structure renovated for modern use in Minneapolis. Restored in 1972-74, it sparked a rejuvenation of the entire area, which in 1982 was named Butler Quarter in its honor. Like other former warehouses, it now contains shops, restaurants, offices, and an atrium in which visitors can see exposed timbers and girders, as in this 1983 view.

Parishioners of Our Lady of Lourdes Church (right background) faced serious difficulties in preserving the historic structure at 21 Prince Street Southeast, Minneapolis, called "the spiritual home for French-Canadian Catholics since 1877." They raised funds for restoration and stablization by selling "tourtières," or meat pies, but the financial problem was still acute in 1983. New construction for "Riverplace" engulfed the church in that year. A parking ramp and a high-rise condominium are going up in the foreground. The tall building under construction in the background near the church is an apartment tower. Left of the tower is the historic Main Street warehouse; renovation plans for the structure include a five-story atrium surrounded by offices, shops, and restaurants.

Lights glowed in 1983 from businesses on Main Street Southeast, Minneapolis, where the old town of St. Anthony began. Left to right are Pracna On Main (an old saloon building converted into a restaurant), the Martin-Morrison Block, the Upton Block, St. Anthony Main (a restaurant-shop complex once occupied by the Salisbury-Satterlee mattress firm), and the Pillsbury A mill.

The John H. Stevens House, the first frame dwelling built on the west bank of the falls in Minneapolis, was moved a few times before it came to rest in 1983 at a new site in Minnehaha Park. With the help of nearly ten thousand school children, it was towed in 1896 from Sixteenth Avenue South, between Third and Fourth streets, to Minnehaha Avenue at Fiftieth Street in the park, close to its present location. The civic event was re-created in 1983 when children helped transfer the house to its present site near the restored Minnehaha Depot. The Junior League of Minneapolis announced plans to restore the house and open it for tours.

Restored "lookalike" houses on Milwaukee Avenue in Minneapolis, occupied in the late nineteenth and early twentieth centuries by working-class families, recalled their original appearance in 1983. Prompt action by preservationists saved the badly deteriorated dwellings when they were scheduled for destruction in 1970. The houses were built on half lots facing an alley between Twenty-second and Twenty-third avenues south, formerly called Twenty-second-and-a-half Avenue. During the project that began in 1972, new basements were dug and exteriors were restored to their original appearance. The avenue is on the National Register of Historic Places.

During the heyday of the lumber industry in Minneapolis, many manufacturers and dealers had offices in the Lumber Exchange Building, 425 Hennepin Avenue, built in 1885 and pictured here in 1983. The Richardsonian Romanesque revival structure designed by Long and Kees is one of two office blocks of this architectural style remaining in Minneapolis. It has been rehabilitated and is again one of the city's important office buildings. The brass revolving door, installed in 1979, once was used to connect New York City's Grand Central Station with the Commodore Hotel. The exterior of the second structure — the Masonic Temple at 528 Hennepin Avenue, built in 1888-89 — has been restored; the interior has been adapted for use by the Hennepin Center for the Arts.

At the annual Victorian Craft Festival on the grounds of the Alexander Ramsey House in 1983, the displays and demonstrations of artisans included weaving, rug braiding, china painting, knitting, crocheting, tatting, lace making, calligraphy, woodworking, and jewelry crafting. The home of Minnesota Territory's first governor, the Victorian mansion at 265 South Exchange Street, St. Paul, is owned and operated as a historic house by the Minnesota Historical Society. It is on the National Register of Historic Places.

On the parade ground at Fort Snelling in 1983 a young tourist learned cannon drill from an actor-soldier. Behind them, visible over the roof of the reconstructed powder magazine, stands the restored round tower, one of three buildings remaining at the post that were constructed by 1824. The site, operated by the Minnesota Historical Society within Fort Snelling State Park, is a National Historical Landmark.

A St. Paul family holds a yard sale of antiques each summer after collecting and restoring them the rest of the year. The growing popularity of such sales at homes, plus larger ones at shopping centers and elsewhere, reflects not only nostalgia but also genuine area-wide interest in craftsmanship and the traditional values of collectibles.

Fireworks and a concert by the Minnesota Orchestra climaxed the three-day celebration called "A Taste of Minnesota" at the state capitol on July 4, 1983. The statue of Christopher Columbus, facing the Historical Building, stands high above the crowd that had tasted delicacies served by Twin Cities restaurants from tents pitched on the Capitol Approach. Pyrotechnics, music, and food have been part of Fourth of July celebrations since territorial days.

Reference Notes

INTRODUCTION

1 United States, *Census, 1980, Population,* vol. 1, part 25, p. 40; Jack Alexander, "The Cities of America: Minneapolis and St. Paul," in *Saturday Evening Post,* April 3, 1948, p. 22.

2 G. Hubert Smith, "First Photographers of Minnesota," 1-3 (ca. 1950), typescript in Minnesota Historical Society (hereafter MHS) Special Libraries Department.

3 For more on the history of photography, here and below, see Alan Thomas, *Time in a Frame: Photography and the Nineteenth-Century Mind,* 7-22 (New York, 1977); Beaumont Newhall, *The History of Photography from 1839 to the Present Day* (Rev. ed., New York, 1982).

4 The quotations are from MHS, *Annual Report, 1872,* p. 15, *Annual Report, 1875,* p. 7, 8.

5 *Minneapolis Journal,* April 30, 1922.

6 Nathan Lyons, ed., *Toward a Social Landscape,* [7] (New York, 1966).

7 Ted Curtis Smythe, "A History of the Minneapolis *Journal,* 1879-1939," 105, Ph.D. thesis, University of Minnesota, 1967.

8 "Autobiography of Clifford Earl Peel," 41, undated typescript in MHS Reference Library; photographer index file, Hibbard Register, and Steven Quaal, "Kenneth M. Wright: A Short Biography," 9, undated typescript — all in Special Libraries Department.

9 Lyons, *Toward a Social Landscape,* [5].

1838-65/River Cities

1 *Minnesota Pioneer* (St. Paul), April 28, 1849; J. Fletcher Williams, *A History of the City of Saint Paul to 1875,* 204-207 (Repr. ed., St. Paul, 1983).

2 *Minnesota Pioneer,* August 23, 1849; June D. Holmquist and Jean A. Brookins, *Minnesota's Major Historic Sites: A Guide,* 1, 9 (Rev. ed., St. Paul, 1972); William W. Folwell, *A History of Minnesota,* 1:218, 427 (Repr. ed., St. Paul, 1956).

3 Folwell, *Minnesota,* 1:217-224.

4 Lucile M. Kane, *The Waterfall That Built a City: The Falls of St. Anthony in Minneapolis,* 12-14 (St. Paul, 1966).

5 Kane, *Waterfall,* 14; Williams, *Saint Paul,* 146, 147.

6 Kane, *Waterfall,* 19; Williams, *Saint Paul,* 184, 185; Minnesota Territory, *Acts, Joint Resolutions and Memorials,* 1849, p. 99-102, and *Laws,* 1855, p. 10-18; *St. Anthony Express,* September 24, 1853. On Sibley, see *Northwest Magazine,* March, 1891, p. 12.

7 Kane, *Waterfall,* 30-34; Folwell, *Minnesota,* 1:423-426, 429.

8 Folwell, *Minnesota,* 1:352, 359, 363, 2:22, 344 (Repr. ed., St. Paul, 1961); E[phraim] S. Seymour, *Sketches of Minnesota, the New England of the West,* 125 (New York, 1850); Kane, *Waterfall,* 29, 44-47, 191; Minnesota Secretary of State, *Annual Report,* 1865, p. 94.

9 *Minneapolis Chronicle,* August 25, 1866; Kane, *Waterfall,* 35-39, 57, 60; Minnesota Secretary of State, *Annual Report,* 1865, p. 94.

10 Williams, *Saint Paul,* 208, 349, 381; Folwell, *Minnesota,* 1:352; Minnesota Secretary of State, *Annual Report,* 1865, p. 101.

11 H[enry] W. Hamilton, *Rural Sketches of Minnesota, the El Dorado of the Northwest,* 20 (Milan, Ohio, 1850); Kane, *Waterfall,* 18, 26-28, 37.

12 Kane, *Waterfall,* 42-47, 49-57.

13 Kane, *Waterfall,* 54, 58-60, and "Rivalry for a River: The Twin Cities and the Mississippi," in *Minnesota History,* 37:309-323 (December, 1961).

14 *Minnesota Pioneer,* April 28, 1849; Rhoda R. Gilman, Carolyn Gilman, and Deborah M. Stultz, *The Red River Trails: Ox Cart Routes Between St. Paul and the Selkirk Settlement,* 14 (St. Paul, 1979).

15 *Northwest Magazine,* July, 1890, p. 13; Folwell, *Minnesota,* 1:353, 359-361; *Minnesota Pioneer,* October 20, 1853, May 27, 1854; *St. Anthony Express,* May 10, 1856.

16 *Northwest Magazine,* April, 1886, p. 1; *Minnesota Republican* (St. Anthony), September 10, 1857; Lucile M. Kane, "Governing a Frontier City: Old St. Anthony, 1855-1872," in *Minnesota History,* 35:123 (September, 1956); Journal of the Town Council, August 16, 1858, June 7, July 11, 1859, July 8, 1861, in Minneapolis Municipal Archives.

17 On public buildings, see Williams, *Saint Paul,* 279-281, 363; Henry A. Castle, *History of St. Paul and Vicinity,* 1:153 (Chicago, 1912); Kane, in *Minnesota History,* 35:122; Marion D. Shutter, ed., *History of Minneapolis, Gateway to the Northwest,* 1:136 (Chicago and Minneapolis, 1923). Quoted materials are in [Alix J. Muller and Frank J. Mead, comps.], *History of the Police and Fire Departments of the Twin Cities,* St. Paul, 45 (Minneapolis and St. Paul, 1899); *Minnesota Republican,* September 10, 1857.

18 Examples of vigilantes and home guards are in [Muller and Mead, comps.], *Police and Fire Departments,* St. Paul, 45, 48; *Minnesota Republican,* July 23, 1858; *Minnesota State News* (St. Anthony), May 4, 1861. On fire companies, see Shutter, ed., *Minneapolis,* 1:124; Kane, in *Minnesota History,* 35:124; *Minnesota State News,* September 17, 1859; [Muller and Mead, comps.], *Police and Fire Departments,* St. Paul, 175-189, Minneapolis, 144-159; Minnesota Territory, *Session Laws,* 1854, p. 38, 1858, p. 275.

19 On bridges at the falls, see Kane, *Waterfall,* 40; Minnesota Territory, *Session Laws,* 1852, p. 19-21, 1854, p. 87-89; *Minnesota Republican,* April 23, 1857, February 12, 1858; *Weekly Pioneer and Democrat* (St. Paul), March 11, 1858; *Daily Minnesotian* (St. Paul), June 30, 1859; *St. Anthony Express,* December 30, 1854 (quotation). On St. Paul street lighting and bridge, see Williams, *Saint Paul,* 378; *Weekly Pioneer and Democrat,* December 11, 1856; St. Paul Common Council, *Proceedings,* 1856-57, p. 67, 77, 1858, p. 51, 91, 97, 1859, p. 159. On street lighting in the falls communities, see *Minneapolis Daily Tribune,* November 22, 1870; Minneapolis City Council, Proceedings, October 19, 1870, in Minneapolis Municipal Archives.

20 St. Paul Common Council, *Proceedings,* 1856-57, p. 37; Shutter, ed., *Minneapolis,* 1:155; Philip D. Jordan, *The People's Health: A History of Public Health in Minnesota to 1948,* 125-127 (St. Paul, 1953). For examples of official actions, see St. Paul Common Council, *Acts of Incorporation, Standing Rules & Proceedings,* 1854-55, p. 67, and *Proceedings,* 1859, p. 48; Kane, in *Minnesota History,* 35:126; St. Anthony City Council, Proceedings, April 13, 1859, in Minneapolis Municipal Archives.

21 On St. Paul's treatment of the mentally disturbed and its law on the "diseased and destitute," see St. Paul Common Council, *Proceedings,* 1859, p. 173, 177, and *Acts of Incorporation, Standing Rules & Proceedings,* 1854-55, p. 81; *Daily Minnesotian,* June 30, 1859; *Daily Pioneer and Democrat,* September 10, 1861. For examples of legislative actions, see Minnesota Territory, *Acts, Joint Resolutions and Memorials,* 1849, p. 128-130; Minnesota Legisla-

ture, *Laws,* 1864, p. 48-58; Petitions, City of St. Anthony, October 13, 1860, and St. Anthony City Council, Proceedings, June 13, 1854, both in Minneapolis Municipal Archives; St. Paul Common Council, *Proceedings,* 1854-55, p. 81, 1858, p. 155, 1859, p. 92; Kane, in *Minnesota History,* 35:125.

²² Castle, *St. Paul and Vicinity,* 2:582. On private physicians, see *Minnesota Pioneer,* July 28, 1853; Shutter, ed., *Minneapolis,* 1:494. For examples of medical advertisements, see *Weekly Minnesotian* (St. Paul), December 25, 1852; *St. Anthony Express,* June 18, 1852; list prepared from *Minnesota State News,* January-May, 1861, in author's possession.

²³ The description of the university is in *Minnesota Republican,* February 12, 1858; see also James Gray, *The University of Minnesota, 1851-1951,* 3 (Minneapolis, 1951). On early public and parochial schools, see Castle, *St. Paul and Vicinity,* 2:454-456, 516; Shutter, ed., *Minneapolis,* 1:393-398, 580. Examples of advertisements for "select" schools are in *St. Anthony Express,* December 6, 1851, April 1, 1853; *Daily Minnesotian,* October 11, 1854.

²⁴ E. Osmer to Henry H. Sibley, April 18, 1835, Henry Hastings Sibley Papers, Division of Archives and Manuscripts (DAM), Minnesota Historical Society (MHS); Holmquist and Brookins, *Minnesota's Major Historic Sites,* 15, 20; Folwell, *Minnesota,* 1:186-189, 192-195, 205-207; United States, *Census,* 1860, *Mortality and Miscellaneous Statistics,* 415-417. Other religious groups, including the German Lutherans at the falls, organized congregations without building churches.

²⁵ Warren Upham and Rose Dunlap, comps., *Minnesota Biographies,* 539 *(Minnesota Historical Collections,* vol. 14, 1912); Minnesota Territory, *Acts, Joint Resolutions and Memorials,* 1849, p. 45, and *Session Laws,* 1852, p. 12-18; Daniel R. Noyes, "Charities in Minnesota," in *Minnesota Historical Collections,* 12:172 (St. Paul, 1908). For examples of church activities and foreign-language services, see *Minnesota Republican,* January 15, 1858; *St. Anthony Express,* March 11, 1854, March 8, 1856; *Weekly Minnesotian,* August 21, 1852; Castle, *St. Paul and Vicinity,* 2:541.

²⁶ For examples of lending libraries, newspapers, magazines, and books, see *St. Anthony Express,* May 31, 1856; J. Fletcher Williams to Samuel W. Williams, November 23, 1856, original in Samuel Williams Papers, Ohio Historical Society, photocopy in John Fletcher Williams Papers, MHS; *St. Anthony Express,* July 26, August 23, 1851; Isaac Atwater, ed., *History of the City of Minneapolis, Minnesota,* 65 (quotation) (New York, 1893). On early libraries, see Castle, *St. Paul and Vicinity,* 2:478; Minnesota Territory, *Acts, Joint Resolutions and Memorials,* 1849, p. 106; Betty L. Engebretson, "Books for Pioneers: The Minneapolis Athenaeum," in *Minnesota History,* 35:222 (March, 1957); *St. Anthony Express,* May 13, 1853; *Minnesota Republican,* February 19, 1858; *Minnesota State News,* January 5, 1861.

²⁷ For examples, see *Minnesota Pioneer,* January 29, 1852 (quotation), January 12, 1854; *St. Anthony Express,* December 9, 1854; *Minnesota Republican,* January 15, 1858; *Minnesota State News,* March 25, September 10, October 22, 1859.

²⁸ Lawrence J. Hill, "A History of Variety-Vaudeville in Minneapolis, Minnesota, From Its Beginning to 1900," 32-38, Ph.D. thesis, University of Minnesota, 1979; *Minnesota Pioneer,* May 27, 1854; *St. Anthony Express,* September 24, 1857.

²⁹ For examples, see "Spring Comes to the Frontier: Reminiscences of Mrs. Joseph Ullmann," in *Minnesota History,* 33:196 (Spring, 1953); *St. Anthony Express,* June 28, 1851, April 10, June 4, 1852; *Minnesota Pioneer,* February 26, 1852; *Minnesota Chronicle and Register* (St. Paul), December 22, 1849; *Weekly Pioneer and Democrat,* July 9, 1857; "Menu Collection," in pamphlet collection, MHS Reference Library.

³⁰ John G. Rice, "Old Stock Americans," in June D. Holmquist, ed., *They Chose Minnesota: A Survey of the State's Ethnic Groups,* 58 (St. Paul, 1981); *Minnesota Republican,* November 6, December 18, 25, 1857, March 19, 1858 (quotation); *Minnesota Pioneer,* March 24, 1853.

³¹ *Minnesota State News,* April 20, 27, 1861; *Daily Pioneer and Democrat,* June 22, 23, 1861.

³² For examples of city council votes, see St. Anthony City Council, Proceedings, April 27, 1861, in Minneapolis Municipal Archives; St. Paul Common Council, *Proceedings,* 1861, p. 121, 1862, p. 40, 1863, p. 56, 59, 63, 94; Folwell, *Minnesota,* 2:164. On volunteer activities, see *Minnesota State News,* April 27, June 22, 1861, Jan-

uary 4, March 1, 1862. The St. Anthony meeting is reported in *Minnesota State News,* July 27, 1861.

³³ *Minneapolis Daily Tribune,* June 20, 1867; *St. Anthony Express,* April 15, 1854; *Minnesota Pioneer,* February 26, 1852; *Weekly Minnesotian,* February 19, 1853. For comparisons of eastern and western mannerisms, see *St. Anthony Express,* June 21, August 2, 1851, June 18, 1852.

³⁴ *Minnesota Pioneer,* January 13, 1853.

³⁴ Kane, *Waterfall,* 40, 60; Mildred L. Hartsough, *The Development of the Twin Cities (Minneapolis and St. Paul) As a Metropolitan Market,* 31-33 (Minneapolis, 1925); U.S., *Census,* 1860, *Manufactures,* 278-280.

³⁴ *Daily Pioneer and Democrat,* September 10, 1861; *St. Paul Daily Press,* June 29, 1862.

1865-80/ *The Railroad Age*

¹ *St. Anthony Express,* December 31, 1853. See also Hartsough, *Development of the Twin Cities,* 77-81.

² Richard S. Prosser, *Rails to the North Star,* 11-21, [188] (Minneapolis, 1966); Hartsough, *Development of the Twin Cities,* 84-86, 206. For an example of the communities' enthusiasm for railroads, see *Minneapolis Daily Chronicle,* December 27, 1866; on ethnicity of railroad crews, see Ann Regan, "The Irish," in Holmquist, ed., *They Chose Minnesota,* 136.

³ Tables giving statistics for the region (Minnesota, Dakota Territory, Montana Territory) on cereal crop production and population are in Hartsough, *Development of the Twin Cities,* 203, 205. Discussions of the fur trade, mining, agriculture, sheep raising, cattle raising, and settlements in Dakota and Montana are in Harold E. Briggs, *Frontiers of the Northwest: A History of the Upper Missouri Valley* (New York, 1940). Maps showing population density in Minnesota in 1870 and 1880 are in R[obert] W. Murchie and M[errill] E. Jarchow, *Population Trends in Minnesota,* 10, 11 (University of Minnesota Agricultural Experiment Station, *Bulletin,* no. 327 — [St. Paul], 1936).

⁴ For examples of co-operation, see *Minneapolis Tribune,* July 8, September 8, 1879; Mildred [L.] Hartsough, "Transportation as a Factor in the Development of the Twin Cities," in *Minnesota History,* 7:229 (September, 1926); *Minneapolis Daily Chronicle,* January 24, 1867. Examples of arguments over railroads and trade areas are in *Minnesota State News,* January 26, 1861; *St. Paul Daily Press,* March 20, 1863; *Minneapolis Daily Chronicle,* November 20, 22, 1866, April 28, 1867; *Minneapolis Daily Tribune,* August 4, 1869, August 8, 1873, June 2, 1877; December 11, 12, 13, 1878, March 4, 1880. On the "St. Paul system," see St. Paul Chamber of Commerce, *Annual Report,* 1867, p. 7. On the Minneapolis and St. Louis, see Hartsough, *Development of the Twin Cities,* 86; Kane, *Waterfall,* 100.

⁵ Kane, in *Minnesota History,* 35:119, 129; *Minneapolis Daily Tribune,* February 14, 1872. For examples of new terms for the cities, see *St. Paul Dispatch,* December 30, 1876; *St. Paul Globe,* January 7, 1880; *Northwest Magazine,* September, 1891, p. 41.

⁶ *Minneapolis Daily Tribune,* August 22, 1869; Kane, *Waterfall,* 99, 103-105; Charles B. Kuhlmann, *The Development of the Flour-Milling Industry in the United States,* 120, 126, 150-153, 289-291 (New York, 1929).

⁷ Kane, *Waterfall,* 59, 106-111; Shutter, ed., *Minneapolis,* 1:377; *Minneapolis Daily Tribune,* August 4, 1870.

⁸ Kane, *Waterfall,* 62-80.

⁹ Kane, *Waterfall,* 102.

¹⁰ *Minneapolis Daily Tribune,* September 21, 1873; Kane, *Waterfall,* 112; St. Paul Chamber of Commerce, *Annual Report,* [1879], p. 5; Minneapolis Board of Trade, *Annual Report,* 1879, p. 46; Hartsough, *Development of the Twin Cities,* 33-35.

¹¹ Kane, *Waterfall,* 92-96; U.S., *Census,* 1870, *Wealth and Industry,* 535, and 1880, *Manufactures,* 412, 434.

¹² *Northwest Magazine,* February, 1892, p. 23; U.S., *Census,* 1880, *Manufactures,* 412, 434.

¹³ Here and below, see "Electric Railways of Minneapolis & St. Paul," in *Interurbans* (Los Angeles), vol. 11, no. 2, p. 4-6 (Interurbans Special No. 14 — December, 1953); U.S., *Census,* 1880, *Report on the Social Statistics of Cities,* 2:690, 699; *Minneapolis*

Tribune, August 23, 1878; Stephen A. Kieffer, *Transit and the Twins*, 5 ([Minneapolis], 1958). On trains shuttling between the cities, see *St. Paul Globe*, September 7, 1880.

[14] For complaints about the lack of a direct route, see *Minneapolis Tribune*, April 6, 1878, October 18, 1879; *St. Paul Dispatch*, April 29, 1874. The planning meeting is described in *St. Paul Press*, February 11, 1873, and *Minneapolis Daily Tribune*, February 14, 1873.

[15] A[nne] H. B[legen], "The Early History of the Telegraph in Minnesota," in *Minnesota History*, 8:172 (June, 1927); *Minneapolis Tribune*, March 3, 1879, March 18, 1880; *Greater Minneapolis*, June, 1955, p. 26; Wayne L. Huffman, "Spanning Time and Space," in *Greater Minneapolis*, January, 1958, p. 38.

[16] *Minneapolis Tribune*, February 24, 1879.

[17] St. Paul Common Council, *Proceedings*, 1856-57, p. 12, 1860, p. 40; Jordan, *People's Health*, 103, 125-135; St. Paul Chamber of Commerce, *Annual Report*, 1869, p. 11; Kane, *Waterfall*, 124.

[18] Josiah B. Chaney, "Early Bridges and Changes of the Land and Water Surface in the City of St. Paul," in *Minnesota Historical Collections*, 12:133 (St. Paul, 1908); *Minneapolis Daily Tribune*, July 10, 1867. The city of St. Paul had been in charge of the Wabasha Street Bridge for several years before it acquired formal ownership. On lighting, see *Minneapolis Daily Tribune*, November 22, 1870, and Chapter 1, note 19, above; on streets, see U.S., *Census*, 1880, *Report on the Social Statistics of Cities*, 2:690, 698.

[19] [Muller and Mead, comps.], *Police and Fire Departments*, St. Paul, 204; Richard Heath, *Mill City Firefighters: The First Hundred Years, 1879-1979*, 7 (Minneapolis, 1981); *Minneapolis Tribune*, July 1, 1879.

[20] [Muller and Mead, comps.], *Police and Fire Departments*, Minneapolis, 34-46, St. Paul, 51-59; Joel Best, "Keeping the Peace in St. Paul: Crime, Vice, and Police Work, 1869-74," in *Minnesota History*, 47:246 (Summer, 1981). For descriptions of the homes, see Castle, *St. Paul and Vicinity*, 2:523; Shutter, ed., *Minneapolis*, 190.

[21] On hospitals, see Castle, *St. Paul and Vicinity*, 1:344; Shutter, ed., *Minneapolis*, 1:505; *Minneapolis Daily Tribune*, March 19, 1871. On organizations, institutions, and poorhouses, see Ethel McClure, *More Than a Roof: The Development of Minnesota Poor Farms and Homes for the Aged*, 10, 20, 24, 40-48 (St. Paul, 1968); Noyes, in *Minnesota Historical Collections*, 12:169, 171-177; Theodore C. Blegen, *Minnesota: A History of the State*, 435 (Minneapolis, 1963).

[22] Castle, *St. Paul and Vicinity*, 344; *Manual of the Church of Gethsemane*, 24 (Minneapolis, 1872); Cottage Hospital, *Annual Report*, 1880, p. 7, 9 (Minneapolis, 1881); "Semi-Annual Report of the Health Office," March 18, 1870, in Minneapolis Municipal Archives; Jordan, *People's Health*, 45; *St. Paul City Directory*, 1879-80, p. 58, 524; *Minneapolis City Directory*, 1879-80, p. 17, 398; Shutter, ed., *Minneapolis*, 505.

[23] *St. Paul City Directory*, 1880-81, p. 44-47; *Minneapolis City Directory*, 1880-81, p. 15; Gray, *University of Minnesota*, 29-68; Merrill E. Jarchow, *Private Liberal Arts Colleges in Minnesota: Their History and Contributions*, 8, 10, 25, 35 (St. Paul, 1973).

[24] *St. Paul City Directory*, 1880-81, p. 38-42; *Minneapolis City Directory*, 1880-81, p. 18; Shutter, ed., *Minneapolis*, 1:583, 598; St. Paul Chamber of Commerce, *Annual Report*, 1883, p. 58, 60; James M. Reardon, *The Catholic Church in the Diocese of St. Paul*, 63, 186 (St. Paul, 1952).

[25] U.S., *Census*, 1880, *Population*, 451, 538-541; Carlton C. Qualey and Jon A. Gjerde, "The Norwegians," 233, Rice, "The Swedes," 262, in Holmquist, ed., *They Chose Minnesota*. Foreign-born residents in Minneapolis in 1870 numbered 4,453 out of a total population of 13,066 and in 1880, 15,013 out of 46,887. The figures for St. Paul are: 1870 — 8,687 out of 20,030; 1880 — 15,075 out of 41,473.

[26] Hildegard Binder Johnson, "The Germans," 169-172, Regan, "The Irish," 140, 142, in Holmquist, ed., *They Chose Minnesota*.

[27] *St. Paul Pioneer*, July 10, 1866.

[28] *St. Paul Pioneer*, September 6, 1866, June 10, June 15, July 6, 1871; Ray P. Speer and Harry J. Frost, *Minnesota State Fair: The History and Heritage of 100 Years*, 12 ([Minneapolis], 1964). For an example of a critic of racing, see Peter Gideon, *Fruit Culture and Fast Horses: The Civilizing Effects of the Former and the Demoralization Caused by the Latter*, 2 ([Minnesota], 1882).

[29] Cecil O. Monroe, "The Rise of Baseball in Minnesota," in *Minnesota History*, 19:162-181 (June, 1938); *St. Paul Daily Press*, August 29, 1866; *Minneapolis Daily Tribune*, July 13, 1867, July 4, 1874, August 26, 1875, August 26, 1876; *St. Paul Dispatch*, October 19, 1876; *St. Paul Pioneer Press*, June 2, 1877; *St. Paul Globe*, July 19, August 11, 1880. On black teams, see *Minneapolis Tribune*, September 18, 1877, August 2, 1878, September 23, 1880.

[30] *St. Paul Pioneer Press*, February 14, 1869; *Minneapolis Daily Tribune*, April 3, 1869, June 29, 1877.

[31] Studies covering theatrical and variety performances during the period are Frank M. Whiting, "A History of the Theatre in St. Paul, Minnesota, from Its Beginning to 1890," Ph.D. thesis, University of Minnesota, 1941; Donald Z. Woods, "A History of the Theater in Minneapolis, Minnesota, from Its Beginning to 1883," Ph.D. thesis, University of Minnesota, 1950; Hill, "History of Variety-Vaudeville." On musical co-operation, see John K. Sherman, *Music and Maestros: The Story of the Minneapolis Symphony Orchestra*, 17 (Minneapolis, 1952); Whiting, "Theatre in St. Paul," 172. For the Pence opening, see Donald Z. Woods, "Playhouse for Pioneers: The Story of the Pence Opera House," in *Minnesota History*, 33:169-173 (Winter, 1952); *St. Paul Pioneer*, June 26, 1867.

[32] U.S., *Census*, 1880, *Population*, 226, 229; *Minneapolis Tribune*, July 16, 1880.

[33] From 1864 to 1880 Hennepin County voted Republican in every presidential election and in every gubernatorial election except in 1873. During the same years Ramsey County voted Democratic in every presidential election and in every gubernatorial race except in 1873. See Bruce M. White *et al.*, comps., *Minnesota Votes: Election Returns by County for Presidents, Senators, Congressmen, and Governors, 1857-1977*, 11-13, 155-161 (St. Paul, 1977).

1880-95/*The Golden Age*

[1] *Northwest Magazine*, December, 1892, p. 20; U.S., *Census*, 1890, *Compendium*, 1:434-440; Matti Kaups, "Europeans in Duluth: 1870," in Ryck Lydecker and Lawrence J. Sommer, eds., *Duluth: Sketches of the Past, A Bicentennial Collection*, 71 (Duluth, 1976).

[2] U.S., *Census*, 1890, *Compendium*, 1:434; State of Minnesota, *Census, 1895*, 21, 45.

[3] Hartsough, *Development of the Twin Cities*, 87, 206; *Northwest Magazine*, April, 1886, p. 16; Frank P. Donovan, *Gateway to the Northwest: The Story of the Minnesota Transfer Railway*, 3, 23 (Minneapolis, 1954). On railroad facilities, see, for example, Kane, *Waterfall*, 147; *Daily Minnesota Tribune* (Minneapolis), March 8, 1884; St. Paul Chamber of Commerce, *Annual Report*, 1884, p. 44.

[4] *Northwest Magazine*, February, 1888, p. 57, February, 1895, p. 19; Minneapolis Board of Trade, *Annual Report*, 1881, p. 56; Minneapolis Chamber of Commerce, *Annual Report*, 1895, p. 125, 126; Kuhlmann, *Development of the Flour-Milling Industry*, 128-138, 161.

[5] *Minneapolis Tribune*, April 1, 1878; *Northwest Magazine*, February, 1892, p. 26; Kuhlmann, *Development of the Flour-Milling Industry*, 141-145; Minneapolis Chamber of Commerce, *Annual Report*, 1896, p. 17; Duluth Board of Trade, *Annual Report*, 1895, p. 70-75; Don W. Larson, *Land of the Giants: A History of Minnesota Business*, 58-65 (Minneapolis, 1979).

[6] Minneapolis Chamber of Commerce, *Annual Report*, 1895, p. 144; Agnes M. Larson, *History of the White Pine Industry in Minnesota*, 229-231, 236-246, 251-256 (Minneapolis, 1949); *Mississippi Valley Lumberman*, January 4, 1895, p. 8.

[7] Briggs, *Frontiers of the Northwest*, 197-199, 203-228, 314-321; Merrill E. Jarchow, *The Earth Brought Forth: A History of Minnesota Agriculture to 1885*, 188-206 (St. Paul, 1949); *Minneapolis Tribune*, November 18, 1882; Minneapolis Board of Trade, *Annual Report*, 1880, p. 66-68; Charles E. Bottemiller, "Meat and Men in Minnesota —The St. Paul Union Stockyards to 1907," p. 17, 44, Master's thesis, Macalester College, 1956.

[8] Bottemiller, "Meat and Men," 27, 36-42; St. Paul Chamber of Commerce, *Annual Report*, 1884, p. 38; Hartsough, *Development of the Twin Cities*, 67.

9 *Northwest Magazine,* December, 1886, p. 13; Bottemiller, "Meat and Men," 42, 47-49.

10 *Minneapolis Tribune,* April 30, 1886; Bottemiller, "Meat and Men," 62-64, 68-72; St. Paul Chamber of Commerce, *Annual Report,* 1895, p. 34; *South St. Paul Kaposia Days, July 2-4, 1976,* p. 12-14 ([South St. Paul], 1976).

11 St. Paul Chamber of Commerce, *Annual Report,* 1888, p. 79-82, 1889, p. 88; Castle, *St. Paul and Vicinity,* 1:249, 2:629-631; *Northwest Magazine,* February, 1888, p. 15, 41, 45.

12 U.S., *Census,* 1890, *Manufactures,* 2:345, 521, 525; St. Paul Chamber of Commerce, *Annual Report,* 1890, p. 60. On Minneapolis suburbs, see Norman F. Thomas, *Minneapolis-Moline: A History of Its Formation and Operations,* 196 ([New York], 1976); Gustav Rolf Svendsen, *Hennepin County History: An Illustrated Essay,* 94 ([Minneapolis], 1976).

13 Hartsough, *Development of the Twin Cities,* 52; *Minneapolis Tribune,* November 29, 1882, September 27, 1890. The St. Paul Chamber of Commerce completely ignored Minneapolis when describing local trade in its *Annual Report,* 1883, p. 10. On world trade, see Kuhlmann, *Development of the Flour-Milling Industry,* 289-294; St. Paul Chamber of Commerce, *Annual Report,* 1881, p. 11, 1883, p. 18; *Northwest Magazine,* May, 1893, p. 42, December, 1894, p. 5, April, 1896, p. 28.

14 *Northwest Magazine,* October, 1886, p. 11, April, 1887, p. 17 (quotation), October, p. 29, November, p. 25 (quotation), both 1895, January, 1896, p. 35.

15 Speer and Frost, *Minnesota State Fair,* 9-20.

16 *Minneapolis Tribune,* September 22, October 19 (quotation), 1885; *Northwest Magazine,* August, p. 23, September, p. 22 (quotation), November, p. 9, all 1886; Shutter, ed., *Minneapolis,* 1:149.

17 [Charles W. Johnson], *A Tale of Two Cities: Minneapolis and St. Paul Compared,* 90 (Minneapolis, 1885); *Northwest Magazine,* January, 1886, p. 15, March, 1887, p. 40, February, 1888, p. 1-9; St. Paul Winter Carnival Assn., *1886-1961, 75th Anniversary of the Fun-Filled St. Paul Winter Carnival,* [1-3, 6, 7] ([St. Paul, 1961?]); St. Paul Chamber of Commerce, *Annual Report,* 1887, p. 74.

18 *Northwest Magazine,* March, 1888, p. 21, February, 1889, p. 2.

19 William W. Folwell, *A History of Minnesota,* 3:480-489 (Rev. ed., St. Paul, 1969); *Northwest Magazine,* October, 1890, p. 39.

20 Calvin Schmid, *Social Saga of Two Cities: An Ecological and Statistical Study,* [71], 387 (Minneapolis, 1937); Goodrich Lowry, *Streetcar Man: Tom Lowry and the Twin City Rapid Transit Company,* 102-107, 115 (Minneapolis, 1979); *Northwest Magazine,* November, 1894, p. 19. On joint associations and boards, see *Northwest Magazine,* December, 1889, p. 17, January, 1890, p. 11; *Minneapolis Tribune,* January 1, 1890.

21 Examples of calls for merger are in *Northwest Magazine,* March, 1888, p. 21, August, 1891, p. 36; *Minneapolis Tribune,* March 29, 1891; *Northwestern Miller,* 31:500 (April 17, 1891). On the Board of Trade rejection, see St. Paul Chamber of Commerce, *Annual Report,* 1891, p. 34-39. The census war was also reported to have broken up the Twin City Commercial Club; see *Commercial West,* August 4, 1906, p. 28.

22 Muriel B. Christison, "LeRoy S. Buffington and the Minneapolis Boom of the 1880's," in *Minnesota History,* 23:222-224, 230 (September, 1942).

23 Shutter, ed., *Minneapolis,* 141-145, 314, 422; Anson B. Cutts, "Metropolitan," in *Twin Citian,* October, 1965, p. 46; *Northwest Magazine,* May, 1893, p. 19.

24 *Northwest Magazine,* November, 1884, p. 9, February, 1888, p. 36, January, p. 30, June, p. 35, both 1892, November, 1894, p. 19, June, p. 30, September, p. 27, both 1896; St. Paul Chamber of Commerce, *Annual Report,* 1886, p. 24.

25 Houses of the wealthy are described in *Northwest Magazine,* January, 1885, p. 4, June, 1892, p. 32; Roger Kennedy, "The Exuberant Eighties," in *Twin Citian,* October, 1965, p. 21. On the cities' clubs, see *Northwest Magazine,* December, 1884, p. 12, February, 1888, p. 22, February, 1889, p. 12; William C. Edgar and Loring M. Staples, *The Minneapolis Club: A Review of Its History 1883 to 1920,* 5, 10, 19 ([Minneapolis], 1974); Harold E. Wood, "The Minnesota Club of the Past," 1, 4 (1949), typescript in MHS Reference Library. On the *Blue Book* and St. Catherine's, see *Dual City Blue Book,* 1885, p. [19]; *Northwest Magazine,* August, 1895, p. 17.

26 *Greater Minneapolis,* October, 1958, p. 12, 19; Shutter, ed., *Minneapolis,* 1:463, 464; Sherman, *Music and Maestros,* 16-36, 50; James Taylor Dunn, "St. Paul's Schubert Club: Musical Mentor of the Northwest," in *Minnesota History,* 39:51-64 (Summer, 1964).

27 *St. Anthony Express,* June 14, 1851; [Theodore C. Blegen], *Horace William Shaler Cleveland: Pioneer Landscape Architect,* [5-9] (Minneapolis, 1949).

28 Shutter, ed., *Minneapolis,* 1:231-247; Castle, *St. Paul and Vicinity,* 1:372; Theodore Wirth, *Minneapolis Park System, 1883-1944,* 20, 39, 219 (Minneapolis, 1945); St. Paul Board of Park Commissioners, *Annual Report,* 1895, p. 11, 26, 29 (St. Paul, 1896).

29 In Minneapolis 36.8% of the population was foreign-born white in 1890; in St. Paul the figure was 39.9%. Schmid, *Social Saga of Two Cities,* 129. On women's contrasting positions, see *Dual City Blue Book, 1885,* p. 28, 31; St. Paul Chamber of Commerce, *Annual Report,* 1873, p. 60; *Northwest Magazine,* June, 1896, p. 31, March, 1900, p. 38. On children, see Atwater, ed., *History of Minneapolis,* 262.

30 Family Service of St. Paul, *A History of Family Service of Saint Paul, Formerly the Associated Charities of Saint Paul and the United Charities of Saint Paul,* 3-11 (St. Paul, [1944]); Associated Charities of Minneapolis, *A Quarter Century of Work Among the Poor, 1884-1909,* 15, 17 (Minneapolis, 1909). An example of private benevolence was the Washburn Memorial Orphan Asylum; see Shutter, ed., *Minneapolis,* 194.

31 George B. Engberg, "The Rise of Organized Labor in Minnesota," in *Minnesota History,* 21:374-394 (December, 1940), and "The Rise of Organized Labor in Minnesota, 1850-1890," p. 52, 55-75, 98-103, 115-119, Master's thesis, University of Minnesota, 1939.

32 Minnesota State Federation of Labor, *Year Book,* 1915, p. 27, 31 (St. Paul, 1915); Lowry, *Streetcar Man,* 95.

33 *Northwest Magazine,* October, 1893, p. 30, November, p. 16, December, p. 28, both 1894; Castle, *St. Paul and Vicinity,* 2:578; State of Minnesota, *Census, 1895,* p. 21, 45, 49; U.S., *Census,* 1890, *Compendium,* 1:434, 436, 438. Stickney was quoted in *Northwest Magazine,* November, 1893, p. 27.

1895-1920/*Passage to the Twentieth Century*

1 *Northwest Magazine,* November, 1894, p. 16; U.S., *Census,* 1900, *Abstract,* 35; 1910, *Abstract,* 23; 1920, *Population,* 1:17, 79. From 1850 to 1890 Minnesota's population grew faster than the nation's and the Twins grew faster than the state. But Minneapolis plummeted from a growth rate of 251% in 1880-90 to 23% in 1890-1900, rose to 49% in 1900-10, then dropped back to 26% in 1910-20. The figures for St. Paul for the same decades were even more sobering — 221%, 22%, 32%, and 9%.

2 U.S., *Census,* 1920, *Population,* 1:62, 64, 67, 80. Minneapolis slipped to nineteenth rank in 1900 and then recovered its previous status in 1910. The suburban communities were South St. Paul, West St. Paul, St. Louis Park, and Edina, whose populations totaled only 13,936.

3 *Northwest Magazine,* July, 1896, p. 30, October, 1897, p. 25; Walter Van Brunt, ed., *Duluth and St. Louis County: Their Story and People,* 1:248, 254-257, 268, 281, 287-289, 316-319, 323 (Chicago, 1921); Larson, *White Pine Industry,* 246, 251-264.

4 *Commercial West,* December 3, 1904, p. 25 (quotation); W[illiam] A. Hartman and J. D. Black, *Economic Aspects of Land Settlement in the Cut-Over Region of the Great Lakes States,* 2-5, 81-84 (U.S. Department of Agriculture, *Circular,* no. 160— Washington, D.C., April, 1931); Larson, *White Pine Industry,* 405. Examples of competition for northern Minnesota's trade are in *Commercial West,* September 26, 1903, p. 25, April 9, 1910, p. 45, May 3, 1913, p. 18; St. Paul Assn., *Official Bulletin,* May 22, 1920, p. [2, 3].

5 *Duluth News Tribune,* July 5, 1905, p. 4; Kane, *Waterfall,* 159-161.

6 Carl H. Chrislock, *The Progressive Era in Minnesota, 1899-1918,* 10-12, 23 (quotation), 29, 107, 109 (St. Paul, 1971); Robert H. Bahmer, "The Economic and Political Background of the Nonpar-

tisan League," 30, 467-470, Ph.D. thesis, University of Minnesota, 1941. See also Robert Morlan, *Political Prairie Fire: The Nonpartisan League, 1915-22* (Minneapolis, 1955). For an example of the Twins' claim of mutual urban and rural interests, see *St. Paul Trade Journal*, February 18, 1893, p. 4.

[7] Theodore Saloutos, "The Rise of the Equity Cooperative Exchange," in *Mississippi Valley Historical Review*, 32:33-36, 53-57 (June, 1945); *Commercial West*, March 22, p. 7, April 12, p. 9, December 27, p. 7, all 1913, February 14, p. 47, February 28, p. 7, both 1914, June 30, 1917, p. 7, September 25, 1920, p. 7, November 20, 1920, p. 7, 9. Investigations of the terminal markets included those conducted by the Minnesota legislature in 1907, 1913, and 1917, the North Dakota legislature in 1907, the U.S. Congress in 1914, and the Federal Trade Commission in the 1920s.

[8] Saloutos, in *Mississippi Valley Historical Review*, 32:31-33, 47-52, 58, 61, and "The Decline of the Equity Cooperative Exchange," in *Mississippi Valley Historical Review*, 34:406, 417 (December, 1947); *Commercial West*, March 28, p. 8, April 4, p. 7, September 12, p. 8, December 5, p. 7 (quotation), all 1914.

[9] U.S., *Census, 1920, Population*, 1:47, 54, 84. The figure for 1880 was calculated from U.S., *Census, 1880, Population*, 66, 226, 229.

[10] Originally published in *Clay County Herald* and reprinted in *Commercial West*, February 1, 1913, p. 24.

[11] For quotations on city versus farm life, see *Northwest Magazine*, February, 1903, p. 34; *Commercial West*, December 30, 1911, p. 8. For examples of efforts to increase rural population, see *Commercial West*, May 14, p. 13, June 18, p. 8, December 3, p. 8, 25, all 1904, October 15, 1910, p. 35, May 13, 1911, p. 10. On rural amenities, see *Northwest Magazine*, February, 1903, p. 34 (quotation); *Commercial West*, August 19, 1905, p. 10, August 21, 1909, p. 7. On education, see *Commercial West*, November 6, 1909, p. 7, November 12, p. 8, December 10, p. 19 (quotation), both 1910, April 8, p. 8, April 29, p. 8, both 1911, November 9, 1912, p. 7.

[12] Chrislock, *Progressive Era*, 113-115; Curtis S. Miller and Mark Starr, *A Summary of Minnesota Labor's First Hundred Years*, 26 ([Minneapolis], 1960); Barbara L. Nelson, "St. Paul and the Progressive Era: The Adoption of Commission Government," 33-50, Master's thesis, Macalester College, 1960; Jessie M. Marcley, *The Minneapolis City Charter, 1856-1925*, 73 (University of Minnesota Bureau of Research in Government, *Publications*, no. 5, — Minneapolis, 1925); William Anderson, *City Charter Making in Minnesota*, 51 (Minneapolis, 1922).

[13] Lincoln Steffens, "The Shame of Minneapolis," in Arthur and Lila Weinberg, eds., *The Muckrakers*, 6-21 (New York, 1961), first published in *McClure's Magazine*, January, 1903; David P. Nord, "Minneapolis and the Pragmatic Socialism of Thomas Van Lear," in *Minnesota History*, 45:3, 6, 8, 10 (Spring, 1976).

[14] Nelson, "St. Paul and the Progressive Era," 37; Regan, "The Irish," in Holmquist, ed., *They Chose Minnesota*, 143; William Mahoney, "Socialism!," [1926?], typescript in William Mahoney Papers, DAM, MHS; *Corning's Quarterly Razoo* (earlier called *Razoo*), 19-21 (Summer, 1920); *St. Paul Daily News*, January 29, p. 8, January 30, p. 2, both 1933; *St. Paul Pioneer Press*, October 12, 1918, p. 1, 4.

[15] *Minnesota Republican*, January 1, 1857 (quotation); Folwell, *Minnesota*, 3:300-303; Chrislock, *Progressive Era*, 77, 86; *St. Paul Pioneer Press*, January 16, p. 1, January 17, p. 1, both 1920 (quotation).

[16] *Minneapolis Daily Chronicle*, April 17, 1867; Folwell, *Minnesota*, 3:227, 4:334-336 (Repr. ed., St. Paul, 1969); *St. Paul Pioneer Press*, September 9, 1919, p. 1; Barbara Stuhler and Gretchen Kreuter, eds., *Women of Minnesota: Selected Biographical Essays*, 340, 342 (St. Paul, 1977).

[17] Folwell, *Minnesota*, 4:336; *St. Paul Pioneer Press*, September 8, p. 10, September 9, p. 1 (quotation), 1919.

[18] Clarence W. Nelson, *Reflections from History: First Half-Century of the Minneapolis Federal Reserve Bank*, 7, 15-25 (Minneapolis, 1964); *Location of Reserve Districts in the United States*, in 63 Congress, 2 session, *Senate Documents*, no. 485, p. 350 (serial 6583).

[19] *Location of Reserve Districts*, 211-266, 319-324, 350; *Commercial West*, April 11, 1914, p. 7. Forty-four additional voters indicated "Twin Cities," with no distinction between Minneapolis and St.

Paul. The Minneapolis brief was prepared by Professor R. H. Hess of Madison, Wisconsin, under the direction of the Minneapolis Civic and Commerce Association, assisted by the Minneapolis Clearing House Association, the Minneapolis Retailers' Association, the Minneapolis Produce Exchange, and the Chamber of Commerce.

[20] Hartsough, *Development of the Twin Cities*, 202; U.S., *Census, 1920, Population*, 1:84; Edwin H. Lewis, *Wholesaling in the Twin Cities*, 6 (University of Minnesota, *Studies in Economics and Business*, no. 15 — Minneapolis, 1952); Larson, *White Pine Industry*, 243, 246; *Commercial West*, October 4, 1919, p. 10. For data on manufacturing, see U.S., *Census, 1900, Manufactures*, 2:446; 1910, *Manufactures, 1909*, 9:612, 614; 1920, *Manufactures, 1919*, 9:746-753.

[21] Bottemiller, "Meat and Men," 70; U.S., *Census, 1920, Manufactures, 1919*, 9:731; Commercial Club of St. Paul, *Bulletin*, June 1, 1915, p. 3; *Northwestern Miller*, 118:1, 119 (June 18, 1919).

[22] *Minneapolis Tribune*, March 26, 29, 1895; Franklin F. Holbrook, *Minnesota in the Spanish-American War and the Philippine Insurrection*, 4-11, 18-31, 46, 115-123 (St. Paul, 1923).

[23] Holbrook, *Minnesota in the Spanish-American War*, 131-133; *Northwest Magazine*, October, 1898, p. 35 (quotation), January, 1899, p. 33.

[24] *Commercial West*, December 5, 1914, p. 9, April 28, 1917, p. 47, May 5, 1917, p. 8 (quotation); *Northwestern Miller*, 101:24, 424 (January 6, February 17, 1915); Franklin F. Holbrook and Livia Appel, *Minnesota in the War with Germany*, 1:13-15, 2:89-143, 220 (St. Paul, 1932). Particularly notable in Belgian relief were the efforts of William C. Edgar, editor of *Northwestern Miller*, who organized donations of flour from millers in twenty-four states and sailed with the cargo to its destination.

[25] Folwell, *Minnesota*, 3:556-575; *Commercial West*, May 11, p. 9, November 9, p. 7, November 30, p. 9, 10, all 1918, January 4, p. 8, August 9, p. 7, September 6, p. 7 (quotations), all 1919.

[26] *Commercial West*, July 13, 1918, p. 7.

[27] Schmid, *Social Saga of Two Cities*, 129, 132-136; *Commercial West*, March 18, 1905, p. 7, November 30, 1918, p. 9, 10, September 16, 1922, p. 8; Holmquist, ed., *They Chose Minnesota*, 3, 10; Carol Aronovici, *Americanization*, 46 (St. Paul, 1919).

[28] *St. Paul Pioneer Press*, November 7, 1906, p. 5; St. Paul Symphony Orchestra, *Descriptive Programs, 1906-1907 Season*, n.p.; Sherman, *Music and Maestros*, 38-40, 54, 131-134; Minnesota Orchestra, *Program*, [October], 1968, p. [4].

[29] *Metropolitan Opera House Programme*, March 11, 1900, p. [8]; May 20, 1906, p. 3; Sam S. Schubert Theater, St. Paul, *Program*, ca. 1911, n.p.; *Commercial West*, November 13, 1915, p. 7.

[30] Allison Danzig and Joe Reichler, *The History of Baseball: Its Great Players, Teams and Managers*, 66 (Englewood Cliffs, N.J., 1959); St. Paul Assn., *Official Bulletin*, April 17, 1920, p. [4]. A brief historical sketch of the American Association is in Robert L. Finch, L. H. Addington, and Ben M. Morgan, eds., *The Story of Minor League Baseball*, 89 (Columbus, Ohio, 1952).

[31] *St. Paul Dispatch*, June 6, 1955, p. 16; *Minneapolis Journal*, November 24, 1938, anniversary sec., p. 90 (quotations); Finch *et al.*, eds., *Minor League Baseball*, 90. *Minneapolis Journal*, cited above, states that Kelley moved in 1921. The poem, "The Return of Kelley" by George K. Foster, is in *Razoo*, September 15, 1908, p. 33.

[32] *Northwest Magazine*, March, 1903, p. 48.

[33] Dorothy V. Walters, "Pioneering with the Automobile in Minnesota," in *Minnesota History*, 26:25, 27 (March, 1945); *Minneapolis Tribune Hustler*, vol. 4, no. 10, p. 18-21 (1908); Castle, *St. Paul and Vicinity*, 2:603; Shutter, ed., *Minneapolis*, 656.

[34] On local manufactures, see Alan Ominsky, "A Catalog of Minnesota-Made Cars and Trucks," in *Minnesota History*, 43:93, 99, 106, 109 (Fall, 1972); *Commercial West*, October 17, 1914, p. 11, April 8, 1916, p. 10, November 7, 1925, p. 11. On early gas stations and mechanics, see *Minneapolis Journal*, November 24, 1938, anniversary sec., p. 28; Walters, in *Minnesota History*, 26:27; *Commercial West*, July 31, 1915, p. 11. On distribution and auto shows in the Twin Cities, see *Commercial West*, September 19, 1908, p. 18, February 18, p. 53, March 11, p. 30, both 1911, February 10, 1917, p. 11, January 28, 1922, p. 10; Ominsky, in *Minnesota History*, 43:96; *Greater Minneapolis*, April, 1952, p. 12. On garages, see ad in *Commercial West*, June 10, 1911, p. 39.

35 *Commercial West,* July 30, p. 23, October 22, p. 22 (quotation), both 1910; December 7, 1912, p. 11 (quotation). On auto thefts, see *Commercial West,* November 1, 1913, p. 9, February 1, 1919, p. 4. On hazards, see *Commercial West,* May 31, 1913, p. 7, January 17, p. 38, May 22, p. 31, both 1920, January 20, 1923, p. 8, February 16, 1924, p. 7. On fuel conservation, see *Commercial West,* November 20, 1915, p. 8, April 1, 1916, p. 30, September 4, 1920, p. 8.

36 *Commercial West,* February 17, 1912, p. 22, December 13, 1913, p. 11, April 3, 1915, p. 21, August 2, 1918, p. 8; Minneapolis City Council, *Proceedings,* 1918-19, p. 416; Kieffer, *Transit and the Twins,* 36, 37; Lewis Olds, "The Way It Was," in *Greater Minneapolis,* March, 1975, p. 26.

37 *Commercial West,* November 5, 1904, p. 9.

38 *Commercial West,* October 7, 1911, p. 8 (quotation), August 27, 1927, p. 7 (quotation); Noel Allard, *Speed: The Biography of Charles W. Holman,* 4-6, 9, 11, 13 (Chaska, 1976); Stephen E. Mills, *More Than Meets the Sky: A Pictorial History of the Founding and Growth of Northwest Airlines,* 13 (Seattle, 1972).

39 *Commercial West,* November 30, 1912, p. 9; Fred A. Sasse, *The Dan Patch Story,* 14, 97 (Harrisburg, Pa., 1957); Commercial Club of St. Paul, *Bulletin,* August 1, 1915, p. 2. The speedway was in receivership by 1916; *Commercial West, July 15, 1916, p. 10.*

1920-29/*The Jazz Age*

1 *Commercial West,* May 17, 1924, p. 7, December 4, 1926, p. 4.

2 George A. Barton, *My Lifetime in Sports,* 46, 55-78, 85-89, 310-313 (Minneapolis, 1957); *Nat Fleischer's All-Time Ring Record Book,* 16 (Norwalk, Conn., 1943); St. Paul Hockey Club, *1927-1928 Season Official Schedule and Program;* Zander Hollander and Hal Bock, eds., *The Complete Encyclopedia of Ice Hockey,* 275 (Englewood Cliffs, N.J., 1974); Dick Cullum, "Americanizing Canada's Sport," in *Saint Paul Magazine,* March, 1929, p. 16.

3 James E. Kelley, *Minnesota Golf: 75 Years of Tournament History,* 9-12, 31, 35, 231 (Minneapolis, 1976).

4 *Minneapolis Tribune,* February 10, 1946, p. 14; *Capitol Theatre Magazine and Programme,* St. Paul, January 28, 1922, n.p.; Capitol Theatre, *Programs,* 1922-23; Ethan Mordden, *That Jazz! An Idiosyncratic History of the American Twenties,* 53 (New York, 1978).

5 *Capitol Theatre Magazine,* March 29, 1924, p. 20; *St. Paul Dispatch,* March 25, 1927, p. 29; *Minneapolis Tribune,* February 10, 1946, p. 14; Mordden, *That Jazz!,* 219.

6 Files of the magazines are in the MHS Reference Library.

7 James Taylor Dunn, "A Century of Song: Popular Music in Minnesota," in *Minnesota History,* 44:133, 136 (Winter, 1974); advertisement for the New Coliseum Pavilion in *Capitol Theatre Magazine,* July 26-August 2, 1924, p. 10; advertisement for the Black Cat Club, [1929], in pamphlet collection, MHS Reference Library.

8 Ted Curtis Smythe, "The Birth of Twin Cities' Commercial Radio," in *Minnesota History,* 41:327-334 (Fall, 1969); *Greater Minneapolis,* November, 1954, p. 40, March, 1962, p. 10-12, 25; *Saint Paul Magazine,* Fall, 1929, p. 10; St. Paul Assn., *News Bulletin,* March 19, 1928, p. [1], and *Official Bulletin,* March 12, p. [2], April 16, p. [1], both 1927; Henry A. Bellows, "The Business of Broadcasting," in Minneapolis Civic and Commerce Assn., *Minneapolis, Metropolis of the Northwest,* February, 1928, p. 5, 6, 43; Mordden, *That Jazz!,* 214.

9 Here and two paragraphs below, see *Gold Medal Radio Station News,* January 1925-March 1927, especially February, 1927, p. 1; Earle R. Buell, "What Is Radio Doing to America?" in *Radio Record,* October, 1928, p. 10; MHS Biographies Project files.

10 *Gold Medal Radio Station News,* January, 1926, p. 3.

11 *Commercial West,* January 7, 1911, p. 8; St. Paul Assn., *Official Bulletin,* November 8, 1918, p. [2]; Allard, *Speed,* 4.

12 Here and below, see St. Paul Assn., *Official Bulletin,* August 14, 1920, p. [1]; *Commercial West,* August 14, 1920, p. 11; Mills, *More Than Meets The Sky,* 13-23; Allard, *Speed,* 62; Harold R. Harris, "Commercial Aviation," in *Minnesota History,* 33:241 (Summer, 1953).

13 *Commercial West,* August 4, p. 42, October 20, p. 12, both 1928, January 19, 1929, p. 11; St. Paul Assn., *Weekly News Bulletin,* April 11, 1930, p. 1; *Minneapolis City Directory,* 1929, p. 2; *St. Paul City Directory,* 1930, p. 921.

14 Allard, *Speed,* 75; *Commercial West,* July 28, 1928, p. 41; St. Paul Assn., *Official Bulletin,* April 17, p. [4], June 19, 1920, p. [1], May 1, p. [1], June 5, p. [2], June 12, p. [3], all 1926; *Greater Minneapolis,* April, 1961, p. 13.

15 Kieffer, *Transit and the Twins,* 36-38; Laurence A. Rossman, *A Romance of Transportation,* 1 ([Grand Rapids, 1940]); Minnesota Railroad and Warehouse Commission, Auto Transportation Company Division, *Biennial Report,* 1925-26, p. 4, 1929-30, p. 307; Arthur S. Genet, *"Profile of Greyhound!" The Greyhound Corporation,* 8-18 (Princeton, N.J., 1958). See also Chapter 4, p. xxx. The Twin City Rapid Transit Company acquired the bus lines in the metropolitan area in the 1920s.

16 *On Parade, East Side,* December, 1928, n.p.; *Commercial West,* March 23, 1929, p. 31; Jerry Boschee, "Hauling People Profitably," in *Greater Minneapolis,* March, 1975, p. 30.

17 Minnesota Railroad and Warehouse Commission, *Biennial Report,* 1929-30, p. 303-306; *Commercial West,* December 28, 1912, p. 45; Russell C. Engberg, "Rural Motor Truck Lines in the Twin Cities," in H. Bruce Price, ed., *The Marketing of Farm Products: Studies in the Organization of the Twin Cities Market,* 366-369, 372, 375-377 (Minneapolis, 1927); *Midway Club Bulletin,* June, 1923, p. 5, January, 1924, p. 5.

18 Engberg, in Price, ed., *Marketing of Farm Products,* 387-389; *Commercial West,* November 21, 1925, p. 32.

19 Cited in *Commercial West,* June 10, 1922, p. 31.

20 St. Paul Assn., *Official Bulletin,* April 5, 1924, p. [1]; *Commercial West,* December 15, 1923, p. 8, January 21, 1928, p. 7; Kieffer, *Transit and the Twins,* 43; Olds, in *Greater Minneapolis,* March, 1975, p. 27.

21 *Commercial West,* November 3, 1923, p. 24; U.S., Census, 1920, *Population,* 1:64, 67, and 1930, *Metropolitan Districts,* 5, 131. Urbanized areas in Anoka, Dakota, Hennepin, Ramsey, and Washington counties were included in the enumeration in both census years. In 1920, however, only areas ten miles from the central cities' boundaries were included. This limitation was not applied in 1930.

22 Andrew W. Crawford, *Plan of Minneapolis Prepared Under the Direction of the Civic Commission MCMXVII by Edward H. Bennett, Architect,* 13, 117 (Minneapolis, 1917).

23 St. Paul Assn., *Official Bulletin,* September 22, 1923, p. [1, 4]; "The Metropolitan and Regional Planning Association of Minneapolis, St. Paul and Environs," June, 1928, typescript in MHS Reference Library.

24 Metropolitan District Planning Assn., "Sewage Disposal in Twin City Area," in *Bulletin of the Minnesota Federation of Architectural and Engineering Societies,* November, 1926, p. 12-24; Metropolitan Drainage Commission, *Report,* 1927, p. 1-11; Jordan, *People's Health,* 144-147.

25 U.S., *Census,* 1930, *Population,* 1:15, 18, 544, 2:19; *Metropolitan Districts,* 131.

26 *Northwestern Miller,* Anniversary Number, December, 1923, p. 1; U.S., *Census,* 1930, *Population,* 1:18, 4:838, *Manufactures: 1929,* 1:298, *Distribution Volume 1: Retail Distribution Part II,* 1343-1346, 1356-1358, *Distribution Volume 2: Wholesale Distribution,* 789, 790; Hartsough, *Development of the Twin Cities,* 202; Ray Vaughn, "Minneapolis vs. St. Paul: The Holy War Between the Twin Cities," in *Haldeman-Julius Quarterly,* 2:155 (January-March, 1928); *Commercial West,* February 2, 1929, p. 15.

27 Kane, *Waterfall,* 175; *Corning's Quarterly Razoo,* Spring, 1925, p. [2]; Virginia Huck, *Brand of the Tartan: The 3M Story,* 2, 31, 57 (New York, 1955); *St. Paul Pioneer Press,* January 4, 1931, p. 3; Nicholas Westbrook, ed., *A Guide to the Industrial Archeology of the Twin Cities,* 67 ([St. Paul], 1983).

28 Charles S. Popple, *Development of Two Bank Groups in the Central Northwest: A Study in Bank Policy and Organization,* 153-155, 165, 174-206 (Cambridge, Mass., 1944); Larson, *Land of the Giants,* 121-123; *Commercial West,* September 1, 1928, p. 16, February 2, p. 8, March 2, p. 11, August 17, p. 41, all 1929, June 14, 1930, p. 18.

29 *Commercial West,* April 30, 1927, p. 20; Popple, *Development of Two Bank Groups,* 149, 156; Marcy Frances McNulty, "Wilbur

Burton Foshay: The Saga of a Salesman," 1-4, 11-89, Master's thesis, Creighton University, 1964.

[30] Galbraith, *The Great Crash: 1929,* 7 (Boston, 1961).

[31] Kane, *Waterfall,* 173; Popple, *Development of Two Bank Groups,* 70-110; St. Paul Assn., *Official Bulletin,* September 25, 1926, p. [3]. For examples of Twin Citians' attitudes toward agricultural problems, see *Commercial West,* December 10, 1921, p. 7, March 10, p. 8, July 21, p. 7, both 1923, February 16, 1924, p. 14, February 27, 1926, p. 8.

[32] Popple, *Development of Two Bank Groups,* 156; *Commercial West,* April 7, p. 6, June 9, p. 7, November 10, p. 9, all 1928, March 16, 1929, p. 17.

[33] *Commercial West,* November 9, 1929, p. 6; McNulty, "Wilbur Burton Foshay," 89-98

1929-45/Depression and War

[1] *Commercial West,* October 4, 1930, p. 6.

[2] Roland S. Vaile *et al., Impact of the Depression on Business Activity and Real Income in Minnesota,* 14-17 (Minneapolis, 1933); Alvin H. Hansen *et al., The Decline of Employment in the 1930-1931 Depression in St. Paul, Minneapolis, and Duluth,* 31-34 (Minneapolis, 1932); U.S., *Census,* 1930, *Population,* 1:18, 2:18; 1930, *Manufactures: 1929,* 1:298; 1930, *Unemployment,* 1:533, 534; 1940, *Manufactures: 1939,* 3:522-526; 1940, *Population,* vol. 1, pp. 16, 32, 63, 555, vol. 3, part 3, p. 689. The population of Minneapolis was 464,356 in 1930 and 492,370 in 1940; for the same years St. Paul's population was 271,606 and 287,736. The population of the metropolitan district in 1930 was 832,258 and in 1940 it was 911,077; the growth rate was 9.5%. The central cities' growth rate was 6%; outside the central cities the rate was 36%.

[3] Minneapolis Dept. of Public Welfare, *Historical Review, Division of Public Relief: Four Years of Depression, 1931-1932-1933-1934,* 4, 5 ([Minneapolis, 1935]); Board of Public Welfare, Ramsey County and St. Paul, *Annual Report,* 1931, p. 4.

[4] Minneapolis Dept. of Public Welfare, *Historical Review,* 1; Board of Public Welfare, Ramsey County and St. Paul, *Annual Report,* 1933, p. 13, 14; *Census of Partial Employment, Unemployment, and Occupations, 1937: Final Report on Total and Partial Unemployment for Minnesota,* 1 (Washington, D.C., 1938).

[5] St. Paul Assn., *Weekly News Bulletin,* October 30, 1931, p. [1]; Raymond L. Koch, "The Development of Public Relief Programs in Minnesota, 1929-1941," 23, Ph.D. thesis, University of Minnesota, 1967.

[6] Koch, "Development of Public Relief Programs," 12-16; *Commercial West,* November 29, 1930, p. 6, December 19, p. 13, August 8, p. 14, both 1931.

[7] George Tselos, "Self-Help and Sauerkraut: The Organized Unemployed, Inc., of Minneapolis," in *Minnesota History,* 45:306-320 (quotations, p. 309, 320) (Winter, 1977).

[8] Minneapolis Citizens Committee on Public Relief and Finance, *Analysis: Public Welfare Programs, City of Minneapolis,* 1, 6, 20, 27 ([Minneapolis], 1939). See also Board of Public Welfare, Ramsey County and St. Paul, *Annual Report,* 1939, p. 79.

[9] Board of Public Welfare, Ramsey County and St. Paul, *Annual Report,* 1935, p. 11, 12; Raymond L. Koch, "Politics and Relief in Minneapolis During the 1930s," in *Minnesota History,* 41:153-170 (Winter, 1968).

[10] For examples, see Board of Public Welfare, Ramsey County and St. Paul, *Annual Reports,* 1929-1939; Minneapolis Dept. of Public Welfare, *Historical Review.*

[11] David L. Rosheim, *The Other Minneapolis or The Rise and Fall of the Gateway, The Old Minneapolis Skid Row,* 115-138 (Maquoketa, Iowa, 1978); Minneapolis Dept. of Public Welfare, *Historical Review,* 31-33; Paul M. Segner, *Minneapolis Unemployed: A Description and Analysis of the Resident Relief Population of the City of Minneapolis from 1900 to 1936,* 42-44 (Minneapolis, 1937); Board of Public Welfare, Ramsey County and St. Paul, *Annual Report,* 1936, p. 27, 1937, p. 23; Minnesota State Emergency Relief Administration, *A Report of the Minnesota State Board of Control as the State Emergency Relief Administration,* 35-43 (St. Paul, 1934).

[12] Carl G. Langland, "What the WPA Did for St. Paul," in Gurdon Simmons and Ralph L. Meyer, comps., *This Is Your America,* 3:104-109 (New York, 1943); Accomplishment Reports, Administrative Files, Works Projects Administration, (WPA), Minnesota, Records, DAM, MHS; Nancy A. Johnson, *Accomplishments: Minnesota Art Projects in the Depression Years,* 1-14 (Duluth, 1976); Writers' Project, WPA, "Achievements of the Minnesota Writers' Project of W.P.A.: The Final Report," 4-10 (N.p., [1942?]).

[13] Board of Public Welfare, Ramsey County and St. Paul, *Annual Report,* 1933, p. 10; William Mahoney, Inaugural Address, June [17?], 1932, Mahoney Papers; Koch, in *Minnesota History,* 41:154-158, 160; George H. Mayer, *The Political Career of Floyd B. Olson,* 120 (Minneapolis, 1951); *Commercial West,* February 27, 1932, p. 6.

[14] Citizens' Alliance of Ramsey and Dakota Counties, *Section "7A" and Employment Relations Policies,* [25] (St. Paul, 1934?); Miller and Starr, *Minnesota Labor's First Hundred Years,* 33-44; William Mahoney to Editor, *Minnesota Union Advocate,* June 1, 1938, Mahoney Papers; Thomas E. Blantz, "Father Haas and the Minneapolis Truckers' Strike of 1934," in *Minnesota History,* 42:5-15 (Spring, 1970); Farrell Dobbs, *Teamster Rebellion* (New York, 1972). Local 574 became Local 544 in the late 1930s; see Dobbs, *Teamster Power* (New York, 1973).

[15] Here and below, see Herman Erickson, "WPA Strike and Trials of 1939," in *Minnesota History,* 42:202-214 (quotation, p. 212) (Summer, 1971).

[16] Schmid, *Social Saga of Two Cities,* 322-330; Nate N. Bomberg, "St. Paul and the Federal Building in the Twenties and Thirties," in Eileen Michels, *A Landmark Reclaimed,* 49, 50 ([St. Paul?], 1977); St. Paul Bureau of Police, Dept. of Public Safety, *Annual Report,* 1939, p. 21, 1945, p. 22; *Commercial West,* September 3, 1921, p. 8, December 9, 1922, p. 8, September 12, p. 11, October 17, p. 8, both 1925, January 16, 1926, p. 4, July 19, 1930, p. 6; *Sheriffs' and Police Review,* April, 1933, p. 13, April, 1934, p. 4.

[17] Fred W. Friendly, "Censorship and Journalists' Privilege: The Case of Near Versus Minnesota — A Half Century Later," in *Minnesota History,* 46:147 (quotation) (Winter, 1978); Bomberg, in Michels, *Landmark Reclaimed,* 52-57. The *Saturday Press,* published by Jay M. Near and Howard A. Guilford, became the basis of a celebrated lawsuit — Near *vs.* Minnesota — that struck down a state law imposing prior restraint of a newspaper and reaffirmed the freedom to publish under the First Amendment to the United States Constitution.

[18] Bomberg, in Michels, *Landmark Reclaimed,* 58-61 (quotation, p. 61); Raymond Moley and Edgar Sisson, "Crime Marches On: St. Paul — Gangster's Paradise," in *Today,* June 23, 1934, p. 3, 22-24; *Sheriffs' and Police Review,* January, 1935, p. 2; *Fortune,* April, 1936, p. 186.

[19] Blegen, *Minnesota,* 535; *Commercial West,* November 19, 1932, p. 18, April 1, p. 13, June 17, p. 13, both 1933.

[20] George W. Garlid, "The Antiwar Dilemma of the Farmer-Labor Party," in *Minnesota History,* 40:365-374 (Winter, 1967).

[21] Elmer A. Benson, *Mobilizing for Peace* (St. Paul, 1937); Millard L. Gieske, *Minnesota Farmer-Laborism: The Third Party Alternative,* 248-251 (Minneapolis, 1979).

[22] George W. Garlid, "Minneapolis Unit of the Committee to Defend America by Aiding the Allies," in *Minnesota History,* 41:267-283 (Summer, 1969).

[23] *Commercial West,* December 13, 1941, p. 6; Virginia B. Kunz, *Muskets to Missiles: A Military History of Minnesota,* 169-182 (St. Paul, 1958); Marilyn Ziebarth and Alan Ominsky, *Fort Snelling: Anchor Post of the Northwest,* 31 (St. Paul, 1970); Masaharu Ano, "Loyal Linguists: Nisei of World War II Learned Japanese in Minnesota," in *Minnesota History,* 45:273, 278-287 (Fall, 1977); Blegen, *Minnesota,* 542.

[24] St. Paul Assn., *News,* December, 1944, p. [1]; June W. Dahl, *Footprints: A History of St. Paul Red Cross,* 106-108 (St. Paul, 1981).

[25] *St. Paul Pioneer Press/Dispatch,* April 5, 1980, p. 8; March 11, 1983, p. 1C.

[26] "When Stars 'Fell' on Minnesota," in *Minnesota History,* 44:108-112 (Fall, 1974); Gray, *University of Minnesota,* 418, 516; *Commercial West,* May 13, 1944, p. 26, November 17, 1945, p. 14; J. Arthur Myers, *Masters of Medicine,* 726-728 (St. Louis, 1968).

[27] *Minneapolis Star Journal,* March 7, p. 21, March 18, p. 15, both 1941; Larson, *Land of the Giants,* 144-151; *Commercial West,* Au-

gust 9, 1941, p. 19, February 27, 1943, p. 8; St. Paul Assn., *News,* May, 1941, p. [1], December, 1944, p. [1]; *Upper Mississippi River Bulletin,* November, 1942, p. [1], May, p. [1], August, p. [1], September, p. [1], all 1943.

28 *Commercial West,* March 8, 1941, p. 34, November 7, 1942, p. 22, June 10, 1944, p. 13; Minneapolis-Moline Power Implement Co., *A Wartime Report: Food, Too, Fights for Freedom,* 5 (quotation) (Minneapolis, n.d.).

29 *Commercial West,* June 27, 1942, p. 15.

30 *Commercial West,* August 18, 1945, p. 7.

31 St. Paul Winter Carnival Assn., *1886-1961, 75th Anniversary,* [9-13]; *St. Paul Pioneer Press,* February 22, p. 1, 2, February 23, p. 1, February 24, p. 1, 22, all 1946.

32 *Greater Minneapolis,* July, 1951, p. 10 (quotation), July, 1963, p. 10, 11, June, 1967, p. 20; *Minneapolis, City of Opportunity,* 134-143 (Minneapolis, 1956).

33 *Sixteenth Annual Ice Carnival: The Hippodrome Skating Club of the Twin Cities,* January 16, 1925, and *Shipstad and Johnson's Ice Revue News,* January 12, 1937, both in pamphlet collection, MHS Reference Library; Russ Davis, "Ziegfelds on Ice," in *Saturday Evening Post,* December 14, 1940, p. 16, 35, 37; L. E. Leipold, *Eddie Shipstad, Ice Follies Star,* (Minneapolis, 1971).

34 St. Paul Assn., *News,* August, 1939, p. [1]; Pop Concert Programs, [1937], [1938], [1940], [1941], [1943], 1945, and [1949]; *1939 National Figure Skating Championships Conducted by United States Figure Skating Association, A.S.U.,* January 19-21, 1939, all programs in MHS Reference Library.

35 Barton, *My Lifetime in Sports,* 284, 313-315; *St. Paul Pioneer Press/Dispatch,* November 17, 1979, p. 5B; John Devaney, *Baseball's Youngest Big Leaguers,* 14 (New York, 1969); National Assn. of Professional Baseball Leagues, *The Story of Minor League Baseball,* 90 (Columbus, Ohio, 1952); Edward Simpkins, *The History of Minnesota State High School Basketball Tournaments, 1913-1963,* 34-79 (Prior Lake, 1964).

36 Gray, *University of Minnesota,* 557-559.

37 Barton, *My Lifetime in Sports,* 299-302 (quotation); Kelley, *Minnesota Golf,* 106, 107, 147; James and Lynn Hahn, *Patty! The Sports Career of Patricia Berg* (Mankato, 1981).

38 Stuhler and Kreuter, eds., *Women of Minnesota,* 339; *Who's Who in America, 1978-1979,* 2:2570 (Chicago, [1978?]); Bernice White, ed., *Who's Who in Minnesota,* 197 (Seattle, 1958).

39 *Greater Minneapolis,* December, 1953, p. 12-14; Sherman, *Music and Maestros,* 227-288 (quotation, p. 227). Ormandy became conductor of the Philadelphia Orchestra upon leaving Minneapolis.

40 Robert A. Stebbins, "The History of Jazz in Minneapolis," 4, 26, undated typescript in MHS Reference Library; David Ewen, *All the Years of American Popular Music,* 284, 285, 322, 393, 410, 431, 474 (Englewood Cliffs, N.J., 1977).

41 Paul Michael *et al.,* eds., *The American Movies Reference Book: The Sound Era,* 1-22, *passim* (Englewood Cliffs, N.J., 1969).

1945-83/Metropolis

1 Thomas J. Abercrombie, "A Tale of Twin Cities: Minneapolis and St. Paul," in *National Geographic,* 158:666 (November, 1980).

2 Here and below, see U.S., *Census,* 1940, *Population,* 1:32, 35, 63, 555; 1950, *Population,* 1:1-65, 1-71, 1-76, vol. 2, part 1, p. 1-67, 1-74; 1960, *Population,* vol. 1, part A, p. 1-66, 1-102, 1-108, 1-117; 1970, *Population,* vol. 1, part 1, section 1, p. 116, 175, 183, 189; 1980, *Census of Housing,* vol. 1, part 25, p. 9, 12, 13. The Minneapolis-St. Paul Standard Metropolitan Statistical Area in 1980 included Anoka, Carver, Chisago, Dakota, Hennepin, Ramsey, Scott, Washington, and Wright counties in Minnesota and St. Croix County in Wisconsin.

3 Kane, *Waterfall,* 173; Larson, *Land of the Giants,* 6; Carol Pine, "From Cheerios to Marvin Gardens," in *Corporate Report,* March, 1976, p. 24-27, 56-61; *St. Paul Pioneer Press/Dispatch,* March 5, 1983, p. 6C; Ken Johnson, "Peavey Moves Out from the Mill," in *Corporate Report,* July, 1977, p. 37-39, 72; *Corporate Report Minnesota,* February, 1983, p. 74; *Minneapolis Tribune,* April 18, 1982, p. 1A. Swift and Company closed in 1969, Armour and Company in 1978, and John Morrell and Company in 1979. See

4 Upper Midwest Research and Development Council, *New Ideas in the Upper Midwest,* 2, 4, 9, 19 (Minneapolis, 1965); Larson, *Land of the Giants,* 20-23, 125-128, 161; *Corporate Report Fact Book,* 1981, p. 175; 3M Co., *Annual Report,* 1982.

5 Larson, *Land of the Giants,* 154-161 (quotation, p. 154); Carol Pine and Susan Mundale, *Self-made: The Stories of 12 Minnesota Entrepreneurs,* 101-124 (Minneapolis, 1982); Robert J. Witt, "The Incomplete Genesis: How Minnesota Almost Became the Computer Capital of the World," in *Corporate Report,* July, 1974, p. 16-19, 74, 75; Milton E. Adams, "World Medical Center," in *Greater Minneapolis,* December, 1972, p. 16; *Corporate Report Fact Book,* 1981, p. 168.

6 J. G. White Engineering Co., *Economic Analysis of the State of Minnesota: Report to Minnesota Resources Commission,* 3:34, 35 (New York, 1945); James M. Henderson and Anne O. Krueger, *National Growth and Economic Change in the Upper Midwest,* 112 (Minneapolis, 1965); Mildred L. Hartsough, *From Canoe to Steel Barge on the Upper Mississippi,* xiii, 220, 246, 277 (Minneapolis, 1934); Kane, *Waterfall,* 175, 176; *Greater Minneapolis,* January, 1953, p. 23; A. D. Strong, "Men of Vision Gave Minnesota a Dependable Waterway to the Sea," in *Greater Minneapolis,* January, 1958, p. 124, 126, 128.

7 *Commercial West,* December 23, 1944, p. 11, June 2, 1945, p. 16; [Northwest Airlines, Inc.], *Northwest Passage Coast-to-Coast* ([N.p., 1945]); Mills, *More Than Meets the Sky,* 87; St. Paul Assn., *News,* August, 1946, p. [1]; *Air International,* November, 1982, p. 223.

8 Here and below, see Burlington Northern Inc., *Annual Report,* 1981, p. 3; Larson, *Land of the Giants,* 10; Steven Leuthold, "Can Amtrak Be Saved?" in *Corporate Report,* September, 1979, p. 78; Westbrook, ed., *Guide to Industrial Archeology,* 77.

9 Kieffer, *Transit and the Twins,* 51, 53; Ronald Abler *et al., The Twin Cities of St. Paul and Minneapolis,* 51 (Cambridge, Mass., 1976).

10 Folwell, *Minnesota,* 1:196; Judith A. Hendricks, ed., *Bloomington on the Minnesota,* 7, 13, 30, 36, 44, 103-105 (Bloomington, 1976). See also U.S., *Census,* 1940, *Population,* 1:542; 1970, *Population,* vol. 1, part 25, p. 17. The count in 1980 was 81,831; *St. Paul Pioneer Press,* March 29, 1981, Metro/Region sec., 2.

11 Metropolitan Council [of the Twin Cities Area], *Industrial Expansion and Migration in the Twin Cities Metropolitan Area, 1960-1970: An Economic Data Report,* 19 (N.p., 1973); St. Paul Assn., *News,* November, 1953, p. 3; Theodore Kolderie, "Twin Cities," in *Suburban Profile,* A-2 (Minneapolis, 1971); Abler *et al., Twin Cities,* 59; *Greater Minneapolis,* November, 1956, p. 36, June, 1960, p. 20.

12 *St. Paul Pioneer Press,* July 2, 1957, p. 6; *St. Paul Dispatch,* February 11, 1976, p. 35.

13 Kolderie, in *Suburban Profile,* A-3; Abler *et al., Twin Cities,* 41; Metropolitan Council, *Industrial Expansion and Migration,* 19; The Joint Program, *Program Notes,* March, 1965, p. 2; St. Paul Area Chamber of Commerce, *Action,* January 1, 1962, p. 6, January 10, 1966, p. 2; *Greater Minneapolis,* November, 1963, p. 14, February, 1970, p. 17. Notable exceptions to the sphere-of-influence expansion were the St. Paul suburbs of Roseville and Eagan, where Minneapolis emigrants were strongly represented.

14 Larry Lindsay, "Urb vs. Exurb," in *Greater Minneapolis,* September, 1973, p. 64; *Greater Minneapolis,* August, 1950, p. 10.

15 *St. Paul Pioneer Press,* September 21, 1969, Leisure sec., p. 1, 5.

16 *St. Paul Pioneer Press,* September 21, 1969, p. 1; Barry Morrow, "The Beltrami Neighborhood Remembered," in *Common Ground,* Spring, 1974, p. 4-10 (quotation, p. 10).

17 Judith A. Martin, *Recycling the Central City: The Development of a New Town-In Town,* ix, xi (Minneapolis, 1978); Gene Struble, "Bombed-Out Look — The Changing Function of Downtown," in St. Paul Area Chamber of Commerce, *Action,* March 7, 1966, p. 2.

18 Marcia Brinkman, "Edward Baker and the Battle for Downtown," Joanna Baymiller, "The High and the Mighty," in *Corporate Report,* January, 1976, p. 29-32, 60, July, 1979, p. 86, 122 (quotations); *Corporate Report,* January, 1975, p. 8; Gurney Breckenfeld, "How Minneapolis Fends Off the Urban Crisis," in *Fortune,* January, 1976, p. 135; Andrew W. Crawford, *Plan of Minneapolis; Greater Minneapolis,* July, 1952, p. 7 (quotation). See also Carol

Pine, "A New Day Downtown," Linda Mack, "Minneapolis Development: Progress, Politics, or Just Plain Chaos?" in *Corporate Report*, July, 1977, p. 23-26, 58-63, April, 1980, p. 67-69, 108, 111, 119-121.

[19] *Commercial West*, August 5, 1944, p. 31; St. Paul Assn., *News*, April, 1945, p. 2; St. Paul Area Chamber of Commerce, *Action*, June 1, 1964, p. 2, May 4, p. 2, July 13, p. 2, 3, both 1969, August 27, p. 2-4, October 9, p. [1], October 23, p. 2, all 1972, January 15, 1973, p. [2]; Carol Pine, "The Rebirth of St. Paul," in *Passages*, April, 1981, p. 24 (quotation) and "Downtown St. Paul: To Be or Not To Be," in *Corporate Report*, October, 1977, p. 70; *St. Paul Pioneer Press*, February 8, 1976, p. 2A (quotation), May 17, 1981, Focus sec., 2.

[20] Pine, in *Passages*, April, 1981, p. 24-30, 34, 36, 38 (quotation, p. 24); *St. Paul Pioneer Press*, October 7, 1980, p. 15.

[21] Baymiller, in *Corporate Report*, July, 1979, p. 122; *Minneapolis Tribune*, May 23, 1981, p. 1S, 4S.

[22] Here and below, see *St. Paul Pioneer Press*, January 17, 1965, p. 8A, May 18, sec. 1, p. 1 (quotation), 8, May 19, p. 1, 4, May 20, p. 1, 6, May 21, p. 1, 4, 5, May 22, p. 1, 4, May 23, p. 1, 4, all 1980, March 2, 1982, p. 6; *Minneapolis Tribune*, October 3, 1982, p. 1G; *Newsweek*, June 29, 1981, p. 82 (quotation). See also Roy M. Close, "The Art of Survival in the Arts," in *Mpls./St. Paul*, July, 1981, p. 62-65; Anson B. Cutts, "Saint Paul Opera Makes History," in *Select Twin Citian*, November, 1962, p. 21.

[23] The survey included performances offered through the media as well as "live" performances; see *Minneapolis Star*, October 9, 1974, p. 6C; *St. Paul Pioneer Press*, May 18, sec. 1, p. 8, May 20, p. 6, both 1980 (quotations). See also Governor's Commission on the Arts, *Minnesota: State of the Arts*, 2-5 (St. Paul, 1977).

[24] Ewen, *American Popular Music*, 463-466, 552-569, 612-617, 631, 632, 645-648; "Discotheque: The Monkey Swims Only with the Watusi," in *Twin Citian*, January, 1965, p. 10-13.

[25] *Commercial West*, April 16, 1927, p. 8; *TV Times: Advance Program Schedules for the Week of July 22 thru July 28, 1950*, 3, and *passim*.

[26] *St. Paul Pioneer Press*, May 10, 1982, p. 1D, 15D; Phil Berger, *Heroes of Pro Basketball*, 27 (New York, 1968); *Greater Minneapolis*, July, 1958, p. 23; Alexander M. Weyand, *The Cavalcade of Basketball*, 239-247 (New York, 1960); Joe Jares, *Basketball: The American Game*, 209, 216 (Chicago, 1971). Professional basketball in the Twin Cities revived briefly in the late 1960s with the Minnesota Muskies and Minnesota Pipers, and in the late 1970s with the Minnesota Fillies, a women's team.

[27] Here and below, see Charles Johnson, "The Story of How Minnesota Got Major League Baseball," in *Greater Minneapolis*, December, 1960, p. 11-13; *St. Paul Pioneer Press*, April 18, 1983, Business sec.

[28] "The Story and Men Behind The 'Vikings' Football Team," in *Greater Minneapolis*, October, 1960, p. 12, 13; Jim Klobuchar, *True Hearts and Purple Heads: An Unauthorized Biography of a Football Team*, 6-20, 25-37 (Minneapolis, 1970).

[29] "The Icemen Cometh," in *Corporate Report*, October, 1975, p. 8 (quotation); Stan Fischler, *The Blazing North Stars*, 16-19 (Englewood Cliffs, N.J., 1972); Hollander and Bock, eds., *Encyclopedia of Ice Hockey*, 137, 343, 698. See also *Minneapolis Tribune*, January 16, 1977, p. 1C.

[30] Allan Holbert, *How We Got Our Kicks*, 9, 10 (Wayzata, 1976); *St.*

Paul Pioneer Press, February 14, 1982, Outlook sec., p. 21, 27.

[31] *Minneapolis Tribune*, March 28, 1982, Dome sec.; *Construction Bulletin*, July 17, 1981, p. 7-9.

[32] *USA Today*, March 11, 1983, p. 1C; *St. Paul Pioneer Press/Dispatch*, March 10, 1983, p. 11F, 21F.

[33] Cited in Breckenfeld, in *Fortune*, January, 1976, p. 131.

[34] For examples of sources on urban problems, see *St. Paul Pioneer Press/Dispatch*, May 10, 1980, p. 1B, 12B; *St. Paul Pioneer Press*, February 29, 1976, Focus sec., 1, 4; John J. Harrigan and William C. Johnson, *Governing the Twin Cities Region: The Metropolitan Council in Comparative Perspective*, 8 (Minneapolis, 1978); "How Syl Davis Sees It: An Interview with Gerald R. Vizenor," in *Twin Citian*, October, 1967, p. 60-62.

[35] John E. Mueller, *War, Presidents and Public Opinion*, 23-32, 38, 39, 155-167, 266 (New York, 1973); *St. Paul Pioneer Press/Dispatch*, November 6, 1982, p. 3A; *Minneapolis Star and Tribune*, April 19, 1983, p. 1A. Mueller states that the difference in opposition to the two wars was vocal and that in other respects it was equal. See also *Dictionary of American History*, 7:182-185 (Rev. ed., New York, 1976); *Vietnam Crisis*, *Minnesota Mobilizer*, and *Minnesota Vietnam News*, newsletters in MHS Reference Library.

[36] *Minneapolis Tribune*, May 17, 1981, p. 15A (quotation); Sarah R. Mason, "The Indochinese," in Holmquist, ed., *They Chose Minnesota*, 580, 584, 586, 588.

[37] *St. Paul Pioneer Press*, October 22, 1979, p. 17, 19, April 7, p. 13 (quotation), May 12, p. 19, May 13, p. 10 (quotation), all 1981. See also *St. Paul Pioneer Press*, July 26, 1981, Metro/Region sec., 1, 5.

[38] Victor Jones, "Foreword," in Stanley Baldinger, *Planning and Governing the Metropolis: The Twin Cities Experience*, vii-ix (New York, 1971); Harrigan and Johnson, *Governing the Twin Cities Region*, 3-9, 14-18.

[39] Theodore Kolderie, *Governing the Twin Cities Area: Background Paper for the Conference on Governmental Structure, St. Thomas College, November 10, 1966*, 1-5, 8-10, Appendix A (N.p., n.d.); Twin Cities Metropolitan Planning Commission, *Biennial Report to the Minnesota Legislature, 1965-1966*, 2; Harrigan and Johnson, *Governing the Twin Cities Region*, 26-30.

[40] Harrigan and Johnson, *Governing the Twin Cities Region*, 30-38; Breckenfeld, in *Fortune*, January, 1976, p. 180 (quotation); Baldinger, *Planning and Governing the Metropolis*, 159-162, 215-219

EPILOGUE/The Cities Remember

[1] Saint Paul Area Chamber of Commerce, *Action*, July 13, 1967, p. 3.

[2] Georgia R. DeCoster, in H. F. Koeper, *Historic St. Paul Buildings*, 4 (St. Paul, 1964); Roger E. Swardson, "Progress Revisited," in *Twin Citian*, January, 1968, p. 11.

[3] Swardson, in *Twin Citian*, January, 1968, p. 11; Anson Cutts, "May It Rest in Pieces," in *Select Twin Citian*, August, 1962, p. 36; Henry L. Prestholdt, *The Story of the Guaranty Loan Building*, v-xv (Minneapolis, 1961).

[4] Holmquist and Brookins, *Minnesota's Major Historic Sites*, vii (quotation).

Picture Credits

PHOTOGRAPHS and other images are reproduced in this book through the courtesy of the institutions named below. Illustrations are credited from left to right and from top to bottom. Key words from the captions are used to facilitate identification.

Photographers and artists are named when their identities are known and not given in the captions. Sources for reproductions of published materials are also listed. Second and subsequent citations of photographers and printed sources are shortened.

Credits for photographs from the collection of the Minnesota Historical Society (MHS) include, when available, the names of the studios or newspapers that employed the photographers. Photographs from the Edward A. Bromley, George Luxton, and Norton and Peel collections are identified as such, although the collections have been interfiled with the society's other photographs.

1838-65/*River Cities*

Page 4: map, Abraham Rees, *Cyclopaedia* ([1806?]); Jefferson, oil by Rembrandt Peale, The New-York Historical Society. **Page 11**: Pike, National Archives; map, Anthony Nau, National Archives; Kaposia, water color by Seth Eastman, about 1850, James Jerome Hill Reference Library. **Page 12**: Fort Snelling, oil by Edward K. Thomas, Minneapolis Institute of Arts; Steele, ambrotype made from charcoal portrait by Philip A. Ott, MHS; Sibley, Sibley House Association of the Minnesota Daughters of the American Revolution; map, National Archives; ferry, stereograph by Whitney's Gallery, about 1860, MHS; "Virginia," oil by Ken Fox, Padelford Packet Boat Company Collection. **Page 13**: chapel, daguerreotype by Joel E. Whitney, about 1855, Catholic Historical Society, St. Paul; St. Paul, pencil drawing with water color on paper, MHS; mills, Benjamin F. Upton, MHS; "Sioux Village, Lake Calhoun, near Fort Snelling," oil by George Catlin, 1835-36, National Museum of American Art (formerly National Collection of Fine Arts), Smithsonian Institution, gift of Mrs. Joseph Harrison, Jr. **Page 14**: St. Paul, water color by Jean B. Wengler, Landesmuseum, Linz, Austria; St. Paul, MHS; tepees and house, MHS; falls, MHS; St. Anthony, enlargement by Charles A. Zimmerman from a daguerreotype by Whitney, MHS. **Page 15**: "Milwaukee," MHS; "Ben Campbell," MHS; miller, MHS; ad, H. E. Chamberlin, pub.,

Commercial Advertiser Directory, for St. Anthony and Minneapolis . . . 1859-1860, 128 (St. Anthony and Minneapolis, 1859). **Page 16**: map, George C. Nichols, 1851, MHS; sketches, gift of Robert O. Sweeny, MHS. **Page 17**: MHS. **Page 18**: Winslow House, engraving by J. O. Lovett, MHS; ad, A. D. Munson, ed., *The Minnesota Messenger, Containing Sketches of the Rise and Progress of Minnesota*, 10 (St. Paul, 1855); panorama, MHS; church, MHS. **Page 19**: city hall, MHS; panorama, MHS; cathedral, R. W. Ransom, MHS. **Page 20**: capitol, Whitney, before 1872, MHS; panorama, MHS; market, Zimmerman Portrait Gallery, about 1870, MHS. **Page 21**: house, MHS; church, St. Paul Dispatch and Pioneer Press; panorama, MHS; jail (detail of panorama), MHS. **Page 22**: all MHS. **Page 23**: hotel, Upton, MHS; panorama, MHS; building, Robert W. Essery, MHS. **Page 24**: both MHS. **Page 25**: both MHS. **Page 26**: church, First Congregational Church; panorama, MHS; university (detail of panorama), MHS. **Page 27**: both MHS. **Page 28**: ad, *St. Anthony Express*, July 22, 1854; panorama, MHS; buildings, Upton, MHS. **Page 29**: tower (detail of panorama), MHS; panorama, MHS; house, Bromley Collection, MHS. **Page 30**: courthouse, Minneapolis Public Library and Information Center; panorama, MHS; mill, William H. Jacoby, MHS; office, sketch by Twiford E. Hughes, MHS. **Page 31**: island view, Whitney's Gallery, MHS; panorama, MHS. **Page 32**: land office, Upton, MHS; panorama, MHS; bridge, MHS. **Page 33**: house, Upton, MHS; panorama, MHS; church, Gordon Ray, MHS. **Page 34**: industrial district, Upton, MHS; map, Orlando Talcott, probably 1857, MHS; Bridge Square views from Bromley, *Minneapolis Album: A Photographic History of the Early Days in Minneapolis* (Minneapolis, 1890). **Page 35**: 1857 view, Upton, MHS; Nicollet Avenue, MHS; Crane Building, Bromley Collection, MHS. **Page 36**: Democrat, Upton, MHS; Washington Avenue, Upton, MHS; masthead, *Minnesota Democrat;* Cataract House print, about 1860, Gibson and Co., Cincinnati, pub., MHS; Sixth Avenue Hotel, MHS. **Page 37**: Second Avenue South, Upton, MHS; school, Bromley Collection, MHS. **Page 38**: Washington Avenue, Upton, MHS; omnibus (detail of hotel photo), MHS; hotel, MHS. **Page 39**: Ramsey's offer, painting by George Overlie, Minneapolis Star and Tribune; home-front volunteers, engraving by Thomas Nast, from Frank B. Goodrich, *The Tribute Book,* 111 (New York, 1865); flag, MHS; soldiers, Upton, MHS; injured, MHS; veterans, MHS. **Page 40**: Mazourka Hall, ink sketch by Sweeny, gift of Sweeny, MHS; Dodge, MHS; Monks Hall, ink sketch by Sweeny, gift of Sweeny, MHS; tipplers, MHS; falls, Upton, MHS. **Page 41**: panorama ad, *St. Anthony Express,* June 17, 1854; building, daguerreotype by John W. Monell, MHS. **Page 42**: steamboats, William H. Illingworth, MHS; cartoon,

William F. Davidson Papers, MHS; ad, *Minnesota Chronicle and Register,* August 12, 1850; "Enterprise," Bromley Collection, MHS. **Page 43**: American House, MHS; *St. Paul City Directory,* 1858-59, p. 26; broadside, MHS; "William Crooks," Moses C. Tuttle, MHS.

1865-80/*The Railroad Age*

Page 44: "Shakopee," Jacoby, MHS. **Page 50**: expedition, MHS; levee, Illingworth, MHS. **Page 51**: all MHS. **Page 52**: train, MHS; depot, A. B. Rugg, MHS; handbill, MHS; map, lithograph by Pioneer-Press Company, in Franklin Steele Papers, MHS. **Page 53**: panorama, MHS; chairs, stereograph by Illingworth, MHS; steamboats, Illingworth, MHS; corner, Illingworth, MHS. **Page 54**: all Illingworth, MHS. **Page 55**: all Illingworth, MHS. **Page 56**: mill, St. Paul Chamber of Commerce, *Annual Report,* 1881, n.p.; crew, MHS; brewery, MHS; Phalen Creek, MHS. **Page 57**: all MHS. **Page 58**: factory, A. T. Andreas, pub., *An Illustrated Historical Atlas of the State of Minnesota,* 35 (Chicago, 1874); roofers, *St. Paul City Directory,* 1871, n.p.; shops, MHS. **Page 59**: military headquarters, MHS; Customs House, National Archives; construction, MHS. **Page 60**: police, Bromley Collection, MHS. **Page 61**: Franklin School, Ransom, MHS; seminary, New York Public Library; reform school, Truman W. Ingersoll, MHS; products, MHS. **Page 62**: bird's-eye view, lithograph by Albert Ruger, Library of Congress; Bridge Square, Norton and Peel Collection, MHS. **Page 63**: market, George Luxton Collection, MHS. **Page 64**: Hennepin Avenue, negative attributed to Charles E. Wales, photo possibly by Alonzo H. Beal, MHS; Johnston Block, MHS; Wagner's, negative attributed to Wales, photo possibly by Beal, MHS; posters, Jacoby, MHS. **Page 65**: Nicollet Avenue, MHS; bank, Illingworth, MHS; map, Alan Ominsky. **Page 66**: industries, MHS; sluice, stereograph by Upton, MHS; map, Ominsky. **Page 67**: coffer dam, MHS; break, MHS; falling mills, MHS; finishing apron, Hennepin County Historical Society; starting apron, MHS. **Page 68**: mill exterior, MHS; mill interior, Jacoby, MHS; mill interior, Jacoby, MHS; sheet music, A. M. Hall and Company, pub., MHS; ruin, Jacoby, MHS. **Page 69**: plow works, Bromley Collection, MHS; Greely, Loye and Company, Bromley Collection, MHS; carriage works, Andreas, *Illustrated Atlas,* 46. **Page 70**: iron works, Andreas, *Illustrated Atlas,* 45; Dean mills, Andreas, *Illustrated Atlas,* 46; meat packers, Minneapolis Board of Trade, *Annual Report, 1877, n.p.; brewery,* MHS. **Page 71**: class, John H. Oleson, MHS; Old Main, Illingworth, MHS; Winthrop, Jacoby, MHS; Central, Jacoby, about 1880, MHS. **Page 72**: barns, engraving from *Northwest Magazine,* May, 1885, p. 16; horsecar, Jacoby, MHS; car 43, Jacoby and Son, MHS. **Page 73**: Tenth Avenue Bridge construction, Norton and Peel Collection, MHS; bridge completion, Jacoby, MHS; Upper Bridge, MHS; Suspension Bridge, Norton and Peel Collection, MHS; Fort Snelling Bridge, Zimmerman, MHS. **Page 74**: fire fighters, [Alix J. Muller and Frank J. Mead, comps.], *History of the Police and Fire Departments of the Twin Cities,* Minneapolis, 169 (Minneapolis and St. Paul, 1899); fire, engraving from sketch by Sweeny, *Harper's Weekly,* 13:141 (February 27, 1869); ruins, Illingworth, MHS; fire company, MHS. **Page 75**: ad, *St. Paul City Directory,* 1867, p. 99; hotel and park, MHS; construc-

tion, Bromley Collection, MHS; completion, Jacoby, MHS. **Page 76**: opera house, Ransom, MHS; broadside, MHS; float, MHS. **Page 77**: parade, MHS; Hayes, engraving from drawing by W. A. Rogers, *Harper's Weekly, 22:788 (October 5, 1878); racing ad, Minneapolis Tribune,* August 10, 1880; circus, MHS. **Page 78**: pavilion, MHS; veranda, Jacoby, MHS; poster, MHS.

1880-95/*The Golden Age*

Page 80: Nicollet and Third, Minneapolis Public Library and Information Center. **Page 87**: *St. Paul Daily Globe,* December 25, 1886; pamphlet, MHS. **Page 88**: Pillsbury, Hennepin County Historical Society; switchboard, MHS; lights, MHS. **Page 89**: Norton and Peel Collection, MHS; plant, H. B. Herington, MHS; letterhead, William F. Davidson Papers, MHS; cartoon, *St. Anthony Hill Graphic,* February 21, 1890. **Page 90**: parade, Jacoby, MHS; arch, Illingworth, MHS; bridge, MHS; boardwalk, Bromley Collection, MHS. **Page 91**: wagon, Hennepin County Historical Society; Washburn mills, drawn and lithographed by Louis Haugg, MHS; Pillsbury trade-mark, in Official Letters, Communications and Railroad Liens, 4:77, Secretary of State Records, Minnesota State Archives, MHS; Pillsbury A, Bromley Collection, MHS. **Page 92**: sawmill, stereograph, Underwood and Underwood, London, pub., MHS; map, Ominsky; fire, MHS. **Page 93**: traders, MHS; bank run, MHS. **Page 94**: depot, MHS; seamstresses, *Northwest Magazine,* June, 1896, p. 1; office, Ingersoll, MHS. **Page 95**: excursion ad, MHS; jobbers, Ingersoll, MHS; stockyards, *Northwest Magazine,* January, 1896, p. 35; buyers, MHS. **Page 96**: hotel, Bromley Collection, MHS; menu, Hennepin County Historical Society; parade, Library of Congress; Metropolitan, MHS; Donaldsons, MHS; interior, MHS; library, MHS. **Page 97**: city hall, Bromley Collection, MHS; Mannheimer exterior and interior, *Northwest Magazine,* February, 1888, p. 30, July, 1890, p. 15; hotel exterior, St. Paul Dispatch, MHS; interior, MHS. **Page 98**: class, Norton and Peel Collection, MHS; Minnie, MHS; Judson, Hennepin County Historical Society. **Page 99**: Macalester, MHS; Hamline, Frank T. Wilson, MHS; farm campus, F. E. Haynes, MHS. **Page 100**: all MHS. **Page 101**: (A) and (B), MHS; (C), Pioneer View Company, MHS; (D), Essery and Brown, MHS; (E) through (H), MHS; (I), Harry Shepherd, MHS. **Page 102**: Summit Avenue, engraving from sketch by Charles D. Winsor, *Northwest Magazine,* July, 1890, p. 27; Scheffer house, MHS; Lowry house, Bromley Collection, Minneapolis Public Library and Information Center; Fair Oaks, MHS. **Page 103**: all MHS. **Page 104**: all MHS. **Page 105**: Swede Hollow, MHS; women, Charles V. Sarnblad, MHS; Tivoli, engraving from *Northwest Magazine,* February, 1889, p. 9. **Page 106**: street railway, *Northwest Magazine,* July, 1890, p. 31; Hopkins, MHS; North St. Paul, engraving from sketch by H. Kratzner, *Northwest Magazine,* January, 1892, p. 31. **Page 107**: Lake Harriet, MHS; Rice Park, engraving from *Northwest Magazine,* April, 1886, p. 1; Sullivan, John Wood, in R. F. Dibble, *John L. Sullivan: An Intimate Narrative,* opposite p. 64 (Boston, 1925); Patti and rink, engravings from photos by Henry Farr, *Northwest Magazine,* December, 1885, p. 23, January, 1885, p. 9. **Page 108**: fountain, MHS; bicycle riders, H. B. Norton, Hennepin County Historical Society; bicycle shop, Hennepin County Historical Society. **Page 109**: poster, MHS; Wildwood, Haas Bros., MHS; ball park, Bromley Collection, MHS. **Page 110**: theater exterior, MHS; theater interior, Jacoby, MHS; Booth company, Bromley Collection, MHS; amateurs, Bromley Collection, MHS. **Page 111**: battle, Hennepin County Historical Society; building, engraving from *Cooke, Howard & Co.'s Map and Business Guide of Minneapolis, Minn.,* inside cover (Baltimore, Md., [1888]); Nushka Club, Ingersoll, MHS; restaurant, MHS. **Page 112**: race track, MHS; balloon, Jacoby, MHS; fruit, Jno. H. Dickey, MHS; fairgrounds, MHS. **Page 113**: convention, engraving from drawing by Thure de Thulstrup and Charles Graham, *Harper's Weekly,* 36:560 (June 11, 1892); Nicollet Avenue, Jacoby and Son, MHS; Exposition Building, MHS. **Page 114**: sheet music, cover lithography by H. M. Smyth Printing Company, St. Paul, MHS; palace, Arthur C. Warner, MHS; parade, Ingersoll, MHS.

1895-1920/*Passage to the Twentieth Century*

Page 116: generator, Louis D. Sweet, MHS. **Pages 124 and 125**: St. Paul and Minneapolis panoramas, Detroit Publishing Company, Library of Congress. **Page 126**: lumberyards, Sweet, MHS; linseed elevators, Charles P. Gibson, MHS; ad, *Ladies Home Journal,* October, 1897, p. 26. **Page 127**: warehouse, Sweet, MHS; wholesale row, Hennepin County Historical Society; brickmakers, MHS. **Page 128**: railroad yards, MHS; barges, St. Paul Dispatch, MHS; syrup, *Log Cabin Recipes* (St. Paul, 1915); syrup train, Haas Bros., MHS. **Page 129**: coal haulers, MHS; foundry, C. P. Gibson, MHS; shoemakers, MHS. **Page 130**: bank construction, C. P. Gibson, MHS; brokers, MHS; cartoon, Charles Bartholomew (Bart), in Bart Cartoon Collection, MHS. **Page 131**: cartoon, Dearborn Melvill, in Hagstrom Political Scrapbooks, 1892-98, MHS; capitol site, St. Paul Dispatch and Pioneer Press, MHS; architects, MHS. **Page 132**: capitol construction, MHS; dedication and cathedral, C. P. Gibson, MHS. **Page 133**: city hall, Bromley Collection, MHS; clock, Minneapolis Journal, MHS; council chamber, MHS. **Page 134**: Third Avenue Bridge, MHS; Franklin Avenue Bridge, from postcard published by St. Marie's Gopher News Company, Minneapolis-St. Paul, about 1960, MHS; High Bridge, Haas and Wright, MHS. **Page 135**: band, MHS; McKinley, Bromley, MHS; Roosevelt, MHS. **Page 136**: O'Connor, Quam and Drydale, MHS; Nash, MHS; float, George E. Luxton, Hennepin County Historical Society; sheet music, © 1918 (Renewed 1946) Leo Feist Inc., international copyright secured, all rights reserved, used by permission. **Page 137**: auto show, Luxton, Minneapolis Journal, MHS; Waverley, MHS; parking, August D. Roth, MHS. **Page 138**: airship, Luxton, MHS; Johnson, Bromley Collection, Minneapolis Public Library and Information Center; Edison, MHS. **Page 139**: cigar maker, Frank P. D. Bruce, MHS; tenement, MHS; grocery, MHS. **Page 140**: poster, printed by Willwerscheid and Roith, MHS; Groechel, The Flash-Lighters, Hennepin County Historical Society; secretaries, Charles J. Hibbard, in Norton and Peel Collection, MHS; picnic, Hibbard, in Norton and Peel Collection, MHS. **Page 141**: newsie, Bromley Collection, Minneapolis Public Library and Information Center; Rice Park crowd, St. Paul Daily News, MHS; Townley, MHS; poster, cartoon by Lou Rogers, Leslie-Judge Company, pub., MHS. **Page 142**: MHS. **Page 143**: all

MHS. **Page 144**: nurses, MHS; wiremen, Library of Congress; Pitroff, Hibbard, in Norton and Peel Collection, MHS. **Page 145**: parade, MHS; artificial limbs, C. P. Gibson, MHS. **Page 146**: carnival king and chancellor, Zimmerman, MHS; banquet, Brown's Photo Craft Studio, MHS; fireworks, Joseph Pavlicek, MHS. **Page 147**: "Hiawatha," MHS; soda jerk, MHS; card party, Luxton Collection, MHS; photographer, MHS; lawn party, Sweet, MHS. **Page 148**: bowling, MHS; Wonderland, MHS; lily pond, Ingersoll, MHS; skating, Hibbard, in Norton and Peel Collection, MHS; seals, MHS. **Page 149**: ski jump, MHS; iceboat, Arus S. Williams[?], MHS; crew, MHS; dancers, MHS. **Page 150**: gridiron, C. P. Gibson, MHS; football, Bromley Collection, MHS; spectators, Luxton Collection, MHS; Millers, Marceau and Bassett, Indianapolis, MHS; Kelley, MHS. **Page 151**: ad, *Minneapolis Journal,* January 20, 1896, p. 3; Palace Museum, Arthur B. Rugg, MHS; Dan Patch, MHS; Paderewski, Theo. Marceau, Hennepin County Historical Society; Lynder, Hennepin County Historical Society; Arthur, Elmer Chickering, Boston, Hennepin County Historical Society; Skinner, Morrison, Chicago, Hennepin County Historical Society. **Page 152**: piano store, MHS; music, drawing by Corydon G. Snyder, MHS; orchestra, MHS; theater, MHS. **Page 153**: Danz band, C. P. Gibson, MHS; Apollo Club, Minneapolis Tribune, MHS; gallery, MHS.

1920-30/*The Jazz Age*

Page 154: MHS. **Page 160**: Kilbourn, Norton and Peel, MHS; Goodwin, MHS; school, MHS. **Page 161**: Riviera, MHS; Strand, MHS; Capitol, MHS; Brunswick, C. P. Gibson, MHS. **Page 162**: Queens, Celebrity, Chicago, MHS; Arcadia, Hibbard, MHS; fox trot, Minneapolis Star-Journal, MHS; orchestra, MHS. **Page 163**: *Whiz Bang,* MHS; newsstand and magazine detail, C. P. Gibson, MHS. **Page 164**: window, MHS; model, MHS; beauty shop, Norton and Peel, MHS; cooks, Minneapolis Star-Journal, MHS; automat, MHS. **Page 165**: parade, MHS; Peterson's troupe, MHS; circus, MHS; auto camp, Brown (unknown first name), St. Paul Daily News, MHS. **Page 166**: ball park, St. Paul Daily News, MHS; boys, MHS; Millers, Minneapolis Journal, MHS; hockey, MHS. **Page 167**: Rober, Hennepin County Historical Society; ball, Ominsky; parade, MHS; marble game, MHS. **Page 168**: Coleman's Station, Norton and Peel, MHS; fire horses, St. Paul Dispatch, MHS; auto, John Banks, MHS; assembly line, Norton and Peel[?], MHS. **Page 169**: picnic, MHS; road work, Hennepin County Historical Society; bus depot, MHS. **Page 170**: stockyards, Peter Schawang, MHS; airfield, MHS. **Page 171**: air mail, MHS; plane, Bruce Sifford Studio, Inc., MHS; wreck, Hibbard, Library of Congress. **Page 172**: (A), MHS; (B), St. Paul Daily News, MHS; (C), MHS; (D), Minneapolis Journal, MHS; (E) and (F), MHS; (G), Minneapolis Journal, MHS; (H) through (J), MHS. **Page 173**: (K), MHS; (L), Ray-Bell Films, Inc., MHS; (M), Minneapolis Journal, MHS; (N), MHS; (O), Norton and Peel, MHS; (P), St. Paul Dispatch Pioneer Press, MHS; (Q), MHS; (R) and (S), St. Paul Daily News, MHS; (T), MHS. **Page 174**: billboards, The Sweet Studios, MHS; Junior League, St. Paul Dispatch, MHS; babies, MHS. **Page 175**: child abuse, Wilbert Mills and Charles Bell, MHS; backyard, The Sweet Studios, MHS; settlement house, The Sweet Studios, MHS. **Page 176**: laborers, MHS; elder, Norton and Peel, MHS; group, MHS; woman,

MHS. **Page 177**: mall, Minneapolis Journal, MHS; lab, University of Minnesota Archives; crowd, Minneapolis Journal, MHS. **Page 178**: panorama, Paul W. Hamilton, St. Paul Pioneer Press, MHS; trains, MHS; Seven Corners, MHS. **Page 179**: University Avenue, Northwestern Photographic Studios, Inc., MHS; bridge, MHS. **Page 180**: downtown, Norton and Peel, MHS; railyards, Hamilton[?], MHS. **Page 181**: Hiawatha corridor, Hamilton[?], MHS; Bridge Square, Norton and Peel, MHS; flats, C. P. Gibson, MHS. **Page 182**: elevator, C. P. Gibson, MHS; Powderhorn, MHS; Nokomis, Hibbard, MHS. **Page 183**: capitol plan, MHS; Minneapolis plan, Andrew Wright Crawford, *Plan of Minneapolis Prepared . . . by Edward H. Bennett Architect,* following p. 150 (Minneapolis, 1917). **Page 184**: politicians, MHS; headquarters, MHS; Coolidge, Pacific and Atlantic Photos, Inc.[?], New York, MHS. **Page 185**: league, Pacific and Atlantic Photos, Inc., MHS; liquor store, Franklin F. Holbrook, MHS; raid, St. Paul Daily News, MHS. **Page 186**: poster, MHS; National Guard, St. Paul Daily News, MHS; Klan paper, MHS; cross, St. Paul Daily News, MHS. **Page 187**: YMCA meeting, Brown's Studio, MHS. **Page 188**: drawing, Hennepin County Historical Society; Foshay Tower, Norton and Peel, MHS; Scherzo, MHS; auction, Minneapolis Star, MHS.

1930-45/ *Depression and War*

Page 190: St. Paul Pioneer Press, MHS. **Page 198**: unemployed, oil by Edwin Nooleen, MHS; queue, MHS; headquarters, Mando Studio, MHS. **Page 199**: demonstration, Minneapolis Tribune, MHS; poster, MHS; Farm Holiday marchers and capitol rally, St. Paul Daily News, MHS. **Page 200**: all MHS. **Page 201**: NRA parade, St. Paul Daily News, MHS; CCC workers, St. Paul Dispatch, MHS; typists, St. Paul Daily News, MHS. **Page 202**: sewer work, St. Paul Daily News, MHS; treatment plant, Charles Moore, MHS; razing, Joseph Zalusky, MHS; data processing, MHS; signal, St. Paul Dispatch, MHS. **Page 203**: god of peace, St. Paul Daily News, MHS; assembling statue, MHS. **Page 204**: Tuohy, St. Paul Daily News, MHS; Karpis, Associated Press, MHS; beer trucks, Luxton Collection, MHS; saloon, MHS. **Page 205**: riot and funeral, Minneapolis Tribune, MHS; Glazer, MHS; brochure cover, MHS. **Page 206**: bank, Harry C. Voss, MHS; tape, St. Paul Daily News, MHS; elevator, MHS. **Page 207**: butter, John Vachon, Farm Security Administration, Library of Congress; lumber, Napoleon N. Nadeau, Photo Art Shop, MHS; elevators, Vachon, Farm Security Administration, Library of Congress. **Page 208**: gas station, Minneapolis Star, MHS; fashions, Roth, MHS; supermarket, Lawrence E. Schreiber, MHS. **Page 209**: Hiawatha, Kaufmann and Fabry Company, Chicago, MHS; schedule, *Commercial West,* June 8, 1935, p. 23; tableware, St. Paul Daily News, MHS; plane, MHS. **Page 210**: ambulance, MHS; auto show and roads, St. Paul Daily News, MHS. **Page 211**: wagon, MHS. **Page 212**: dancers, St. Paul Dispatch, MHS; singers, Minneapolis Journal, MHS; parade, MHS; banquet, Kenneth M. Wright Studios, MHS; class, MHS. **Page 213**: Catholics, St. Paul Dispatch and Pioneer Press, MHS; Methodists, Minneapolis Tribune, MHS; Orthodox, Minneapolis Tribune, MHS; billboards, Vachon, Farm Security Administration, Library of Congress; baptism, Minneapolis Star, MHS. **Page 214**: Minneapolis, J. E. Quigley Aerial Photographs, MHS; elms, MHS; signal, Minneapolis Star, MHS;

city limits, MHS. **Page 215**: St. Paul, Holmberg Air Mapping Company, Chicago, MHS; hospital, Kenneth M. Wright Studios, MHS; bungalows, St. Paul Pioneer Press, MHS; Cedar Street, John W. G. Dunn, Jr., MHS. **Page 216**: sleepers and celebrators, St. Paul Daily News, MHS; tree sitter, Minneapolis Star, MHS; ad, MHS; marathon, MHS. **Page 217**: KSTP, St. Paul Dispatch and Pioneer Press, MHS; girls, St. Paul Daily News, MHS; phonograph, MHS; parade, St. Paul Pioneer Press, MHS. **Page 218**: New Year's Eve, Minneapolis Star, MHS; Orpheum and contest, St. Paul Daily News, MHS; Ice Follies, Fred Hess and Son, MHS. **Page 219**: regatta, Minneapolis Tribune[?], MHS; Adams, MHS; Zephyrus, Robert Beveridge, MHS; parade, MHS. **Page 220**: (A), Luxton, Minneapolis Star, MHS; (B), St. Paul Dispatch; (C), Luxton Collection, MHS; (D), St. Paul Pioneer Press, MHS; (E), St. Paul Daily News; (F), MHS; (G), United Press International. **Page 221**: (H), MHS; (I), Jack Delano, Office of War Information, MHS; (J), Minneapolis Tribune; (K), MHS; (L), Minneapolis Tribune; (M), MHS; (N), Universal Pictures Company, Inc., Minneapolis Public Library and Information Center. **Page 222**: all MHS. **Page 223**: Auditorium crowd, St. Paul Daily News, MHS; appeal, from Records of the Committee to Defend America by Aiding the Allies, Minneapolis Chapter, MHS. **Page 224**: headline, *Minneapolis Tribune,* December 8, 1941; navy, Minneapolis Star-Journal, MHS; kiss, Jack Loveland[?], MHS; draftees, MHS; gun crew, U.S. Navy, MHS. **Page 225**: trailer camp, T. J. Strasser, St. Paul Pioneer Press, MHS; "Genesee," MHS; factory, Robert Yarnall Richie, U.S. Office of Emergency Management, Library of Congress; side gun, Northwest Airlines, Inc., Records, MHS; autopilot, Ominsky, MHS. **Page 226**: poster, Saul Tepper, MHS; siren, Loveland[?], St. Paul Pioneer Press, MHS; coupons, MHS; queue, St. Paul Dispatch, MHS. **Page 227**: soldier, Minneapolis Journal, MHS; scrap drive, St. Paul Dispatch, MHS; caravan, MHS. **Page 228**: both MHS. **Page 229**: United Nations, Kenneth M. Wright Studios, MHS; fruit, Powell Krueger, Minneapolis Daily Times, MHS.

1945-83/ *Metropolis*

Page 230: MHS. **Page 238**: map, Ominsky. **Page 239**: dancers, Minneapolis Tribune, MHS; family night, St. Paul Pioneer Press, MHS; float, Minneapolis Tribune, MHS; Shopp, MHS. **Page 240**: WTCN, Norton and Peel, MHS; visitor, MHS; family, MHS. **Page 241**: loans, Ray, MHS; Dayton's, Norton and Peel, MHS. **Page 242**: children, MHS; Wang, U.S. Information Agency, National Archives; Hungarians, MHS. **Page 243**: Millers, Minneapolis Tribune, MHS; Lakers, MHS; Little League, MHS; skaters, MHS. **Page 244**: all St. Paul Dispatch and Pioneer Press, MHS. **Page 245**: Gateway building, Norton and Peel, MHS; redevelopment aerial, Minnesota Department of Transportation; sign and demolition, Minneapolis Star, MHS. **Page 246**: Metropolitan, Strasser, St. Paul Dispatch and Pioneer Press, MHS; mall, Greater Minneapolis Chamber of Commerce, Minneapolis City Archives; university, University of Minnesota Archives. **Page 247**: hole and demolition, Hymie Paul, St. Paul Dispatch and Pioneer Press; eagle, MHS. **Page 248**: blighted dwelling, Norton and Peel, MHS; rectory, St. Paul Dispatch, MHS; flood, MHS; Mt. Airy, Norton and Peel, MHS. **Page 249**: billboard, Minneapolis

Housing and Redevelopment Authority; laying pipe, Don Berg, MHS; lots near Lake Nokomis, Norton and Peel, MHS; Roseville houses, MHS. **Page 250**: Miracle Mile, Norton and Peel, MHS; Lexington Plaza, St. Paul Dispatch and Pioneer Press. **Page 251**: Miracle Mile, Norton and Peel, MHS; Southdale, MHS; 1958 view, Norton and Peel, MHS; 1983 view, Ominsky, MHS. **Page 252**: streetcars, St. Paul Dispatch and Pioneer Press, MHS; ramp, Norton and Peel, MHS; school parking, Shell Oil Company, MHS; auto teller, MHS; White House, Norton and Peel, MHS. **Page 253**: Cottage Grove, St. Paul Dispatch and Pioneer Press, MHS; bus, MHS; meeting, Don Church, St. Paul Dispatch and Pioneer Press, MHS. **Page 254**: hatchet, St. Paul Dispatch and Pioneer Press, MHS; bridge, Minnesota Department of Transportation; traffic jam, Spencer Hollstadt, St. Paul Dispatch and Pioneer Press. **Page 255**: freeway bridge, Minnesota Department of Transportation; St. Paul aerial, Ominsky, MHS. **Page 256**: airport, Norton and Peel, MHS; stadium and ticket line, Gerald Brimacombe, Minneapolis Tribune, MHS; hockey, MHS. **Page 257**: 1960 view, MHS; 1983 view, Ominsky, MHS. **Page 258**: press, Brown and Bigelow News Bureau, MHS; newsroom, U.S. Information Agency, National Archives; bank, St. Paul Dispatch and Pioneer Press, MHS. **Page 259**: upper locks, Norton and Peel, MHS; Delmonico's, Carlson Companies; truck, Ominsky, MHS. **Page 260**: Gamble-Skogmo, MHS; General Mills, General Mills Photo Service, MHS; balloon, Strasser, St. Paul Dispatch and Pioneer Press, MHS; Univac, Norton and Peel, MHS. **Page 261**: Honeywell, Honeywell Inc.; Medtronic, Medtronic, Inc.; Control Data, Control Data Corporation. **Page 262**: Gateway and aerial view,

Ominsky, MHS. **Page 263**: all Ominsky, MHS. **Page 264**: Guthrie, Brimacombe, Minneapolis Star and Tribune, MHS; hall, Minnesota Orchestral Association; Science Museum and Ordway, Ominsky, MHS. **Page 265**: Beatles, fans, and be-in, Neale Van Ness, St. Paul Dispatch and Pioneer Press, MHS; Sorry Muthas, MHS. **Page 266**: protest, Van Ness, St. Paul Dispatch and Pioneer Press, MHS; police, Minneapolis Tribune, MHS; McCarthy, MHS; march, Krueger, Minneapolis Star and Tribune, MHS. **Page 267**: Naftalin, Krueger, Minneapolis Star and Tribune, MHS; clock, Sally French; Amtrak, Ominsky, MHS; Humphrey, Bruce M. White; plant, Hollstadt, St. Paul Dispatch and Pioneer Press, MHS. **Page 268**: Fourth of July, MHS; federation, MHS; Hmong student, Michael Kieger, MHS; children, Wendy Gilbert, Red School House, MHS. **Page 269**: Goodrich, Strasser, St. Paul Dispatch and Pioneer Press, MHS; book sale, White; Vikings and tailgaters, Hollstadt, St. Paul Dispatch and Pioneer Press, MHS.

Epilogue/*The Cities Remember*

Page 270: Godfrey House, Ominsky, MHS. **Page 273**: Gibbs Farm, Hollstadt, MHS; "Three Sisters," Ominsky, MHS; "Jonathan Padelford," Padelford Packet Boat Company. **Page 274**: Energy Park, Irvine Park, and Landmark Center, Ominsky, MHS; play, Great North American History Theatre. **Page 275**: all Ominsky, MHS. **Page 276**: all Ominsky, MHS. **Page 277**: all Ominsky, MHS. **Page 278**: fireworks, Ominsky, MHS.

Index

Note: Numbers in italics refer to picture pages. Abbreviations used in this index are Mpls (Minneapolis); StP (St. Paul); and TC (Twin Cities).

ACADEMY OF MUSIC, Mpls, 75
Actors Theatre of St. Paul, 235
Adams, Cedric, broadcaster, *219,* 236
Adams, R. H., art curator, *153*
Adlerika Co., StP, products, *216*
Advertising, *154,* 156; campaigns, 83; firms, *143, 179, 258*
Agribusiness, 231
Agriculture, equipment, *58, 69, 143, 172;* farmers' protest movements, 82, 117, *199;* education, *99,* 234; cutover lands, 117; urban-rural tension, 118; decline, 159, 231; buildings, *253*
Air conditioning, natural, *161*
Airplanes, pilots, 122; exhibitions, *144, 229;* accidents, *171;* war equipment, 195, *225*
"Alhambra," steamboat, 10
Ambassador Restaurant, StP, 119
Ambulances, *210*
America First Committee, 194, *222*
American Ballet Theatre, 235
American Fur Co., post, *16*
American House, StP, hotel, *43*
American Legion, conventions, *165, 217*
American Locomotive Co., engines, *209*
American Red Cross, 120, *144, 174,* 194
Americanization, YMCA classes, *187*
Ames, Dr. Albert Alonzo, Mpls mayor, 118, *136*
Amidon Marble Yards, StP, *16*
Amtrak, established, 232; depot, *267*
Amusement, *see* Games and amusements
Ancker Hospital, StP, *215*
Anderson, Elmer L., governor, *256*
Anderson, ———, magician, *64*
Anderson, Victor E., district attorney, 193
Andrews Sisters, singers, 197, *221*
Anoka County, suburban growth, 284n21, 286n2
Antiques, *277*
Anti-Saloon League, 119
Anti-Semitism, *186,* 194. *See also* Jews
Antiwar movement, pacifism, 194, *242;* World War II, *222, 223;* Vietnam War, 235, 237, *266;* Korean conflict, 237
Apollo Club, Mpls, choral group, 121, *153,* 235
Apollo Hall, StP, *16*
Aquatennial, Mpls, events, 195, *219, 239*
Arcadia Dancing Academy, Mpls, *162*
Arcadia Palace, Mpls, dance hall, *162*
Archer-Daniels-Midland Co., Mpls, *126*

Architecture, office buildings, 84, *130, 260, 262, 276;* houses, *253, 273. See also* Houses and housing, Preservation, Urban renewal
Arden Hills, gas pipeline, *249*
Armenians, at folk festival, *212*
Armour and Co., meat packers, 120, 286n3
Aronovici, Carol, quoted, 121
Art and artists, historical aspects, 1; panorama, 41; theater curtains, *76, 154;* galleries, 84, *96, 153,* 235; mural, *133;* drawing, *188;* sculpture, *188, 203, 247, 278;* fairs, *269, 277*
Arthur, Julia, actress, *151*
Associated Charities of Minneapolis, 85
Associated Charities of St. Paul, 85
Auerbach, Finch, Culbertson and Co, StP, *54*
Augsburg College, Mpls, 48, *71,* 84
Auteria Co., StP, *164*
Automobiles, popularity, 121, 122, 168, 232; related industries, 122, *169, 208;* shows, *137, 210;* affect suburban growth, 157, 158, 232; manufactured, *168;* affect shopping habits, *208, 250, 251, 252;* accidents, *210, 211. See also* Parking, Roads and highways, Traffic, Transportation, individual makes and manufacturers
Aviation, *138,* 156, 157, 192, 232, 237
Ayres, Lew, actor, 197

BABLER, BERNICE, telephone operator, *173*
Bagley confectionery, Mpls, *35*
Bailey, C. M., dentist, *100*
Bajakian, Rebecca, dancer, *212*
Bakers, *173*
Baldwin School, StP, *19, 99*
Ball and Naylor, Mpls, *100*
Ballooning, ascensions, 9, *112,* 196, *220, 260*
Bandana Square, StP, development, *272, 274*
Bangotch, Aukinsé, dancer, *212*
Banks and banking, buildings, *55, 130, 180, 206, 252, 258;* in depressions, *93, 201;* mergers, 159. *See also* Federal Reserve Bank
Baptist church, 8, *22*
Baptist Hill, StP, *1, 22*
Barber Block, Mpls, *36*
Barbers, 35
Barfuss, Gustave H., commissioner of public safety, *202*
Barges, *128, 178, 225*
Barker, Kate ("Ma"), gangster, 193
Barker brothers, gangsters, 193, 194
Barnum, P. T., circus, 77

Baseball, 49, *150,* 156, 236. *See also* individual teams
Basilica of St. Mary, Mpls, *132*
Basketball, high-school, 196 237. *See also* individual teams
Bassett, L. B., entertains old soldiers, *39*
Bassi, John, store, *215*
Battle Creek Park, StP, 196
Bazille, Charles, house builder, *23*
Beal, Alonzo H., gallery owner, *50*
Beatles, singing group, 235, *265*
Beaupre and Kelly, StP, *54*
Beauty shops, *164*
Becker, George L., StP mayor, 47
Belmont Lane, Roseville, *249*
Beltrami ("Dog Town"), Mpls, 234
"Ben Campbell," steamboat, *15*
Benson, Elmer A., governor, 194
Benz, George, house, *244*
Berg, Patricia ("Patty"), golfer, 196, *221*
Berman, Dorothy, teacher, *212*
Berry, J. C., and Co., Mpls, mill, 66
Bethany Home, Mpls, 48
Bicycles, *108, 109, 113,* 226; velocipedes, 49
Bierman, Bernard ("Bernie"), football coach, 196, *220*
Bijou Theater, Mpls, *154*
Billiards, *35, 54, 100*
Birkerts, Gunnar, and Associates, architects, *262*
Black, John I., storekeeper, *34*
Black Cat Club, roadhouse, 156
Blacks, baseball team, 49; status in TC, *199,* 237, *266*
Black's Corner, Mpls, *35*
Blacksmiths, StP, *17;* Mpls, *36*
Blair, Anna, automobile owner, *168*
Blodgett and Osgood, StP, *57*
Bloomington, 232, 233, *257*
Bloor, Ella Reeve, antiwar activist, *222*
Boardinghouses, Mpls, *30, 38*
Boardman, Kathryn, quoted, 234
Boating, *149, 219*
Boeckmann, Carl L., artist, *153*
Bohemian Flats, Mpls, *98, 104*
Bohn, Haskell, kidnaped, 193
Bomberg, Nate, reporter, 194, *204*
Bookstores, *16, 41*
Booth, Edwin, actor, *110*
Boston Block, Mpls, 84
Boundaries, Fort Snelling, 5; of TC, *11, 12, 214*
Bowell, Capt. William, 272, *273*
Boxing, *107,* 121, 155, 156, *220*
Boy Scouts, *218, 227*
Breckenridge, railroad, *51*
Bremer, Edward, kidnaped, 193
Breweries, 48, *56, 70, 204. See also* Liquor

Bridge Square, Mpls, *34, 35, 62, 65, 88, 181*
Bridges, at Falls of St. Anthony, 8, 47; at Fort Snelling, *12, 73;* toll, *25;* railroad, *51, 64,* 81, *90, 104;* designs, *134;* on interstate highway, *254*
Brissman, Gustave, city official, *226*
British Americans, in Mpls, 48
Brittin, Col. Lewis H., 157
Bromley, Edward A., photographer, 2, *17*
Brown, William, labor leader, *221*
Brown, Willie Gertrude, welfare worker, *175*
Brown and Bigelow, StP, *179, 239, 258*
Bruce, John J., clothier, *100*
Brunswick-Balke-Collender Co., Dubuque, Iowa, *161*
Buck, Albert O., photographer, *100*
Buffalo, N.Y., flour milling, 159
Buffington, LeRoy S., architect, *78, 84, 91, 96*
Bullock, Walter, aviator, 122
Burbank, James C., house, *22*
Burkhard, William R., shop, *114*
Burlington Northern Inc., *232, 267*
Burnham, Daniel H., architect, *183*
Buses, city, 122, 157, *239, 246,* 253; interstate, 157, 232; depot, 169. *See also* Omnibuses
Business, *see* Commerce
Butler Brothers, Mpls, *127, 275*
Butler Quarter, Mpls, *275*
Butler Square, Mpls, *127, 272, 275*
Butters, W. A., aviator, *171*

CABLE PIANO CO., Mpls, *152*
Cahill, W. F., drugstore, *41*
Calhoun Yacht Club, Mpls, *149, 219*
Cambodians, immigrants, 237
Cameras, *see* Photographs and photography
Camp, John H., wholesaler, 55
Camp Ramsey, StP, 120
Camp Ripley, Morrison County, 195
Camp Savage, Scott County, 194
Campbell, Marion, *219*
Camphor Memorial Methodist Church, StP, *228*
Canadian Pacific Railway, 81
Canals, at Falls of St. Anthony, *15, 34, 91,* 232
Canary, Martha Jane ("Calamity Jane"), tour, *151*
Capital Mills, StP, flour mill, 56
Capitol Area Architectural Planning Commission, *272*
Capitol Avenue, StP, *215*
Capitol Meat Co., StP, *226*
Capitol Square Building, StP, *215*
Capitol Theatre, StP, 155, *161*
Cappelen, Frederick W., engineer, *134*
Cappelen Memorial Bridge, Mpls, *134*
Capt. Billy's Whiz Bang, published, 123, 155, *163*
Cardiff, Patrick ("Patsy"), boxer, *107*
Cargill, Samuel, grain merchant, 81
Cargill, William, grain merchant, 81
Cargill, Inc., Wayzata, 231; builds ships, 195, *225*
Carlson, Curtis L., entrepreneur, 234, *259*
Carlson, Don, basketball player, *243*
Carlson, George, in World War II, *224*
Carlson, Mrs. George, *224*
Carver County, suburban growth, 286n2

Cataract Hall, St. Anthony, theater, *41*
Cataract House, Mpls, hotel, *36, 66*
Cataract mill, Mpls, *34, 36, 66, 91*
Cathedral of St. Paul, 59, *272;* sites, *19;* present structure, *132, 174, 219, 263. See also* Chapel of St. Paul
Catholic church, 8, 48, *186, 213, 223, 248*
Catlin, Elizabeth, clubwoman, *174*
Catlin, George, artist, *40*
Cedar Avenue, Bloomington, *257*
Cedar Lake Ice Co., Mpls, *172*
Cedarette Cafe, StP, *215*
Cedar-Riverside Area, Mpls, 234
Celebrations, capitol dedication, *132;* war victories, *145, 228;* Lindbergh's flight, *170;* golf championship, *167;* end of prohibition, *204;* ethnic, *212, 264, 272;* end of Great Depression, 218; last streetcar run, *252. See also* Parades, various holidays
Centennial Building, StP, *244*
Central Avenue, Mpls, *33*
Central City Market, Mpls, *127*
Central High School, Mpls, *71;* StP, *147*
Central House, StP, hotel, *16*
Central (Loring) Park, Mpls, 85
Central Park, StP, *114*
Central Park Methodist Episcopal Church, StP, *21*
Central Presbyterian Church, StP, *20, 244*
Central School, Mpls, *71*
Chalmer Bros., Mpls, hardware store, *34*
Chapel of St. Paul, 8; built, 5, 6, *13;* razed, *271. See also* Cathedral of St. Paul
Chapman, Rev. Ervin S., speaker, *136*
Chapman, Joseph, banker, 118, *188*
Charles, Mpls, clothing store, *208*
Charlie's Cafe Exceptionale, Mpls, *188*
Charnley, Mitchell V., professor, *242*
Chase, Guy, *216*
Chase, Mrs. Guy, *216*
Cheever, William A., builder, *29*
Cherokee Tourist Camp, StP, *165*
Chicago, Ill., trade, 45, 81, 82; railroad, *209, 267*
Chicago, Burlington and Quincy railroad, *219*
Chicago, Milwaukee and St. Paul railroad, routes, *52;* depot, *52, 53;* elevator, *66;* yards, *90;* engine, *209*
Children, at play, *66, 105, 167, 216, 217, 269;* in labor force, 85, *141;* welfare, 85, *174, 175;* sports, *166, 243;* special programs, *264, 273;* move Stevens House, *276*
Children's Protective Society, Hennepin County, *175*
Children's Theater, Mpls, 235
Chimera Theater, StP, 235
Chisago County, suburban growth, 286n2
Christ Child Community Center, StP, *212*
Christ Episcopal Church, StP, *24*
Christian Aid Society, Mpls, 48
Chrysler automobile, *210*
Church, Elihu, 158
Churches, *18,* 48; activities, 8, *160, 187;* baptismal ceremonies, *172, 213. See also* individual denominations
Churchill, The, Mpls, apartments, *270*
Chute, Richard, memorial, *270*
Chute Building, St. Anthony, *28*
Cigars, manufactured, *139*
Circuses, Barnum's, 77; side show, *165*
Citizens Alliance, Mpls, 118, 192, 193
City Hall, StP, 7, *19, 21,* 84, *97, 203,* 226,

263; Mpls (Municipal Building), *62,* 84, *125, 133, 180, 181, 188, 199,* 271
"City of St. Paul," steamboat, *53*
City planning, in TC, 158, *183*
Civil rights movement, 235, *266, 267*
Civil War, 9, *39*
Civil Works Administration, 192, *199*
Civilian Conservation Corps, 192, *201*
Cleveland, Horace W. S., landscape architect, 85
Clifford, Nina, madam, *274*
Climate, winter, 5, *78,* 83, *269;* thaws, 5, *213, 217;* tornado, *134;* weather reports, 156; spring snowstorm, *199;* summer, *216*
Clothing, men's, *12,* 48; retailers, 16, *24, 97, 100, 101, 208;* Indian, *40;* women's, 48, *173, 241;* wholesalers, 55, *94;* manufacturers, 55, *172;* for cycling, *108;* underwear, *126;* footwear, *129*
Cloudman, Dakota Indian leader, *13,* 233
Coal, *128, 129, 173*
Coleman, Carl J., service station, *169*
Coliseum Ballroom (Pavilion), StP, 156, *162, 166,* 196
College of St. Thomas, StP, *106*
Collier, Barron G., Inc., advertising firm, *143*
Columbia Park, Mpls, 85
Comité de Reconstrucción, *212*
Commerce, StP, entrepôt, 7, *12;* public markets, *20;* wholesalers, 46, 82, 95, 119, *127;* traveling salesmen, 83; international, 83; Duluth, 117; brokerage firms, *130;* Mpls dominance, 158; antipathy to organized labor, 193; impact of depression, *208;* suburban, *252, 257;* antique sales, 277
Committee to Defend America by Aiding the Allies, 194
Communist party, *186,* 193, 194
Community Chest, funds raised, *174*
Como Park, StP, 85, *148, 153, 220;* in song, *152*
Computers, data processing, *202;* developed, 231, *260, 261*
Comstock, Castle and Co., StP, 55
ConAgra, Inc., Omaha, Neb., 231
Confectioners, *35, 100, 101, 108*
Congress of Industrial Organizations, activities, *205*
Construction industry, materials, 16, 58, *127*
Contests, tree sitting, *216;* dance, *216, 239;* movie star doubles, *218;* Miss America, *239*
Control Data Corp., Bloomington, 232, 233, *261, 263*
Conway, J. C., dance hall, *162*
Conway's Arcadia Dance Palace, Mpls, *162*
Coolidge, Calvin, president, *184*
Coolidge, Grace, visits state fair, *184*
Co-operatives, dairy, *207*
Cottage Grove Township, Washington County, population, *253*
Cottage Hospital of the Brotherhood of Gethsemane, Mpls, 48
Cotton, manufactured, *66*
Council of Twin Cities Metropolitan Area Chambers of Commerce, 233
Courts, municipal, *20;* quarters, 59, *271*
Cousineau, Joseph, saloon, *113*
Covert, Bernard, actor, *40*
Crafts, revival, *272;* demonstrated, *277*
Cramsie's Blacksmith and Wagon shop, StP, *17*

Crane jewelry store, Mpls, *35*
Cricket Theater, Mpls, 235
Crime, "fallen women," 7, 48; on river front, 7, *60;* liquor-related, 7, 159, 193, 194; punishments, 47, *186;* juvenile, *61;* auto theft, 122; in city government, *136;* against women, *140;* strike violence, 193, *205;* gangsterism, 193, 194; kidnaping, 193, *204;* Mpls, 195. *See also* Jails
Crittenden, M. H., manufacturer, *58*
Crosby, John, miller, *91*
Crown Iron Works Co., Mpls, *172*
Cummins Diesel Sales, Inc., Roseville, *259*
Customs House, StP, *59*
Cyclorama Building, Mpls, *111*

Daguerreotypes, studios, *16, 24. See also* Photographs and photography
Dain Tower, Mpls, *180*
Dairies, urban deliveries, *173;* co-operatives, *207*
Dakota County, suburban growth, 284n21, 286n2
Dakota Indians, *14;* land cessions, 5, 7; villages, 8, *11, 13;* photographers' models, *40*
Dakota Territory, 45
Dakota War of 1862, refugees, 9; troops, *39*
Dams, Falls of St. Anthony, 6, *14, 15, 29, 34,* 46, 259; Hennepin Island, 67. *See also* High (Ford) Dam
Dan Patch, race horse, 123, *151*
Dance, social, *41,* 156, 197, 235; halls, *162;* school, *162;* ballet, *188,* 235; folk, *212;* contests, *216, 239*
Daniels, John K., sculptor, *203*
Danz, Frank, Jr., orchestra leader, *153*
Darrow, Clarence S., lecturer, *109*
Davidson, William F., steamboat owner, *42*
Davies, Dennis Russell, orchestra leader, 235
Davis, Cushman K., peace commissioner, 120
Day and Jenks, StP, drugstore, *24*
Dayton Co., 233; Mpls store, *164, 180, 241;* StP store, *234, 247*
Dean, Joseph, lumberman, *70*
De Camp, Jack, fruit dealer, *101*
DeCoster, Georgia R., quoted, 271
Delano, Francis R., railroad man, *43*
Delmonico's, Mpls, grocery store, *259*
Demarest, James H., locksmith, *101*
Democratic party, 49, 119, *230,* 266, 267
Demonstrations and rallies, *186, 199, 222,* 266
Dempsey, Jack, boxer, 155, 156, *220*
Dentists, *100*
DePalma, Ralph, aviator, 156
Depression, 1930s, 159, 190-194, 197, *218,* 237; relief measures, 192, *200-202, 210;* effects, *198, 208, 209,* 231. *See also* Panics
Dickinson, Charles, 156
Dillinger, John, gangster, 193, 194
Dinkytown, Mpls, antiwar rally, *266*
Discrimination, *120, 186,* 194, *199,* 237, *266*
Division of Public Relief, Mpls, 192
Dobbs, Farrell, labor leader, 193
"Dr. Franklin No. 2," steamboat, 5, 6
Dodge, Ossian E., theater manager, *40*
Donaldson, L. S., Co., Mpls, department store, 84, *173, 180*

Donaldson, Lawrence, store, *96*
Donaldson, William, store, *96*
Donnelly, Ignatius, criticizes railroads, *52*
Dow, Daniel E., house, *106*
Downtown Auto Park, Inc., Mpls, *252*
Drive-ins, *252*
Drugstores, StP, *16, 24, 54, 147;* Mpls, *38, 64, 100;* St. Anthony, *41;* merchandise, 55, *216*
Dry goods, retail, *34, 40, 100;* wholesale, *54, 55*
Drycleaners, Mpls, *173*
Dual City Blue Book, social list, 84
Duesenberg automobile, 122, 123
Duluth, 82, 158, 236; railroad, 45, 46, *267;* rivalry with TC, 81, 117; population, 81, 86
Duluth Board of Trade, grain marketing, 117
Duluth Eskimos, football team, 236
Dunne, Miles, labor leader, 193, *221*
Dunne, Vincent, labor leader, 193, *221*
Dunwoody, William H., 84
Dunwoody Institute, Mpls, 122, *143, 144*
Dylan, Bob, musician, 235

Eagan, growth, 286n13
Eames, Henry, store, *53*
Earhart, Amelia, aviator, *220*
Eastman, Seth, artist, 1, *13*
Eastman, William W., *36, 46,* 66
Ebenezer Home, Mpls, *176*
Edgar, William C., editor, 283n24
Edina, *251,* 282n2
Education, 48, *187;* private schools, 8, *19, 24,* 84; students, *61, 242, 268;* courses, *71, 242, 273. See also* individual schools
Eighteenth Amendment, 119, 194
Eisenhower, Dwight D., president, *230*
Electric power, 80; used, 84, 88, 89, *107, 114, 137, 148, 151, 161;* generated, 85, 89, *116,* 259
Elevators, storage, 50, *54, 64,* 66, *126, 181, 182, 206, 207, 214, 215, 263;* passenger, *62, 84,* 96
Elfelt's Clothing Store, StP, *24*
Elfelt's dry-goods store, StP, *40*
Elizabeth Peabody Primary School, Mpls, 98
Elms, on streetscape, *214, 269*
Elvgren, A. A., *216*
Elvgren, Mrs. A. A., *216*
Emanuel, Nathan B., orchestra leader, 121
Emanuel Lutheran Church, StP, *244*
Emergency Relief Appropriation Act, 193
Emmett, Lafayette, lawyer, *16*
"Empire Builder," train, *267*
Energy Park, StP, 236, 272, *274*
Engine House No. 13, StP, *168*
Engineering Research Associates, StP, 232, 260
Englewood Avenue, StP, *215*
"Enterprise," steamboat, *42*
Equity Cooperative Exchange, 118
Erickson, Wally, Coliseum Orchestra, *162*
Ethnic groups, 48, 85, 118; assimilation, 120, 121. *See also* individual groups
Exposition Building, Mpls, *113, 125, 138, 153*

Fabel, Philip, store, *101*
Fair (store), Mpls, *100*

Fairs, in TC, *77, 112. See also* Minnesota state fair
Falls of St. Anthony, 11, 12, *125;* power source, 1, 5, 6, *69;* collapse, 1, *46, 66, 67;* milling, *15, 91, 138;* map, 66; electric plant, *116,* 271
Family, The, singers, 265
Farmer-Labor party, 194, *198*
Farmers' Alliance, 117
Farmers and Mechanics Bank, Mpls, *93*
Farmers and Mechanics Grocery Assn., 55
Farmers' Holiday Assn., rally, *199*
Farmers Union Terminal Assn., 159, *206*
Farnham and Lovejoy, Mpls, sawmill, *30,* 67
Fawcett Publications, Robbinsdale, 155, 156, *163*
Federal Building, StP, 271
Federal Courts Building, StP, 271
Federal Emergency Administration of Public Works, *202*
Federal Emergency Relief Administration, 192
Federal Highway Administration, *134*
Federal Reserve Bank, ninth district, 119, *130,* 262. *See also* Banks and banking
Federal Surplus Relief Corp., *200*
Federal Trade Commission, 283n7
Felt, Reuben, farmer, *199*
Fenn, John, playwright, *274*
Ferguson, Dr. James C., 226
Ferries, 6, *12, 25,* 73
Ferrin, Arnie, basketball player, *243*
Fifth Street, StP, *19*
Finkelstein and Ruben, theater operators, *173*
Finn, John J., tailor, *100*
Fire and Police Alarm Telegraph, air raid siren, 226
Fire fighting, 20, 47; equipment, 7, *74, 168*
Firearms, in World War II, 225
Fires, *20, 74,* 92
First Amendment, 285n17
First Bank System, Inc., 159
First Baptist Church, StP, *14*
First Congregational Church, Mpls, *26*
First Methodist Church, Mpls, *27*
First Minnesota Volunteer Infantry, 9, *39, 42*
First National Bank, Mpls, *38,* 65, *180;* StP, *206, 258*
First Presbyterian Church, StP, *14, 17*
First State Bank of St. Paul, *252*
Fitzgerald, F. Scott, author, 155
Flags, *39, 132*
Flandrau, Charles E., Boreas Rex, *146*
Floods, Mississippi River, *248*
Flour milling, at St. Anthony, 6, *14, 15, 69;* process, *34,* 45, 68; Mpls district, 45, 81, *91,* 120, *138, 180, 181, 259, 263;* StP, 56; Duluth, 117; decline, 159, *207,* 231
Flying Tigers airline, 229
Foley, T. H., cartoonist, *187*
Folkets Vel temperance society, *136*
Food, wholesale, *16, 54, 101, 127;* retail, *36, 64, 101, 139, 172, 181, 208, 215, 226, 227, 259;* menu, *96;* ethnic, *105, 275;* transported, 157, *229;* packaged, *164;* given to needy, *200;* rationed, 226; cookbook, *269. See also* Restaurants
Foot, Schulze and Co., StP, *129, 172*
Football, *see* Minnesota Vikings, University of Minnesota: football
Forbes, William H., trader, *16*
Ford, John, *pseud., 240*
Ford automobiles, *137*

Ford (High) Dam, Mississippi River, *128, 158, 232. See also* Dams
Ford Motor Co., 122, 157; StP plant, 159, *168,* 173
Forepaugh and Tarbox, StP, 55
Fort St. Anthony, *see* Fort Snelling
Fort Snelling, 5, 6, 8, 11, 12, *18, 201;* buildings, *59, 73;* in World War II, 194, 224; restoration, 271, 272, *277*
Foshay, Wilbur B., 159, *188*
Foshay Tower, Mpls, 159, *180, 188, 206, 234*
Fossum, Syd, artist, *205*
Foster, George K., poet, 283n31
Fountain Cave, 5, *12*
Fourteenth Street, StP, 234
Fourth of July, celebrated, 9, *76, 109, 146, 268, 278*
Fourth Street, StP, *17, 23, 24, 254*
France Avenue, Edina, *251*
Franklin Avenue Bridge, Mpls, *134*
Franklin School, StP, *61*
Franklin Steele Square, Mpls, *243*
Freeman, Orville, governor, *242*
Freemasons, in TC, 9, 77
Freewill Baptist Church, Mpls, *38*
Freie Presse, offices, *100*
Fridley, Russell W., MHS director, 272
Frishmuth, Harriet, sculptor, *188*
Fuller House, StP, hotel, *21*
Furniture, manufactured, *18, 172, 276;* warehouse, *36*

Gale, Edward C., speaker, *203*
Gale, Harlow, realtor, *63*
Galley, George, manufacturer, *18*
Galtier, Father Lucien, *13*
Gamble-Skogmo, Inc., 159, *260*
Gambling, *16,* 49. *See also* Crime
Games and amusements *39, 66, 167, 216, 217;* shows, *41, 64, 151*
Garland, Judy, actress, 197
Gateway Building, Mpls, *181, 245*
Gateway Center, Mpls, *245, 246*
Gateway District, Mpls, 192; urban renewal, *234, 241, 262*
Gateway Park, Mpls, *181*
Gaynor, Janet, actress, *218*
Gehan, Mark, StP mayor, *210, 218*
General Drivers and Helpers Union, Local 574, 193
General Mills, Inc., 159, 195, 231, 233, *260, 263. See also* Washburn-Crosby Co.
"Genesee," ship, *225*
German-American Red Cross Society of Minnesota, 120
Germania Life Insurance Co., *143*
Germans, 9, 280n24; in StP, 48, *104;* in brewing industry, 56; in World War I, 120, *143*
Gibbons, Mike, boxer, 155
Gibbons, Thomas ("Tommy"), 155, 195, *220*
Gibbs Farm Museum, Falcon Heights, *273*
Gibson, Charles P., photographer, 2
Gibson, James, photographer, 39
Gilbert, Cass, architect, *131, 177, 183,* 272
Gilbert, Woodland H., executive, *164*
Gill, Mrs. ——, school, *24*
Gillette, Mrs. A. J., contest promoter, *174*
Gillis, Lester, gangster, 193
Girard Terrace, Mpls, *248*
Glass Block Store, Mpls, 96

Glazer, Joe, labor leader, *205*
Gleckman, Leon, kidnaped, 193
Glenwood district, Mpls, *248*
Glenwood (Theodore Wirth) Park, Mpls, 85, *149*
Gluek Brewing Co., Mpls, *204*
Glyn, Elinor, author, 155
Godfrey, Ard, *30;* house, *29, 270,* 271
Goheen, Frank ("Moose"), hockey player, 155, *166*
Gold Bond Stamp Co., Mpls, *259*
Golden Valley, 233, *260*
Golf, 155, *167,* 196, *221*
Goodhue, James M., publisher, *16*
Goodrich Avenue, StP, *269*
Goodwin, Hugo P., organist, *160*
Gorman, Willis A., 9, *20*
"Governor Ramsey," steamboat, *42*
Grain, marketed, 81, *93,* 117-119, 159, *206;* transported, 157; raised, 158; storage, *182, 207;* feed mills, *214. See also* Flour milling
Grain Terminal Assn., 159, 231
Grand Army of the Republic, *135*
Grand Opera House, StP, *110;* Mpls, *110*
Grant, Jim ("Mud Cat"), baseball player, *256*
Gray, Carl R., Jr., 195
Great Atlantic & Pacific Tea Co., *208*
Great North American History Theatre, StP, *274*
Great Northern railroad, 81, *128, 187, 209, 232, 267*
"Great Northwest," balloon, *112*
Great Northwestern Exposition, *112*
Great Western Band, trip, 95
Greater Amusements, trade magazine, 155
Greater Minneapolis Chamber of Commerce, 233
Greely, Loye and Co., Mpls, *64, 69*
Green, Eugene ("Eddie"), gangster, 194
Greyhound Corp., bus company, 157
Griffin, Hach S., bicycle school, *109*
Griffith, Calvin, baseball team owner, 236
Groechel, Frieda (Mrs. Frederick), aids women, *140*
Grote's Tivoli, StP, hall, *105*
Groveland Park, StP, developed, *106*
Guaranty Loan Building (Metropolitan Building), Mpls, *84, 96, 246,* 271
Guardian Life Insurance Co., *143*
Guerin, Jules, city planner, *183*
Guerin, Vital, *20, 22*
Guernsey, A. T., and Son, StP, *147*
Guilford, Howard A., publisher, 285n17
Guthrie, Sir Tyrone, *264*

Haeberle, Arle, TV performer, 236
Hagen, Margaret, *217*
Hall, Lawrence, commissioner, 256
Hallie Q. Brown Community Center, StP, *176*
Hamilton, Charles, aeronaut, *138*
Hamilton airplane, *171*
Hamline University, StP, 48, 84, 99
Hamm, Marie, clubwoman, *174*
Hamm, Theodora, clubwoman, *174*
Hamm, Theodore, brewer, 56, *70*
Hamm, William, Jr., kidnaped, 193, *204*
Hand, Cal, singer, *265*
Hankinson, Richard H., 47
Hardware, retail, *34;* wholesale, 55, *94*
Hargreaves, Mrs. Richard T., *185*
Harriet Island, Mississippi River, *124, 178, 273*

Harris, Philip, chamber of commerce executive, *254*
Harrison, Benjamin, president, 96
Hartman, Sam, junk dealer, *211*
Harvest States Cooperatives, 159, 231
Haugsrud, Oluf, 236
Hawley, David, critic, 235
Hayes, Rutherford B., president, 77
Haynes, James C., Mpls mayor, *138*
Health conditions, 8, *216. See also* Hospitals, Medicine
Heart of the Earth Survival School, Mpls, *268*
Heath, "Frankie," waitress, *173*
Heath, Tommy, baseball manager, *243*
Hedlund, Christian T., family, *146*
Heffelfinger, F. Peavey, 195
Helstein, Ralph, labor leader, *205*
Hennepin Avenue, Mpls, *33,* 64
Hennepin Avenue Bridge, Mpls, *180, 245*
Hennepin Avenue Methodist Episcopal Church, Mpls, *72, 213*
Hennepin Center for the Arts, Mpls, *276*
Hennepin County, 7, *30,* 48; politics, *184, 230;* suburban growth, 284n21, 286n2
Hennepin County Courthouse, *30, 84, 125, 133, 180, 188, 199,* 271
Hennepin County Government Center, *263*
Hennepin County Historical Society, photograph collection, 3
Hennepin County Territorial Pioneers Assn., *29*
Hennepin Island, Mississippi River, 6, *14, 29, 30, 67, 125*
Herman, Keith, teacher, 268
Herrmann, Louis T., stenographer, *94*
Hersey, Harry, *151*
Hess, R. H., professor, 283n19
"Hiawatha," steamboat, *147*
Hiawatha Avenue, Mpls, *181, 182*
"Hiawatha No. 1," railroad engine, *209*
Hibbard, Charles J., photographer, 2
Hibbing, bus line, 157
High Bridge, StP, *104, 134*
High (Ford) Dam, Mississippi River, *128, 158, 232. See also* Dams
Hill, Francis, miller, *15*
Hill, I. P., miller, *15*
Hill, James J., *50,* 274; house, *84, 102*
Hill, Louis W., revives Winter Carnival, *146*
Hi-Lo project, Mpls, *249*
Hilton Hotel, StP, 233, 234
Himmelsback, Casper, undertaker, *100*
Hinck, Clarence, aviator, 122
Hinkley, Bill, singer, *265*
Hippies, *265*
Historic Hill District, StP, *272, 273*
Historic sites and houses, marker, *13;* Stevens House, *14, 32, 276;* Le Duc House, *16;* Godfrey House, *29, 270;* Hill House, *102;* Third Avenue Bridge, *134;* Robert ("Fish") Jones House, *148;* Hill District, *273. See also* Houses and housing, Preservation
Hmong, immigrants, 237, *268*
Hockey, 155; high-school, 237. *See also* individual teams
Hodgson, Laurence C., StP mayor, *170, 179, 184*
Holbrook and Co., meat packers, *70*
Hollywood Victory Caravan, theatrical troupe, 227
Holman, Charles ("Speed"), aviator, 122, 156, 157, *171*
Holman Field, StP, airport, 157, *171, 215, 225*

Home for the Friendless, StP, 48
Honeywell, Inc., Mpls, 159, 195, 231, 237; products, 225, 232, 261
Hoover, Herbert, president, 184, 198
Hoover, J. Edgar, 204
Hopkins, 82, 106
Horace Mann School, Mpls, 160
Horihan, Raymond, house, 240
Horse racing, 49, 77, 112, 151
Horsecars, see Street railways
Horses, stables, 35; supplies, 36, 64, 69; work, 46, 48, 52, 74, 121, 168; in accident, 211
Hospitals, Mpls, 27, 48, 119, 173, 221, 269; StP, 48, 215. See also Medicine
Hotel Leamington, Mpls, 188
Hotel Lyndale, Mpls, 78
Hotel Radisson, Mpls, 218
Hotels, StP, 16, 18, 21, 23, 43, 53, 54, 75, 97, 263, 274; built, 27, 40, 246; St. Anthony, 29; Mpls, 38, 66, 77, 78, 173, 181, 188, 218; fires, 74; resort, 78; events, 96
House of the Good Shepherd, StP, 48
Houses and housing, early StP, 21, 23; early Mpls, 33, 36; immigrant, 48, 104, 139; of the wealthy, 102; furnishings, 103, 164; apartments, 103, 181, 270; for workers, 106, 276; public projects, 202, 248, 249, 274; middle-class, 215, 269; trailer camp, 225; suburban tracts, 253; condominiums, 262, 270, 275. See also Architecture, Historic sites and houses, Preservation
Hubbard, Stanley, radio executive, 211
Hubert H. Humphrey Metrodome, Mpls, 237, 263, 269
Hudson, Wis., road, 210
Humphrey, Hubert H., 229, 252, 266, 267
Hungarians, refugees, 242
Huse, "Widow," house, 28
Hutchinson Hun Hunters, 143
Hyatt Regency Hotel, Mpls, 262

IDS Center, Mpls, 234, 263, 270
Ice Follies, 218
Ice industry, 172
Ice skating, 148, 243; shows, 196, 218
Illingworth, William, photographer, 2, 54
Immigration, 104, 121; after World War II, 237, 242
Independent Grain Exchange, 118
Indians, education, 268. See also individual tribes
Indochinese, immigrants, 237
Industrial Exposition, Mpls, 113
Industry, in Mpls, 34, 46, 119, 158, 214, 246; in StP, 57, 119, 215; power sources, 66, 69; war contracts, 120, 195, 225; decline, 191, 233; high-technology, 231, 232. See also Breweries, Commerce, Flour milling, Livestock, Lumber industry
Ingersoll Hall, StP, 40
Interlachen Club, Mpls, 155
International Hotel, StP, 74, 75
International Institute, StP, festivals, 212
International Stock Food Co., Mpls, 151
Interstate Commerce Commission, 232
Ireland, Archbishop John, 89, 120, 132
Irish, 9, 45, 48, 104, 105; in politics, 48, 136
Iron industry, manufacturers, 66, 70, 129, 172; mining, 117, 231

Irvine, John R., donates park, 107
Irvine Park, StP, restored, 274
Island mill, Mpls, 15, 67
Italia Club, StP, building, 212
Italians, 104, 212, 259
"Itasca," steamboat, 42

Jackson Street Bridge, StP, 16
Jackson Street Methodist Church, StP, 3, 21
Jacoby, William H., photographer, 2
Jails, 7, 8, 16, 21, 30
Japanese, 194
Jaros, Tony, basketball player, 243
Jarvis, Dr. William H., 1, 16
Jeep, developed, 195
Jefferson, Kenny, 268
Jerrard, Frederick, fruit dealer, 101
Jewelers, Mpls, 35; StP, 55
Jewish Educational Center, StP, 212
Jewish Home for the Aged, StP, 176
Jews, 48, 139, 186, 194, 212
Joesting, Herb, football player, 196
John Ireland Boulevard, StP, 255
Johnson, Frank A., brickmaker, 127
Johnson, Ivan ("Ching"), hockey player, 166
Johnson, John A., governor, 138
Johnson, Lyndon B., president, 192
Johnson, Oscar, ice skater, 196, 218
Johnston, Harrison ("Jimmy"), golfer, 155, 167
Johnston Block, Mpls, 64
Jokers Wild, singers, 265
"Jonathan Padelford," steamboat, 272, 273
Jones, Bobby, golfer, 155, 196
Jones, Harry Wild, architect, 127
Jones, Robert ("Fish"), zoo owner, 148
Jordan, Corinne, radio musician, 156
Jordan, Charles M., house, 103
Jordan, Mrs. Charles M., 103
"Josiah Snelling," steamboat, 272
Joy, Charles W., barber, 35
Judson, Abby A., educator, 98
Judson Female Institute, Mpls, 98
Junior League of Minneapolis, 276
Junior League of St. Paul, 174
Junior Pioneer Assn., 214

KSTP, StP, radio station, 156, 160; television station, 217
Kalman, Peggy, clubwoman, 174
Kalmon, Lion, and Son, StP, 55
Kaposia, Dakota Indian Village, 8, 11
Karpis, Alvin ("Creepy"), gangster, 193, 194, 204
Kauffman, Beverly, student, 212
Kay, Emily Grace, suffragist, 119
Keljik, Sossy, dancer, 212
Keller, Herbert P., StP mayor, 119
Keller family, lumber dealers, 57
Kelley, Michael J., baseball coach, 121, 150, 196
Kellogg Boulevard, StP, 254
Kelly, Anthony, and Bro., Mpls, 35
Kelly, George ("Machine Gun"), gangster, 193
Kelly, June, tree sitter, 216
Kennedy, John A., sculler, 149
Kenny, Sister Elizabeth, 221
Keys, Ancel, professor, 195
Kidder, William, 157
Kilbourn, Leona Wood, pianist, 160

Killebrew, Harmon ("Killer"), baseball player, 236
King, Martin Luther, Jr., 266
King, Samuel Archer, aeronaut, 112
King, William S., 49, 112
Kingsbury, A. B., stable, 35
Kittel, Jean, 217
Kittenball, invented, 167
Kline, Marvin L., mayor, 224
Knabenshue, Roy, airship, 138
Knights of Labor, 85
Knights of Pythias, parade, 77
Kolstad, John ("Papa"), singer, 265
Korean War, 237, 242
Ku Klux Klan, 159, 186

La Belle Saloon, StP, 16
Labor, 104, 176, 201; employment services, 35, 140, 175; unions, 85, 109, 118, 120, 141, 159, 186, 193, 195, 205, 221; women, 143, 195; workers, 172, 202; unemployed, 198, 199, 261
Labor Day, observance, 85
Ladies' Musicale, StP, 84
Lake Calhoun, Mpls, Dakota Indian village, 8, 13, 233; street railway, 47; park, 85; iceboating, 149
Lake Calhoun Pavilion, Mpls, 49, 78
Lake Calhoun Yacht Club, Mpls, 149, 219
Lake Harriet, Mpls, 8, 47, 85, 107, 153
Lake Minnetonka, Hennepin County, 78
Lake Nokomis, Mpls, 182, 213
Lake of the Isles, Mpls, 85
Lake Park Hotel, Excelsior, 78
Lake Street Auditorium, Mpls, 162
Lake Superior Museum of Transportation, Duluth, 43
Land O'Lakes Creameries, Inc., Mpls, 207, 231
Landmark Center, StP, 271, 274
Lanpher, R. A., and Co., StP, 55
Lao, immigrants, 237
Lao Family Community, 268
Larson, Judy, singer, 265
Latimer, George, StP mayor, 234
Laurel Avenue, StP, 273
Lawyers, 16, 40, 41
Leach, George, Mpls mayor, 170
League of Women Voters, 185
Le Bon Ton, StP, restaurant, 55
Le Claire, Michel, land claim, 5
Le Duc, William G., bookseller, 16
Lee, Robin, ice skater, 196
Legg, Harry, golfer, 155
Leith, Ron, teacher, 268
Leuthold, Stephen, quoted, 232
Lexington Food Arcade, StP, 208
Lexington Park, StP, sports field, 121, 166
Lexington Plaza, Roseville, 250
Liberty Bonds, 144
Libraries, rental, 9. See also Minneapolis Public Library
Lillibridge, H. F., store, 100
Lindbergh, Charles A., Jr., 122, 170, 222
Lindstrom, Elizabeth, 217
Linseed oil industry, 120, 126
Liquor, whisky sellers, 5, 12, 185; criminal aspect, 7, 185, 193, 194; consumption, 40, 105; wine store, 100. See also Breweries, Prohibition, Saloons
Little Crow (Che-tan-wakan-mani), Dakota Indian leader, 11
Little League, children's baseball, 243
Livestock industry, 82, 157, 170. See also

Meat packing
Lockheed "Electra," plane, *209*
Locksmiths, *101*
Log Cabin syrup, *128*
Long, Dick, orchestra, *162*
Long and Kees, architects, *133, 276*
Longfellow, Henry W., poet, *40, 148*
Longfellow Gardens Zoo, Mpls, *148*
Loring, Charles M., park commissioner, 85
Loring Green East, Mpls, *262*
Loring Park, Mpls, 85, *131, 262, 265*
Louisiana Purchase, map, *4*
Love, James W., boilerman, *173*
Lower Bridge, Mpls, *73*
Lower Dam, Mpls, *259*
Lower Levee, StP, 7, *263;* transportation center, *42, 50, 52, 53. See also* Upper Levee
Lowry, Thomas A., *89, 102, 150*
Lowry Hill, Mpls, *102*
Lumber Exchange Building, Mpls, *276*
Lumber industry, at St. Anthony, *14, 31, 66;* factories, *28, 30, 57, 70, 126;* markets, *37,* 119; mill production capacity, *46, 82, 92;* map of fire area, *92;* in Duluth, 117; decline, *207,* 231; offices, *276*
Lund, Francis ("Pug"), football player, 196
Lutheran church, 8, *48, 71, 176, 244*
Lynder, Sylvia, actress, *151*
Lyons, Nathan, quoted, 2

MACALESTER COLLEGE. StP, 48, 84, 99
McCarthy, Eugene J., senator, *266*
McFadden, Eddie ("Father Tom"), *204*
McFarlane, William K., realtor, *32*
McGrath, John, business executive, *226*
McGuire, Marie (Mrs. Arthur J.), *185, 229*
McKinley, William, president, *135*
McKnight, Mrs. Sumner T., *185*
McLeod, Minnie, student, *98*
McMeekin, Thomas W., lawyer, *204*
McNulty and Dafoe, Mpls, automobile dealers, *171*
Macomber, Clara, actress, *40*
Macomber, Emma, actress, *40*
McQuillan, P. F., and Co., StP, *54*
Magazines, variety, 156, *163*
Mahoney, William, StP mayor, *212*
Mail service, 5, 43; by air, 156, 157, *171*
Main Street, Mpls (St. Anthony), *29, 32, 272, 275*
Mamer Air Transport, 157
Mannheimer Bros., StP, store, 84, *97*
Manufacturers' Loan and Investment Co., 82
Maplewood, 233
Maps, Louisiana Purchase, *4;* Pike's expedition, *11;* Fort Snelling reservation, *12;* StP in 1851, *16;* Bridge Square in Mpls, *34;* TC railroads, *52;* Falls of St. Anthony, *66;* Mpls lumber district fire, *92;* highway, 158; TC metropolitan area, *238*
Marienhof, Benjamin, tailor, *100*
Marigold Gardens, Mpls, ballroom, 196
Market House, StP, *20;* Mpls, *63*
Market Street Methodist Episcopal Church, StP, *18, 59*
Markets, public, *20*
Marsh, K. H., farmer, *199*
Marshall, Joseph, merchant, *16*
Marshall, William R., *16, 25*
Martin, Slater, basketball player, 236, *243*
Martin-Morrison Block, Mpls, *275*
Masonic order, *see* Freemasons
Masonic Temple, Mpls, *276*
Masqueray, Emmanuel L., architect, *132*

Maternity Hospital, Mpls, 119
Maun, Joseph, *254*
Mays, Willie, baseball player, *256*
Mazourka Hall, StP, theater, *40*
Meat-packing industry, *70, 82, 95, 120, 186, 231. See also* Livestock industry
Mecklenburg, Rev. George H., 192
Medicine, patent remedies, 8, *216;* disease treated, *221, 261. See also* Health conditions, Hospitals
Medtronic, Inc., products, 232, *261*
Mendota, 5, 8, *12,* 271
Merchants Hotel, StP, *23,* 53
Merchants National Bank, StP, *128, 130*
Merriam Park, StP, developed, *106*
Merrill, Elijah W., teacher, *26*
Methodist church, 8, *27, 48,* 99, *213,* 228
Methodist Episcopal Church, StP, *18, 21*
Metropolitan Airports Commission, 238
Metropolitan and Regional Planning Assn., 158
Metropolitan area, government, 237, 238; map, *238. See also* Twin Cities
Metropolitan Building, Mpls, 84, *96, 246,* 271
Metropolitan Council, 238
Metropolitan District Planning Assn., 158
Metropolitan Drainage Commission, 158
Metropolitan Opera, 156, 235
Metropolitan Opera House, Mpls, 121
Metropolitan Sports Center, Bloomington, 236, *256*
Metropolitan Stadium, Bloomington, 236, *256, 265, 269*
Metropolitan Theater Orchestra, conductor, *153*
Metropolitan Transit Commission, *253*
Mexican Americans, *212,* 237, *268*
Mickey's Diner, StP, *194*
Midland Linseed Products Co., Mpls, *126*
Midway district, businesses, *207, 215, 274;* housing, *215, 274;* railroad depot, *267*
Midway Stadium, StP, 236
Mikan, George, basketball player, 236, *243*
Mikkelson, Vern, basketball player, 236, *243*
Milch, Adeline, musician, *162*
Milch, Arma, musician, *162*
Milch, Margaret, musician, *162*
Miles, Charles C., locksmith, *101*
Miles Theater, Mpls, shows, *152*
"Mill City," *see* Minneapolis
Milles, Carl, sculptor, *203*
Millinery, shop, *38*
"Milwaukee," steamboat, *15*
Milwaukee and St. Paul railroad, *see* Chicago, Milwaukee and St. Paul railroad
Milwaukee Avenue, Mpls, restoration, 272, *276*
Milwaukee Road, *see* Chicago, Milwaukee and St. Paul railroad
Minikahda Club, Mpls, 155
Minneapolis, name, 6; incorporated 6, 47; platted, *32;* oldest church, *33;* first newspaper, *36;* eclipses St. Anthony, *62;* politics, 118, *136;* as financial center, 119, *130;* in song, *152;* aerial view, *180, 214, 255, 262;* first house, *276*
Minneapolis and St. Louis railroad, 45, *128*
Minneapolis Artificial Limb Co., *145*
Minneapolis Athenaeum, 9
Minneapolis Auditorium, events, 196, *239*
Minneapolis Bedding Co., *172*
Minneapolis Board of Park Commissioners, 85, *182*
Minneapolis Board of Public Welfare, 192

Minneapolis Board of Trade, 84
Minneapolis Chamber of Commerce, 233, 236, 283n19; grain exchange, 81, 82, *93,* 117, 118
Minneapolis Civic and Commerce Assn., 283n19
Minneapolis Clearing House Assn., 283n19
Minneapolis Club, founded, 84
Minneapolis cotton mill, 66
Minneapolis Council of Social Agencies, *174*
Minneapolis Dry Goods Co., *140*
Minneapolis flour mill, 66
Minneapolis Gas Light Co., 47
Minneapolis General Electric Co., plant, *116*
Minneapolis General Hospital, employees, *173*
Minneapolis Heritage Preservation Commission, 272
Minneapolis-Honeywell Regulator Co., Mpls, *see* Honeywell, Inc.
Minneapolis Hook and Ladder Co. No. 1, *74*
Minneapolis Housing and Redevelopment Authority, *245*
Minneapolis Institute of Arts, 235
Minneapolis Journal, 2, 150
Minneapolis Lakers, basketball team, 236, *243*
Minneapolis, Lyndale and Lake Calhoun railroad, 46, *78*
Minneapolis Mill Co., 6, *15*
Minneapolis Millers, baseball team, *109,* 121, *150, 166, 196, 221, 240, 243, 256*
Minneapolis Millers, hockey team, 155, *166*
Minneapolis Millers Assn., 81
Minneapolis-Moline Power Implement Co., 195, *225*
Minneapolis paper mill, 66
Minneapolis Produce Exchange, 283n19
Minneapolis Public Library, 84, *96,* 200; photograph collection, 2, 3
Minneapolis Retailers' Assn., 283n19
Minneapolis, St. Paul and Sault Ste. Marie (Soo) railroad, 81
Minneapolis-St. Paul International Airport, 233, 256
Minneapolis-St. Paul Sanitary District, 158, 238
Minneapolis School of Fine Arts, 96
Minneapolis Society of Fine Arts, 84
Minneapolis Soldiers' Aid Society, *39*
Minneapolis Steel and Machinery Co., *143*
Minneapolis Stockyards and Packing Co., 82
Minneapolis Street Railway Co., 46, *72*
Minneapolis Symphony Orchestra, 84, 121, *153, 156, 161, 196,* 235; conductors, *220. See also* Minnesota Orchestra
Minneapolis Threshing Machine Co., *106*
Minneapolis Trades Assembly, 85
Minneapolis Tribune, 62, 258
Minnehaha Carriage Works, Mpls, *69*
Minnehaha Depot, Mpls, *276*
Minnehaha Falls, Mpls, *40*
Minnehaha Park, Mpls, *276*
"Minnesota," steamboat, *53*
Minnesota Academy of Natural Sciences, 96
Minnesota Agricultural and Mechanical Assn., 77
Minnesota Boat Club, *149;* in song, *152*
Minnesota Chicano Federation, *268*
Minnesota Club, StP, 84
Minnesota College Hospital, Mpls, *27*
Minnesota Commission of Public Safety, 120

Minnesota Committee to End the War in Vietnam, 237, *266*
Minnesota Dance Theatre, Mpls, 235
Minnesota Democrat, Mpls, offices, *36*
Minnesota Dept. of Highways, *179*
Minnesota Fighting Saints, hockey team, 236
Minnesota Fillies, basketball team, 287n26
Minnesota Garden Flower Society, *147*
Minnesota government, office buildings, *244*
Minnesota Historical Society, *18,* 271; collections, 1, 2, 3, *39, 43, 137;* building, *244, 278;* sites, *277*
Minnesota Iron Works, Mpls, *66*
Minnesota Kicks, soccer team, 236
Minnesota legislature, *190,* 271; activities, 118, 119, 155, *199,* 238, 272, 283n7
Minnesota Magdalen Society, 48
Minnesota mill, *15*
Minnesota Mining and Manufacturing Co., 159, 192, *206,* 232, 233
Minnesota Municipal Commission, *253*
Minnesota Museum of Art, StP, 235
Minnesota Muskies, basketball team, 287n26
Minnesota Mutual Life Insurance Co., StP, *263*
Minnesota National Guard, *135, 186,* 195, *266;* armory, *137*
Minnesota North Stars, hockey team, 236, *256*
Minnesota Opera Co., 235, *264*
Minnesota Orchestra, 121, 235, *264, 278. See also* Minneapolis Symphony Orchestra
Minnesota Packet Co., *15*
Minnesota Pioneer, StP, office, *16*
Minnesota Pipers, basketball team, 287n26
Minnesota Public Radio, 235
Minnesota Railroad and Warehouse Commission, 157
Minnesota River, shipyards, *225*
Minnesota State Capitol, *124, 178, 190, 263, 278;* first, *53;* removal controversy, 120, *131;* second, *131, 132;* approach area, *183, 230, 244,* 272; rally site, *193, 199,* 237
Minnesota State Employment Service, *198*
Minnesota state fair, *214;* locations, 83, *112;* events, *112,* 122, 123, *229;* buildings, *112, 166;* grounds used, *212, 213, 221*
Minnesota State Federation of Labor, 85
Minnesota State Reform School, *61*
Minnesota State Unemployment Compensation, office, *198*
Minnesota Street, StP, *21*
Minnesota Territory, 5, 6; capitol, 7, *16, 20,* 271; centennial, *239*
Minnesota Transfer Railway Co., 81, 82, 119
Minnesota Twins, baseball team, 236, *256*
Minnesota Vikings, football team, 236, *269*
Minor Heir, race horse, *151*
Miracle Mile, St. Louis Park, *250*
Miske, Billy, boxer, 155
Missions and missionaries, 8, *13,* 233
Mississippi Bridge Co., *32*
Mississippi River, 46, 271; navigation, 6, 7, *42, 128,* 159, *225,* 232; explored, *11;* reservoirs, 117. *See also* Bridges, Dams, Ferries, Steamboats and steamboating
Mitropoulos, Dimitri, symphony conductor, 196, *220*
Mix, Edward Townsend, architect, *96*

Moffet, Lot, hotelkeeper, *16*
"Moffet's Castle," StP, hotel, *16*
Monitor Plow Works, Mpls, *69*
Monks Hall, StP, clubhouse, *40*
Montana Livestock Co., 82
Montgomery Ward, StP, *214, 215*
Morrell, John, and Co., meat packers, 286n3
Morrison, Clinton, 84
Morrison, Dorilus, mill owner, 6
Morrison, J. C., clerk, *43*
Morrison Mills, Mpls, planing mill, *66*
Moss, Henry L., lawyer, *16*
Motion pictures, popularity, 121, 155, 197; theaters, *154, 161, 173, 218, 264*
Moulton, ———, mill owner, *67*
Mounds Park, StP, *186*
Mt. Airy Homes, StP, *248*
Mount Sinai Hospital, Mpls, *269*
Mueller, August, store, *101*
Multifoods Tower, Mpls, *270*
Municipal Building, *see* City Hall: Mpls
Munsing, George, manufacturer, *126*
Munsingwear, Inc., Mpls, *126, 172*
Murphy Motor Freight Lines, Inc., StP, 157
Music, 95, *107,* 239; bands, 9, *18,* 51, *135, 153, 162, 165, 188, 217;* performing groups, 9, 49, *153, 221, 265;* stores, *40, 152, 161;* songs about TC, *67, 114, 152;* concerts, *107,* 196; popular songs, *136, 165,* 195, 235, *265;* published, 156; radio broadcasts, 156, 160; recordings, 161, *217;* buildings, *264. See also* individual musical groups
Myers and Scholle, StP, *94*

NAFTALIN, ARTHUR, Mpls mayor, 256, *267*
Nagurski, Bronko, football player, 196
Nankin Cafe, Mpls, *162*
Nash, Michael W., county commissioner, *136*
Nash, Nancy, cover girl, *163*
Nassig, Louis, ice man, *172*
National Aeronautics and Space Administration, 196, *261*
National Archives, photograph collection, 3
National Basketball League, 236
National German American Bank, StP, *130*
National Historic Engineering Landmark, bridge, *90*
National Historic Landmarks, *91,* 277
National Recovery Administration, 192, *218*
National Register of Historic Places, *127, 133, 273, 274, 276, 277. See also* Historic sites and houses
National Science Foundation, project, *260*
National Woman's party, 119
Near, Jay M., publisher, 285n17
Near v. Minnesota, lawsuit, 285n17
Neill, Rev. Edward D., 8, 9, *18, 19,* 99
"Nellie Kent," excursion boat, *78*
"Nelson, Baby Face," gangster, 193
Nelson, Rev. Clarence T. R., *228*
Nelson, Capt. Harry, policeman, *173*
Nelson, Nels T., coal hauler, *129*
Ness, Henry B., death, *205*
Nevens Co., Mpls, drycleaning plant, *173*
New Brighton, 82, 120, *249*
New Englanders, club, 9
New Garrick Theater, Mpls, *152*
New Year's, celebrated, *218*
New York Life Insurance Co., *247*
Newman, Peter, farmer, *199*
Newspapers, 9, *36, 141,* 285n17; offices, *16, 258*

Newsstand, offerings, *163*
Nichols, George C., map maker, *16*
Nicollet Avenue, Mpls, *35, 65, 80,* 113
Nicollet Hotel, Mpls, *77, 173, 181*
Nicollet House, Mpls, hotel, *38*
Nicollet Island, Mississippi River, 6, 46, *180*
Nicollet Mall, Mpls, 234, *246, 262*
Nicollet Park, Mpls, 121, *166, 243*
Nicols and Dean, StP, 55, *94*
Nineteenth Amendment, 119
Nixon, Richard M., president, 266
"Noah's Ark," Mpls, apartments, 48
Nonpartisan League, 117, 120, *141*
North Central Airlines, 232
North Dakota, 88, 283n7
North Minneapolis, *180;* lumber center, 70, 92, *126;* ethnic groups, *139,* 266; urban renewal, *202,* 261
North St. Paul, 82, *106*
"North Star," train, *267*
North Star Iron Works, Mpls, *70*
North Star Woolen Mills, Mpls, *66,* 195
Northeast Minneapolis, *249, 259*
"Northern Belle," steamboat, *9*
Northern Federal Savings and Loan Assn., StP, *247*
Northern Pacific railroad, 232; constructed, 50, 59, 81, *90;* bridge, *104;* buildings, *128, 267, 274*
Northern States Power Co., *169, 267*
Northrop Field, Mpls, *150*
Northrup King and Co., Mpls, *172*
Northwest Airlines (Airways), Inc., 157, *220,* 225, 232; planes, *171, 209*
Northwest Bancorporation, 159
Northwest Crossing, StP, shopping center, 234
Northwest Magazine, StP, offices, *97*
Northwest Theatre Circuit, Inc., Mpls, *173*
Northwestern Consolidated Milling Co., 81
Northwestern Knitting Co., Mpls, *126*
Northwestern National Bank, Mpls, *65, 180*
Northwestern National Life Insurance Co., *262*
Northwestern Stove Works, Mpls, *100*
Northwestern Telegraph Co., 47, *62*
Northwestern Telephone Exchange Co., *88*
Norton, Charles, photographer, 2
Norwegians, 48, *105, 184*
Nowack, Michael, photographer, *73*
Noyes Bros. and Cutler, StP, 55
Nuclear power, plants, *267*
Nurses, in armed forces, 120, 194
"Nushka," sailboat, *111*
Nushka Club, StP, *111*
Nye, Dennis B., photographer, *103*
Nye family, *103*

OBERHOFFER, EMIL, orchestra conductor, 121
O'Connor, Richard T., political boss, 119, *136*
Odd Fellows, Independent Order of, 9, 77
O'Dowd, Mike, boxer, 155
Office of Naval Research, projects, *260*
Ojibway Indians, 5, 14
Old Betz (Bets), in song, *152*
Oldfield, Barney, aviator, 157
Olson, Floyd B., governor, 2, *190,* 191, 193, *198, 202,* 210, 220
Omnibuses, *38, 54, 94. See also* Buses, Street railways
100 Washington Square, Mpls, condominiums, *270*
Opera House, StP, 49, *76*

Orange Blossom flour, advertisement, 56
Orchestra Hall, Mpls, 235, 264
Ordway Music Theater, StP, 235, 264
Organized Unemployed, Inc., Mpls, 192
Ormandy, Eugene, orchestra leader, 196
Orpheum Theater, StP, 218
Orth, John, brewer, 70
Orth's Brewery, Mpls, 70
Osborn Plaza, StP, 234
O'Shaughnessy Auditorium, StP, 235
Oswald's Corner, Mpls, 34
Our Lady of Guadalupe Catholic Church, StP, 212
Our Lady of Lourdes Catholic Church, Mpls, 33, 275
Ousdigian, Arne, dancer, 212
Oustad, Kristoffer Olsen, engineer, 134
Overland automobiles, 137
Oxford Properties, Inc., 234

Pabst, Georg, meat seller, 101
Pacific and Atlantic Telegraph Co., 55
Pacific Mills, Mpls, lumber firm, 70
Packard automobile, 137
Padelford Packet Boat Co., StP, 273
Paderewski, Ignace, pianist, 151
Palace Museum, Mpls, 151
Panics, 1857, 6; 1873, 45; 1893, 85, 93, 117.
    See also Depression
Panoramas, St. Anthony, 3, 26-33; StP, 3, 17-26, 53, 124; as entertainment, 41; Mpls, 124
Paper, manufacture, 30, 66
Parades, 47, 76, 77, 90, 96, 113, 135, 136, 170, 201, 217; as ethnic celebrations, 9, 212, 272; at bridge openings, 32, 179; Winter Carnival, 83, 114, 195, 219; World War I, 143, 144, 145; American Legion, 165, 217. See also Celebrations
Paramount Theater, StP, 218
Parker Brothers, game manufacturers, 231
Parker Paine and Co., StP, bank, 258
Parking, lots, 137, 244, 245, 248, 250, 251, 252, 269; ramps, 247, 252, 275
Parks, 192, 237; StP, 75, 85, 107, 114, 186, 220, 274; Mpls, 85, 107, 181, 182, 196, 243, 262, 268, 276; White Bear Lake, 109; amusement, 148
Parrant, Pierre ("Pig's Eye"), 5
Parson, Bert, soda jerk, 147
Pascual, Camilo, baseball player, 236
Patti, Adelina, singer, 107
Pawnshop, Mpls, 241
Peavey, Frank H., grain merchant, 81
Peavey Co., Mpls, 231
Pedestrians, 137; aided by traffic signals, 202, 214; mall, 246
Peel, Clifford, photographer, 2
Pellegrini, Sebastiano, confectioner, 101
Pence Opera House, Mpls, 49, 64
Penney, J. C., Co., 159
People's party, 117
Peterson, Elsie, 214
Peterson, Hildur, 214
Peterson, Hjalmar, theater manager, 165
Peterson, Mrs. N. C., 185
Peterson, P. Kenneth, politician, 267
Peterson, Shirley, carnival queen, 195
Petroleum Service Co., service station, 208
Phalen Creek, StP, 56, 57, 105
Phalen Park, StP, 85
Phonographs, 138, 161, 217
Photographs and photography, 100; technology, 1, 2, 17, 147, 178; subjects, 1,

168; popularization, 2; collections, 3. See also Daguerreotypes
Phyllis Wheatley Settlement House, Mpls, 175, 200
Piccard, Jean, balloonist, 196, 220
Piccard, Jeannette, balloonist, 196, 220
Picnicking, 109; business sponsored, 140, 169
Pig's Eye, original StP settlement, 5, 6
Pigs Eye Lake, Ramsey County, 158, 202
Pike, Lt. Zebulon M., 5, 11
Pike Island, Mississippi River, 11
Pillsbury, C. A., and Co., Mpls, 66, 88, 91, 231
Pillsbury, Charles A., office, 88
Pillsbury A mill, Mpls, 91, 125, 275
Pillsbury-Washburn Flour Mills Co., Mpls, 81, 91
Pioneer Building, StP, 128
Pioneer life, 9, 203
Pitroff the Escape Artist, magician, 144
Placide's Varieties, theatrical troupe, 40
Pless, Rance, baseball player, 243
Plymouth Avenue Bridge, Mpls, 73
Plympton, Maj. Joseph, 5, 12
Poles, housing, 104
Police, TC departments, 47, 60, 173, 193, 194; crowd control, 199, 205, 266
Politics, corruption, 118, 136; use of media, 156, 267. See also individual political parties
Pollard, Jim, basketball player, 236, 243
Pond, Gideon, missionary, 13
Pond, Samuel, missionary, 13
Ponds, for geese, 34
Population, St. Anthony, 6; Minnesota, 6, 45; TC, 6, 49, 81, 83, 118, 119, 158, 191, 231; Duluth, 81, 86; Hopkins, 106; metropolitan district, 117, 158, 191, 231; Bloomington, 233; Richfield, 252; Cottage Grove Township, 253
Post office, StP, 19, 59, 201, 263; Mpls, 34, 62, 245
Postmasters, St. Anthony, 30
Postum Cereal Co., Battle Creek, Mich., 164
Powderhorn Park, Mpls, 85, 182, 268
Pracna On Main, Mpls, restaurant, 275
Prairie Island, nuclear-power plant, 267
Prendergast Bros., StP, 55
Presbyterian church, 8, 17, 20, 99, 244
Preservation, business buildings, 247, 274, 275, 276; houses, 270, 273, 274, 276. See also Architecture, Historic sites and houses, Houses and housing, Urban renewal
Preus, Jacob A. O., governor, 186
Prince, John S., StP mayor, 10
Prince's Block, StP, 53, 55
Printing, graphic arts, 258
Progressive movement, comments on urban life, 118
Prohibition, temperance movement, 8, 9, 16, 40, 136; legalized, 119, 185; opposed, 136; violations, 159, 185, 193; repealed, 204. See also Liquor
Protestant Episcopal church, 8
Protestant Orphan Asylum, StP, 8
Public utilities, 118, 159; waterworks, 8, 47, 66, 158, 192, 237; gas, 8, 47, 249. See also Electric power
Public works, see Streets, Sewers and sewage
Public Works Administration, 192
Publishers, StP, 57
Purdy, Mrs. Milton D., 185

Queens of Syncopation, jazz band, 162
Quong, Gin, Lung and Co., StP, 84

Rader, Luke, evangelist, 213
Radio, 156; broadcasts, 160, 177, 213
Radisson Hotel, StP, 234, 263
Radisson Plaza, StP, 234
Raft, George, actor, 197, 220
Railroads, 50, 105; built, 10, 45, 81; advertisements, 43, 151; depots, 51, 52, 53, 81, 94, 232; criticized, 52; map, 52; passenger trains, 178, 209, 232, 267; intracity tracks, 180, 181, 182, 214, 263
Rainbow Nymphs, dance troupe, 188
Raines, R. J., aviator, 229
Ramsey, Alexander, 39; house, 274, 277
Ramsey County, county seat, 7; welfare, 48, 192; donates fair site, 83; politics, 184, 230; unincorporated area, 253; acquires Landmark Center, 271; suburban growth, 284n21, 286n2
Ramsey County Board of Commissioners, 237
Ramsey County Courthouse, 7, 22, 24, 84, 97, 203, 226, 263
Ramsey County Historical Society, 271, 273
Rand, Alonzo, mayor, 47
Rand Tower, Mpls, 180
"Rangers," volunteer guards, 193
Raspberry Island, Mississippi River, 149
Ravel, Marietta, actress, 76
Raymond, Floyd, 122
Real estate, agents, 32, 40
Reardon, Elizabeth, 216
Reardon, Helen, 216
Red Coach Line, stagecoaches, 43
Red Cross Society of Minnesota, 120
Red School House, StP, 268
Refrigeration, 208
Religion, see Churches
Remington Rand, Inc., 232
Rentfrow, Milton L., songwriter, 68
Reo automobiles, 137
Republic Airlines, Inc., 232
Republican party, 49, 96, 113, 119, 230
Restaurants, 278; StP, 55, 119, 194, 215; Mpls, 111, 173, 188, 275; automat, 164
Rian, Clifford John, broadcaster, 240
Rice, Henry M., donates park, 107
Rice House, StP, hotel, 43
Rice Park, StP, 107, 274
Richard Chute Square, Mpls, 270
Richfield, population, 252
Richfield High School, 252
Richfield Road, Hennepin County, paved, 169
Rickenbacker, Eddie, aviator, 157
Riheldaffer, Rev. John G., 18, 61
Riley, Rev. William B., 187
Ringling Bros. and Barnum and Bailey Circus, 165
Ripley, Dr. Martha, suffragist, 119
River-Lake Gospel Tabernacle, Mpls, 213
Riverplace, Mpls, developed, 275
Riviera Theater, StP, 161
Roach, Frederick, bicycle shop, 108
Roads and highways, good-roads movement, 157, 158, 169, 170, 210; interstate system, 233, 234, 237, 244, 251, 254, 255, 257, 263. See also Streets
Rober, Lewis, invents kittenball, 167
Robert, Louis, trader, 21, 23
Robert Street Bridge, StP, 179, 263
Robertson, Daniel A., 16, 47
Robinson, Hugh, aviator, 122

Rochat, Henri, jeweler, 55
Rochester, air-mail service, 157
Rogers, R. C., miller, *30*
Rohrer, Daniel, bookseller, *16*
Roosevelt, Franklin D., president, *184,* 192,
  193, *198, 220*
Roosevelt, Theodore, president, *135*
Rose, Anson H., druggist, 55, *100*
Rose, Bert, football manager, 236
Rosedale Shopping Center, Roseville, *269*
Roseville, *249, 250,* 286n13; truck termi-
  nals, 233, *259*
Rothschild, Maurice L., and Co., Mpls, *172*
Rowan, Carl, journalist, *258*
Rubinstein, Artur, pianist, *220*
Russell, Roswell P., house, *33*
Russian Orthodox church, Mpls, *213*
Rutherford, Dr. W. C., *216*
Ryan Hotel, StP, 84, *97*

St. Anthony, early growth, 5, *14;* plat, 6, *16,
  29;* public works, 7; city council, 9; rail-
  road, 10, 45; panorama, *26-33;* first
  house, *33;* union with Mpls, *73*
St. Anthony Falls Water Power Co., 6, *30*
St. Anthony Hill, StP, *132*
St. Anthony Main, Mpls, 272, *275*
St. Anthony Mill Co., partners, *30*
St. Anthony Park, StP, 85, *126*
St. Barnabas Hospital, Mpls, 48
St. Catherine's, StP, Episcopal school, 84
St. Croix County, Wis., suburban growth,
  286n2
Saint-Gaudens, Augustus, sculptor, *247*
St. Joseph's Hospital, StP, 8, 48
St. Louis Park, 82, *260,* 282n2
St. Luke's Catholic Church, StP, *248*
St. Luke's Hospital, StP, 8, 48
St. Mary's Russian Orthodox Greek Catholic
  Church, Mpls, *213*
St. Patrick's Day, parades, 9, 272
St. Paul, townsite purchased, 5, 6, *12, 16,
  21;* name, 5, 6, *13;* early growth, 7, *13,
  14;* city council, 8, 9; first house, *23;*
  politics, 118, 119, *136;* aerial views, *178,
  214, 215, 255, 263;* anniversary, *239;*
  city historic districts, *273, 274*
St. Paul and Minneapolis Street Railway
  Employees' Union, 85
St. Paul and Pacific railroad, *43, 51, 58, 62,
  64, 69*
St. Paul Arts and Science Center, 235
Saint Paul Association of Commerce, 191
St. Paul Auditorium, 196, *210, 223*
St. Paul Board of Park Commissioners, 85
St. Paul Board of Public Welfare, 192, 193
St. Paul Bridge Co., 25
St. Paul Chamber of Commerce, *57,* 82, 84,
  87, 233, 236, 271, 282n13
St. Paul Chamber Orchestra, 235, *264*
St. Paul City Railway Co., 46, *72*
St. Paul Civic Center, 237, *284*
St. Paul Civic Opera, 196
St. Paul Commercial College and Tele-
  graphic Institute, 55
St. Paul Committee for Unemployment In-
  surance, *199*
St. Paul Community Chest, 191
St. Paul Daily News, 167, 194
St. Paul Dispatch, 76, 192
St. Paul Driving Assn., 49
St. Paul Female Seminary, *61*
St. Paul Figure Skating Club, 196
St. Paul Fire and Marine Insurance Co., 53,
  55

St. Paul Foundry Co., *129*
St. Paul Gas Light Co., 8
St. Paul Harvester Works, 58
St. Paul Heritage Preservation Commis-
  sion, 272
St. Paul History Theatre, *274*
St. Paul Hotel, *40, 274*
St. Paul House, StP, hotel, *23*
St. Paul Jobbers' Union, 95
St. Paul Library Assn., 9
St. Paul Manufacturing Co., 57
St. Paul, Minneapolis and Manitoba rail-
  road, *90*
St. Paul Omnibus Line, *54*
St. Paul Park, 82
St. Paul Pioneer Press, 101, 192
St. Paul Pleasure Park, 75
St. Paul Port Authority, 234
St. Paul-Ramsey Medical Center, 234
St. Paul Red Cross Aid Society, 120
St. Paul Roller Mill Co., 56
St. Paul Saints, baseball team, *109,* 121,
  150, 166, 196, *240, 243*
St. Paul Saints, hockey team, 155
St. Paul Society for Improving the Condi-
  tion of the Poor, 48
St. Paul Street Railway Co., 46, *72*
St. Paul Symphony Orchestra, 120
St. Paul Trades and Labor Assembly, 85
St. Paul Type Foundry, parade float, *76*
St. Paul Union Stockyards Co., 82, 95
St. Paul Water Co., 47
St. Rose of Lima Catholic School, Roseville,
  249
St. Thomas College, StP, 84
Salisbury-Satterlee Co., Mpls, *275*
Saloons, *40, 150;* StP, *16,* 55; St. Anthony,
  29; Mpls, *113, 275;* post-prohibition
  celebrations, *204*
Sanitary Food Manufactury Co., StP, *149*
Saturday Press, scandal sheet, 193
Sault Ste. Marie ("The Soo"), Mich., rail-
  road, 81
Savage, Marion W., horse owner, *151*
Savage, 195
Savory and Johnston, Mpls, *64*
Sawmills, at Falls of St. Anthony, 6, *15, 29,
  33, 34, 116,* 271. *See also* Lumber
  industry
Scandinavians, 45, *104, 264*
Schaber and Wendt, StP, millers, 56
Schade, Fred H., park owner, *148*
Schaefer, Herman, basketball player, *243*
Schaeffer, Gustav ("Gloomy Gus"), gang-
  ster, *204*
Scheffer, Albert, house, *102*
Schiek, Frederick, restaurant, *111*
Schoch, Andrew, Grocery Co., StP, *172*
Schubert Club, StP, 84, 235, *264*
Schwartzbauer, Rita, *217*
Science Museum of Minnesota, StP, 235,
  264
Scott, Anna M., dance teacher, *162*
Scott, Capt. Martin, 5
Scott County, suburban growth, 286n2
Screen Secrets, movie magazine, 156
Seattle, Wash., airline, *209, 220;* railroad,
  267
Secombe, D. A., lawyer, *41*
Second Avenue, Mpls, *37*
Selby-Dale district, StP, *266*
Selective Training and Service Act, *224*
Sevareid, Capt. Paul, *224*
Seven Corners, StP, *178*
Seventh Street, StP, *20, 215, 239;* Mpls, *137*

Severance, Mrs. Cordenio A., suffragist, 119
Sewers and Sewage, 158, 192, *202,* 237
"Shakopee," railroad engine, *44*
Sheraton-Ritz Hotel, Mpls, *246, 262*
Sherman House, StP, hotel, *54*
Shipstad, Eddie, ice skater, 196, *218*
Shipstad, Roy, ice skater, 196, *218*
Sholom Home, StP, *176*
Shopp, Beatrice ("BeBe"), beauty queen,
  239
Shoreview, gas service, *249*
Shotwell, Clerihew and Lothmann, Mpls, 85
Shriners, *220*
Sibley, Henry H., 6, *12, 32;* house, 271
Sieloff, William H., milkman, *173*
Sixth Avenue Hotel, StP, *36*
Sixth Minnesota Volunteer Infantry, *39*
Sixth Street, StP, *263*
Sixth Street Bridge, StP, *105*
Skiing, *149,* 196
Skinner, Otis, actor, *151*
Skoog, Whitey, basketball player, 236
Skyways, TC system, 234, *263*
Sleighing, 84, *103*
Sligo Iron Store, StP, *16*
Solvaks, immigrants, *104*
Smilow, Joseph W., pawnbroker, *241*
Smith, Alfred E., candidate, *184*
Smith, Bruce, football player, 196
Smith, C. A., Lumber Co., sawmill, *92*
Smith, C. H. F., and Co., StP, *130*
Smith, J. George, soda fountain, *137*
Smith, Robert, milling interests, 6, *32*
Smith, Parker, and Co., Mpls, 66
Snelling, Col. Josiah, *12*
Snyder, Simon P., realtor, *32*
Soccer, professional, 236
Social life, 97, *103,* 240; pioneer, 9, *41;* of
  unmarried adults, *40, 140;* group out-
  ings, *78, 107, 111, 147, 239, 269;* clubs,
  84, *111, 147;* of women, 85, *175;* among
  Germans, *105*
Social Security Administration, *201*
Socialist party, 118, 120
Societta Italia di Mutuo Soccorso, StP, *212*
Soda fountains, *108, 137, 147*
Softball, origins, 167
Soo Line Terminal Elevator, Mpls, *182*
Sorry Muthas, singers, *265*
Sousa, John Philip, composer, 159, *188*
South Dakota, 88
South Minneapolis, temperance society,
  136
South St. Paul, livestock industry, 82, *95,*
  120, *170, 186,* 231, 286n3; as suburb,
  282n2
Southdale, Edina, 233, 234, *251*
Southeast Minneapolis, industry, *126, 182,
  246*
Spanish-American War, 120, *135*
Spencer, Rose, *221*
Sperry Rand Corp., Univac division, 232,
  233, *260*
"Spirit of St. Louis," airplane, *170*
Spooner's Building, St. Anthony, *41*
Sports, 84; roller skating, *107;* bowling,
  148; winter, 148, *149;* playground facil-
  ities, *243. See also* individual sports
Spread Eagle Bar, StP, 55
Stagecoaching, *43*
Standard Metropolitan Statistical Area,
  population, 231
Starkweather, Mary, aids women, *140*
Stassen, Harold E., governor, *221*
Stassen, Mrs. Harold E., *221*

State Eight Hour League, 109
State Office Building, StP, 244
Steam power, 69; generates electricity, 89, 116
Steamboats and steamboating, 5, 7, 8, 42, 43, 50; arrivals, 15, 22, 53. See also individual steamboats
Steele, Franklin, 12, 32, 270; land claim, 5, 6; dam builder, 14, 29; builds mill, 15, 30, 33, 271; memorial, 243
Stelnicki, Bob, singer, 265
Stevens, John H., 6, 32; house, 14, 32, 271, 276
Stevenson, Adlai E., politician, 230
Stewart, William Scott, lawyer, 204
Stickney, Alpheus B., 82, 85
Stickney Motorette, 122
Stone Arch Bridge, Mpls, 90, 104, 180, 259
Stores, 23, 33; department, 96, 140, 164, 180, 241, 247. See also various kinds of stores and items sold
Stoves, manufactured, 55; retailers, 100
Strand Theater, StP, 161
Street railways, horsecars, 46, 47, 72, 90; urban service, 82, 84; electrified, 84, 89; cable cars, 97; Mpls system, 102, 118, 249; StP system, 106, 178; competition, 108, 122; conductor, 172; system ended, 232, 239, 252
Streets, paved, 7, 48, 85, 254; lighting, 8, 47, 88, 113; traffic signals, 202, 208, 214; tree-lined, 214, 269
Strong, Hackett and Chapin, StP, 55
Struble, Gene, 234
Suburbs, development, 106, 158, 232, 251; population, 158, 231; shopping centers, 233, 250, 251; relations with TC, 233, 252, 253; commercial growth, 233, 257; map, 238; idealized, 240; public utilities, 249; housing, 253
Sullivan, John L., boxer, 107
Summit Avenue, StP, 102, 106, 272
Summit flour mill, Mpls, 67
Summit-Hill district, StP, 269
Sumner Field Housing Project, Mpls, 202
Superior National Forest, CCC camp, 201
Suspension Bridge, Mpls, 32, 73, 181
Swans Down, flour, 164
Swanson, Frederick T., composer, 152
Swardson, Roger E., 271
Swede Hollow, StP, 48, 56, 105
Swedes, 48, 105, 212, 272
Sweeny, Robert O., artist, 16, 40
Sweet, Louis D., photographer, 2
Swift and Co., South St. Paul, 82, 286n3

Tailors, 55, 100
Taliaferro, Maj. Lawrence, 13
Tarkenton, Francis ("Fran"), football player, 236
Telegraph, 47, 53, 55, 62, 150; wireless, 138
Telephones, 80, 88, 238; early calls described, 47
Television, 217, 235, 236, 240, 260, 267
Temperance House, StP, hotel, 16
Temperance movement, see Prohibition
Tenney, E. B., tailor, 55
Tenth Avenue Bridge, Mpls, 73
Theaters, 84; troupes, 9, 40, 49, 110, 165; St. Anthony, 41; Mpls, 64, 75, 235, 264; StP, 76, 235; interiors, 110; visiting performers, 144, 151; vaudeville, 152; historical, 274

Theodore Wirth Park, Mpls, 85
Third Avenue Bridge, Mpls, 134, 180, 245
Third Street, StP, 55; Mpls, 80
Thirteenth Minnesota Volunteer Infantry, 120, 135
Thompson, Lt. James L., map maker, 12
Thompson, Wayne, quoted, 237
3M, see Minnesota Mining and Manufacturing Co.
Thye, Edward J., governor, 229
Tidewater Oil Co., service station, 208
Tobacco, products manufactured, 139
Toltz, King and Day, architects, 179
Toro Co., Bloomington, 233
Tourism, southern visitors, 27, 78; at Minnehaha Falls, 40; in lake district, 78; effect of climate, 83; camps, 165; information center, 181; river sightseeing, 273
Towboats, built, 225
Towers, St. Anthony, 29; electrified, 148; water, 251, 253
Towle, Patrick J., wholesaler, 128
Towle Syrup Co., StP, 128
Town and Country Club, StP, 147, 155, 216, 254
Town Square, StP, 234
Townley, Arthur C., politician, 141
Trade, see Commerce
Traeger, August, wine merchant, 100
Traffic, congestion, 127, 134, 137, 254; signals regulate, 202, 208, 214; on freeways, 263
Transportation, see Automobiles, Buses, Omnibuses, Railroads, Roads and highways, Steamboats and steamboating, Street railways, Trucks
Tremont House, St. Anthony, hotel, 28
Trinity Lutheran Church, StP, 244
Tri-State Employment Co., Mpls, 35
Trucks and trucking, industry developed, 122, 157, 170; drivers' strike, 193, 205, 221; terminals, 233, 259
True Confessions, magazine, 156
Truman, Harry S, president, 228
Tufenk, Togue, dancer, 212
Tunney, Gene, boxer, 155, 156, 220
Tuohy, Roger ("Terrible"), gangster, 193, 204
Turners, band, 51
Turpin, Eulalie, 21
1200 on the Mall, Mpls, condominiums, 262
1225 La Salle, Mpls, condominiums, 262
Twin Cities, characterized, 1, 49, 231; rivalry, 10, 45, 49, 82, 83, 87, 112, 118, 119, 207, 233, 236, 238, 254; name, 45; census war, 83, 115; proposed merger, 84
Twin Cities Metropolitan Planning Commission, 238
Twin Cities Ordnance Plant, New Brighton, 225
Twin City Aero Corp., 157
Twin City Bankers Assn., 84
Twin City Commercial Club, 84, 282n21
Twin City Flying Field, 157
Twin City Freight, Inc., 259
Twin City Mandolin Orchestra, 152
Twin City Motor Speedway, Mpls, 156, 170
Twin City Motor Transit Co., 122, 157
Twin City Rapid Transit Co., 84, 107, 141, 158, 239, 252, 284n15
Twin City Ski Club, 149
Twin City Wonderland Park, 148
Tyrone Guthrie Theater, Mpls, 235, 264

Ueland, Clara, suffragist, 119
Ulmer, Rock, announcer, 217
Undertakers, 100
Union Bus Depot, Mpls, 169
Union City Mission, Mpls, 176
Union Depot, StP, 128, 178, 184, 194
Union flour mill, Mpls, 66
Union of Swedish Singers, 212
Union School, Mpls, 37
United and Ancient Order of Druids, 77
United Nations, 197, 229, 242
United States, land purchase, 4; government mill, 6, 28; builds bridge, 73; New Deal, 191, 192; urban-renewal programs, 238, 271, 272; bicentennial observed, 270
U.S. Army, posts, 11; Department of Dakota, 59; in Spanish-American War, 120, 135; World War I veterans, 145, 198; in World War II, 224, 227
U.S. Census, 1849, 6; 1857, 6; 1865, 6; 1880, 45, 49; 1895, 81; 1890, 82, 83; 1920, 117, 119, 158; 1930, 158; 1950, 231; 1960, 231; 1970, 231; 1980, 231
U.S. Congress, investigates grain trade, 283n7
United States Figure Skating Assn., 196
U.S. Navy, servicemen, 224
Universal Aviation Corp., Mpls, 157
Universalist Church, St. Anthony, 33
University Avenue, Mpls-StP, 27, 47, 179
University of Minnesota, 48, 84; established, 8; buildings, 26, 71, 156, 177, 196, 246; students, 26, 71, 246; farm campus, 99; football, 150, 156, 177, 196, 220, 236; radio station, 156; faculty, 195, 196; antiwar rallies, 194, 222, 237, 266
Upper Bridge, Mpls, 73
Upper Levee, StP, 7, 15, 104, 128, 248. See also Lower Levee
Upper Midwest American Indian Center, Mpls, 268
Upton, Benjamin F., photographer, 2, 17, 22, 26, 30, 33, 40
Upton Building, St. Anthony, 28; Mpls, 275
Urban renewal, downtown Mpls, 181, 234, 235, 241, 245, 246, 262, 271, 275; housing projects, 202, 248, 249, 274; capitol-approach area, 230, 244; beginnings, 233; downtown StP, 234, 235, 247, 271

Vadnais Heights, 253
Valesh, Eva McDonald, labor leader, 274
Van Brocklin, Norman, football coach, 236
Van Cleve Park, Mpls, 148
Van Dyke, Arthur A., postmaster, 201
Van Lear, Thomas, Mpls mayor, 118, 120
Van Meter, Homer, gangster, 194
Van Sant, Samuel R., governor, 146
Vavoulis, George, StP mayor, 254, 256
Vietnam War, protested, 235, 237, 266
Vietnamese, immigrants, 237
"Virginia," steamboat, 12

WCCO, Mpls, radio station, 156, 160, 162
WDGY, Mpls, radio station, 156, 213
WLB, Mpls, radio station, 156
WTCN-TV, Mpls, 240
Wabasha Street, StP, 17, 19, 25, 239
Wabasha Street Bridge, StP, 8, 47, 53, 77, 178, 263; built, 25
Wagner, D. R., store, 64
Wales, W. W., bookstore, 41
Walker, R. O., storekeeper, 16

303

Walker, Thomas B., art collector, 84, *153*
Walker Art Center, Mpls, 84, 235
Walsh, Judith, boardinghouse keeper, *38*
Wampler, A. J., druggist, *54*
Wang, Tan Ming, student, *242*
"War Eagle," steamboat, 9, *42*
Warehouses, StP, *50, 215;* Mpls, *127, 180, 275;* St. Louis Park, *260*
Warman, John A., Block, Mpls, *103*
Washburn, Cadwallader C., mill owner, 6, *91*
Washburn, William D., mill owner, 6, 82, *91;* house, 84, *102,* 271
Washburn A mill, Mpls, explosion, 1, 46, 68; in song, *152*
Washburn-Crosby Co., Mpls, 81, *91,* 156, 159. *See also* General Mills
Washburn Memorial Orphan Asylum, Mpls, 282n30
Washburn Mill Co., Mpls, *66, 91*
Washington Avenue, Mpls, *36, 38, 64, 90*
Washington Avenue Bridge, Mpls, 232, *246*
Washington County, *224,* 284n21, 286n2
Washington Roller Rink, Mpls, *107*
Washington School, StP, *22*
Water power, used in flour milling, 6, 15, 45, 46, 56, 66, 69, 91; generates electricity, *89,* 116, 159, *259*
Water supply, *see* Public utilities
Waverley automobile, *137*
Weeds, The, singers, *265*
Wefald, Knud, legislator, 118
Welfare, agencies, 8, 48, 85, *175,* 176; soldiers' aid societies, 9, *39;* fund raisers, *78, 174, 269;* war relief, 120, *145,* 195; in 1930s Depression, 191-193, *199, 200, 202;* for refugees, 237

Wengler, Jean Baptiste, artist, 1
Werden, Perry ("The Moose"), baseball player, *150*
West, John B., and Co., StP, *57*
West Hotel, Mpls, *96*
West Minneapolis (Hopkins), suburb, 82, *106*
West St. Paul, suburb, 82, 282n2
West Side, StP, celebrations, *212*
Western Avenue, StP, *103*
Western Freight Traffic Assn., StP, *140*
Weyerhaeuser Timber Co., StP, office, *207*
White Bear Lake, *109, 253*
White Bear Township, Ramsey County, *253*
White House, Golden Valley, *252*
Whitney, Joel E., photographer, 1, *24*
Wildwood Park, White Bear Lake, *109*
Wilfahrt, John ("Whoopee John"), orchestra leader, 156, 236
Wilhelm, Hoyt, baseball player, *243*
Will, C. H., Motors, Inc., 157
"William Crooks," locomotive, 10, *43,* 45
Williams, J. Fletcher, quoted, 2
Williams, J. P., *228*
Williams, Mrs. J. P., *228*
Williams, Ted, baseball player, *221*
Willius Bros. and Dunbar, StP, *55*
Willys-Overland automobile, 122, 137, *168*
Wilmot, Walter, baseball manager, *150*
Winnebago Indians, *14*
Winslow, James M., hotelkeeper, *18, 27*
Winslow House, StP, hotel, *18, 40;* St. Anthony (Mpls), *27, 28, 99*
Winter Carnival, StP, 83, *114, 146, 152,* 195, *219*
Winthrop School, Mpls, *71*
Wold-Chamberlain Field, 157, *170,* 194, 233

Wolfe automobile, 122
Woman suffrage, 119, *141, 184*
Woman's Christian Temperance Union, 119
Woman's Club of Minneapolis, *29, 270*
Women, *164, 237;* war work, *39, 143,* 194, *225;* occupations, 85, *94, 140, 162, 173,* 195, 196, *200, 261;* social life, 85, *147, 175;* in sports, *108,* 196, 287n26
Wood, Harold E., 158
Woodman, Ivory, builder, *37*
Woodman Block, Mpls, *37*
Woodruff, Hal, singing-club director, *153*
Works Progress Administration, projects, 192, 196, *200, 220;* strike, 193
World Court, supporters, *185,* 229
World Theater, StP, 235
World War I, 120, 122, *142-145, 198*
World War II, 191, 194, 195, 197, *219, 222, 228,* 232
World's Fair Store, StP, *23*
Wright, Kenneth M., photographer, 2
Wright County, suburban growth, 286n2

Yamasaki, Minoru, and Associates, architects, *262*
Yanz, Griggs and Howes, StP, *101*
Young Men's Christian Assn., 55, *187*
Yount, Allen, *260*

Zimmerman, Charles A., photographer, 2
Zoos, StP, *124, 220;* Mpls, *148*
Zuckerman and Co., Mpls, *100*
Zukerman, Pinchas, orchestra leader, 235

ST. ANTHONY'S FALLS AND THE MILLING DISTRICT. MINNEAPOLIS, MINN.